D1712300

Topics in Information Systems

Editors:
Michael L. Brodie
John Mylopoulos
Joachim W. Schmidt

Springer Series
Topics in Information Systems

M. L. Brodie, J. Mylopoulos, J. W. Schmidt (Eds.): On Conceptual Modelling: Perspectives from Artificial Intelligence, Databases and Programming Languages. XI, 510 pages, 25 figs., 1984

W. Kim, D. S. Reiner, D. S. Batory (Eds.): Query Processing in Database Systems. XIV, 365 pages, 127 figs., 1985

D. C. Tsichritzis (Ed.): Office Automation: Concepts and Tools. XII, 441 pages, 86 figs., 1985

M. L. Brodie, J. Mylopoulos (Eds.): On Knowledge Base Management Systems: Integrating Artificial Intelligence and Database Technologies. XXI, 660 pages, 89 figs., 1986

L. Bolc, M. Jarke (Eds.): Cooperative Interfaces to Information Systems. XIV, 328 pages, 62 figs., 1986

M. P. Atkinson; P. Buneman, R. Morrison (Eds.): Data Types and Persistence. XVI, 292 pages, 10 figs., 1988

J. W. Schmidt, C. Thanos (Eds.): Foundations of Knowledge Base Management: Contributions from Logic, Databases, and Artificial Intelligence Applications. XIV, 579 pages, 84 figs., 1989

K. R. Dittrich, U. Dayal, A. P. Buchmann (Eds.): On Object-Oriented Database Systems. X, 422 pages, 87 figs., 1991

Klaus R. Dittrich Umeshwar Dayal
Alejandro P. Buchmann (Eds.)

On Object-Oriented
Database Systems

With 87 Figures

Springer-Verlag

Berlin Heidelberg New York
London Paris Tokyo
Hong Kong Barcelona
Budapest

Series Editors

Michael L. Brodie
GTE Laboratories Incorporated
40 Sylvan Road, Waltham, MA 02254, USA

John Mylopoulos
Department of Computer Science, University of Toronto
Toronto, Ontario M5S 1A7, Canada

Joachim W. Schmidt
Fachbereich Informatik, Johann Wolfgang Goethe-Universität
Robert-Mayer-Straße 11-15
W-6000 Frankfurt a. M. 11, Fed. Rep. of Germany

Volume Editors

Klaus R. Dittrich
Universität Zürich, Institut für Informatik
Winterthurerstraße 190, CH-8057 Zürich

Umeshwar Dayal
Digital Equipment Corporation, Cambridge Research Laboratory
One Kendall Square, Building 700, Cambridge, MA 02139, USA

Alejandro P. Buchmann
GTE Laboratories Incorporated
40 Sylvan Road, Waltham, MA 0234, USA

ISBN 3-540-53496-2   Springer-Verlag Berlin Heidelberg New York
ISBN 0-387-53496-2   Springer-Verlag New York Berlin Heidelberg

Library of Congress Cataloging-in-Publication Data
On object-oriented database systems/Klaus R. Dittrich, Umeshwar Dayal,
Alejandro P. Buchmann, eds.
  p. cm. – (Topics in information systems)
Includes bibliographical references and index.
ISBN 3-540-53496-2 (Springer-Verlag Berlin Heidelberg New York)
ISBN 0-387-53496-2 (Springer-Verlag New York Berlin Heidelberg)
1. Data base management.   2. Object-oriented data bases.
I. Dittrich, Klaus R.   II. Dayal, Umeshwar.   III. Buchmann, Alejandro P.   IV. Series
QA76.9.D3049 1991   005.75–dc20   90-26851   CIP

© Springer-Verlag Berlin Heidelberg 1991
Printed in the United States of America

47/3140-543210 – Printed on acid-free paper

Topics in Information Systems

Series Description

Computer Science is increasingly challenged to deliver powerful concepts, techniques, and tools for building high quality, low cost information systems. In the future, such systems will be expected to acquire, maintain, retrieve, manipulate, and present many different kinds of information. Requirements such as user-friendly interfaces, powerful reasoning capabilities, shared access to large information bases, and cooperative problem solving all with high performance are becoming ever more popular to potential information system users. More fundamentally, there is an ever increasing need for powerful environments for the design and development of such information systems.

Software technology for building these systems is far from meeting these requirements. Despite major achievements in every area of Computer Science, the gap between what is expected and what Information System technology can deliver is widening. This is in marked contrast to dramatic advances in individual research areas such as hardware technology, knowledge-based systems, distributed processing, graphics, user-interfaces, etc. The critical challenge in meeting the demand for high quality, low cost information systems cannot be addressed successfully by individual technologies. Rather, it critically depends on our ability to integrate technologies. One reason for the urgency of this task is that dramatic advances in hardware technology have made computers available to an ever-growing community of potential users all of whom have definite information processing needs.

The Topics in Information Systems (TIS) series of books focuses on the critical challenges of technology integration for information systems. Volumes in the series will report recent significant contributions to the conceptual foundation, the architectural design, and the software realization of information systems. The series is based on the premise that these tasks can be solved only by integrating currently distinct technologies from different areas of Computer Science such as Artificial Intelligence, Databases and Programming Languages. The required dramatic improvements in software productivity will come from advanced application development environments based on powerful new techniques and languages. The resulting new technologies should allow us to transform our conceptions of an application domain more directly and efficiently into operational systems utilizing conceptual modelling methodologies, new languages for requirements, design and implementation, novel environments, performance analysis tools, and optimization techniques.

The *concepts*, *techniques*, and *tools* necessary for the design, implementation, and use of future information systems is expected to result from the integration of those being developed and used in currently disjoint areas of Computer Science. Several areas bring their unique viewpoint and technologies to existing information processing practice. One key area is *Artificial Intelligence* (AI) which provides knowledge representation and reasoning capabilities for knowledge bases grounded on semantic theories of information for correct interpretation.

An equally important area is *Databases* which provides means for building and maintaining large, shared distributed databases grounded in computational theories of information for efficient processing. A third important area is *Programming Languages* which provides a powerful tool kit for the construction of large, efficient programs and programming environments to support software engineering. To meet evolving information systems requirements, additional research viewpoints and technologies are or will be required from such areas as *Software Engineering, Computer Networks, Machine Architectures* and *Office Automation.*

Although some technological integration has already been achieved, a quantum leap is needed to meet the demand for future information systems. This integration is one of the major challenges for Computer Science in the 1990s.

The TIS series logo symbolizes the scope of topics to be covered and the basic theme of integration. The logo will appear on each book to indicate the topics addressed. The book *On Knowledge Base Management Systems: Integrating Artificial Intelligence and Database Technologies*, edited by Michael L. Brodie and John Mylopoulos, for example, deals with concepts and techniques in AI and Databases and has the logo

	Artificial Intelligence	Databases	Programming Languages
Concepts	●	●	
Techniques	●	●	
Tools			

All books in the series provide timely accounts of ongoing research efforts to reshape technologies intended for information system development.

Michael L. Brodie
John Mylopoulos
Joachim W. Schmidt

Preface

The past decade has witnessed an intensity of research and development on the part of computer scientists in the realm of object-orientation. It is, therefore, not surprising to learn that many members of the database community are focussing their interests in understanding the notions and concepts underlying object-orientation. The impact of relational database systems as evidenced in the widespread success of "real" applications now faces competition from this promising research area. Even though still in the experimental phase and lacking any commonly agreed definition, object-orientation engenders much discussion and debate - a well-known precursor to significance and success.

To date, object-oriented database systems have been approached primarily withthe following two intentions in mind:

• improving the support of new application areas (CAD/CAM, office automation, knowledge engineering, etc.) where units of interest in the real world are composed of dissimilar units in a more or less arbitrary way, and where abroad variety of application-specific unit types (including appropriate operations) has to be dealt with;

• overcoming the impedance mismatch between data models and programming languages that has always presented a severe problem with relational, network, and similar models.

As a result of these considerations the notion of object-orientation in database systems is broader than that found in programming languages. Although data model concepts furnish the decisive features for object-oriented database systems, aspects found in other systems need to be reconsidered when seeking solutions to the above goals. They include, for example, transactions, optimization, formalization, the inclusion of rules, system architecture and interoperability.

A number of research prototypes and commercial systems have been developed and are now available. Approaches to extend databases using object-oriented capabilities as well as, vice versa, attempts to extend object-oriented programming languages by integrating database features are being investigated and involve the active participation of both database and programming language people in the field. This volume covers a broad range of topics in object-oriented database systems.The first part equips the reader with a definition and classification considered useful for the discussion and comparison of various approaches. A collection of issues that need to be addressed are described. Many of them are taken up in later sections of the book.

Part II addresses data model concepts, especially with respect to the representation of complex objects, user-defined types including their operations, inheritance, and constraints. A comparison of objects and database views is given.

Part III is devoted to the language aspects of object-oriented database systems. Different approaches are presented which either extend object-oriented programming languages by using database system features, or combine such languages with a database system to achieve persistence and reliability for the language objects.

In Part IV, the user interface aspect of object-oriented databases is discussed and two different solutions are presented in detail. Part V considers object-oriented database systems from an application point of view. Examples taken from two specific applications are presented and the important issue of database design is addressed briefly.

The remainder of the book emphasizes internal aspects of object-oriented databases. First, Part VI examines architectural issues, including approaches to extensible database systems, object servers, and database system generation. A discussion of some specific topics regarding object-oriented database implementation follows, namely, associative access, derived data, and techniques to support complex objects.

Part VIII concludes the volume with a brief summary, a perspective of current achievements, and, finally, a prediction of future developments and trends in the area.

The contributions to this book originated from papers presented at the First International Workshop on Object-Oriented Database Systems held in Asilomar, California. The editors requested the revision of the original workshop papers, including specifically the results of the intensive discussions held in Asilomar. Although this request along with the review procedure involved considerable time, we are convinced that this volume justifies all the efforts and presents a comprehensive and balanced account of a major area of contemporary database system research and development.

We would like to thank all contributing colleagues for their collaboration and patience during the production of this book, as well as all those participants of the lively discussions at Asilomar. Margot Just and Tassilo Fieg deserve our special thanks for doing an outstanding job in preparing the camera-ready copies of all contributions thus enabling a uniformity of appearance. Finally, our thanks go to Ingeborg Mayer and Dr. Hans Woessner of Springer-Verlag who never lost hope in getting the book into print some day. Well, here it is!

Klaus R. Dittrich
Umeshwar Dayal
Alejandro P. Buchmann

Contents

Part I

Introduction

1
Object-Oriented Database Systems:
The Notion and the Issues

Klaus R. Dittrich

Abstract

Since half a decade or so, object-oriented database systems have become an extremely hot topic of database research and development. At many places all over the world, people work on individual aspects or complete system prototypes. Already, some systems have even reached the marketplace. However, the notion of "object-orientation" in the context of database systems is unfortunately still widely unclear and means different things to different people.This paper tries to bring some clarification to this terminological problem by promoting a definition that recently has been put together by a number of researchers from six different "schools". Afterwards, it establishes a classifications of approaches that do not (yet) meet all criteria requested by this ideal definition, but are in one way or the other close to it. Finally, a number of issues are given that need special consideration in the context of object-oriented database systems.

1   Introduction

At least since the first publications on Smalltalk appeared in the popular computer science press [Gold81], the notion of "object-orientation" has started to become one of the major buzzwords of the field, at first in the context of object-oriented programming (languages) and object-oriented system design. As it is the case with most buzzwords, "object-orientation" unfortunately suffered (and in many respects still suffers!) from misconceptions, overestimation and glorification on one side, and at the same time from ignorance of the "déjà vu"-style at the opposite extreme. Typical symptoms include (slightly exaggerating) that

– everybody cries for mature products that have it already (without always knowing what it exactly is and what it is potentially good for),

-   in the marketplace (and sometimes in research, too), everybody`s system claims to have it, or at least everybody claims to work on it,
-   old stuff reappears under the new label (which may, in some rare cases, even be justified!).

When the database community got attracted little later and started to carry over object-orientation to databases/database management systems, this situation did of course not at all improve. On the contrary, due to somewhat different intentions, approaches and attitudes, object-oriented database systems (or ooDBS for short) today are even in a less consolidated state than e.g. object-oriented programming languages.

Past experience (e.g. from the development of relational database systems) indicates that it takes some 15 years or more from the first (published!) ideas of a new software-related technology until the widespread use of efficient and reliable products in large-scale applications. Given the fact that it is now only half a decade or so since ooDBS are being researched and developed, it is obvious that no satisfactory degree of maturity can be expected today. What has been achieved so far is that

-   a relatively large number of groups all over the world (including some of the most respected database people) are working on individual ooDBS aspects and/or complete system prototypes; as a result, a number of issues have been clarified, first-shot solutions have been tried out (and have partially triggered improved solutions); some systems – mainly produced by start-up companies – are even already offered for sale.
-   considerable interest in ooDBS has been created; technical people and managers from numerous potential application areas are eager to acquire information and training; conferences, workshops, and professional seminars on the topic attract large numbers of participants.

However, there are also a number of issues on the negative side:

-   The history of relational database systems started with a clear concept and a formal basis (at least as far as the data model itself is concerned), and all important system prototypes have been developed on these common grounds. In contrast, the origins of ooDBS were a set of vague ideas that immediately lead to a number of prototypes with quite different underlying concepts. Consequently, it is now hard to even agree on a common definition of an ooDBS (apart from a very superficial one), and to some extent also on what the real issues in system development are.
-   We do not yet have any major experience in making real use of ooDBS, especially when it comes to applications of realistic size.

Clearly, for the second problem it is just a question of time to get solved. Nevertheless, one should neither underestimate the effort it will take to introduce this (or any other) new technology to users, nor expect that all pitfalls will be known beforehand.

The much more serious problem is the first one. Unfortunately, history is no transaction which would allow us to undo its effects. The only way to arrive at a common basis will thus be that the various groups working in the field get together and try to unify their views, and there is hope that such a process is already underway. Once a generally accepted understanding of the ooDBS concepts has been established, it will certainly be possible to come up with the appropriate formal basis and to compete for the best solutions for specific problem areas.

2   Towards a Common Definition

In the sequel, we present and explain a list of features and characteristics that an ideal ooDBS should have and that together constitute a definition of the notion "object-oriented database system". It is the result of joint work of six people representing groups that have all taken different approaches so far. The original publication is "The Object-Oriented Database System Manifesto (A Political Pamphlet)" [Mani89]; this chapter contains a very condensed summary (partially in a rearranged form and with some reinterpretation).

Like a relational database system is one which is based on the relational data model, we define an **object-oriented database system** to be **a database management system with an object-oriented data model**.

To fall into the category of database management systems means to have the following features (apart from the data model question to be discussed separately):

*   **persistence**
*   **disk management**
*   **concurrency control**
*   **recovery**
*   **ad hoc query facility**

Access control and distribution (if an issue) might be added. All these features are presented in every good database textbook and do not need much further explanation. Note, however, that we have listed the characteristics that are required and not the mechanisms by which they are provided (e.g. locking, transactions etc. for concurrency control, recovery, ...). Disk management includes such things like access paths, clustering, or buffering; they are not directly visible to the user, but no realistic DBMS can fulfill its task without them. Under an ad hoc query facility, we understand any means that allows access to database data without the necessity to go through the usual cycle of programming, compilation, execution, and debugging. For example, a descriptive query language, a graphical browser or some "fill in the form"-facility would do that job.

The list of characteristics we require for an object-oriented data model is much more controversial. First of all, the concept of data model itself has to be understood in a broad sense as a framework in which to express real world semantics in a database system. Though this is not at all a novel view, traditional data models offer rather limited means and do not address at all some features for advanced semantic capture. They should thus not be taken as a yardstick for understanding what a data model is. With this remark in mind, our requirements include the following which will be discussed one by one in the sequel:

*   **composite objects**
*   **user-definable types**
*   **object identity**
*   **encapsulation**
*   **types/classes**
*   **type/class hierarchies**
*   **overloading/overriding/late binding**
*   **computational completeness**

The units an ooDBS deals with are called **objects**. They have a representation, i.e. a (possibly structured) value or state (sometimes also called a set of instance variables), and a set of operations that are applicable for that object. **Composite objects** (or, synonymously, complex objects, structured objects, molecular objects) are built from (among others) components that are objects in their own right and may be composite themselves. The presence of this characteristic especially means that objects of any level of composition have to be supported in a uniform way, that object constructors (e.g., for tuples, sets, lists) have to exist, and that specific operations to dynamically modify and exploit object structures (both, in their entirety and specific parts of them) are needed.

Every data model comes with a number of predefined data types (which are usually simple ones like integers, characters, strings). Above that, traditional record-oriented data models provide some sort of "parameterized" types with fixed sets of generic operators. In the relational model, for example, there is the parameterized type "(homogeneous) set of (flat) tuples", called a relation. The only parameters to be chosen for a relation by the user are the number of attributes, their names, and their (predefined, simple) types (plus the name of the relation itself). In contrast, the **user-definable types** requirement means that really new types can be introduced to the system by its users, and afterwards dealt with in the same way as with predefined ones. This includes particularly that mechanisms are needed to program new operators and register them with the system.

Object identity means that the existence of an object is independent of its value. It is thus possible within the database to distinguish between the equality of two objects (i.e. they happen to have – at a given point in time – the same value) and their identity (they really are – always – the same object). An object thus has to be considered as a pair (<OID>, <value>) where <OID> is an object identifier and <value>, according to the above, may be simple or composite. Obviously, an OID has to be system-wide unique, must not change during the object`s lifetime, and even after its deletion, it is should be guaranteed foreever that any other object may not have the same identity. Object identity (even when not explicitly made visible in a system) is an underlying concept for shared objects (i.e. objects that are components of two or more objects); it is also necessary for easily and correctly reflecting updates of real world entities in the database. Otherwise, if e.g. a person gets married and at this occasion changes his/her name which has been used as a key for the respective database object, how could one tell whether the updated object would still represent the same real world entity as before? Obviously, the current practice is to have the user introduce artificial attributes like employee numbers etc. and thus make it his task to deal with identity. It is now recognized that the database system can cope much better and more reliably with this problem.

When a user defines a new type, he has to choose a representation for the values of its instances, he specifies the operator interfaces, and he programs their bodies (in terms of the representation). In this case, it usually does not make sense that users of this type may look at the representation details or at the operator codes; all they need to know to use objects of the type is its interface, i.e. the operator specifications. **Encapsulation** provides for information hiding in this abstract data type flavor. Note, however, that this should not be made an "all or nothing" principle: in some cases, one may well want to define a new type just on a representational basis and adopt the (generic) operators of the representation (e.g. direct access to the attributes of a tuple) for the type interface, maybe augmented by one or two additional operators that are user-defined.

The requirement for **types/classes** as such is not that new for database systems, but it has an extended meaning for ooDBS and the notion of a class has been carried over from the programming language area. Whatever the favorite definitions (and there is some dispute about different characteristics or just synonymous use), types/classes include the following:

- the specification of the commonalities of a set of objects with the same properties (i.e. their operators and representational structure),

- a mechanism to create instances (objects) of the type/class ("object factory"),

- mechanisms to query and manipulate the set of instances currently in existence for a type/class (the extension; "object warehouse").

The real novelty with respect to types/classes in ooBDS is that they can be organized in **hierarchies** and thus allow to express that one type is considered a subtype of another one, i.e. that it is specified in more detail (with respect to representational structure and/or operators) than the supertype. The standard example is a type *person* with attributes like name, address, age etc., and subtypes *employee* (with additional attributes for salary, department, ...) and *student* (semester, courses, grade points, ...). Along with type hierarchies goes the concept of **inheritance** in that objects of a subtype inherit the properties (again, structure and/or operators) from the supertype, in addition to those properties that have been specified with the subtype itself. Of course, inheritance propagates all the way to the top of the hierarchy if there are more than just two levels. There are various solutions to particular questions arising in this context that are beyond the scope of our discussion here, for example on how to resolve ambiguities if multiple supertypes are allowed. In summary, with type hierarchies and inheritance, more semantics can be expressed than without, it introduces an additional modeling discipline (refinement!), and it may even save coding effort because operators need not always be recoded.

Closely connected are the requirements for **overriding**, **overloading**, and **late binding**. Overloading means that the same operator name (and interface) may be used for different operations in different types. This allows to reimplement ("override") an inherited operator for a subtype, taking into account the additional semantics that may be known there. The advantage one gains is that users that deal with objects of various subtypes of a given supertype do not have to program tedious case selections to find out the exact type of any object and apply the appropriate operator; they may uniformly use the operator specified for the supertype, and the system will automatically determine which implementation to execute. Obviously, this mandates late binding: the system cannot bind names to programs prior to runtime. However, this is again not that much different from traditional approaches (consider e.g. the "find" operator in a network database system).

Finally, **computational completeness** relates to the language facilities provided for programming the operators of user-defined types. We require that arbitrary algorithms may be coded, and thus mere query language facilities will typically not be enough for this purpose.

Discussion and classification

The list of characteristics we have presented above is only a first attempt to give a comprehensive definition of an ooDBS. Though it contains most features that up to now have evolved in the area, we did not specify how they should orthogonally cooperate. This is not a superfluous requirement: it may be much easier to provide an uncoordinated potpourri of the above features than an elegant, streamlined system that has them all. However, only the latter will be easy to comprehend and to use, and thus stand a chance to find wide acceptance.

Also, we have defined an "ideal" ooDBS; most system prototypes and products that are available today do not (yet) fulfill it entirely, and for the majority of those, this is due to the data model requirements listed. In order to nevertheless allow a better evaluation of current and upcoming proposals, it makes sense to establish a coarse classification of object-oriented data models on the basis of the presented definition. It assumes that the first two criteria, composite objects and user-definable types, are the decisive ones, i.e. if a model does not incorporate any one of those, but supports some of the others, this is not considered enough progress to existing approaches to justify a new name. On the other hand, once composite objects and/or user-definable types are available, the data model is already a big step forward compared to record-oriented ones, even if some of the other goodies are missing.

In this respect, [Ditt88] introduced the following classification: A data model is called

- **structurally object-oriented** if it supports composite objects,
- **behaviorally object-oriented** if it supports user-defined types,
- **fully object-oriented** if it supports both *and* has all the other features as explained above.

Full object-orientation matches the comprehensive definition as introduced. Of course, the provision of the other six data model features (where applicable; some of them do not make sense for structural object-orientation) does not hurt for the first two classes either. In fact, at least most behaviorally object-oriented models do adhere to most of them. A structurally object-oriented database system etc., then, is again a database system (remember the list of criteria) with an appropriate data model.

3   Issues

Obviously, the criteria to be met as given above – even if they are all adhered to – do not define *the* one and only object-oriented data model (in contrast to e.g. the relational model which defines exactly one such thing). In consequence, various ways of providing the individual concepts and mechanisms can be (and have been) investigated. The same holds true for the other database system issues, and many of them do have to be reconsidered in the light of the data model that is now different from classical ones. And finally, several additional aspects resulting mainly from the application areas object-oriented systems are primarily aiming at should be (and already are) investigated in this context. Altogether, this leads to a long list of topics that need attention; to give an impression, we mention a few of them in random order, without any claim for completeness (see e.g [Kim90, ZdMa90, Moss89] for other collections of issues):

- Within the framework as introduced, concrete ways have to be found to present all the necessary features of full object-orientation in a coherent and orthogonal fashion. Quality criteria will comprise, among others, expressive power and ease of comprehension and use.

  A specific subtopic pending clever solutions is how to best integrate composite objects (with full-fledged support as sketched in section 2) with user-definable types (including encapsulation). Furthermore, most present approaches offer just one uniform mechanism to express object composition (i.e. the generic IS-PART-OF-relationship which its very specific semantics) as well as object referencing (as a means to model all kinds of other – typically rather "loose" – associations between objects). Unfortunately, this conceals apparant differences of real world facts and is thus counterproductive to the goal of offering highly expressive data modeling facilities.

- Beyond composite objects, applications are often concerned with object versions (i.e. multiple representations of the same semantic entity, to account for different states, different times of validity or creation, alternative or hypothetical information etc.). Appropriate modeling mechanisms and operations should be integrated into an object-oriented database system.

- How is query processing integrated into object-oriented database systems (both, at the conceptual – how do ad hoc queries interact with e.g. encapsulation? – and at the implementation level)?

- When processing objects comprising large amounts of data, transactions (seen as closed, meaningful units of work, from a user's perspective) may become much longer than usual. Concepts are therefore needed to accomodate long-lived transactions (often called "long transactions", "design transactions" etc.); they will have different properties than the transactions as supported by today's systems (which follow the ACID-principle, i.e. compoundly guarantee for atomicity, consistency, isolation and durability) by separating recovery, synchronization and consistency control issues.

- How do the notions of database views and consistency transfer to object-oriented data models?

- Protection issues have to be based on the notion of object which is the natural unit of access control in this framework.

- For databases containing large numbers of data, archiving may become an important issue. Again, objects (and their versions, if any) form the natural unit for this activity.

- Powerful implementation techniques are needed to provide object-oriented database systems that perform efficiently. These may partly be carried over from the wealth of approaches developed for relational and other traditional systems, but undoubtedly further concepts will need to be considered, e.g.
    - specialized access paths for composite objects,
    - storage structures for composite objects (e.g. clustering, delta storage for versions),
    - object-oriented main memory buffering.

  Also, how do the ideas of extensible database system architectures (e.g. [CaDV88] relate to the special case of object-oriented database systems?

- How do the concepts of active [McDa89] and deductive [CeGT90] database systems tie in with object-oriented database systems?

- High quality database design is a rather tedious job even for record-oriented database systems. It appears that it is even more difficult within the framework of object-oriented database systems as the target application areas show a much higher degree of complexity which may easily exceed the gain in modeling power. Appropriate design metho-dologies and tools that support them have to be developed.

- In contrast to the development of the relational data model, formal foundations for object-oriented data models are still missing. As several research groups became interested in this area (cf. e.g. [KiNN89]), there is justified hope that these deficiencies are going to be remedied with in the near future. However, care has to be taken that theory addresses full-fledged object-oriented data models and not just the easier issues.

- Finally, what migration paths can be meaningfully offered for the users of today's relational database systems in order to enable them to benefit from the advantages of object-oriented ones? How can heterogeneous distributed DBMSs help?

4   Conclusions

This paper has first tried to propagate a commonly acceptable definition of an object-oriented database system, together with a classification scheme for systems that do not completely match the full definition at this time. We have also sketched some issues where further investigations and experiments by means of prototyping seems to be promising. While a lot of work into these directions is already well underway, more will have to be done in the future. Especially, real application experiences are still missing. Only when having them will we be able to answer the questions of whether the set of concepts of object-oriented data models is appropriate as it is, whether in some cases, structural or behavioral object-orientation are perfectly sufficient, and many more.

5   References

[CaDV88], [CeGT90], [Ditt88], [Gold81], [KiLo89], [Kim90], [Mani89], [McDa89], [Moss89], [ZdMa90]

Part II

Data Model Concepts

2

An Overview of PDM: An Object-Oriented Data Model

Frank Manola, Umeshwar Dayal

Abstract

This paper describes the development of the data model of PROBE, a knowledge-oriented DBMS being developed at CCA. The data model, called PDM, is an extension of the Daplex functional data model that illustrates an integration of functional, relational, and object-oriented approaches. The extensions are primarily those required to handle the requirements of new database applications, such as engineering applications and cartography, having spatial or temporal semantics.

1   Introduction

The application of database technology to new applications, such as CAD/CAM, geographic information systems, software engineering, and office automation, is an extremely active area of database research. Many of these new applications deal with highly structured objects that are composed of other objects. For example, a part in a part hierarchy may be composed of other parts; an integrated circuit module may be composed of other modules, pins, and wires; a geographic feature such as an industrial park may be a complex composed of other features such as buildings, smokestacks, and rail lines; and so forth. Moreover, many of the objects dealt with in these applications have spatial or temporal properties, or have conventional properties that vary in time or space. For example, a mechanical part has a geometric shape; the altitude of the earth's surface varies with the latitude and longitude.

A number of papers have proposed extensions to conventional record- or tuple-oriented data models to deal with these applications, e.g. [LoPl83]. However, another approach has been the development of *object-oriented* data models for these applications [Loch86, DiDa86]. This paper describes the development of the data model of PROBE, an object-oriented DBMS being developed at CCA [DaSm86, Daya87, DDGO87, MaOr86, MaDa86, MaOD87,

This work was supported by the Defence Advanced Research Projects Agency and by the Space and Naval Warfare Systems Command under Contract No. N00039-85-C-0263. The views and conclusions contained in this paper are those of the authors and do not necessarily represent the official policies of the Defense Advanced Research Projects Agency, the Space and Naval Warfare Systems Command or the U.S. Government.

Mano87, Oren86, OrMa88, Rose86]. Our approach has been to start from DAPLEX, a functional data model and query language [Ship81], and to enhance DAPLEX to meet the requirements of these new database applications. We refer to the enhanced model as PDM (PROBE Data Model).

There were two reasons for our interest in starting with DAPLEX. First, DAPLEX already incorporates many of the features generally associated with object-oriented models, and considered as advantages in the new DBMS applications, including:

- the concept of an *entity* or *object* that has existence independent of any properties or relationships with other entities it might have.

- object- and set-valued properties of entities (in DAPLEX, entity- and set-valued *functions*); this in turn allows the structure of complex objects to be modeled directly [Daya87].

- the concept of an *entity class* or *type*, together with *generalization* (subtype) *hierarchies* (with property inheritance) among classes.

- a method for incorporating *entity behavior* and *derived properties* in the model; this is provided by functions in DAPLEX (although in DAPLEX functions are generally only used as a notation for referring to stored data, rather than computed data).

The advantages of DAPLEX in spatial data modelling are described in [NoMi86].

Our second reason for starting with DAPLEX was our prior experience with both the design of DAPLEX, and its implementation in several DBMS systems. This gave us a basis for implementing PDM in the PROBE system. The implementation of the basic DAPLEX model, including support for entities, functions (typically implemented by pointers), referential integrity, and generalization hierarchies, is described in [Chan82].

Our specific goals for PDM extensions were to provide:

- a smooth incorporation of multiargument functions and computed functions (general procedures) into the model.

- an algebra-based formal data model definition (along the lines of the relational model) for use as a foundation for query optimization, view mapping, and query language development studies.

- a clean way of extending the model with objects having unconventional semantics, particularly spatial and temporal semantics.

Multiargument and computed functions are important as representations for time- and space-varying entity properties, and in the integration of derived data, general procedures, and operations into the model. A variant of relational algebra (that did not explicitly incorporate computed functions) had been used previously as an informal target interpretation of Daplex in the study of query optimization techniques (e.g., [Ries83]). It was felt that a more explicit definition of such an algebra would be useful for PDM.

In this paper (which is a revised and updated version of [MaDa86], we first describe the basic characteristics of the model. We then describe aspects of an algebraic definition of the model and some issues related to the definition. Next, we briefly describe other facilities of the model, such as rule facilities and recursion, and finally we describe current work in progress. Our intent is to describe the general characteristics of PDM objects. We do not consider in this paper the special characteristics of particular object classes that have been investigated for PROBE, such as spatial/temporal entities, or their functions (for a description of such entities and functions, see [MaOr86, MaOD87].

2   PDM Data Objects

There are two basic types of data constructs in PDM, *entities* and *functions*. An *entity* is a construct that denotes some individual thing (and corresponds to an *object* in other object-oriented models). The basic characteristic of an entity that must be preserved in the model is its distinct identity. An entity is represented in the database by a surrogate (or by its value if it is a "primitive", such as an integer).

Entities with similar characteristics are grouped into collections called *entity types* (e.g., **PART, PERSON**). Properties of entities, relationships between entities, and operations on entities (behavioral aspects) are all uniformly represented in PDM by *functions* (which correspond to *methods* in other object-oriented models). In order to access properties of an entity or other entities related to an entity, or to perform operations on an entity, one must evaluate a function having the entity as an argument (this corresponds to sending a message specifying a method to an object). In PDM, a function is a relationship between collections of entities. The example below illustrate some of the aspects of PDM functions (the syntax used is illustrative only):

*   the single-argument function **PART_NUMBER (PART) -> STRING** allows access to the value of the part number attribute of a **PART** entity. Similarly, the function **ADVISOR (STUDENT) -> INSTRUCTOR** allows access to the advisor attribute of a student (whose value is another entity).

*   the multi-argument function **COLOR (X,Y,PHOTO) -> COLOR_VALUE** allows access to the color values at particular points in a photograph.

*   the function **LOCATION (CONNECTION,LAYOUT) -> (X,Y)** allows access to the value of the coordinates of a connection in a diagram (note that a function can return a complex result).

*   the function **UNION (3DSOLIDPART, 3DSOLIDPART) -> 3DSOLIDPART** provides access to a union operation defined for 3-dimensional solid models of parts.

*   the set-valued function **COMPONENTS (PART) -> set of PART** allows access to the component parts of a group part (assembly).

*   the set-valued function **QUANTITY_ON_HAND (DEPOT) -> set of (MATERIAL, INTEGER)** shows a function that returns sets of complex results.

Functions may also be defined that have no input arguments, or that have only Boolean (truth-valued) results. For example:

*   the zero-argument function **PART() -> set of ENTITY** is implicitly defined for entity type **PART**, and returns all entities of that type (a corresponding function is implicitly defined for each entity type in the database).

*   the function **ADJACENT(PART,PART,ASSEMBLY) -> BOOLEAN** defines a predicate that is true if two parts are adjacent within a given assembly. All predicates within PDM are defined as Boolean-valued functions.

Specializations (subtypes) of entity types may be defined, forming an *inheritance (isa) hierarchy*. For example, the declarations:

entity PART

function PART_NUMBER (PART) -> STRING

function WEIGHT (PART) -> REAL

entity 3DSOLIDPART isa PART

function UNION (3DSOLIDPART, 3DSOLIDPART) -> 3DSOLIDPART

define a **PART** entity type having two functions, and a subtype **3DSOLIDPART** having an additional function. Because **3DSOLIDPART** is a subtype of **PART** any **3DSOLIDPART** entity is also an entity of the **PART** supertype, and automatically "inherits" the **PART_NUMBER** and **WEIGHT** functions. (All user-defined entity types are subtypes of the generic type **ENTITY**).

The same entity may be associated with one or more entity types in the database, as defined by database declarations, and may move in and out of types as a result of database operations. Thus, if **STUDENT** and **INSTRUCTOR** are defined as subtypes of **PERSON**, an entity might move from subtype **STUDENT** to **INSTRUCTOR** (e.g., if a former student was hired as an instructor), or be both a **STUDENT** and an **INSTRUCTOR** simultaneously (whether or not this is allowed is controlled by constraint declarations).

The use within PDM of functions allowing multiple input and output arguments has a number of notational and semantic effects. First, because it is possible for functions to have more than one output argument, the function name and its input parameters do not always denote a single output value (or a set of such values), as in conventional functional languages: sometimes they denote a *tuple* of output argument values (or a set of such tuples). Because it is necessary to be able to refer to individual output values within such tuples, PDM functional notation provides each argument with a label. This acts like a formal parameter name in a procedure defined in a programming language.

Second, because of the way PDM functions are defined as relationships between *collections* of entities, it is possible to have function arguments that serve as both input and output parameters. For example, given a 3-ary relationship **QUANTITY_ON_HAND** between depots, materials, and amounts of materials stored at depots, one could imagine both the functions

QUANTITY_ON_HAND_1 (DEPOT,MATERIAL) -> INTEGER

and

QUANTITY_ON_HAND_2 (DEPOT) -> set of (MATERIAL,INTEGER)

being useful, even though they are based on the same 3-ary relationship (a similar issue is addressed in [LyKe86]). This notation appears to define two different functions, but the only real difference is that **MATERIAL** is an input variable in one and an output variable in the other. A PDM function corresponding to the two functions above would be declared:

QUANTITY_ON_HAND (D: in DEPOT, M: in out MATERIAL,

QUAN: out INTEGER)

This notation is essentially that used in declaring an Ada[1] subprogram, using "in" and "out" declarations to specify how the parameter may be used, as well as giving a parameter label and the required parameter type. (As in Ada, parameters may be supplied to functions using either "keyword" or positional references.) The general notation is:

function_name (label1: {in/out/in out} type1, ..., labeln: {in/out/in out} typen)

(This notation applies to the concrete syntax being used to define the PDM model. A query language based on the model might very well adopt a different convention). Cardinality constraints may also be specified in function definitions to control the appearance of parameter values in PDM functions. For example, a constraint would be specified in the definition of **QUANTITY_ON_HAND** above to indicate that there must be a single integer value corresponding to each pair of **DEPOT** and **MATERIAL**. These are similar to constraints specified on relationships in many ER models.

PDM's functional notation allows general procedures to be included in the model. For example, a finite element analysis routine might be included as:

function FE_ANALYSIS(MODEL: in FE_MODEL, LOADS: in FE_LOAD,

       OPTION: in   INTEGER,   DEFORMED_MODEL: out FE_MODEL)

In this function, the parameters labeled **MODEL**, **LOADS**, and **OPTION** are input-only parameters, while **DEFORMED_MODEL** is an output-only parameter. Similarly, a conventional entity property might be defined by:

function AGE (PERSON: in out PERSON, RESULT: in out INTEGER)

a function in which either argument can be an input or output parameter (in this example, the first appearance of **PERSON** is a formal parameter name, the second is an entity type name). In this case, the function may be invoked with a value for either parameter, to produce a value for the other. Functions can also be used to model arbitrary operations on entity types, such as rotating a part through an angle, or computing its union with another part, as described above.

2.1 Computed versus Stored Functions

Functions in PDM may be either *intensionally-defined*, with output values computed by procedures (such as the **UNION** function above), or *extensionally-defined*, with output values determined by a conventional database search of stored data (such as the **PART_NUMBER** function above). If the function is intensionally-defined, the body of the function is stored in the DBMS metadata. If the function is extensionally-defined, the extent (the stored data) is a database relation containing a tuple for each combination of legal input and output values (or entity surrogates). Set-valued functions are viewed as being "flattened" into tuples in such relations in the normal relational style. Conceptually, the column names of these relations are the lables of the parameters defined in the function definitions. An exception is made for the 0-argument functions that represent entity types. An entity type is

---

[1] Ada is a trademark of the Department of Defense (Ada Joint Program Office).

represented by a unary stored relation which contains all surrogates of entities defined to be of that type. Conceptually, the column name of a relation representing an entity type is the entity type name itself.

Effectively, the difference between the two classes of functions is that an extensionally-defined function can be evaluated with any combination of arguments assigned "input" values, in order to derive values for the remaining arguments. This is reflected in parameters of stored functions being generally declared as "in out". This may not always be possible for intensionally-defined functions, since these are often designed assuming that certain arguments are always input, and certain other arguments are always output.

For extensionally-defined functions, the function definitions, in addition to defining the form of the underlying database relations, also define implicit referential integrity constraints among the columns of the relations. For example, in the function

AGE (PERSON: in out PERSON, RESULT: in out INTEGER)

the **PERSON** column of the underlying relation must contain surrogates of **PERSON** entities (which appear in the unary relation representing the **PERSON** entity type).

In PDM, references to all functions are treated syntactically as if they were references to intensionally-defined functions, even when a stored extent exists, rather than either treating all functions as if they corresponded to stored relations, or treating the two classes of functions differently. (The next section describes the effect this has on the definition of algebraic operations). This functional interpretation matches the functional syntax intended for query languages based on the model (similar to DAPLEX) more closely than a relational interpretation would. It has also assisted in understanding problems related to integrating computed functions into the model (discussed in the next section).

It may be observed that, in the general case, PDM functions are mathematically relations (since they may have multiple output values), and those with stored extents are database relations in the sense of the relational data model. We will continue to refer to these objects as "functions", because syntactically they will be "applied" like (computed) functions. However, the description above suggests that PDM could equivalently be considered a form of *entity-* (or *object-*) *relational* model, along the lines of RM/T [Codd79]. (In fact, [Date83] has suggested that simpler functional models based on similar ideas might be referred to as "directed binary relational models").

3   PDM Algebra

Generic operations on objects (entities and functions), such as selection, function application, set, operations, and formation of new derived function extents, have been defined in the form of an algebra similar in many respects to the algebra defined for the relational data model. Like the relational algebra, this *PDM algebra* provides a formal basis for the definition of general database operations. In particular, the algebra serves to define the semantics of expressions in PROBE's query language, *PDM Daplex*, involving functions and entities, such as:

for P in PART, for D in DRAWING

print (PART_NUMBER (P)) where

WEIGHT (P) > 5 AND SQ_INCHES (AREA(P,D)) < 10

The following sections provide further details of this algebra.

3.1 Basic Characteristics of PDM Algebra

PDM algebra is defined for the objects (entities and functions) described in the last section by adopting a "functional interpretation" for operations of a modified relational algebra, and considering these operations as built-in functions (actually, *functionals*) on function objects. (For extensionally-defined functions, this interpretation is consistent with the one normally associated with the relational model). These operations are viewed as operating on functions and returning functions (effectively relations, as noted above). The arguments of these returned functions are defined in terms of the input functions in the same way that columns of output relations are defined for conventional relational algebra operations. (To illustrate the "functional interpretation" of relational operators, the projection of F(X,Y) on X can be interpreted as asking "what values of argument X are defined for function F(X,Y)?" It is possible to imagine that in some cases projection could be defined for intentionally-defined functions as well as for conventional relations. Metadata specifications can be used to indicate whether or not such a built-in function applies to a given function in the database.)

PDM algebra contains operations for projection, Cartesian product, and set operations (and their "outer" variants [Codd79]). (For set operations, the usual union-compatibility constraints are not applied, in order to allow formation of new generalizations). Selection is defined as in the relational algebra, with the selection condition being a Boolean function evaluation. This function may be a complex expression including functions implementing the usual predicates allowed in relational theta-joins, and logical connectives, as well as function arguments ("columns") containing truth values.

As suggested above, in PDM algebra, all functions are treated as if they were intensionally-defined (computed). The key operation in integrating such functions into the algebra is "apply function (and append results)", which applies a function to arguments contained in tuples of another function. The result is a new function formed conceptually by *appending* columns to the argument function containing the results of the function evaluation. This operation plays a role in the PDM algebra corresponding to that of join in the relational algebra, and in the case of extensionally-defined functions, the interpretation of an **apply** operator is that of a relational (outer, natural) join of the relation containing the arguments (the argument function) to the relation representing the function extent. This approach to integrating (intensionally-defined) functions with (extensionally-defined) relations borrows somewhat from the treatment of functions in [Piro76], and also somewhat resembles the approach described in [HaHT75]. In particular, the **apply** operation is similar in some respects to the "relational composition" operator defined in [Hall84].

The **apply** operator can be described as follows:

Let P be an (extensionally-defined) argument function of the form P (A,B), and F be an (intensionally- or extensionally-defined) function of the form F (I,O), where A, B, I, and O are sets of argument labels, the labels in I are declared either "in" or "in out", and the labels in O are declared either "out" or "in out". Let C be a set of argument labels not currently defined in P, and let @ be a "null", whose meaning will be described in the next section. Then the application of F to P.

apply (P, F (..., Ij: Aj, ... , Ok: Ck, ...))

is a new (extensionally-defined) function R (A,B,C) whose value is the set of tuples t such that t is the concatenation of a tuple tp of P and a distinct tuple of entities (with elements labeled C) returned by evaluating function F with its input arguments I instantiated to the entities of tp with labels in A as specified in the **apply**. If F for some reason cannot produce a result for the given input arguments from tp, tp is concatenated with a tuple of @ (with elements labeled C) to form a result tuple. More formally, the value of R is given by:

$$\{tp + tf[O] \mid tp \in P \; \& \; tf \in F \; \& \; tp[A] = tf[I]\} \; U$$

$$\{tp + @ \mid tp \in P \; \& \; \sim exists \; tf \in F \; (tp[A] = tf[I])\}$$

(where + denotes concatenation, and t[X] denotes the projection of a tuple t on its elements with labels in the set of labels X).

To illustrate a simple use of **apply**, suppose an argument function **T1** contained an argument (column) labeled **P** containing **PERSON** entities, and an **AGE** function was defined as:

function AGE (PERSON: in out PERSON, RESULT: in out INTEGER)

Then **apply (T1,AGE(PERSON:P,RESULT:A))** would result in a new function (say **T2**) having all the columns of **T1**, plus an additional column labeled **A**. Each tuple of **T2** would consist of a tuple from **T1** concatenated with the result (labeled **A**) of evaluating the **AGE** function using the value of the **P** column in that tuple of **T1**.

Including function application within an algebraic framework allows the function "built up" by a sequence of operations in an algebraic expression to serve as the context for the evaluation of subsequent functions. In particular, it retains associations (possibly indirect) between input and output arguments that can be useful in constructing complex results, such as those found in view definitions and other types of derived data. PDM algebra appears to be an effective integration of strictly functional capabilities such as those in [BuFN82] with relational and object-oriented ones. The identification of functional and object-oriented capabilities with relational ones seems particularly important in suggesting implementation strategies and query-optimization techniques.

To illustrate these ideas, the query "print the names of persons whose age is less than ten", which would be expressed as **print (NAME({P in PERSON where AGE(P) < 10}))** in a Daplex-like query language, would be expressed in PDM algebra as:

T1:	apply	**(,PERSON:P)**
T2:	apply	**(T1,AGE(PERSON:P,RESULT:A))**
T3:	select	**(T2,LT(A,10))**
T4:	apply	**(T3,NAME(PERSON:P,RESULT:N))**
T5:	print	**(T4,N)**

(The operations have been separated for clarity.) The sequence of operations is similar to that which would be used in the relational algebra in an RM/T-like database, except for the use of **apply** instead of join. The initial **apply** in T1 denotes the evaluation of entity type **PERSON** as a 0-argument function returning a set (column) of entities of that type. The functional interpretation of this is that each new **apply** of a user-defined function appends additional columns to the function denoted by the algebraic expression, as a relational join would do to a relation. We believe that intensionally-defined functions fit more naturally into this framework than "joining" them as if they were relations (although the difference is largely a matter of taste, provided the semantic issues, as discussed below, are dealt with). The functions that can be applied in this way are not restricted to functions taking simple tuples of values, but also include more complex forms, such as aggregate functions. The technique for integrating them is described in [Piro76, MPBR82, Mano87].

3.2 Semantics of Function Application

In order to fully integrate intensionally- and extensionally-defined functions in PDM algebra, a number of issues relating to the semantics of partial functions and incomplete information must be addressed. In the relational model (and therefore for extensionally-defined functions), these issues have to do with the semantics of the "join" operation (including the various forms of "outer join"), and the inclusion of various types of "null values" (or "marks", in a more recent formulation [Codd86]).

The first of these issues can be characterized in functional terms as "how should functions deal with missing information in function applications?" Specifically, what should be the result when (a) the function is applied to a tuple of input arguments for which it is not defined (intensionally-defined functions) or for which it has no tuple with matching argument values in its extent (extensionally-defined functions); (b) the function is defined for tuples of input arguments that are not actually supplied as arguments in the call? Situations of missing information in function applications, or inapplicable function applications, cannot always be eliminated by type checking at compile time (particularly in an object-oriented model) if the system is to retain necessary flexibility and ease of use. For example, suppose **STUDENT** and **INSTRUCTOR** are defined as subtypes of **PERSON** and the function

ADVISOR (STUDENT:in out STUDENT, RESULT:in out INSTRUCTOR)

is defined. It seems unreasonable to forbid evaluating **ADVISOR** over a set of **PERSON** entities, even though some of them may not be students. However, what the function does in these cases must be defined.

Case (a) above refers, in relational terms, to the choice between an ordinary join and a "left outer join" (using terminology from [Merr84]). To see this, consider the operation

apply (T1,ADVISOR (STUDENT:P,RESULT:A))

which applies an **ADVISOR** function to an argument function **T1** having a column **P** containing **PERSON** entities. The corresponding relational operation would be:

T1 (...,P,...) join ADVISOR (P,A)

In a conventional join, any input tuple of T1 for which the **ADVISOR** function was undefined would not appear in the result. However, in the case of intensionally-defined functions, disappearance of input arguments might be considered an unconventional side effect of trying to apply a function to a set of arguments. A more normal result for functions involving computations would be for the function to return some form of error condition. The null value (or mark) produced by a left outer join in this case can be considered a form of error return from a function call, indicating that, for some reason, the function was unable to return a normal value. Moreover, by defining how other operators of the algebra deal with such abnormal results (as in [Codd79, Codd86]), the approach can ensure that the query does not abort in the middle of a set-oriented expression. For this reason, the **apply** operator in PDM is defined as having semantics similar to an outer join. That is, functions are defined as returning null values corresponding to argument tuples for which it is (for some reason) not able to produce a normal result. A variant of **apply** is also defined that behaves more like a conventional join, in that tuples corresponding to argument values for which the applied function returns an abnormal result do not appear in the result.

A number of papers have identified the need for more than one type of "null" in order to deal with missing information requirements in databases. In particular, [Codd79] notes that the type of null to be returned by the outer join operation depends on whether the relation involved is interpreted according to a "closed world" or "open world" interpretation. The same holds true for functions: the function may be interpreted either as not being defined for particular arguments, or as being defined for the arguments but having insufficient information to return a known result. To support these requirements, two types of "null values" (described in [Merr84]) are currently supported in PDM. The *"don't care" null* behaves like a special value, with properties similar to those of non-null values. Thus, every domain contains this null as a potential value, and a three-valued logic is not required. The *"don't know" null* can be used as the default value of stored functions for which no explicit value has been supplied. The use of the "don't know" null requires the definition of a three-valued logic. The one currently being used is that defined in [Merr84], although this remains under investigation. An additional parameter of the **apply** operator is available to specify what type of null is to be returned when an abnormal condition arises. If the parameter is not explicitly specified, the "don't know" null is returned by default.

The use of "nulls" as an indication of abnormal results in evaluating PDM functions is similar to the notion of "error values" defined in some functional programming languages as a way of indicating errors [Weth82]. The programming language facilities must be much more precise in identifying the exact cause of the error (e.g., "zero divide"), and thus they usually involve more than two "error values". Papers such as [Codd86] seem to agree that in the *general case* a more general mechanism than "nulls" would be needed, although it might not be very justifiable in normal database practice. Moreover, papers such as [Weth82] and [Codd86] agree in emphasizing the need to define the algebraic characteristics of the error values they use. This appears to be a potentially important area of research for the integration of intensionally-defined functions into database systems.

Case (b) described above refers, in relational terms, to the choice between an ordinary join and a "right outer join". To see this, consider the application of the **ADVISOR** function to the argument function **T1** in the previous example. In a conventional join, any tuple of **ADVISOR** for which there was no corresponding argument tuple supplied in **T1** would not appear in the result. A right outer join would preserve this information. While these semantics may not seem very important when considering intensionally-defined functions, a form of **apply** is defined having these semantics to ensure power corresponding to the relational model for dealing with extensionally-defined functions. Taken together, provision of these variants of **apply** extends to intensionally-defined functions the sort of control over the appropriate interpretation that the various "join" variants do for relations in the relational model.

Another issue relating to the semantics of function application has to do with the form of the extents of extensionally-defined functions, and the semantics of updates to functions (primarily of concern for extensionally-defined functions). This issue encompasses a number of problems. For example, the semantics of a multiargument, extensionally-defined function such as

QUANTITY_ON_HAND (D: in DEPOT,
M: in out MATERIAL, QUAN: out INTEGER)

normally include the idea that the function is defined for all possible values of the input argument types, i.e., that **QUANTITY_ON_HAND** can be evaluated for any pair of **DEPOT** and **MATERIAL**. The stored extend for this function might then be thought to include all possible tuples of input arguments. Of course, if only a few materials were stored in each depot, actually storing a tuple for each combination of material and depot might not be very reasonable. Moreover, if a user added a new **MATERIAL** entity, the user might be expected to explicitly supply a value for the function for each existing **DEPOT** entity, in order to "complete" the stored extent. This is clearly unrealistic, from both the user and implementation perspectives. In a corresponding relational database, only the combinations of **DEPOT** and **MATERIAL** for which quantity information was available would be explicitly represented in tuples. Other combinations would be dealt with using the "missing information" facilities described earlier ("nulls" and operations with "outer" semantics). The same approach is used in PDM. As noted above, PDM allows explicit specification in the **apply** operator of the type of null to be returned, in case such a value is appropriate. The discussion here indicates that in some cases it might be preferable to associate information about the intended completeness of the function with the function definition itself, rather than with the **apply** operator. Thus a function might be declared as either *partial* or *total*. A function declared as total might then have a less-than complete extent, and would by default generate "don't know" nulls if applied with input argument values not present in its stored extent. The same function declared as partial, with the same stored extent, would generate "don't care" nulls under similar circumstances.

It is particular important to have defined the semantics of missing information in functions whose values are partially stored and partially computed, or when stored extents of functions may be constructed for optimization purposes. For example, the function

ALTITUDE (TERRAIN_MODEL,LATITUDE,LONGITUDE) -> REAL

in a geographic database would typically be based on a matrix of height values measured at various latitudes and longitudes. The function would return a stored value where one existed for an input latitude and longitude; otherwise, it would compute a value by interpolation. Thus, for this function, a missing tuple in the extent does not mean that the function is "undefined", or that a particular type of "null" should be returned. Moreover, tuples can be explicitly added to such a function extent, provided they satisfy any defined constraints. In fact, for extensionally-defined functions, the extent (together with any specification of whether the function is total or partial) effectively defines the function and an update of either effectively changes the definition of the function. This functional view of updates emphasizes the need for access controls on certain types of updates and is consistent with the observation in [Codd86] that special facilities should exist to control user changes in null values (or "marks"). In general, the problem of updating functions is similar to the problem of updating views in the relational model, and semantic issues must be carefully addressed.

3.3 Other Aspects of PDM Algebra

Operations for creating and destroying entities, duplicates removal, expressing quantification, etc., are also provided in the algebra. For example, given a function P(L1, ..., Ln), **createobj(P,L)** returns a function P1(L1, ..., Ln,L) obtained by concatenating each tuple of P with a new entity (surrogate) as a value of argument L. Effectively, **createobj** is a built-in function defined for entities of type **ENTITY** and may be specialized for particular entity types (e.g., to perform specialized initialization procedures). As suggested by the discussion in the last section, a complete set of update operations is also defined.

Like the operations of the relational algebra, the operations of PDM algebra define dynamically-created entity types and functions that have no explicit database metadata (the metadata is implicit in the algebraic expressions). In order for such entity types or functions to become permanent parts of the database, however, explicit metadata must be created and stored. PDM metadata is represented using entities and functions, so that PDM algebra can also be used in operating on metadata. The structure of this metadata is a hybrid between that used in the LDM [Chan82] and RM/T [Codd79]. Unlike RM/T, which requires operators to translate between names and relations. PDM allows direct functions between metaentities and extensional objects (e.g., database entities). Thus, some of the special operators defined in RM/T for use in mixed metadata/data queries are unnecessary.

PDM algebra as currently defined is powerful enough to perform arbitrary manipulations of PDM databases, including formation of generalization hierarchies, new entity types, and multiargument functions, enabling it to support both query language and view definition requirements. A number of complex test cases demonstrating these capabilities have been worked out, although space precludes presenting them here. The full model definition is given in [Mano87].

4   Other PDM Capabilities

4.1 Extensibility

New data types and operations can be added by defining them as new entity types and functions. The physical realization of these types and their operations may be invisible to the users through an abstract data type mechanism (as in [StRG83]). Essentially this provides a straightforward way of interfacing specialized hardware or software processors to the DBMS. The data types and operations implemented by these processors are defined in the schema as entity types and functions that can be used in queries and transactions exactly like the entity types and functions that are "directly" implemented by the DBMS. At the moment, if the procedures to be added cannot be defined entirely using PDM algebra, they can be written in a conventional programming language and linked into the system. We are also investigating the possibility of extending PDM algebra to make it a complete functional programming language.

Since metadata is also represented by entities and functions, extensibility could potentially also be applied to metadata. This might, for example, be used to create multiple metadata levels, although this has not yet been investigated to any great extent.

Recognizing that many of the objects that occur in the applications to be supported by PROBE deal with spatial and temporal data, we have given special treatment to spatial and temporal modeling. This is accomplished through the definition of special entity types, with appropriate behavior, to model spatial and temporal properties of objects. The following simple example illustrates the basic ideas. More thorough discussions of PDM spatial data modeling capabilities can be found in [MaOr86, MaOD87, OrMa88]. Our approach to *implementing* spatial objects is described in [Oren86, OrMa88]. .

entity PART

function PART_NUMBER (PT: in PART, NUM: out STRING)

function SHAPE (PT: in PART, SHP: out PTSET)

function COLOR (PT: in PART, EXTENT: in PTSET, CLR: out COLORVALUE)

entity PTSET

function CONTAINS (P: in PTSET, Q: in PTSET, O: out BOOLEAN)

Briefly, entities of type **PTSET** that have the semantics of points or point sets (such as lines, areas, or volumes) are defined in the model. These serve as the values of spatial attributes, such as "shape" or "boundary", of ordinary database entities, such as "parts". Subtypes of **PTSET** can be defined to represent general classes of point sets (e.g., 2D and 3D point sets), and specific types of objects within those general classes (e.g., 2D lines and 3D solids). (Points and intervals can also be defined in the same way to represent temporal objects.) For each subtype, appropriate functions can be defined to represent the properties and operations appropriate to the type of object being represented. Note that both spatial and non-spatial attributes (such as **PART_NUMBER**) to be associated with the same database entities in a straightforward way.

Attributes, such as **COLOR** or **DENSITY**, that vary over the shape of the part may be handled in two ways. First, the attribute, e.g. **COLOR**, can be defined as a multiargument function (in this case, as taking a part and a portion of its boundary, and returning a color value). Alternatively, a separate entity could be defined. In this model, object versions (which have received special treatment in some models) are treated as temporal objects. The model is general enough to support many different notions of space and time.

4.2 Rule Specification

PDM incorporates a general facility for specifying situation-action rules or "triggers". This facility can be used to specify rules for propagating changes to derived functions, for propagating operations on some entities to other entities to which they are related (hence, for propagating operations from a complex object to its components, and vice versa), for specifying how and when to check constraints, for invoking exception handlers, etc. Constraints can be specified either as rules that assert some invariants over the database or indirectly through procedures that check whether some desired conditions are satisfied.

4.3 Recursion

The inclusion of recursion in DBMSs, especially to support PROLOG-style deduction over relational databases, has become an extremely active area of research. However, general recursive PROLOG-style rule processing for large, stored databases is potentially inefficient, and not guaranteed to terminate. For practical problems involving recursion in databases, we have identified a special class of recursion, called *traversal recursion* [Rose86], for inclusion in PROBE. Traversal recursion generalizes transitive closure computations on the database viewed as a graph, and has two important properties. First, it is powerful enough to express the recursive computations needed for practical applications. Second, very efficient algorithms, based on graph traversal, exist for performing these computations.

The various forms of traversal recursion are integrated into the model as multiargument functions, which are invoked in the usual way. The parameters of these functions are used to specify properties of the graph (e.g., acyclic or cyclic, disjoint or not), properties of functions to be evaluated during the graph traversal (e.g., whether they are monotonic, whether components are spatially enclosed within their parent objects), and other properties of the computations (see [Rose86] for details).

4.4 Views

As discussed in previous sections, PDM algebra provides the basis for powerful capability for defining new entities and functions in terms of existing database entities and (intensionally- or extensionally-defined) functions. This capability can be used both in providing a conventional database view facility, and also in providing facilities for defining new objects in terms of existing ones, such as usually exist in object-oriented programming systems. Using a combination of these facilities, "internal" entities and functions can be defined that are inaccessible except within specified entity or function definitions, thus providing the type of "encapsulation" generally found in object-oriented programming.

5   Current Work

Work related to PDM is ongoing in a number of areas, some of them mentioned in previous sections. We are continuing to investigate the semantics of function application in the context of set-oriented queries. We feel particularly that being able to deal consistently with partial functions will be of assistance in integrating user-defined extensions (including functions defined for individual objects as opposed to whole types) into the framework. A breadboard implementation of the Probe Data Model and algebra (on both Sun and Symbolics machines), and of some spatial query processing and traversal recursion algorithms, has been completed [DDGO87]. Extensions to this breadboard are now in progress.

6   Acknowledgements

We express our thanks to Alex Buchmann, Upen Chakravarthy, David Goldhirsch, Sandra Heiler, Jack Orenstein, and Arnie Rosenthal for their contributions to the development of PDM.

7   References

[BuFN82], [Chan82], [Codd79], [Codd86], [Dani82], [DaSm86], [Date83], [Daya87], [DDGO87], [DiDa86], [HaHT75], [Hall84], [Loch86], [LoPl83], [LyKe86], [MaDa86], [Mano87], [MaOD87], [MaOr86], [Merr84], [MPBR82], [NoMi86], [Oren86], [OrMa88], [Piro76], [Ries83], [Rose86], [Ship81], [StRG83], [Weth82].

3

Views, Objects, and Databases

Gio Wiederhold

Abstract

Objects provide a useful abstraction in programming languages; views provide a similar abstraction in databases. Since databases provide for persistent and shared data storage, view concepts will avoid problems occurring when persistent objects are to be shared. Direct storage of objects disables sharing.

1 Introduction

The intention of this article is twofold. First of all, I show intrinsic differences in the underlying concepts of access to persistent storage in databases and current extensions of object-oriented programming systems intended to incorporate persistence [DiDa86, Loch86]. Since the objectives of both paradigms are similar, I develop a connection between *object* concepts in programming languages and *view* concepts in database systems.

Secondly, I propose an architecture that exploits the commonality of objects and views, and indicate research and development directions needed to make the bridge viable. Such an architecture seems to be especially suitable for computer-aided design tasks.

Engineering information systems, or EISs, and systems for similar applications must provide suitable abstractions of real-world objects for their users and support long-lived transactions [KaLe84]. The complexity of the design process and the number of specialized individuals needed to bring major projects to completion are driving the search for more systematized solutions than those provided by the file mechanisms now in use in operational precursors of EISs. The issues being raised here pertain to systems with large quantities of data and long lifetimes. Design tasks that can be handled by single individuals are not likely to benefit from EIS technology.

2 Databases and Views

Database concepts provide independence of storage and user data formats. The schema describes the form of the database contents, so that a variety of

---

First published in IEEE Computer 19 (1986) 12; reprinted with permission.

users can satisfy their data requirements by querying the shared database using nonprocedural declarations of the form:

SELECT what-I-want WHERE some-set-of-conditions-is-true

A database administrator integrates the requirements of diverse users. The shared database can be changed as long as the schema is changed to reflect such changes. Concepts of database normalization help avoid redundancy of storage and anomalies that are associated with updates of redundantly stored information.

The principal formal database mechanism to obtain selected data for an application is a view specification. A view on a database consists of a query that defines a suitably limited amount of data. A database administrator is expected to use predefined views as a management tool. Having predefined views simplifies the user's access and can also restrict the user from information that is to be protected. We are interested here only in the first objective, and not in the protections aspects associated with views.

Views have seen formal treatment in relational databases, although subset definitions without structural transformations are common in other commercial database systems. I will hence describe views from a relational point of view, without implying that a relational implementation is best for the underlying EIS databases.

A view is defined in a relational model as a query over the base relations, and perhaps also over other views. Current implementations do not materialize views, but transform user operations on views into operations over the base data. The final result is obtained by interpreting the combination of view definition and user query, using the description of the database stored in the database schema.

The view, like any relational query result, is a relation. However, even when the base database is fully normalized, say to Boyce-Codd normal form, the view relation is, in general, only in first normal form. Views are in that sense already closer to objects: related data has been brought together.

The issue that views present data not in second or third normal form seems to be ignored in database research, except for the update complications that result [Kell86]. I have no evidence that the unnormalized views are uncomfortable to a user expecting a normalized relational representation. Acceptance of unnormalized views can be taken as a partial validation of the acceptability of structures more suitable to represent objects than normalized tables. Some current research is addressing unnormalized relations independent from the view aspect.

3   Objects

Object-oriented programming languages help to manage related data having a complex structure by combining them into objects. An object instance is a collection of data elements and operations that is considered an entity. Objects are typed, and the format and operations of an object instance are inherited from the object prototype.

The prototype description for the object type is predefined and the object instances are instantiated as needed for the particular problem. The object prototype then provides a meta description, similar to a schema provided for a database. That description is, however, fully accessible to the programmer. Internally an object can have an arbitrary structure, and no user-visible join operations are required to bring data elements of one object instance together.

The object concept covers a range of approaches. One measure is the extent to which messages to external operation interfaces are used to provide access and manipulation functions. Objects may be active, as in the Actors paradigm, or passive, as in CLU, or somewhere in between, as in Simula or Smalltalk in terms if initiating actions.

The use of objects permits the programmer to manipulate data at a higher level of abstraction. Convincing arguments have been made for the use of object-oriented languages and some impressive demonstrations exist. Especially attractive is the display capability associated with objects. Object concepts can of course be implemented using nonspecialized languages, for instance in Lisp or Prolog. The tasks in EISs seem to match object-oriented concepts well and many successful demonstrations have been conducted.

4   Objects and Databases

Let us assume a database is used for persistent storage of shared objects. A database query can obtain the information for an object instance, and an object-oriented programming language can instantiate that object. An interface is needed, since neither can perform the task independently. A view can define the information required for a collection of objects, but the data will not be arranged as expected for a collection of objects. Linkage to the object prototype and its operations is performed in the programming system. The program queries the database nonprocedurally to remain unaffected by database changes made to satisfy other users.

The query needed to instantiate an object may seem quite complex to a programmer. A relation is a set of tuples, and, from an idealized point of view, each tuple provides the data for some object. However, normalization often requires that information concerning one object be distributed over multiple relations, and brought together as needed by join operations. The base relations must contain all the data required to construct the view tuples; the composition knowledge is encoded into the Select expressions used to construct the views. An ideal composition of an object should allow its data to be managed as a unit, but unless non-first-normal form relations - supporting repeating groups - are supported for views, multiple tuples are still required to represent one object in a relational view.

Hence storage of objects is not easy in databases, as indicated by the extensions proposed to Ingres for such tasks [StRo86]. A further complexity is that objects themselves may be composed from more primitive objects. In hierarchical databases records may be assembled from lower level tuples, but in relational databases the programmer has to provide join specifications externally to assemble more comprehensive relations from basic relations.

There is some hope that formal semantics being extended for databases can permit the management of the information required to manage objects. Performance remains a bottleneck, and I will consider this issue later with my proposal. The database community has to be careful not to promise too much too soon to the object-oriented folk.

5   Sharing Information in Objects

More serious are the problems I see in the management of shared information within the object-oriented paradigm. I consider two problems:

1.   The growth of objects that contain information for multiple design tasks.

2.   The conflict when object configurations differ for successive design tasks.

Let us first consider the simpler case, where multiple users deal with the same configuration of objects. I will draw my examples from EIS, and consider that the objects are components of a circuit.

In using an EIS the level of abstraction for the objects changes during the process of design. First the objects are simple logic elements and the process of design refines these objects to circuit components and, eventually, to simple geometric elements projected from each layer of the chip. The final objects will carry many data elements not needed at the higher levels. The sketch in Fig. 1 symbolizes how objects grow and lose their vitality.

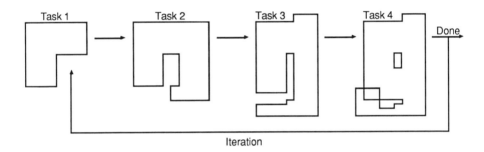

Fig. 1:   *Growth of Objects as they try to satisfy multiple Design Tasks*

As the design process moves from one subtask to the next, successor objects are constructed out of earlier objects. Each new generation has new data fields appended.

Unfortunately, since design often requires cycles, old information cannot disappear. An unacceptable geometry may require a change at the circuit level, say adding an inverter to change a polarity. If design is iterative, then successive transformations of objects must not lose information. This means that objects suitable for one task must contain information relevant to all tasks that may be successors, although much information may be irrelevant to the task at hand. The information may be hidden within the object, but must be passed on correctly, so it remains available when needed.

The objects become big, and no longer have the qualities associated with the object-oriented paradigm. A solution to this problem of overloaded objects is to have super-objects, owned by an object czar. Objects for each user task type are created by projection from the super-object. Updating privileges must be well defined.

This solution does not solve the second class of problems, namely sharing object information when the object configuration differs. Now, to create objects for a user task objects may have to be created from combinations of several and, perhaps, different objects or super-objects.

I show in the next section an EIS example having components and nets connecting them. These present different configurations of the same information. In aircraft design the objects serve design tasks as aerodynamics, structures, power, fuel, control, etc., and it is obvious that their configuration is quite different. Even in a simple commercial credit-card operation there is the customer as an object for some tasks and the stores are the objects wanting to be paid in other tasks. No single hierarchy can structure the data.

Because of these problems, I present later a proposal that will not try to store to objects directly in persistent form. I prefer a new approach to satisfy the demands of database style sharing and object concepts.

6   Looking at one Example of Distinct Object Configurations

To clarify the issue I will take a simple device, a D-type latched flip-flop. At some level of abstraction it is an object; at a lower level it is composed of several gate objects of only three types: AND, INV, NOR, and contacts to the external world. The graphical representation of Fig. 2 shows the component objects of the flip-flop at the gate level and the interconnection nets. The components are capitalized and the nets have lowercase labels.

D-type latched Flip-Flop

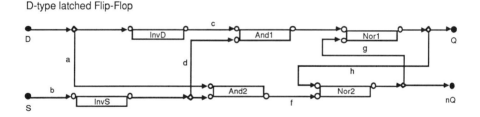

Fig. 2:   *Latched D Flip-Flop*

A fully normalized database storing the information describing this circuit requires several relations. I show in Fig. 3 the two library relations, which describe the types of gates (Gates) and their connection points (Gate-connects). Many other values will be kept in such a library. The ruling part or key attributes of each relation are placed ahead of a separator symbol :>.

Fig. 4 presents a nonredundant representation for the specific circuit using two more relations, one for each gate instance and one giving the net connections for each gate. Other design-specific information can be kept within these relations.

Relation   Gates:

Gate-type:>	Function,	Area,	No-pins,	Power,	Delay, . . .;
Inv	x = 1/a	30	2	. . .	
And	x = a ∧ b	40	3	. . .	
Nor	x = a ▽ b	35	3	. . .	
Cntct	a	900	1	. . .	

Relation   Gate-connects:

Gate-type,	C-no :>	C-id,	IO;
Inv	1	a	in
Inv	2	x	out
And	1	a	in
And	2	b	in
And	3	x	out
Nor	1	a	in
Nor	2	b	in
Nor	3	x	out
Cntct	1	a	inout

Fig. 3: *Relations describing the Gates Library*

Relation Components:

Id:>	Type,	Role,	Position, . . . ;
D	Cntct	Data in	1/1
S	Cntct	Sense in	3/1
InvD	Inv	Data inverter	1/2
InvS	Inv	Sense inverter	3/2
And1	And	And data	1/3
And2	And	And sense	3/3
Nor1	Nor	Nor to Q	1/4
Nor2	Nor	Nor to nQ	3/4
Q	Cntct	State out	1/5

Relation Connections:

Id,	Pin:>	net;
D	1	a
S	1	b
InvD	1	a
InvD	2	c
InvS	1	b
InvS	2	d
And1	1	c
And1	2	d
And1	3	e
And2	1	a
And2	2	d
And2	3	f
Nor1	1	e
Nor1	2	g
Nor1	3	h
Nor2	1	h
Nor2	2	f
Nor2	3	g
Q	1	h
nQ	1	g

Fig. 4: *A fully normalized Description*

The representation of the design shown is quite complete, but also fairly unclear. I need to create views that place all relevant data into coherent tuples. A view is needed to analyze the components and their loads; another view is needed to look at the nets; and other views will be needed for timing analysis, heat dissipation, etc.

In Fig. 5 I extract two views, ComponentsView and NetsView for the database of Fig. 4, using also the library relations shown in Fig. 3. The ComponentsView is intended to be appropriate for checking components and their sources and sinks. It primarily accesses the Components relation, and joins with its tuples data about the connected components and from the libraries.

```
CREATE VIEW ComponentsView (ID, Pin, IdC:> Type, N, IO, IOC)
       AS SELECT C.Id, C.Pin, CC.Id, CM.Type, T.No-pins, G.IO, GC.IO
              FROM Connections C CC, Components CM, Gate-connects G GC, Gates T,
       WHERE C.Id = CM.Id AND C.Net = CC.Net AND C.Type = T.Gate-Type
              AND C.Type = G. Gate-type AND CC.Type = GC.Gate-type;
CREATE VIEW NetsView (Net, Dev. Pd:> IOd)
       AS SELECT C.net, C.Id, C.Pin, GC.IO
              FROM Connections C, Components CM, Gate-connects G GC, Gates T,
       WHERE C.Id = CM.Id AND CM.Type = T.Gate-type;
```

ComponentsView :=							NetsView :=			
Id,	Pin,	IdC :>	Type,	P,	IO,	IOC;	Net,	Dev,	Pd:>	IOd;
D	1	InvD	Cntct	1	inout	in	a	D	1	inout
D	1	And2	Cntct	1	inout	in	a	InvD	1	in
S	1	Inv1	Cntct	1	inout	in	a	And2	1	in
InvD	1	D	Inv	2	in	inout	b	S	1	inout
InvD	2	And1	Inv	2	out	in	b	InvS	1	in
InvS	1	S	Inv	2	in	inout	c	InvD	2	out
InvS	2	And1	Inv	2	out	in	c	And1	1	in
InvS	2	And2	Inv	2	out	in	d	InvS	2	out
And1	1	InvD	And	3	in	out	d	And1	2	in
And1	2	InvS	And	3	in	in	d	And2	2	in
And1	2	And2	And	3	in	in	e	And1	3	out
And1	3	Nor1	And	3	out	in	e	Nor1	1	in
And2	1	D	And	3	in	inout	f	And2	3	out
And2	1	InvD	And	3	in	out	f	Nor2	2	in
And2	2	InvS	And	3	in	out	g	Nor2	3	out
And2	2	And1	And	3	in	in	g	Nor1	2	in
And2	3	Nor2	And	3	out	in	g	nQ	1	inout
Nor1	1	And1	Nor	3	in	out	h	Nor1	3	out
Nor1	2	Nor2	Nor	3	in	out	h	Nor2	1	in
Nor1	2	nQ	Nor	3	in	inout	h	Q	3	inout
Nor1	3	Nor2	Nor	3	out	in				
Nor1	3	Q	Nor	3	out	inout				
Nor2	1	Nor1	Nor	3	in	out				
Nor2	1	Q	Nor	3	in	inout				
Nor2	2	And2	Nor	3	in	out				
Nor2	3	Nor1	Nor	3	out	in				
Nor2	3	nQ	Nor	3	out	inout				
Q	1	Nor1	Cntct	1	inout	out				
Q	1	Nor2	Cntct	1	inout	in				
nQ	1	Nor2	Cnct	1	inout	out				
nQ	1	Nor1	Cntct	1	inout	in				

Fig. 5: *Component View and Net View*

The NetsView is intended to generate data on the interconnection nets for an application doing checking. The primary relation for the NetsView is the Connections relation, augmented with library information for the connected components.

The number of objects in ComponentsView is equal to the cardinality of the component relation (10), but the augmentation makes the result much larger (30). The eight nets are represented in the primary relation and in the view by 20 tuples, one per connected point (∘) or external contract (•). In both views I present the tuples in a logical order.

This view is still awkward, since single component objects require multiple tuples. A more reasonable presentation would delete redundancies and add implicit non-first-normal-form bindings by rearranging columns according to the source relations. The Nor1 component shown within Fig. 5 would then have a object data strucure as shown in Fig. 6. I add a column N, which gives the number of connected components. The computation of N using SQL requires Group By and Count operations.

Id,	Type,	P	Pin,	N,	IO,	IdC,	IOC;
Nor1	Nor	3	1	1	in	And1	out
			2	2	in	Nor2	out
						nQ	inout
			3	2	out	Nor2	in
						Q	inout

Fig. 6:   *Reduced Datastructure for a View Object*

```
enum io {IN, OUT, INOUT};
  class Cpin;
class CCpin;
  class ComponentsView
  {
        char          Id [8];
        char          Type [6];
        short         P; // Component pin count
        Cpin* Pin;
  };
  class Cpin
  {
        io            IO;
        short         N; // Connected component count
        CCpin* C;
  };
  class CCpin
  {
        char*         IdC;
        io            IOC;
  };
```

Fig. 7:   *C++ Datastructure for Component Objects*

I now describe in Fig. 7 this structure in the object-oriented extension of C, namely C++ [Stro86]. In C++ structures have to be mappable at compile time, so arrays of dynamic extent cannot be embedded: Since it is permissible in C++ to have a dynamic array as the last element of a class by writing an appropriate constructor, it is possible to bring the CCpin array inboard.

A similar reasoning could lead to a NetsView hierarchical structure. At the leaves of both hierarchies we would find the same data. Only one of these could be active at any time.

7   Views and Objects

Let us now reconsider the similarities between views and object concepts. Both are intended to provide a better level of abstraction to the user, although the database user is seen to manipulate sets of objects in a nonprocedural notation while the objects are manipulated procedurally and iteratively.

The *collection* of tuples of a view is defined by the query that generates the set, and described by the relation-schema associated with the view query. The set of objects is defined by the user-initiated action of generation and described by the prototype. Object-oriented languages may have a ForAll primitive to rapidly generate collections of objects of some type.

The description of the relation has to be available to the relational user, since no implied operations can be kept in the relation-schema. There are proposals to store object-defining procedures in relational schemas, but these have not yet been tested [StRo86].

Both tuples and objects can be selected based on any of multiple criteria, and interrogated to yield data for processing. View update may be severely restricted because of ambiguities in base relation update. Object update can be restricted by having only limited access functions, but otherwise no constraints are imposed on the programmer, although consistency problems can easily arise among users sharing objects.

Basic, of course, is the difference in persistence. Databases, and hence views over them, persist between program invocations. Objects must be explicitly written to files to gain persistence. Related to persistence is the critical issue to be addressed, namely the multiplicity of views that can be derived from a base relation. Fig. 5 showed a view of "components" and a view of "nets" derived from the relations of Fig. 3 and 4.

8   The Proposed Architectural Unit: View-Objects

I now propose to combine the concepts of views and objects, as discussed above, into a single concept: view-objects. This proposal is motivated by noting that systems suitable for engineering information problem support require both sharability and complex abstract units, i.e., both views and objects. I use the concept of views to generate a working set of objects corresponding to projections of the entities described in the database [Cart86]. The generators may need to access multiple relations to reconstruct the entities hidden to the relational representation. Components of the architecture are

1. a set of **base relations** and

2. a set of view-object generators.

In a complete version of this approach I also require the inverse function of 2., namely,

3. a set of view-object decomposers and archivers.

The conceptual base relations serve as the persistent database for aplications under this architecture. They contain all the data needed to create any specified object type. Conventional database technology should be adequate for development, but eventually performance demands may drive users to specialized databases. I will consider the options for physical organization later.

Concurrent access by long-lived transactions will require a capability to conveniently access prior versions of the data. Where database management systems do not serve that need intrinsically, the database must be configured with additional time-based attributes. As experience is gained, this service will be included in specialized systems being built.

The view object generator is the new component in this architecture. It performs the following steps:

a. The view-object generator extracts out of the base database data in relational form as needed - as is now done by a query corresponding to a view. A view tuple or set of view tuples will contain projected data corresponding to an object. A view tuple or set of view tuples will contain projected data corresponding to an object. A view relation will cover a selected set of objects.

b. The view-object generator assembles the data into a set of objects. The objects will be made available to the program by attaching them to the predefined object prototype.

The view-object generator needs information other than the data, i.e., knowledge to perform its functions:

a1. The query portion identifies the base data.

a2. The specification of the primary relation identifies the object-entities.

a3. The object prototype specifies the structure and linkages of the data elements within an object, and the access functions for the object.

Initially the view-object generators will be implemented as code, closely following the translation programs in use now to convert persistent storage representations of engineering data files into representations suitable for specific tools. For experiments a relational database can be used for storage of the base data, but expect that ongoing developments in EIS will provide systems with more appropriate functionality and performance.

The goal is to eventually provide non-procedural access for object-oriented approaches as well. By formalizing the semantics of the objects required by the tools, and interpreting the object type description, I believe that the view-object generators may be automated. The programmer then only provides the object type declaration and the Where clause defining the desired set of object instances.

With increased storage of data semantics in extended schemas one may advance further. With structural or dependency information about the base relations, automatic generation of the internal structure of an object type may become feasible. Since access to the objects by the tools is still procedural, the performance benefits of automated object generation would be minor. The major benefit is in the control of access and consistency that may be gained.

9   Justification

I am proposing a major extension to database and object-oriented concepts, with the intent to obtain the joint benefits that each approach provides separately today. The effort must justified by these benefits.

Sharable access to objects. The proposed architecture supports procedural access to objects, as expected by object-oriented programming systems. Access to the base data is automatic, and nonprocedural. This permits base data to be effectively shared, since no single application or combination of applications imposes a structure on the base relations.

Growth of the system. New object types can be defined by adding new view-object generators. As is expected in databases, new data instances, types, and entire relations can be added without affecting other users' programs. Data can be reorganized without changing the object generator code since only the views will be involved. Such flexibility is essential for growth and multiuser access.

Support for a wide variety of representations. When simple tabular results are to be obtained from the database, a view-object generator can easily generate tables for direct inspection and manipulation. A graphics object-generator can project the attributes needed for visual display.

High-performance access from the database. To achieve this goal new database interfaces must be developed that make the benefits of the set-oriented database retrieval concepts available to programming languages. Current database interfaces create a bottleneck when delivering data to programs. A common method for relational systems is to accept a query that specifies a set, but then require repeated invocations that deliver only single values or records at a time. This access mode, because of conventional programming techniques, is clearly inadequate.

The data from the databases is to be inserted into sets of objects at a time. For the object-oriented programmer such a set is best defined as a super-object. A program typically cannot proceed until the set is complete. The object generators need only be invoked once for all the data needed to compose a super-object. An effective view-object generator hence needs an interface at a deeper level into the existing relational functions.

Updating from objects. The programs can freely update the contents of the objects. Some applications require that these changes be made persistent and hence be moved from its object representation to the base database.

To achieve update I envisage a third architectural component, the view-update generator. This component can be invoked at commit-time, when results affecting the objects are to be made persistent. I envisage that such a process will only update from objects that have changed, and only replace values that were changed.

Where views have been constructed using joins, aggregation operators, and the like, automatic view update can be ambiguous. Restrictions on object update are one solution. However, as shown by Keller [Kell86], such ambiguities can be enumerated and a choice can be made when the view-update is generated. The view update generator can also take advantage of the semantic knowledge available to an advanced view-object generator. An important source of knowledge constraining updates is authorization information.

10 Cost trade-offs

What costs and benefits will this architecture provide other than what I see as its structural advantage? I will now review areas where performance may be gained versus one of the two underlying approaches - database use or object-oriented programming - alone.

Set-based data access. A single invocation of a view-object generator will instantiate all specified objects. The overhead of programmed access to relations, typically requiring an initial Call giving the query and then iterated Calls to obtain the result piece by piece, is avoided. Also, no sequence of object instance-generating Calls, as seen in object-oriented programming, is needed. Of course, one invocation of the object generator will be a major operation, but only one call should be needed per object type.

The object generator may also perform the so-called macro-generator function, where instances of design objects are generated based on a general prototype and parameters. The source of such information is a library of cell descriptions, permitting, say, the generation of a series of cells making up a register.

The view-object generator will be more complex than either a database retrieval alone or an object prototype. It will provide a very clear definition of the mapping from base data to objects and do so in a localized manner. A partial example was given, using the SQL approach to describe the view in Fig. 5 and then using C++ to define the storage structure for the objects in Fig. 7.

Binding of retrieved data. The ability of the view-object generator to bind the object will pay off in processing time. No joins are needed at execution to bind relational tuples, and no search operations are needed to assemble tuples belonging to the same object. Since the required information exists at view generation time, no search cost is expended. The only requirement is that the object's internal data structure permit retention of the information.

Task allocation that matches hardware system components. Implicit, but not essential, to my proposal are the complementary concepts of database servers and design workstations. They will be linked by a powerful, but often still bandwidth-limited, communication network. In such an architecture I expect that most of the retrieval and restriction operations will be carried out on the machine serving the database and the object generation and use will occur in the workstation.

Optimization in the file server. The file server can select optimum retrieval strategies and reduce the data volume needed to convey the information. Keeping data in sorted order and removing redundant fields as shown in Fig. 6 is straight-forward and effective. All operations are specified nonprocedurally and can be arranged and interleaved as needed to handle requests from the users. Concurrency control and version management are tasks best handled in the file server.

Communication minimization. The data volume is reduced in the file server. Communication bandwidth between server and workstation can be used fully for information, rather than for data to be ignored in the workstation.

High performance on workstations. The workstation only needs to assemble the information obtained into the desired object configuration. It is desirable that all objects for an application task can be placed into the real memory of the working processor [Holl85]. The objects now do not contain data fields irrelevant to the process at hand. Since these working objects are now compact, the probability that they will all fit into a modern workstation is increased. Virtual memory management can be invoked if needed, but the capacities of modern machines are such that there should be adequate memory space for working storage of the required objects. However, I can envisage several techniques to exploit having the data independence provided by view generators to improve locality for virtual memory management.

11 Physical organization of the database

Performance issues are considered critical in EISs, and experiments with relational databases have not given me confidence that adequate performance is easy to obtain. Performance will furthermore be impacted by the extentions, such as version support, that are needed in the engineering environment [KaLe84]. Many of these extensions will also be useful for broader objectives, so that there is a motivation to share the development and maintenance costs of relational database systems extensions.

Objects are seen as a means to solve the performance problem, because data is bound in a user-sensible manner. I believe that such binding can indeed be significant in workstations, although our own experiments have not given proof of that assumption when external storage is used [Wilk85]. There are obviously many more factors to be considered simultaneously when building comprehensive systems, but storing data in relational tables is often seen as a critical issue, of clarity and maintainability versus efficiency.

The fully normalized model of the representation has as its objective the minimization of redundancy and the avoidance of a number of anomalies that can occur. It also supports a very simple storage structure, as seen in our example, that can lead to a large number of relations. Retrieval from such an organization will require a large number of joins, as seen in the example leading to Fig. 5.

Updates seem to require less work in a relational database than in our proposal. However, when the database has to obey interrelational constraints, expensive joins must also be executed when the data are updated. For instance, it is necessary to ensure that the components exist and that the connections are valid when a net connection is in an EIS to be changed.

There is, of course, no requirement for the physical storage structure to mimic literally the logical relational structure. Specifically, information from multiple tuples may be stored in one record. Denormalization has been formally considered, but is not supported by current DBMSs. It is commonly employed in practical relational databases. Preserving correctness in a denormalized database often requires additional transformation and care: records may have repeated fields and at other times some fields may be replicated in multiple records. Sometimes here work is required as well: dependent tuples, as connection points for a component, will automatically be deleted if they were implemented as a repeating group. I expect to profit here from ongoing research on nested relation databases.

In my architecture, where I expect that the object generator is the primary means for accessing data, complexity issues discouraging use of a non-normalized storage structure are moot. The object generators can be adjusted, probably eventually automatically, to any storage structure chosen. It is likely that the most efficient storage structure will be similar to the dominant object structure.

With such an organization I have provided the two primary objectives favoring the concept of object-oriented programs for computer-aided-design:

1.   The concept of a view-object provides the desired clean and compact user interface.

2.   The flexibility of the storage structure can provide the locality needed to achieve high performance in source data access.

I can now provide these objectives for multiple users, and share selected information in a controlled fashion. I gain greatly from the flexibility obtained by interposing the object generator operating on a persistent base storage structure, I am no longer bound to an optimal data storage structure bound to an optimal object format. It is likely that in any design project the data retrieval loads will change over time. The object types that dominate use during initial design phases are not likely to be the object types used during the maintenance phase of the designed devices. A physical storage reorganization is now possible, as long as the view-object generators are adjusted correspondingly.

Replication, the primary tool to improve performance, can be utilized as well. A high-demand subset of the database can be replicated and made available to improve the performance of the object generators. Object update functions can use primary copy token concepts to update all copies consistently and synchronously.

12 Summary

I argue that direct storage of objects, to make them persistent, is not appropriate for large, multi-user engineering information systems. I propose storage using relational concepts, and an interface that generates objects. To test the validity of the concept, initial versions of the interface may be coded directly. In the longer range I look toward knowledge-driven transformations.

Generation of objects from base data brings the advantages of sharing persistent information to an object-oriented program. It also provides a better interface from programs to databases, recognizing that access by programs, large or small, will remain essential for data analysis and complex transactions.

The separation of storage and working representation will also simplify the development of new approaches to engineering desing [HaMa85]. The object generator can be viewed as a system component utilizing knowledge to select and aggregate data for the information objectives. An implementation has been developed at SRI - Sarnoff-Laboratory [CoMu88].

13 Acknowledgments

This paper has benefited from interaction with a VHSIC program-sponsored project to define information models for engineering information systems, although it certainly does not reflect the consensus of the group. Comments by Tony Gadient of the USAF, WPAFB, Arnold Goldstein of MCC, and Professor Alice Parker of USC were constructive and helped focus the issues. Earlier presentations of these concepts at Workshops for Integrated Design and Manufacturing Processes at the Naval Postgraduate School in Monterey, Calif., April 1986, and at the Object-Oriented Database Workshop [DiDa86] engendered useful feedback. David Beech, from Hewlett-Packard, visiting the Stanford Center for Integrated Systems, provided motivation to consider the object-oriented approach and gave constructive criticism to earlier versions of this paper. He also provided the C++ example for Fig. 7. Support for this research was provided in part by DARPA contract N39-84C-0211 for Knowledge Based Management Systems and in part by the Air Force through a contract with UES F33615-82-C-1716.

14 References

[Cart86], [CoMu88], [DiDa86], [HaMa85], [Holl85], [KaLe84], [Kell86], [Loch86], [StRo86], [Stro86], [Wilk85].

4

Inheritance Issues in Computer-Aided Design Databases

Randy H. Katz, Ellis E-Li Chang

Abstract

Object-orientated concept, particularly inheritance mechanisms, appear to be of wide use in non-standard database applications. However, we believe that conventional type-instance inheritance is too limited for computer-aided design data. We propose alternative inheritance semantics that are better suited for propagating data and constraint definitions around a lattice of computer-aided design objects.

1   Introduction

Object-oriented systems provide a natural way to structure applications and their data. Data is defined in terms of abstract data types, with the operations for data manipulation implemented in the type definition. Further, it is possible to propagate data definitions and attribute values within the lattice formed from instances, types, and supertypes through inheritance mechanisms. Because applications-specific operations can be associated with the data, the object-oriented approach is attractive for structuring non-traditional databases. Several research groups are applying these concepts for computer-aided design databases [Atwo85, BaKi85, Harr86], as well as databases for office applications [Zdon84].

Our work has been motivated by computer-aided design for VLSI circuits. Although it is possible th think of an individual layout geometry or logic gate as an object, for the purposes of data management we find it more useful to aggregate these into larger units. Thus, objects correspond to named design units, such as an arithmetic logic unit (ALU) or a register file, which consist of potentially large numbers of primitives in particular representation types, such as layout or logic. Objects can also be defined in terms of compositions of more primitive objects, e.g. a datapath layout object can be composed from an ALU layout object and a register file layout object. The composition relationships among objects are called *configurations* in our model. Over time, an object may undergo revision, and several versions of it may be created. Each is an object in its own right, but it is important to keep track of the

Reseach supported under N.S.F. grants ECS-8403004 and ECS-8352227, with matching support from the Microelectronics and Computer Technology Corporation.

relationships among versions, such as which was derived from which. We call these version histories. Further, an artifact like "the ALU" actually has several physical realizations: an ALU layout, an ALU logic description, an ALU transistor decription, etc. Again, each of these are objects in their own right, but the relationshipts among them are modelled by *equivalences*. Thus, it can be seen that a design database is a complex hierarchical collection of interrelated objects, spanning time (via versions) and representations (via equivalences).

Inheritance provides powerful mechanisms for organizing a computer-aided design database, especially as it *evolves over time.* New versions of design objects are very much like their ancestors. Inheritance mechanisms can reduce the amount of information that needs to be specified to describe a new version.

Inheritance, as it is normally defined, provides scoping for data and operation definitions through a taxonomic hierarchy of instances belonging to types, which in turn belong to supertypes (i.e., types of types). For example, if a variable is accessed from an instance, and is not defined there, then its associated type is searched for the definition. If it is not defined in the type, the process recurses to the supertype, and so on until the root of the type lattice. More advanced models support *mix-ins*, i.e., they allow types to be instances of more than one supertype and provide mechanisms for disambiguating multiple definitions.

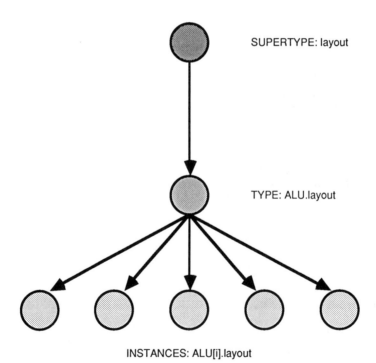

Fig. 1:   *Supertype/Type/Instance*
The figure shows the taxometric relationship among instances (versions) of the ALU layout "type", wihich is in turn an instance of the supertype of layouts

From the viewpoint of computer-aided design applications, inheritance is most useful for defining default values for new version instances. For example, consider the "type" of ALU layouts, which is a subtype of the supertype layout (see Fig. 1). All ALU layout instances share a set of data manipulation operations common to all layout objects, which are inherited from the layout supertype. In addition, they share common attributes and values for those attributes, such as ther interface and behavioral descriptions (e.g., the arithmetic and logical operations they support). This common data can be factored out of the instances and stored with the ALU layout subtype. In creating a new instance of the ALU layout, the values of these common attributes can be inherited from the ALU layout type without being explicitly specified.

However, conventional type-instance inheritance provides only one of many ways to propagate defaults to new versions, albeit the most widely used and best understood. For example, a new version might inherit attributes from its immediate ancestor version. Alternatively, since design objects are used as components within other objects, an object can inherit attributes from the composite object that uses it. Further, design objects are associated with other objects that are alternative representations of the same real-world artifact, such as the layout, netlist, and functional objects to inherit from one of these equivalents. In other words, inheritance between instances along arbitrary relationships is of use in the CAD environment.

The rest of this paper is organized as follows. In Section 2, we point out the limitations of conventional type-instance for modeling CAD objects. Section 3 gives examples of how other kinds of inheritance can prove to be more useful. Section 4 discusses some implementation issues, while Section 5 contains our summary and conclusions.

2   Problems with Type-Instance Inheritance

Object-oriented models provide a logical data organization in which taxonomic relationships are maintained between instances and their associated type, and recursively between types and supertypes. Observe that it is not possible to propagate data directly from one instance to another. Interestingly enough, object-oriented models have descended from arbitrary semantic networks, which usually provide capabilities for propagating data along arbitrary relationships (e.g., see [Brac83, Fox79]). No doubt the restrictions were introduced for implementation efficiency. We will have more to say about this in Section 4.

Instance-to-instance inheritance is important in computer-aided design databases, since a new version tends to resemble its immediate ancestor. It is useful if a new version can inherit its attribute values, and more importantly its constraints, from its ancestor. For example, if ALU[5].layout[1] is equivalent to ALU[3].netlist, then a new descendent of ALU[5].layout should inherit this constraint.

Type-instance inheritance provides a rudimentary mechanism for propagating common data to versions. [BaKi85a, BaKi85b] have used the type concept to group together versions of the same real world artifact, e.g., the type of ALU layouts. A new version instance can inherit a default from the ALU

---

[1]   We adopt the notation object-name [version#].type to name an instance in a computer-aided design database.

layout type. But it is not possible to inherit from the type definition constraints that can vary on an instance to instance basis. While it is possible to associate a generic constraint like "every ALU layout should be equivalent to some netlist instance" with the ALU layout type, this is insufficient to identify to which instance of the netlist a given layout is equivalent.

Mix-ins can support a limited kind of instance-to-instance inheritance (see Fig. 2). A new subtype is introduced for each equivalence class of instances under each constraint. For example, all ALU layout versions that share an equivalency constraint with ALU[3].netlist could be members of the same subtype. A new member of the subtype would inherit the constraint when it was created. Other attributes could be recursively inherited from the ALU layout type. Obviously this leads to an undesirable proliferation of subtypes, greatly complicates the type lattice, increases the runtime overhead, and makes it difficult for the instance's creator to understand of which subtypes a new instance should become a member.

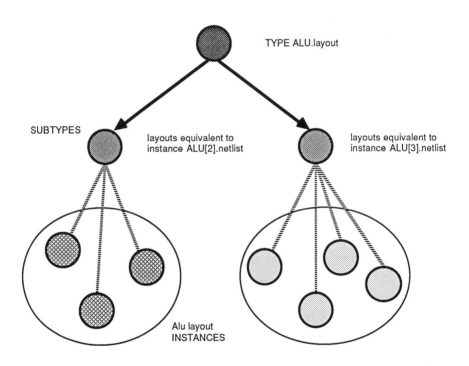

Fig. 2:   *Handling Instance-to-Instance Inheritance with Subtypes*
              A subtype is created for each group of instances that shares a common attribute or
              constraint. Obviously this leads to an undesirable proliferation of subtypes.

Other researchers have made similar observations, and have proposed the concept of *prototypes* to replace types [MiBK86, Born86, Lieb86]. Instances are associated with a prototype object, and are defined to behave like it unless the instance overrides some aspect of its definition. The difference between prototypes and types is primarily conceptual. Advocates of this approach point out that it is often difficult to completely define an abstract type in advance, while it is relatively easy to provide an example of instance of the type, which can serve as the prototype. An advantage is that there are no distinguished objects to represent types: any instance can serve as a prototype. By providing mechanisms such as delegation, which is essentially message passing, it is possible to implement inheritance-like propagation directly among instances. An attempt to access an instance's attribute which is not locally specified is forwarded to its prototype. Typically, when a new version is created, its ancestor can be its prototype. To support mix-ins, it should be possible to have more than one prototype for different aspects of an instance's behaviour.

The interesting thing about prototypes is that they provide a better model for how a design undergoes evolution than that provided by types. Designers do not first define an abstract type, identifying the attributes that will be common to all versions, and then proceed to create concrete instances of the type, allowing these to inherit default values. Rather, common attributes and their values can only be *generalized* to the type once a number of concrete instances have been created. Thus, the "type" is more like a generic description of the concrete instances that can vary over time. This is in contrast to the strict concept of type found in programming languages, i.e., a collection of constraints that define type membership. The first version serves as a prototype to its immediate descendents, which serve as prototypes to their descendents, and so on. Once several instances are in place, one could imagine the type serving as the prototype for any attributes that could be generalized across all instances, while the ancestor serves as the prototype for the attributes that cannot be generalized. However, determining which attributes to generalize is tantamount to deducing the type definition from examples, a well-known (and difficult!) problem in artificial intelligence.

3   Other Kinds of Inheritance and their Uses

The relationship between an instance and its type is only one of several that an instance can participate in (see Fig. 3). As alluded to in the introduction, we have developed a version data model that identifies three kinds of relationships among versioned objects [Katz87]. An object instance **is-a-descendent-of** some parent instance. In turn, it **is-an-ancestor-of** some child instances. These are *version history* relationships. In addition, an instance **is-composed-of** component object instances, and **is-a-component-of** some other higher-level instance. These are *configuration* relationships. Finally, an instance in one type **is-equivalent-to** instances in other types. These are *equivalence* relationships or constraints. It would be useful if default values could be propagated along any of these relationships.

In the previous section, we presented an example of constraint inheritance from an ancestor. In general, the source of most default values and constraints should be from the ancestor of a new version. Since equivalences are constraints among instances, these cannot come from the type, and must come from the ancestor. Of course, the first version could inherit its attribute defaults from the type (i.e., the prototype of the first instance is the type).

There are situations in which inheritance along configuration relationships is also important. Some of the details of the interface description can only be determined from the context in which an object is used, rather than from its type. The types of the input and output ports of a design object could be inherited from the composite object that incorporates it. Procedurally defined design objects often operate by adapting to their environment, for example, resizing the layout of their internal circuitry when presented with a large output load to drive.

Similarly, hints to CAD tools, such as how to place and route cells, can only be determined by the context in which the cells are used. Such information can be propagated to the object from its containing composite. Finally, change propagation strategies, i.e., how a composite object is to react to a change in one of its components, can also be inherited from its containing composite (e.g., see [KaCh87]).

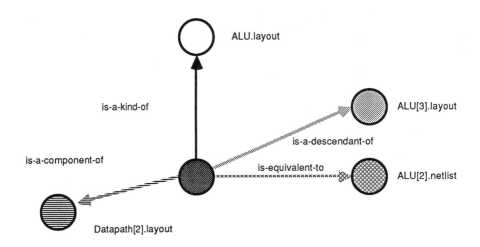

Fig. 3: *Lattice of Relationships Among Design Objects*
Besides being taxonomically related to its type (i.e., is-a-kind-of), a design object can be related to its ancestor, (i.e., is-a-descendant-of), to the objects that use it (i.e., is-a-component-of), or to equivalent objects in other representations (i.e., is-equivalent-to).

The final method of inheritance is from equivalent objects. In most design domains, there is one representation from which the others are derived, either automatically or by hand. For VLSI design, this is the functional representation. For example, major portions of the functional interface description, such as the names and general types of the input/output connection ports, can be propagated to the netlist and layout descriptions. As mentioned above, local configuration information may override, or more fully specify the interface description. As in the case of mix-ins, it is important to specify the priority of inheritance for the different places from which default values can come.

4   Implementation Issues

In object-oriented programming languages, the advantage of type-instance inheritance is that the procedure for propagating values to instances can be determined at compile-time. Of course, the actual instance, type, and supertype objects will have to be examined at run-time while inheritance is being performed. On the other hand, implementing inheritance along arbitrary instance-to-instance interconnections requires considerable run-time interpretative overhead, and this is perhaps why it has not been implemented in the past. However, in a design database, this can be tolerated since inheritance is invoked to fill in default values only when a new instance is created. The additional overhead is incurred once, and does not affect normal access to the instance once it has been created.

Apart from the implementation overhead, language designers argue that users have difficulty understanding the added complexity of arbitrary instance-to-instance inheritance. This is somewhat ameliorated by the design object model alluded to in this paper, since objects exist within a limited lattice of relationships (i.e., **is-a-kind-of**, **is-a-descendent-of**, **is-a-component-of**, and **is-equivalent-to**).

There is no question that the instance's creator is presented with a complex mix-in problem, since default values can conceivably come from four different places: the type, the ancestor, the composite instance that uses it, or equivalent instances. In our Version Server [Katz87], a new version is created by first *checking-out* an existing instance from an archive into a private workspace, where it can be modified and later returned via *check-in*. Inheritance takes place at check-out time. Currently, only inheritance from ancestor to descendent is supported, and we do not yet have the ability to inherit operations. However, we are extending the system to permit the attachment of operations to objects, and will provide support for the more general inheritance mechanisms described in this paper.

If a new instance is to inherit from a containing composite object or an equivalent object, it is necessary to establish the relationships with these as part of a check-out context. The format of the context-dependent check-out command is as follows:

check-out <object-name>

    equivalent-to {<list of equivalent instances>}

    contained-within {<list of composite instances>}

    {list of the following:

        <attribute-name> like

        [GENERIC, ANCESTOR, EQUIVALENT, COMPOSITE]};

(NOTE: "GENERIC object" is the Version Server's terminology for type, e.g., ALU.layout is a generic object). For example, assuming that ALU layouts have three attributes, *input-port*, *output-port*, and *behavior*, the following check-out command:

check-out ALU[3].layout

    equivalent-to ALU[2].netlist,

    contained-within Datapath[2].layout

        input-port like ANCHESTOR,

        output-port like COMPOSITE,

        behavior like EQUIVALENT;

would create the version ALU[4].layout of Fig.1, whose input-port attribute would be inherited from ALU[3].layout, whose output-port would come from Datapath[2].layout, and whose behavior attribute would be from ALU[2].netlist. While it looks laborious to specify what should be inherited, note that the default is to have exactly the same inheritance behavior as the instance's immediate ancestor. The detailed specifications are only necessary if the default inheritance is to be overridden. The description of the check-out context can also be reduced by relying on defaults (e.g., a new instance is equivalent to the same instances as its immediate ancestor, and is to be used where its ancestor has been used), as well as the Version Server's browsing interface, which allows the user to "click-on" icons to specify the equivalent-to and contained-within lists. The order of the instances within the equivalent-to and contained-within lists is used to disambiguate multiple inheritances: the first object found within the list that has the described attribute will furnish its value in the new instance. The LIKE clause can mention a specific instance name if this simple form of disambiguation is not sufficient.

5   Summary and Conclusions

Type-instance inheritance provides a powerful mechanism for propagating information from supertypes to types to instances. It provides a useful form of abstraction, in that common attribute values are factored out of instance definitions and are placed elsewhere in types (or supertypes). It significantly simplifies the task of creating a new instance, since an instance's default values can be filled-in from its associated type. The semantics of type-instance inheritance are well understood, implementation strategies have been developed, and a number of programming systems (e.g., Smalltalk-80, Loops, Flavors) support it.

The problem with type-instance inheritance is that it is not possible to inherit values directly among instances. Unfortunately, this is the most natural way to describe a design database, since new version instances are sure to inherit most of their attributes from their ancestor version. In fact, we have identified three relationships in addition to **is-a-kind-of** along which information in a CAD database can propagate: version histories (as described above), configurations, and equivalences. As with mix-ins, it is necessary to define which path dominates if more than one is used to define an attribute of a given instance.

We are now completing the implementation of a Version Server for computer-aided design data that organizes the versions of a design across time. It is essentially a sophisticated but passive electronic filing cabinet for design data. The next goal is to make the system more active, in particular, more reactive to changes, by incorporating mechanisms for change propagating, described in [KaCh87], and inheritance as described here.

6   References

[Atwo85], [BaKi85a], [BaKi85b], [Born86], [Brac83], [Fox79], [Harr86], [KaCh87], [Katz87], [Lieb86], [MiBK86], [Zdon84].

5

Object Management in Postgres using Procedures

Michael Stonebraker

Abstract

This paper presents the object management facilities being designed into a next-generation data manager, POSTGRES. This system is unique in that it does not invent a new data model for support of objects but chooses instead to extend the relational model with a powerful abstract data typing capability and procedures as full-fledged data base objects. The reasons to remain with the relational model are indicated in this paper along with the POSTGRES relational extensions.

1   Introduction

This paper presents the mechanisms in POSTGRES [StRo86a] to support object management. This system does not invent a new data model for manipulation of complex objects, but rather extends the relational model with a powerful abstract data typing system and support for procedures as a fundamental data type. With these constructs, most application specific data models can be easily simulated. A companion paper illustrates this fact by showing how a shared, multiple-inheritance, object hierarchy can be implemented on POSTGRES [Rowe]. Hence, POSTGRES appears to easily support a wide variety of application specific needs without compromising the simplicity of the relational model for conventional business data processing applications.

In section 2 we briefly review a collection of data modeling proposals intended for support of non-traditional applications. We also argue that there is no small common collection of ideas on which to base the data model of a general purpose next-generation data base system. Consequently, the thrust of next-generation systems should be to efficiently simulate a variety of application specific data models.

In Section 3 and 4 we discuss the specific approach taken in POSTGRES which utilizes an abstract data typing capability and procedures as full-fledged data base objects. Section 5 closes with a summary of the capabilities of our approach.

This research was sponsored by the U.S. Air Force Office of Scientific Research Grant 830021 and by the Naval Electronics Systems Command Contract N00039-84-C-0039.

2   The Case for the Relational Model

This section briefly discusses three reasons to retain the relational model as the backbone of a next-generation system.

2.1 The Semantic Poverty Argument

It is often argued (e.g. [Zani83] that the relational model is semantically impoverished, and should be replaced by a data model with additional semantic constructs. Over the last ten years there has been considerable research toward identifying such a model, and in this section we briefly list some of the constructs proposed.

Without attempting to be very rigorous at classification or exhaustive in coverage of proposals, the following list is easily assembled from the literature.

ENRICHED COLLECTION OF OBJECTS

entities, attributes and relationships [Chen76]
classes [HaMc81]
roles [BaDa77]
objects with no fixed type or composition [CoMa84]
set valued attributes (repeating groups) [Zani83]
unnormalized relations [Lum85]
class variables (aggregation) [SmSm77a]
category attributes and summary tables [Ozso85]
molecular objects [BaKi85a]

TYPES OF RELATIONSHIPS

"is-a" hierarchies [SmSm77a, GoRo83]
"part-of" hierarchies [Katz85]
convoys [Codd79, HaMc81]
associations [WoKa80]
referential integrity (inclusion dependencies) [Date81]
grouping connections [HaMc81]
equivalence relationships [Katz86]

OTHER CONSTRUCTS

ordered relations [Ston83a]
long fields [LoPl83]
hierarchical objects [LoPl83]
multiple kinds of nulls [Kent83a]
multiple kinds of time [SnAh85]
versions [WoSt83]
parameterized versions [BaKi85a]
snapshots [AdLi80]
synonyms [Lohm83]
table names as a data value [Lohm83]
automatic sampling [Rowe83]
recursion or at least transitive closure [Ullm85]
windows or universal relations [Kort84]
semantic attributes [Spoo84]
unique identifiers [Codd79, Powe83]
demons [Ston85a]

Two conclusions are evident:

1. There is a large collection of constructs, each relevant to one or more application specific environment

2. The union of these constructs is impossibly complicated to understand and probably infeasible to implement with finite resources

Hence, it appears inappropriate to look for a single universal data model which will support all non-traditional applications. In short, what the CAD community wants is different from what the semantic modeling community wants which is different from what the expert data base community wants, etc. Consequently, such users should build application specific data models containing the constructs needed in their environment.

The thrust of a next-generation data base system should be to provide a support system that will efficiently simulate these constructs. The next section discusses the POSTGRES capabilities which will be seen to be considerably more powerful than other proposals with the same general intent.

Since the relational model has found such widespread acceptance, it should be the task of the proponents of some other data model to demonstrate that their choice provides the same degree of simplicity and simulation power as provided within the relational context by POSTGRES.

2.2 The Simplicity Argument

There are many drawbacks to using a complex tool rather than a simple one in a data base environment. First, the user manual is longer and harder to write, and training customers to use the tool is more costly. Second, a more complex tool has inherently higher technical support costs than one which is simpler. Additionally, there is often more than one construct that can be used to model a particular real world situation. Hence, advice is needed on which one to use and the performance implications of the choice. A logical and physical design tool is thereby harder to construct.

All other data models are more complex than the relational model. Clearly, constructs should be included in a data model only if the power provided overwhelms the cost of the added complexity in a variety of application environments. In my opinion, this power/complexity case has not been persuasively made by the advocates of most of the specific constructs in the previous section.

Stated differently, this author considers simplicity a good idea. The remarks of [Codd70] on the subject seem as valid now as they did when written fifteen years ago.

2.3 Compatibility

It is conceded by most that the relational model provides a good fit to the needs of the business data processing community. Such data will clearly gravitate from older technology data managers into relational data bases over the next decade.

It is also obvious that users will demand the ability to correlate data in multiple data bases managed by multiple software packages. For example, consider a CAD data base containing the design of a particular printed circuit board. This PC board contains packages which are bought from outside suppliers. Hence, it is certainly appropriate to ask the total cost of packages contained in the PC board. This query requires the ability to correlate data in the CAD data base with data on suppliers and parts. This latter data base is business data processing data and will presumably be in a relational system. As a result, one will need to correlate a relational data base with whatever data base system manages the CAD data.

This problem was addressed by Multibase. Moreover, it is obvious that problems of heterogeneity become increasingly severe the further one strays from the relational model. Hence, compatibility issues are an additional reason to retain the relational model unless overwhelming case can be made to displace it.

3   The POSTGRES ADT System

POSTGRES supports object management within the relational model with two facilities, an abstract data type (ADT) facility and procedures as a data type. The ADT system has been described in [Ston83b, Ston86], and is briefly reviewed in this section. POSTGRES support for procedures is considered in detail in the next section.

POSTGRES allows a user to implement a new data type which can then be used as the type of any column in any relation in the data base. Moreover, operators specific to the new data type can be included in the query language by writing a procedure to evaluate the operator. This capability is useful for all kinds of objects normally found in engineering applications (e.g. boxes, lines, polygons, points, line-groups, complex numbers, vectors, bitmaps, etc). For example, the proposal of [Ston83b] discusses the inclusion of box as a data type along with a collection of operators (e.g. intersection, area-of, to-the-left-of, etc.) appropriate to the new type. The facility is also useful in business data processing applications. For example, many commercial system implement date and time as data type (e.g. INGRES, FOCUS, NOMAD) along with operators on this type (e.g. subtraction). Unfortunately, the normal definition of subtraction for dates is not appropriate for some segments of the financial community which utilize a 360 day year and 12 equal length months. Only an ADT system allows a user community to implement a different definition of subtraction.

In summary the collection of data types and operators provided by most current data base systems are appropriate to the needs of business data processing applications. One need only allow an extensible type system to support the needs of others.

This ADT proposal is extended in [Ston86] with constructs that allow a heuristic query processor to optimize query language expressions containing new operators and new data types. Preliminary discussion of support for new access methods was also included. In the interest of brevity, these proposals are not summarized as they are not relevant to the following discussion.

An ADT facility meets the needs of a variety of object management applications. However, it fails in three important situations:

objects with many levels of subobjects
objects with unpredictable composition
objects with shared subobjects

Consider a mechanical CAD application which stores a particular building in a data base. An object in such a data base might be an office desk. However, the desk is in turn constructed of subobjects (e.g. drawers), which are in turn constructed of subobjects (e.g. handles). This "part-of" hierarchy is prevalent in many engineering applications. A user often wishes to "open up" an object and access specific subobjects. For example, he might want to find the handle on the lower left-hand drawer. The ADT proposal noted above would force a user to write an operator for each such access he wanted to perform. A very large number of operators would result that would be exceedingly hard to use. In summary, a user wants the query language to assist with "opening up" complex objects and searching for qualifying subobjects; he does not want an operator for each particular search.

The second problem concerns unpredictable composition of objects. This issue is noted in [CoMa84], and can be easily illustrated with the desk data. Suppose the data base contains objects that are on top of the desks in the example building. In particular, some desks have flowers, some have simple phones, some have switchboard phones, etc. In this case, a subobject of a desk may be one or more objects from a huge set of possible desk accessories. It is unreasonable to require a user to write an operator to extract any object from such an unpredictable collection.

The third problem concerns shared subobjects. Consider a heating duct in the building that is accessible from several rooms in the building. One would want to store the duct once, and then have it be a shared subobject in higher level objects (rooms). The ADT proposal noted above has no ability to share subobjects in this fashion.

To support objects with any of these requirements, POSTGRES supports procedures as full-fledged data base objects. In the next section we indicate the specific procedural support that we are constructing.

4   POSTGRES Procedures

POSTGRES supports the notion of a registered procedure which can be used in query language commands as well as two different procedural data types, namely:

> POSTQUEL procedure
> parameterized POSTQUEL procedure

These are discussed in turn below.

4.1 Registration of Procedures

A procedure in a general purpose programming language can be **registered** to POSTGRES by indicating the following information.

> the name of the procedure
> the implementor of the procedure
> the data types of its parameters
> the data type of its result
> the programming language it is written in
> the source language representation of the code for the procedure
> a type-checking flag
> a precomputation flag

Registration of a procedure is a POSTQUEL utility command which fills the above information into two system relations, one for the procedure information and one for the parameters. After registration, the procedure is compiled asynchronously by POSTGRES and can be used in the POSTQUEL query language anywhere that a function is currently allowed in QUEL.

For example the code for "is-overpaid" could be registered as taking a float and an integer as arguments and returning a boolean. With this definition the following query can be expressed for the standard EMP relation:

retrieve (EMP.all) where EMP.age > 35
and is-overpaid (EMP.salary, EMP.age)

A second example would be a "progress" procedure which accepts a float and an integer and returns an integer between 1 and 10. The employees whose progress is greater than 4 who are over 35 would be expressed as follows:

retrieve (EMP.all) where EMP.age > 35
and progress (EMP.salary, EMP.age) > 4

This mechanism is a straightforward extension of hard-wired functions currently supported in QUEL (e.g. sin, cos, log, sqrt, etc.).

Registered procedures have the types of their arguments installed in a system relation. Consequently, type checking is done on the arguments to any registered procedure. If a type mismatch is discovered, then argument conversion takes place. This conversion is guaranteed to succeed, because part of registering a data type to POSTGRES is specifying two operators which will convert ascii to the new type and then back. Hence, if T is the type of argument expected and Y is the type of the actual argument, then POSTGRES need only apply the Y-to-ascii function followed by the ascii-to-T function.

In order to avoid a double conversion, we may experiment with a special class of functions called **conversion functions**, which convert between data types. If there exists such a registered function which has Y as the type of its argument and produces T as the type of its result, then that function can be used in place of the two functions noted above.

Note that the implementor of a registered procedure can turn type checking off by specifying the type checking flag as "no checking". This setting is appropriate in two situations. First, commands may come from an application program which can (somehow) guarantee that the arguments are the correct type. In this situation, run-time type checking of the parameters by POSTGRES generates needless overhead, and should be turned off. The second situation would be a user defined procedure which expected a variety of argument types and contained code to do its own type checking and coercion. In this case POSTGRES type checking should also be disabled.

The other flag that can be set by the implementor of a procedure declares it to be **precomputable**. In this case, POSTGRES is allowed to evaluate the procedure before receiving a request from a user. This precomputation is a central optimization for POSTGRES and is useful in a variety of circumstances as will be presently seen. In the present context, procedures with no arguments are sometimes precomputable. for example, consider the following functions:

user()
time()
group()
command()
machine-type()
factorial-10()

These functions return the current user, current time, the group of the current user (if defined), the command he is currently running, the type of machine on which he is running, and the factorial of 10 respectively. Notice that the last two functions can be precomputed and the result of the procedure cached, while the others will generate the incorrect result if precomputed.

In the system relation containing registered procedures there is one additional flag besides those settable by the implementor. This flag declares a procedure to be safe. In this case, POSTGRES will call the compiled version of this procedure by linking the code into the POSTGRES address space and performing a local procedure call. This call is unprotected, and an errant or malicious procedure can bring down POSTGRES (by zeroing the disk or doing a wild branch into POSTGRES code). However, no performance penalty need be paid to call such procedures. On the other hand, unsafe procedures are called by spawning another process, loading the procedure into the created process and performing a remote procedure call. This protected version will incur considerably more overhead.

All registered procedures are initially unsafe and can be debugged without far of crashing POSTGRES. The POSTGRES super-user (the person with the POSTGRES password) can update the safety flag to make a procedure trusted. Presumably, he does this only after inspecting the code or talking with the implementor of the procedure.

4.2 Procedural Data Types

4.2.1 POSTQUEL Fields

A column of a relation may be declared to be of type POSTQUEL procedure; e.g.:

```
create EMP (name = c10,
    age = i4,
    hobbies = POSTQUEL)
```

Each ADT has an associated external to internal conversion routing, and the one for POSTQUEL procedures will accept a quoted string containing the POSTQUEL code. With a registered procedure, file, which accepts the name of a file and returns the contents, we can express the following append command:

```
append to EMP (name = "Mike",
    age = 10,
    hobbies = file("/usr/myfile"))
```

The code in "/usr/myfile" is a collection of retrieve commands which access appropriate relations in the data base to get hobby tuples for Mike. An example collection of commands might be:

```
retrieve (windsurf.all) where windsurf.name = "Mike"
retrieve (softball.all) where softball.name = "Mike"
```

POSTQUEL procedures are automatically (and asynchronously) compiled and the answer is optionally precomputed and cached if the procedure is a retrieval. The cache is invalidated, if necessary, using the mechanisms in [StRo86]. Moreover, the "nested dot" notation can be used to address into the objects which are represented by POSTQUEL, procedures as suggested in

[Ston84]. The following POSTQUEL command finds the batting average of Mike on the softball team.

retrieve (EMP.hobbies.batt-avg)
where EMP.name = "Mike"

Notice that any procedural object can access tuples which in turn contain procedures, so an object hierarchy can be constructed. Objects can be shared by being referenced in multiple procedural fields. Next, the contents of a POSTQUEL field can be any query, so unpredictable composition of objects is readily supported. Finally, the nested dot notation allows the query language to be used to search inside of complex objects. Consequently, all objections to the ADT paradigm can be overcome with POSTQUEL procedures.

Moreover, one can easily perform operations that are difficult with explicit data hierarchies, such as the ones in [HaMc81, Ship81]. For example, the following POSTQUEL query will find all hobby data for Mike:

execute (EMP.hobbies) where EMP.name = "Mike"

To use a semantic data model, one can declare employees to be an object type and then declare a large collection of subtypes (e.g. softball-emp, windsurf-emp, etc.). In order to find all the hobby information for Mike, one would have to iterate over all possible subtypes at great expense to answer the above query. Hence, POSTQUEL procedures can effectively simulate object hierarchies and also perform certain operations that are difficult with other approaches.

The remaining subsection suggests a variation of procedural types that is useful in a variety of circumstances.

4.2.2 Parameterized POSTQUEL Fields

In many instances one requires a column of a relation to be of type POSTQUEL procedure. However, all values for the column use the same procedure, differing only by the parameters used as arguments in the call. For example, suppose a second DEPT relation is added to the data base and a field "dept" is added to the EMP relation. The value of "dept" for each EMP tuple is the query:

retrieve (DEPT.all) where DPT.dname = $1

The "$1" is simply a parameter to the query which changes from employee to employee and indicates his department. It is certainly possible to store the same query as the value for "dept" for each tuple in the EMP relation. However, space will be economized and integrity of the column will be enhanced if the procedure is "factored out" of the column and stored elsewhere.

More exactly, if the above procedure is registered using the mechanism of the previous subsection, then the EMP can be specified by:

create EMP (name = c10,
     age = i4,
     dept = POSTQUEL[pname])

"Pname" is simply the registered name of the above POSTQUEL procedure. With EMP so defined, a new employee can be added to the data base by:

```
append to EMP (name = "Mike",
      age = 10,
      dept = "shoe")
```

The value specified by the user for the "dept" field is the parameter to the procedure. POSTGRES converts "shoe" to the correct type and stores the parameter in the actual field. Of course, registered procedures must be extended modestly to allow POSTQUEL commands with run-time parameters to support the above capability.

There are several advantages to parameterized POSTQUEL fields, as noted in [Ston87]. First, the user can specify queries with a nested dot notation rather than using a join. For example the query

```
retrieve (EMP.dept.floor) where EMP.name = "Mike"
```

finds the floor on which Mike works. Moreover, one obtains a particular kind of referential integrity by using a procedure because all employees who belong to a non-existent department have a query which returns nothing and thereby automatically have a null department. Lastly, the query optimizer can coalesce the user command with the definition of the procedure to "flatten out" the user command and then optimize the resulting composite query. Hence, one is not restricted to processing nested-dot commands in a particular order. The flattening algorithm is discussed in [Ston87].

Parameterized POSTQUEL fields and registered procedures bear some resemblance to Smalltalk methods. In Smalltalk, there are a collection of methods (procedures) defined for an object which are stored external to the object instances. In parameterized POSTQUEL, there is exactly one method associated with an object which is separately stored. A registered procedure is similar to a Smalltalk method; however, our registered procedures are "global" to the data base rather than bound to a specific object and inherited by other objects as in Smalltalk.

In the remainder of his section we indicate one further generalization of parameterized POSTQUEL procedures. Consider the case of procedures that cannot be expressed solely in POSTQUEL. This may result from the necessity to perform computations that are not expressible easily in POSTQUEL or to format output data in some peculiar way. A good example is the "progress" of employees noted earlier. This computation might be quite involved and perhaps require accessing other relations in the data base. In order to support precomputing of the value for "progress", one would like to define a field in EMP that was associated with a procedure written in a general purpose programming language.

The solution is to register a procedure in the data base for "progress" and then specify a second POSTQUEL procedure:

```
retrieve (result = progress(EMP.salary, EMP.age))
where EMP.name = $1
```

Then, the user can create the EMP relation as:

```
create EMP (name =c10,
      age =i4,
      progress = POSTQUEL[name])
```

"Pname" corresponds to the above registered POSTQUEL procedure. Hence, one can insert a new employee by:

```
append to EMP (name = "Mike",
      age = 10,
      progress = "Mike")
```

Clearly, it is undesirable to require the constant "Mike" to be specified twice in the append command. The following generalization of registered POSTQUEL procedures allows a more compact notation.

Suppose the parameters to a POSTQUEL, command can be denoted "$1" to indicate the i-th parameter found in the POSTQUEL field itself or "$string" to indicate that the parameter is to come from the column in the same tuple with the name "string". Hence, the above POSTQUEL retrieve command should be specified as:

retrieve (result = progress(EMP.salary, EMP.age))
where EMP.name = $name

With this specification, Mike can be added to EMP as follows:

append to EMP (name = "Mike", age = 10)

The user can now find the progress of Mike in two different ways. First, he can use the registered procedure "progress" as follows:

retrieve (value = progress(EMP.salary, EMP.age))
where EMP.name = "Mike"

This will execute the registered procedure at the time that Mike's tuple is accessed. On the other hand, one can also access the field in EMP corresponding to "progress", i.e.:

retrieve (value = EMP.progress.result)
where EMP.name = "Mike"

This second form has on important advantage, namely the procedure for Mike may have been precomputed since all POSTQUEL fields are candidates for precomputation. If the registered procedure "progress" was flagged as precomputable, then the above POSTQUEL command may have cached answers for a variety of employees. Hence, if the progress of Mike is in the cache, the result is returned directly and no run-time computation need be performed. This is an important optimization if "progress" is a long computation.

The following example suggests another situation in which precomputation of POSTQUEL procedures containing registered procedures in a general purpose programming language is a crucial optimization. Consider a forms management application whereby an individual form is composed of various trim features and fields, each with a collection of attributes. It is desirable that forms be stored in the data base so they can be easily shared by multiple applications. However, it is also important that forms be compiled into an efficient main-memory representation appropriate to the run-time forms management code. Currently, users of INGRES [RTI86] must explicitly compile a form after they are through constructing it. If the form is changed, they must explicitly recompile it anew.

With POSTGRES , one can register a procedure "compile" which accepts as its single argument, the identifier of a form. Then one can register the following POSTQUEL command:

retrieve (result = compile(FORMS.identifier)
where FORMS.identifier = $id

Lastly, one need only declare a FORMS relation as follows:

create FORMS (id = i4, compiled =POSTQUEL[pname])

The compiled version of a form will be created asynchronously by caching the value of the POSTQUEL command. Since the definition of forms changes slowly, the cache will be only infrequently invalidated. Moreover, the user is spared from the difficulty of remembering to compile form definitions. In all cases he simply executes the following retrieve:

retrieve (computation = FORMS.compiled.result)
where FORMS.id = xxx

We close this section by discussing the reasons for not extending the POSTQUEL procedural data types of this section to ones written in a general purpose programming language. First, if a column of a relation was of data type "arbitrary procedure", then there would be no way of knowing the data type of each argument expected by the procedure or the data type of the result. Hence, it is necessary to register all procedures in a general purpose programming language to obtain this information. For POSTQUEL procedures, registration is not necessary because POSTGRES can ascertain the data types of all arguments and the composition of all the result relations.

There are two difficulties with extending parameterized procedures to allow any registered procedure instead of only those written in POSTQUEL. First, the "multiple dot" notation allows fields to be selected from the output of a procedure by name, and the registration step does not contain a mechanism to name fields in procedural output. Second, the $string notation discussed above cannot easily be extended to registered procedures. Both difficulties do not arise in POSTQUEL procedures.

5   Discussion

This section briefly reviews the power available in the procedural fields described in the previous section.

First, note that a variety of data hierarchies can be effectively modeled. One approach is discussed in a companion paper which uses a single relation to store the form of the type hierarchy and a second relation to store the operators that can be applied to any given object in the hierarchy [Rowe]. However several others approaches can also be utilized. For example, one can use one or more procedural fields in the relation that corresponds to any given object to assemble the objects which are "inherited" by any given object. This inheritance can be of arbitrary composition, and is not limited to "is-a" hierarchies.

Registered operators must have unique names, so it is not possible to have several operators of the same name and then inherit the one which is "closest" to a given object in some object hierarchy. We considered allowing operators to be multiply defined; however, that would have given us all the messy problems that come with multiple inheritance (i.e. determining which operator to actually use in a specific instance).

Lastly, notice that procedures can be used for many different purposes (e.g. storage of user commands, triggers, rules, data base procedures, the code of operators, etc.). Hence, we feel that utilizing a single powerful construct is a better approach than extending the data model with more anemic capabilities.

6   References

[AdLi80], [BaDa77], [BaKi85a], [Chen76], [Codd70], [Codd79], [CoMa84],

[Date81], [GoRo83], [HaMc81], [Katz85], [Katz86], [Kent83a], [Kort84],

[Lohm83], [LoPl83], [Lum85], [Ozso85], [Powe83], [Rowe83], [Rowe], [RTI85], [Ship81], [SmSm77a], [SnAh85], [Spoo84], [Ston83a], [Ston83b], [Ston84], [Ston85a], [Ston86], [Ston87], [StRo86], [Ullm85], [WoKa80], [WoSt83], [Zani83].

6

Handling Constraints and their Exceptions: An Attached Constraint Handler for Object-Oriented CAD Databases

A.P. Buchmann, R.S. Carrera, M.A. Vazquez-Galindo

Abstract

An attached constraint handler that can be invoked from an object-oriented CAD-DBMS is described. Constraints and their exceptions are treated uniformly, and are stored and updated as instances of predefined constraint classes. This allows for dynamic constraint definition, deferred constraint checking, and uniform handling of constraints and exceptions, which are relaxations of the constraints. The paper analyzes constraint classes typically encountered in CAD environments, discusses the problems of dynamic constraint definition and deferred evaluation, and based on this discussion, introduces the design and implementation details of the constraint and exception handler.

1   Introduction

Semantic data models have gained in popularity mainly because of the modeling power they provide, a feature that is most useful for non-conventional knowledge-oriented database applications, such as CAD, cartographic databases and office automation [Daya85]. The increased modeling power is derived from the ability of these models to handle semantically meaningful objects rather than normalized tuples or single records. The main mechanism by which a data model can capture better the semantics of the objects that are being modeled is through the use of constraints that are an integral part of the data model. These constraints can be structural or value based constraints. The first type is used to enforce the composition of the modeled objects while the second kind is used to enforce the correctness of values assigned to a variety of attributes of the objects. There is, however, a grey zone when dealing with objects that are composed of multiple component objects that present inheritance and aggregation of attributes, since the very structure of the object will determine the values the inherited or upwards aggregated attributes can take.

In non-conventional applications it is not only important to be able to handle constraints effectively, but it is also necessary to deal with exceptions. Exceptions shall be viewed in this context as relaxations of constraints. The same rationale that motivates the inheritance of attributes in a semantic data model has to be applied to the handling of constraints and exceptions: both have to be inherited by the constituent objects. This is necessary since constraints are often specified at high levels of abstraction. For example, in a CAD application concerned with the design of a computer one may want to define a constraint at the project-level, in which case the restriction will be applicable to all the components of the computer, or we may decide to define a constraint for a single board or a certain type of chip.

A review of the literature shows that several attempts have been made to handle integrity constraints in databases. However, most of these attempts have been made in the context of tuple or record oriented database systems [HaMc75, Ston75, BeBC80]. On the other hand, exception handling has been linked most prominently to programming languages and only recently an interest for managing exceptions has been noticeable in the database community [Borg85]. The approach taken so far for constraint and exception handling in databases relies mostly on strongly typed languages in which the constraints are specified and compiled in the schema definition. A different approach is taken by expert systems. They allow addition of new rules to a rule-base, thereby refining the system as new insight is gained and additional facts are known.

As new semantic data models are developed and full DBMSs that are based on them are implemented, it becomes increasingly necessary to handle the constraints that are an integral part of these models. Strong typing, on which both, traditional data base approaches and programming languages depend for constraint enforcement, has two basic consequences:

1. constraints have to be checked always and cannot be deactivated temporarily, and

2. the database designer (or programmer) has to anticipate all possible constraints under penalty of having to recompile the definition.

Recompilation is a minor task when dealing with application programs and when the users of the environment are sophisticated programmers, but it is totally unrealistic to recompile the schema frequently in a turn-key CAD environment in which the end-users often have to supply the constraints but have little idea of the inner workings of the CAD system and its underlying database. Therefore, a flexible mechanism is required for constraint and exception handling that does not depened on schema recompilation and laborious application-program rewriting, i.e. a mechanism that allows dynamic specification of constraints along the lines of a rule base. Independently of how constraints are defined, either as instances of well defined types of constraints (as shown here) or as rules, we like to point out a basic difference between an expert system and an (object-oriented) DBMS with extensive constraint and exception handling capabilities: The expert system suggests (or should suggest) a solution to a problem deriving the solution from a set of rules which is assumed to be complete; an enhanced DBMS requires that a particular solution be given by the user (either human or an application program) and uses the constraints to ensure consistency with other portions of the design, to the extent that constraints exist. Given the magnitude of a large design and the difficulty of defining a *complete* set of rules we consider the expert system approach somewhat unrealistic for most large CAD applications, while the use of an enhanced DBMS which only supports the decision making process of the user is feasible in then near term, given the current state of the art in database technology and programming language development.

Based on this reasoning we present in this paper an analysis of constraints and their exceptions as a necessary preliminary task for the design and implementation of a generalized constraint handler. We discuss next the scope of constraints and exceptions and in Section 3 and 4 the issues of dynamic definition and deferred evaluation for constraints and exceptions. Finally, we present design and implementation issues for the generalized constraint handler in Section 5 and Section 6 deals with some of the extensions that will be needed at the programming language level to include constraints into the object-oriented language TM [GeBu85]. We conclude with our current status and future plans.

2   Analysis and Classification of Constraints and Exceptions in a CAD Environment

The environment in which the present work is embedded is an object-oriented DBMS which we are developing for CAD applications. The underlying model is a semantic data model that is based on the notion of molecular aggregates [BaBu84]. A molecular aggregate can be viewed at different levels of abstraction and consists of one object which represents the aggregate as a whole and any number of constituent objects. The component objects are linked to the object which stands for the whole aggregate and among themselves through a variety of roles of aggregation which can be specified by the user and which carry the semantics of aggregation. There are a few basic roles of aggregation whose semantics are implicitly supported by the model, such as IS_A hierarchies and COMPONENT_OF aggregation, but other roles which are not of these types can be defined. The two basic types of roles of aggregation are used for support of constraint and exception inheritance. Each molecular object can have any number of constraints associated with the object and the constraints can either be value-based constraints or structural constraints acting on the roles of aggregation. An initial description of the data model has been presented elsewhere [BuCe85]. Here we shall concentrate on the definition and handling of the constraints and exceptions to them.

The examples we shall use in the remainder of this paper are taken from the CAD applications we are most familiar with. We decided to use these examples, even at the risk of them being unfamiliar to some readers, simply because they are real cases we have encountered and we think they represent a given situation better than artificially concocted examples.

The constraints we are dealing with can be classified according to a variety of criteria: type vs. instance constraints; violatable and non-violatable constraints; and value vs. structure constraints. In our application we have a fourth grouping according to the scope of the constraints which divide them into universal constraints and particular constraints; this is a special case of the type vs. instance classification.

Type Constraints vs. Instance Constraints

We speak about *type constraints* if the restriction is defined on the whole class of objects. Similarly we speak about *instance constraints* if these are defined on a single object including its constituent objects.

As an example let us consider the object class `process_stream` which is defined as illustrated in Fig. 2.1. The definition is in TM [GeBu85] but we have, on purpose, downplayed the sections that do not define the object's structure.

The example shows the definition of the object class `process_stream` and its `components`. Every process stream consists of one or more components for which we want to constrain the concentration. If concentration x_comp is expressed as a fraction, a constraint applicable to the whole class of components is:

$0 \leq x\_comp \leq 1$

In addition we may want to constrain the concentration of a given component by stating:

$0 \leq x\_comp(1234) \leq 0.05$

While many (but usually not all) constraints defined for whole object classes can be defined during database-design time, instance-specific constraints are defined while using the database, i.e. during product-design time. They have to be observed by subsequent design activities.

Violatable vs. Non-Violable Constraints

As soon as we contemplate the possibility of exceptions to constraints, it is imperative to distinguish between constraints that can be violated and those which cannot.

In the above example it is clear that a negative concentration, or a concentration of more than 100% makes no physical sense and violates our definition of concentration. The constraint $0 \leq x\_comp \leq 1$ is, therefore, a *non-violatable* constraint. On the other hand, the constraint $0 \leq x\_comp(1234) \leq 0.05$ may have been defined only for economic reasons and may be violated or relaxed in certain cases. It is, thus, a *violatable* constraint.

The definer of a constraint should indicate for every constraint, as it is defined, whether exceptions are allowed (violatable constraint) or not (non-violatable constraint).

Value vs. Structural Constraints

This classification of constraints is common and most DBMSs support a limited form of both, value-based and structural constraints. Most commercial DBMSs only support a few basic types and related format specifications for values; mapping correspondences are limited in most cases to 1:1 and 1:N correspondences for structures. However, we have found that in order to model objects adequately in a CAD environment additional facilities are needed.

```
/* Partial definition of the administrator for the class "process */
/* stream" */

process_stream

/* declaration of public part, i.e. procedures and variables that are */
/* visible from the outside */
{
Public
     to_instance
          update =>
          ←.boolean;
          insert =>
          ←.boolean;
          delete =>
          ←.boolean;
     end_instance
end_public

/* definition of internal structure and procedures */

Private
     instance
          stream_id: string.
          service: string.
          P_op: float.
          P_dis: float.
          T_op: Tconst.
          T_dis: Tconst.
          comp: component.    fields

/* note nesting of the component field which is a user-declared class */
/* Tconst is a constrained set of reals defined by the user of the */
/* language declaration of body of procedures */

          to_instance
               update =>
               instance <= check constraint
               .
               .
               .
               end

/* other procedure bodies */

     end instance
end private
}
/* declaration of the structure of the objects of class "component" */
/* procedure declarations and bodies are omitted */
.component
     Private
          instance
               comp_id: fix.
               comp_name: string.
               x_comp: float.          fields
```

Fig. 2.1: *Declaration of the Object-Class "process-stream" Using Basics of the TM Notation*

Value-based Constraints

Value-based constraints are those that applied to the values an attribute can take and are subdivided in our system into:

- range constraints (e.g. $0 \leq x \leq 1$);

- enumeration constraints (e.g. {Carbon-steel, SS-304, SS-316} $\supseteq$ material);

- relationship constraints (e.g. P_design $\leq$ P_operation * 1.15).

Range and enumeration constraints have the commonly accepted semantics. Relationship constraints establish the correct relationship between two or more attributes that are stored in the database. The attributes involved in the relationship may belong to the same object or to different objects. This kind of constraint can range from the very simple, as the one stated above, to rather complex consistency constraints involving many attributes and complex evaluation procedures. Therefore, these constraints are best viewed as routines that are invoked through a trigger mechanism.

A recurring problem when dealing with objects that allow the definition of superclasses and subclasses is the definition of inherited and aggregated attributes. Inheritance is fairly clear when an IS_A generalization hierarchy exists between classes of objects. In that case the subclass can inherit all of the attributes and constraints that are not explicitly overwritten in the subclass. The problem gets more difficult, as we try to model objects that have a COMPONENT_OF relationship to their superclass. Take, for example, a pipeline which consists of pieces of pipe, flanges, fittings and valves. The diameter of every component should be the same as the diameter of the superclass pipeline and one might be tempted to inherit the diameter to the components. But other attributes that might at first appear to behave likewise, for example the material of construction, do not always comply with the inheritance. The material of construction will be the same for carbon-steel pipelines and its fittings but not so for glass-fiber or stainless steel pipe. The difficulty in distinguishing between these cases under a COMPONENT_OF role of aggregation has prompted us to require a facility for storage of these attributes both at the class and its superclass with explicit equality constraints between redundant attributes.

Structural Constraints

Structural constraints represent the connectivity between the components of an object and are defined at the class level. We have identified three types of structural constraints:

- component classes;

- number of component objects;

- structural relationship between component objects.

Structural constraints on component classes are given in the basic class definitions. We shall not discuss them further.

Constraints on the number of components. These constraints specify how many instances of the component objects make up another object. Examples of this kind of constraints are:

- a heat exchanger has exactly one shell-side fluid and one tube-side fluid;
- a 4_AND gate has always exactly 4 input pins and exactly one output pin.

Structural constraints between component objects. These constraints define the topology of the objects and can include specifications of the legal order of component objects or correspondences between objects at different levels of abstraction.

An example of legal order specification for a pipeline would be:

threaded valve preceded by {pipe}
threaded valve followed by {pipe,NIL}
flanged valve preceded by {flange}
flanged valve followed by {flange, NIL}
pipe preceded by {pipe, T, L, flange, threaded valve}
pipe followed by {pipe, T, L, flange, threaded valve, NIL}

An example of correspondence specification is the 4_AND gate that consists of three 2_AND gates. In this case a constraint could be the definition of correspondence between the input pins of the first two 2_AND gates to the input pins of the 4_AND gate and the correspondence of the output pin of the third 2_AND gate to the output pin of the 4_AND gate.

Exceptions

The exceptions we consider are strictly defined as relaxations of a given constraint. We do not intend to include in the exceptions any new type definitions nor objects with additional or special properties. For those cases we consider it necessary to define a new class or subclass.

The question has been raised if exceptions could be treated as a special case of constraints. We think that exceptions and constraints are opposite concepts:

- a constraint, of whichever type, limits the values that an instance can assume;
- an exception is defined to allow a value which was previously excluded by a constraint.

For example, pipes could be made in any conceivable diameter. However, in practice only a finite set of diameters is manufactured, namely {0.5", 0.75", 1", 1.5", 2", 3", 4", 6", 8", ...}. A valid constraint would limit the allowable values for pipe to the values enumerated above. In order to standardize their stock a company may only allow pipes of diameters {1, 2, 3, 4} and this is expressed in an additional constraint. If piping of 1.5" is essential for a certain portion of the design an exception can be defined to allow the previously restricted diameter.

On the other hand, assume that a certain building code does not include any constraints on the type of glass to be used for apartment buildings, but the architect wants to specify thicker glass for the windows facing the playground. This "exceptional" case should not be treated as an exception since no constraint exists that can be relaxed. Instead, this is a particular constraint that is defined only for those windows facing the playground. This example raises the point of scope of a constraint.

3   Scope of Constraints and Exceptions

Current DBMSs enforce constraints usually through declaration of the constraint in the schema. Those constraints are always enforced. Such a mechanism is reasonable for non-violatable constraints that are applicable to the whole class, but not for constraints that are applicable only to a subset of instances of the class or for violatable constraints.

For practical reasons, an instance-constraint should always be defined at the highest possible level in the instance hierarchy and inherited to the component objects to which it applies directly. An example should illustrate this. In environments in which volatile solvents are present all the electric motors have to be spark-protected. We cannot specify the constraint at the class-level for motors, since this would then require all electric motors in the database to be spark-protected. Instead, we can define for the plant XYZ which will require electric motors, that these be spark-protected. In this case the constraint has to be defined at the level of plant XYZ but has to be applied at the level of the motor-objects.

Definition of a subclass spark-protected motors of the class electric_motors does little to solve the problem, since then we have to verify the membership of a motor in a particular plant. All we would accomplish would be to convert an instance-specific value-based constraint to an instance-specific structural constraint.

The main problem that arises with constraints defined on instances is that the constraints have to be inherited to the underlying objects by "instance inheritance", not only by "type inheritance". This means that every time a lower level object is updated, the constraints that were defined for instances further up in the instance hierarchy have to be checked. This is time-consuming and should be avoided if possible. In order to avoid this problem, inheritance can be checked upon insertion of a new object, but as the object is inserted an instance specific constraint can be defined for that particular object to be used in future updates. It is a matter of implementation that will be discussed later.

Another useful scoping mechanism for constraints is the dynamic definition of subclasses based on the value of a particular attribute (this mechanism is conceptually similar to the definition of views for the purpose of defining the constraint on the view). Let us illustrate this through an example. Pipes are available in a variety of materials, diameters and wall thicknesses (or schedules in the engineering jargon). However, not all schedules are available for every material. For pipe made of the most common material, carbon steel, 10 different schedules are available in a given diameter. For pipes manufactured from expensive and seldom used alloys only 2 or 3 different wall thicknesses exist for each diameter. A constraint on available pipe-schedules should reflect this fact and be specific for those instances of the class pipe. Defining a new subclass for each type of material, such as carbon-steel_pipe or stainless-316_pipe is impractical even if every subclass is defined at the time the schema is designed since endless hierarchies of subclasses would make the schema unmanageable. If, in addition, constraints are to be defined dynamically by the user of a CAD-system, then it becomes also necessary to create subclasses dynamically only for purposes of constraint enforcement without impact on the schema and the code of application programs. We call this process *"qualification"* since we are qualifying a constraint to be applicable only in the case that a predicatè is true. In our previous example, a constraint on pipe-schedules can be defined for stainless-316 pipe without having to create in the schema a new subclass. If a transaction updates an object of the class pipe, the constraint will be accessed, the material will be compared to the qualification, and only if both are "stainless-316" is the constraint applied. For any constraint more than one qualification can be defined. In our system the qualifications are also stored as constraint-base occurrences and all the qualifications applicable to a given constraint are chained. From them we can reconstruct the conjunctive predicate and can express constraints on "subclasses" without having to define them formally in the schema. Although this approach carries some overhead it is a method for avoiding changes to the schema and the application programs. The implementation details are given in Section 5.

4   Dynamic Definition and Deferred Evaluation of Constraints and Exceptions

The semantic richness of a database for CAD, which can comprise of the order of 10,000 attributes, makes it impossible to specify at database design time all of the constraints, even those that can typically be defined at the class level. In addition, there is a multiplicity of constraints that have to be specified for a particular project at any level of abstraction. These particular constraints depend on a variety of factors, for example, the client company's design practices, limitations imposed by geographical location, availability of materials and components in foreign countries, local design codes, etc. Many of these constraints are negotiated with the client while the design has already begun in order to save time.

CAD-systems are developed as generic tools and can only be tailored to the needs of a particular company or group of users through a "learning period", during which constraints are added and adjusted so that the system can perform according to the expectations of the users. This is similar to the process by which expert systems, such as R1 [McDe82] have been refined.

The main problem with this approach is, that the engineering companies that buy a turn-key CAD-system rarely have the personnel to make the modifications at the schema level and to perform extensive recompilations and software tests. Therefore, the goal for the DBMS underlying a CAD-system should be a mechanism for dynamic specification of constraints that will require only the pertinent engineering knowledge from the user, and not require extensive knowledge of the DBMS and a new language to define constraints.

Another typical property of CAD databases that has an effect on the constraint checking facility is the length of the transactions. If a constraint is violated in a commercial transaction usually little is lost if the whole transaction is rolled back to the initial point, since commercial transactions are typically short and the constraints to be evaluated are rarely of great complexity. This is not so in a CAD environment, in which transactions are long and a variety of situations can arise:

1.   A transaction often consists of a large number of atomic actions and the designer may want to check the consistency of his work at points other than end-of-transaction.

2.   In design applications a database is just being populated and a constraint defined on one attribute may not yet be enforceable since one or more attributes intervening in the constraint have not been specified.

3.   The complexity of some constraint checks and the interactive nature of the design process makes it often not feasible to evaluate constraints on

the fly, since this may be too time consuming and lead to an interruption of the thought process of the designer.

4. Depending on the stage of the design, a constraint violation may require different responses or actions to be taken. Rolling back a transaction because of a constraint violation may cause the designer to lose the work of many hours or even days. Therefore, the designer should have the option to specify the action to be taken.

5. Violations of some constraints may result in the definition of exceptions. Therefore, the constraint-checking mechanism must allow interactive evaluation of constraints with an escape into the exception-handling mechanism.

6. Many updates to a design database, particularly the work-area database, are only tentative in nature and are later modified or invalidated. Checking constraints on these tentative updates is wasted time.

Since constraint-checking is a time consuming task and many constraints may evaluate to false or undetermined unless the design has proceeded to a certain degree of completion, it is desireable to have a global switch that allows the user to work without constraint checking in his work area database until he wants to verify consistency. The constraint-checking switch should be specified at the beginning of a session. If constraint checking for each update is selected then the user should have the right to specify whether he wants to do retrospective constraint checking before he continues or if he wants to check only from the current state onwards. Each work-area database has a status field which is set to "unreliable" unless all constraints evaluate to TRUE either in their original form or because an exception has been specified. If any update is performed without constraint checking the status is set to "unreliable" until a global constraint check is performed.

One of the assumptions of our architecture [BuCe85] is the distinction of a stable, project-wide database and workareas which extract data from the former according to the library paradigm. Although the only updates that are performed against the project-wide database are those that have passed the approval process in the workareas, constraints may fail when trying to integrate partial designs, because other data that are involved in the constraint have not yet been inserted. In such a case, the enforcement of the constraint has to be temporarily deactivated. To mark data of dubious quality, a status field is included in the header of each object.

If constraint checking was deferred and is to be carried out at a later time several choices should be available:

•   constraint checking for a whole (long) transaction;

•   constraint checking for a specific object or one or more attributes of an object;

•   and constraint checking for a group of atomic actions, i.e. a subtransaction.

Both for the checking of a whole transaction and for parts of a transaction it is necessary to keep a log of the transaction. Not all of the tentative updates that were later reversed need to be kept. Therefore, a consolidated log which contains only the relevant updates should be produced for each transaction. We shall not elaborate here on this point but we assume that such a log will be kept since it is the basis for recovery and reintegration of objects from the work-area into the project-wide database.

When initiating the constraint checking mechanism the user should also be allowed to specify the kind of action to be taken if a constraint is violated. We consider that when the constraints for a whole transaction or a set of atomic actions are checked, then the default actions should consist only in a report of the violations. Based on this report, the user can later run the constraint checks interactively and make the necessary corrections or define the required exceptions for each violation of a constraint individually.

In our current design and implementation we are not including the definition of special actions to be invoked when a constraint fails. However, we can easily include a pointer from our constraint definition to the action routine that should be invoked.

5   Design and Implementation Issues of the Constraint Checker

Constraints on database objects are metadata that up to now have been compiled once through the schema definition and have been off-limits for the users. One way a database schema (and the constraints specified therein) is stored is in the form of cross-reference tables. Instead of elaborating these tables through a compilation process, we can express a variety of constraints by their typical parameters and define the cross-reference tables as database tables. We store each new constraint as a new instance in the form of a tuple of its characteristic parameters. More elaborate constraints, such as relationship constraints that are better enforced through a procedure and cannot be reduced to a simple tuple of parameters should be kept as library routines pointed at from the constraint management tables. The structural constraints, such as correspondences and legal sequences can also be reduced to instances of fairly simple database structures.

The gain in this approach lies in the fact that constraints do not have to be compiled and that a schema does not have to be recompiled whenever a new constraint is specified. Those constraints that could be specified when the database schema was designed could as well be stored in the same homogeneous form from the beginning, even if they were specified through a strongly typed conceptual language. We are fully aware of the possible delays that we are incurring through this very flexible form of handling constraints but we want to recall that much of the constraint checking in the CAD applications that we are familiar with will be done off-line. In addition, if the constraint checker is not used, absolutely no overhead will be paid. Nonetheless, we are trying to streamline the process to speed up the response.

Overall Structure of the Constraint Manager

The constraint management system consists of the Constraint Processor who has access to the schema definition (collection of object class definitions), to the Constraint Base, and the Exception Base. The Constraint Processor has modules that allow the user to define and modify constraints; define and modify exceptions; and handle actions or responses to constraint and exception violations. To facilitate the use of the system by application engineers a fill-in-the-blanks approach is specified for definition of constraints and exceptions. For each constraint and exception the necessary book-keeping data are stored in the data dictionary in order to be able to hold definers of constraints and exceptions accountable for them. Fig. 5.1 illustrates schematically the components of the constraint management system. Fig. 5.2 shows the interaction between user, constraint manager and constraint bases.

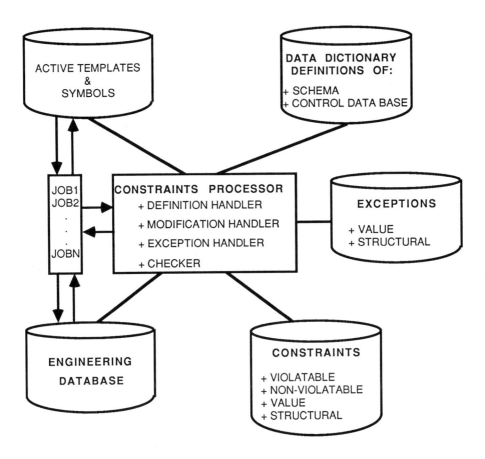

Fig. 5.1: *Components of the Constraint Management System*

The Constraint-Base

Based on the analysis of constraints in a CAD environment we subdivide the constraint base into a portion containing the constraints which are independent of a particular project and those which are project-specific. The constraints which are project-independent are called universal constraints and are always applicable to all instances of a class. Those constraints which are project-specific are the particular constraints. This categorization allows an easy exchange of whole portions of a constraint-base to tailor the system to the conditions of a given project. Particular constraints are instance constraints which are inherited to all of the subclasses and component classes. If they are defined at the highest level of abstraction, this is the project, then they are inherited to all of the objects of the class for which they were defined. If they were defined at a lower level, they may be applicable only to a few objects in a class.

The definition of exceptions is common to both kinds of constraints as far as they are applicable (i.e. the constraint has to be violatable).

The Identification of Objects

Most object-oriented database systems use system-assigned surrogates for internal identification of objects. We shall elaborate a little more on the structure of the object-identifier since we use it extensively in the implementation of the constraint checking mechanism.

An object-id in our system consists of the class identifier and the instance identifier. Associated with each object is a status field. The length of an object-id is 6 bytes: 2 correspond to the class-id and 4 to the instance-id. Two more correspond to the status portion. The class-id and instance-id together are enough to uniquely identify an object and only this portion is relevant in establishing the roles of aggregation between objects.[1] The status portion contains the necessary information on data quality (e.g. whether an update has been made without constraint checking), the existence of inheritable constraints and exceptions, etc.

Identification of Constraints

Constraints are associated with either an object-class or with individual objects. In order to locate the pertinent constraints for a given object or class, a constraint header is kept and indexed on class-id and instance-id. The constraint header consists of:

```
object-id
      class-id
      instance-id
status-portion
attribute
qualification_ptr
constraint_ptr
      constraint_type
      constraint_id
exception_ptr
      exception_type
      exception_id
```

---

[1] Some researchers object to the embedding of class information in the object identifier, since this sacrifices "object-orientedness" by making it impossible to conserve object-identity when an object is moved from one class to another [Kosh86]. However, we opted for this approach for efficiency reasons.

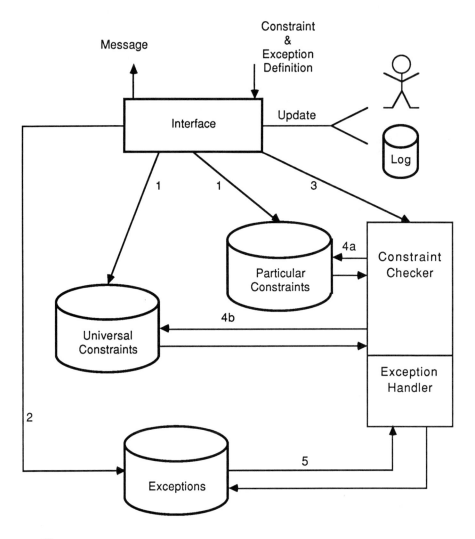

①   Constraint Definition

②   Exception Definition

③   Ask for Constraint Checking

④   Search for Constraint

⑤   Search for Exception

Fig. 5.2:   *Interaction with the constraint manager*

For any insertion or modification operation the headers of the universal constraints are checked. The access is via the object-id and the structure of object-ids is used here. For a class-constraint the instance-id is 0. For constraints defined on instances both the class-id and the instance-id are needed. The header contains also the attribute on which the constraint is defined. The qualification pointer allows us to locate additional qualifications on the class, thereby creating dynamically subclasses for constraint definition and enforcement. Storage structure and application of the qualifications is detailed in the next paragraph. The constraint_ptr is a pointer to a given constraint and consists of a constraint_type and a constraint_id. The constraint_type indicates whether it is a range constraint, an enumeration constraint, etc. The constraint_id is used to identify uniquely the constraint. The exception_ptr serves the same purpose for exceptions defined on a given constraint. For a non-violatable constraint the exception pointer is set to a "non-applicable" value. We should point out that the exception_type may be different from the constraint_type since for a certain constraint, say a range constraint, we may want to define an exception in which we enumerate the exceptional values.

The qualification pointer allows us to know whether any further qualification on a class constraint exists and it is simply an identifier of a tuple which determines the qualification. The qualification has the following structure:

    qualification_id
    attribute
    attribute_value
    next_qualification_id

If the next qualification_id is different from NIL the system assumes that another restriction exists and evaluates the conjunction of the qualifications. If the object for which the constraints are being checked falls into the set determined by the conjunction of all of the qualifications then the constraint is applied. At present we consider only qualifications on attributes within the same class and equality between the attribute's value in the object and the attribute_value in the qualification.

Application of Constraints

According to our view of universal and particular constraints a particular constraint overrides a universal constraint of the same type defined on the same attribute. By analyzing the constraint headers of the class and the object we can immediately tell whether there exists a particular constraint that is more restrictive than the class constraint. In that case we can ignore the universal constraint since the particular constraint is more restrictive. This principle is not applied for relationship constraints since several of them can be defined for one attribute of an object. For example, if the universal constraint specifies $0 \leq x \leq 1$ and the particular constraint $0 \leq x \leq 0.5$ exists, then there is no point in evaluating the universal constraint. However, the same attribute x can participate in two different relationship-constraints $x = y$, which is universal and $x > z$, which is particular. Neither constraint can claim priority over the other and both have to be evaluated.

If an exception is defined for an object on a given attribute we can immediately tell from the header and need not check the constraints but can proceed directly to the exception.

Inheritance of Particular Constraints

As we have discussed in a previous section, not all of the particular constraints will be defined directly at the level of the object at which they will be applied. Therefore, whenever a new object is inserted into the database the constraint checker (if the global switch is turned on) has to verify if there exists a particular constraint that has to be inherited and was defined at a higher level. This is a rather time-consuming task and therefore we try to minimize the upwards checking. Since we cannot set any flags for the objects just being created we keep track of the need for inheritance in the status portion of the class. If the flag is set for the class, then the constraint checker looks for a defined constraint at any ancestor-instance. Since the constraints have their own identifier, once the corresponding constraint was located at the higher level we create automatically a particular constraint header for the instance and point to the corresponding constraint definition. With this mechanism we check upwards only for those objects where the class has been flagged for the existence of inheritable constraints and once they have been located for an instance during insertion they don't have to be traced later during modification operations.

The tracing of constraints is done along the lines of the roles of aggregation that are of the IS_A or COMPONENT_OF type. Whenever, during an insertion operation, the constraint checker spots the "inherited-constraint" flag in the status portion of the class, it traces the ancestor instances along the COMPONENT_OF and IS_A roles of aggregation in the object class definitions. For "instance inheritance", the relevant portion of the instance hierarchy has to be traversed. In our case the roles of aggregation are being implemented as binary relations of objects identifiers. Each role of aggregation is stored in the form of owner-component pairs of object-ids in two permutations to facilitate traversal in both directions. They are indexed through a B+tree. For each identified ancestor object the pertinent constraints are identified by checking the defined constraints in the attribute field which will show in those cases the object-class and the attribute for which the constraint was defined.

The Structure of Constraints

For each type of constraint a different object-class is defined, and depending on the value of the header attribute "constraint-type" the corresponding structure is accessed to search for the constraint identified by the constraint-id.

Range Constraints

The structural definition of the range-constraint is the following:

```
constraint_id
lower_bound
      lower_bound_value
      lower_bound_close
upper_bound
      upper_bound_value
      upper_bound_close
```

The type for the values is the same as the type for the attribute on which the range is defined. The lower_bound_close and upper_bound_close fields indicate whether the interval is open or closed.

Enumeration Constraints

The enumeration_constraint class has the following definition:

    constraint_id
    number_of_elements
    element_list

In the case of enumeration constraints we are only allowing positive enumeration at present. Exclusion of the form "all except ... " might be added later for the case where a universal constraint exists already.

Relationship Constraints

Relationship constraints are defined both in generic form and for specific instances of objects. Typically we want to verify the consistency between attribute values within the same object or between objects belonging to component classes. In this case the identification of the objects on which to apply the relationship constraint is automatic. However, if we want to specify a constraint that involves two or more objects that have to be explicitly designated, then we have to pass on to the corresponding function a list of objects on which to apply the constraint. A relationship constraint is currently defined as:

    constraint_id
    number_of_objects
    object_list
    function_name
    library_name

In the pilot-implementation we are using libraries of C-functions to implement this kind of constraint. Once the TM environment is fully operational under UNIX we shall substitute the definition and conserve the name of the relationship-constraint-object and the message to be sent to it.

Constraints on Number of Component Objects

Constraints on the number of component objects could be defined easily in the schema but often a designer wants to add these constraints later. The structure is quite simple:

    constraint_id
    superobject_id
    component_object_id
    number_of_components
    type_of_limitation

A new constraint has to be created for each component object whose number of occurrences we want to constrain. The type_of_limitation attribute indicates whether the value of number_of_components is a maximal, minimal or equality constraint.

Constraints on Legal Order

The constraints on legal order are essentially defined at the class level and they include a predecessor list and a successor list of valid object-classes.

    constraint_id
    number_of_predecessors
    list_of_predecessors
    number_of_successors
    list_of_successors

Correspondence Constraints

Correspondence constraints relate objects at different levels of abstraction to one another's counterpart.

    constraint_id
    high_level_object_id
    low_level_object_id

These constraints act on roles of aggregation through which the correspondence property is implemented in a molecular aggregate.

The Structure of Exceptions

Exceptions have the same structure as the basic constraints with the possibility that a particular exception can be of a different type than the original constraint. For example, an exception to a range-constraint can be defined as an enumeration. We do not allow for exceptional values to be of different types than the type definition of the attribute in the schema, since this would cause problems with the application programs.

6   Current status and Future Work

Combining the Constraint Checker with the Object-Oriented
Language TM

The constraint checker that we presented is part of a larger project in which we are designing and implementing and object-oriented DBMS intended as infrastructure for large CAD systems. The ultimate goal is to combine this DBMS with the object-oriented language TM which Mike Gerzso has been developing at IIMAS [GeBu85, BuGe85]. In its present form the constraint checker serves the purpose of learning more about constraint handling to allow us to specify clearly how the TM language should be expanded to include constraint-handling capabilities.

At present, TM provides for subclass definition with attribute inheritance; it also allows arbitrary nestings of classes but does not support as primitive types the roles of aggregation. Constraint enforcement is possible in a limited form, since domains can be declared at the class level.

The way that we envision the first coupling of TM and the constraint checker is through the extension of TM with the necessary classes. By defining an administrator (TM's name for the class code) for constraints we can slip the present version of the constraint checker underneath and define only the message handling interface. In a later stage the constraint can be rewritten in TM. Class constraints can be extracted from the TM class-definition; particular constraints and exceptions are not expected to be integrated as primitive features of the TM language but can be handled as object classes that are defined by the DBMS developers.

Future Development of the Constraint Manager and the Object-Oriented DBMS

Future work on the constraint management system will include resolution of conflicting constraints, definition of additional actions and behavior of constraints in recursive definitions.

Other portions of the DBMS that are being developed are the storage structures for objects, a log for recovery and reintegration of workarea databases into the project-wide database, a mechanism for context definition, a formalization of the molecular aggregate model, and a mechanism for handling CAD-related metadata.

Acknowledgements

We wish to thank Mike Gerzso, Hanna Oktaba, Sergio Cardenas and Pedro Flores for many useful discussions about constraint and exception handling in the TM language. We also appreciate the interaction with Socorro Vargas and Alejandro Ávila.

7   References

[BaBu84], [BeBC80], [Borg85], [BuCe85], [BuGe85], [DaSm86], [Daya85], [GeBu85], [HaMc75], [Kosh86], [McDe82], [Ston75].

Part III

Language Issues

7
Object-Oriented GALILEO

A. Albano, G. Ghelli, M.E. Occhiuto, R. Orsini

Abstract

Programming languages with data types have been used successfully to model databases with the abstraction mechanisms of relational or semantic data models. The benefits of data types for modeling databases with an object-oriented database language has also been considered, but more research is required to isolate the basic features that the type system of the language should have, and to integrate the representation of abstract knowledge with the representation of concrete and procedural knowledge. The point of view is presented that, for a strongly typed, object-oriented database programming language, the following features are relevant: a) a type system with concrete types, abstract data types with assertions and inheritance of operators from the representation type; b) the notion of type hierarchies; c) and object-oriented view of databases, where objects are the only values that can be created, destroyed, and updated. Examples will be given to show how the conceptual language Galileo might be modified to become a strongly typed, object-oriented database language.

1   Introduction

An important feature of programming languages for database applications is the abstraction mechanisms provided for representing the abstract knowledge about the slice of reality being modeled, that is the knowledge about the properties of the concrete knowledge (entities, entity properties, and relationships among entities), and the way in which represented facts can evolve to reflect changes in the reality.

A current research topic is to investigate the effectiveness of an approach based on the use of data types, in the context of a strongly typed programming language, that is a language with the property that the type of each identifier, data structure component, expression, function and parameter can be determined statically, during the translation. When a language is designed with these goals in mind, then it is possible to verify statically that operators are applied to well typed arguments, that a function is invoked with parameters compatible with those declared, that the result of a function is of the type declared, and so on. Of course a strongly typed language is

---

This work was supported by Ministero della Pubblica Istruzione.

interesting as long as it provides also expressive abstraction mechanisms to define useful, application oriented types.

Although any statically detectable error could also be detected at runtime, it is desirable to do static checks for the following basic reasons: Firstly, programs can be safely executed disregarding any information about types; secondly, the language offers considerable benefits in testing and debugging applications, since the type-checker detects a large class of common programming errors without the need of executing programs, while errors at run-time could be detected only be providing test data that cause the errors to be raised. In fact, static type checking is considered an example of consistency check extremely useful to detect frequent semantic errors. For database applications the above benefits are certainly valuable, but static type-checking does not eliminate the need for dynamic testing to enforce value constraints. However, the type-checker is still useful to provide information to the translator to produce specialized testing code.

The benefits of data types for database languages have been discussed in the seminal works of Schmidt [Schm78], Brodie [Brod80] and Biller [BiNe78]. Recently, database programming languages, called *conceptual languages*, have been designed that include features to support the abstraction mechanisms of semantic data models (ADAPLEX [CCA83], Galileo [AlCO85] and Taxis [MyBW80]). An open problem is whether these languages are more effective when based on strongly typing. For instance, Galileo is strongly typed, Taxis is not, while ADAPLEX has been designed starting with ADA, a strongly typed language, but features have been included which prevent static type-checking of operations (e.g. generalization). More investigations are required to settle the question, especially when extensions to these languages are considered to have a full object-oriented view of the database, where objects have the following characteristics:

Objects are different from their name: Objects are all distinct and they might not have an external reference, such as a key, that stands for them.

Objects have state: Objects are the only time-dependent abstractions and are equipped with operators to change their state.

Objects can be shared: Associations among entities are modeled by relating the corresponding objects and not external references, such as foreign keys of relational data model. When objects are updated their modification is reflected in all other objects in which they appear as components.

Objects are "first class" values: Objects can be embedded in data structures, passed as parameters and returned as a value. Therefore access operators to the database return objects and not copies of them, as in current commercial database systems.

Objects are grouped in classes: A class defines the attributes of its instances, as well as constraints on the possible values of the attributes.

Classes of objects are organized into hierarchies: A subclass A shares the structure of its instances with its superclass B, via inheritance, and the objects instances of A are also instances of B.

The key technical concepts that form the common basis of an object-oriented approach to database systems and knowledge based systems can be found in an overview [Zani86]. A collection of papers in this area can be found in [DiDB]. The purpose of this paper is to illustrate an approach to the design of an object-oriented database programming language by extending Galileo, a conceptual language which already supports some of the features deemed fundamental for an object-oriented approach. The present implementation of Galileo, a compiler running under the UNIX™ operating system [AlOO88], shows evidence of the integration in a strongly typed programming language of the following features:

1. *Functional programming*: Galileo is a statically-scoped functional language. Functions are first class values which can be passed as parameters, returned as values and embedded in data structures.

2. *Query language*: Galileo is an interactive language. A Galileo session is a dialogue of questions and answers with the Galileo system. Interaction is achieved by an incremental compiler, which has some of the advantages of interpreted languages (fast turnaround dialogues) and of compiled languages (high execution speed). This feature allows the interactive use of Galileo without the need of a separate query language.

3. *Static type checking*: Galileo is a strongly typed language. Every Galileo expression has a type, which is determined statically. The type of an expression is usually automatically inferred by the system, without need of type definitions. The Galileo type system guarantees that any expression that can be typed will not generate type errors at run time.

4. *Flexible type system*: Galileo has a rich collection of data types and type constructors to define new types, from predefined or previously defined types; they are: tuple, sequence, discriminated union, array, function and abstract data types. In defining abstract types, it is possible to restrict the set of possible values with assertions and to inherit the primitive operations of the representation type (overloading).

5. *Type hierarchies*: Another property of the type system is type inheritance: If a type T is a subtype of a type T', then a value of T can be used as argument of any operation defined for values of T', but not vice versa because the subtype relation is a partial order. Type hierarchy is important to incorporate the generalization abstraction mechanism of semantic data models into a strongly typed programming language.

6. *Database modeling*: Galileo supports the abstraction mechanisms of semantic data models (classification, aggregation and generalization) to model objects of arbitrary structure and complexity, which can have other objects as components.

7. *Transactions and failures handling*: Galileo has mechanisms for modeling transactions and to control exceptions and their handling.

8. *Graphical interfaces*: Galileo has a form oriented interface to input and to display abstract values, in particular database objects, which are a kind of abstract data. The system automatically generates the graphical primitives from the definition of abstract data types.

9. *Values persistence*: Galileo is a persistent language, i.e., a programming language with values persistence as an orthogonal property of the type system: instead of having persistence as a property of values of special types, it is assumed that persistence is a property of any value that is accessible from the top level environment[1].

A proposal which has several aspects in common with Galileo is Trellis/Owl [OBBS86]. The main similarities are in static type-checking, type hierarchies, and the classification mechanism.

---

[1] Secondary storage management, transactions and concurrency control are not yet provided by the present implementation.

The paper is organized as follows. Section 2 and Section 3 describe the type system and the abstraction mechanisms for modeling objects. Section 4 presents the class mechanism used to build an object-oriented view of a database. Section 5 describes the graphical interface for objects. Section 6 describes the use of metadata and Section 7 illustrates the problems to be solved in implementing values persistence. Examples will be given in the framework of Galileo, however the reader should be aware that the examples are used only to make the presentation more precise, since the full definition of the language is out of the scope of the paper.

2   The Type System

The basic features of the type system are:

1. A set of basic types exists together with a set of type constructors to define concrete types: tuple, sequence, discriminated union (variant), and function. For concrete types the following properties hold: a) the type equivalence rule is the so-called *structural equivalence*: User-defined type names are used just as an abbreviation for the structure they represent; b) concrete values cannot be changed, they are immutable.

    use type Point := (X:int **and** Y:int);

    This declaration introduces the identifier Point bound to a concrete tuple type with attributes X and Y of type int. A tuple P with value (X:=3 **and** Y:=5) is of type Point and the result of the expression X of P is 3.

2. The user can define new abstract data types, which are indistinguishable from the system predefined types, together with the operations to create and manipulate values of that type. For abstract types the type equivalence rule is the so-called *name equivalence*: Two user-defined types are always different, as well as an abstract type is different from its representation type.

    use type Age <=> int
    with Newage (a:int): Age :=
        if a>0 **then** mkAge(a)
        else failwith "Positive ages only!"
        and EqAge(a1: Age, a2: Age): boolean :=
            repAge(a1) = repAge(a2)
        and IncreaseAge(a: Age): Age :=
            mkAge(repAge(a)+1) ;

    This declaration introduces an abstract type Age together with three functions: NewAge, EqAge and IncreaseAge. The two primitive functions mkAge and repAge are only available in the definitions that appear in the with part, but they are not exported in the scope of the type declaration. mkAge and repAge are automatically declared to map values of the representation type int into the abstract type Age and vice versa.

3. New abstract types can inherit a subset of the predefined operators on the representation type. The predefined operators retain their names, but this overloading does not introduce ambiguities because the type-checker can infer the meaning of an operator from the type of the operands. A pure abstract type mechanism requires the definition of all the possible operations on its instances. Abstract types with inheritance of all or some of the operations on the representation type make simple the definition of abstract data types. This modeling capability is particularly useful in database applications, where it is often needed to

define semantically different types that have the same representation, but their values should never be mixed in operations. For instance a Salary and a Weight are like integers, but they should never be combined in expressions.

use type Address <->
(Street: string **and** Town: string);

This declaration introduces an abstract type Address, which inherits the primitive operator **of** on the representation type, together with the functions mkAddress and repAddress.

4. New abstract data types can be defined by restricting with an assertion the values of the representation type. The assertion is maintained automatically by the operators inherited from the representation type. When an assertion on a value is violated, an exception is raised and an exception handler can be specified.

use type Weight <-> int
assert self > 0;

This declaration introduces a new type Weight whose values are constrained to be positive numbers, and inherit the operators on integers. Self is an identifier bound to the value.

use X := mkWeight (3)
and y := mkWeight (10)
in X - Y;

The result of this expression is a value of type Weight, but the evaluation of the expression will generate a run-time failure because the result would be negative and the inherited operator "-" enforces the assertion on Weight values.

5. The type system supports the notion of type hierarchy, in that if a type T is a subtype of the (super)type T', written also T' $\supseteq$ T, then a value of T can be seen as a value of T', but not vice versa because the subtype relation is a partial order [Alba83, Card84, AICO85]. For example, a value of T can be used as argument for any function defined for values of T' (*function inheritance*). The type hierarchy is a directed acyclic graph instead of a simple tree, thus implementing multiple hierarchy instead of single hierarchy like in Smalltalk. For concrete types, the subtype relation is automatically inferred by the type-checker according to the following rules:

• Every type is included in itself.

• Every type is included in the type any.

• The type none is included in every type.

• If r and s are tuple types, then s $\supseteq$ r if the set of identifiers of r *contains* the set of identifiers of s, and, if r' and s' are the types of a common identifier, then s' $\supseteq$ r'.

For instance the type

(Name: string **and** Address: (City: string **and** Street: string))

includes

(Name: string **and** Address: (City: string **and** Street: string and Country: string) **and** Age: int)

- If r and s are variant types, then s ⊇ r iff the set of identifiers of r is *contained* in the set of identifiers of s, and, if r' and s' are the types of a common identifier, then s' ⊇ r'.

  For instance the type {|Integer: int **or** Boolean: bool|} includes {|Integer: int|}.

- If r and s are sequence types with elements of types r' and s', then s ⊇ r iff s' ⊇ r'.

- If (r -> s) and (r'-> s') are function types, then (r' -> s') ⊇ (r -> s) iff r ⊇ r' and s' ⊇ s.

  For instance the type

  seq (Name: string **and** Age: int) -> (Name: string)

  includes

  seq (Name: string) -> (Name: string **and** Count: int)

- A type Id <-> t (the same rule applies to <=>) is a subtype of another type Id' <-> t', with primitive types considered as predefined abstract types, when t' ⊇ t, and the subtype relation is declared explicitly to the type-checker as follows:

  Id **is** Id' <-> t" New Assertions.

  For instance the type

  Thing <-> (Name:string)

  includes

  LivingThing **is** Thing <-> (Name: string **and** BirthDate:Date)

  which can be shortened as

  LivingThing <-> (**is** Thing **and** BirthDate:Date)

  Note that the assertions on Id are those of Id' plus New Assertions.

3   Abstraction Mechanisms for Objects

The notion of object-oriented programming originated with Simula 67 [DaNy66], where objects are similar to tuples with functions as components. Nowadays, a standard reference language for object-oriented programming is Smalltalk [GoRo83]: every value of the language is an object, and the only control structure is based on message passing between objects. Smalltalk is type-free and dynamically-scoped, and stresses interactive and incremental programming. For a survey of the field see [StBo86, Rent81, Sigp86]. The key characteristics of the object-oriented programming paradigm are:

1. A program is a collection of *objects* which are software entities with a local state and a number of *methods* that are local procedures: the only way to interact for these objects is through method activation.

2. A program is defined by:
   - a set of *object* definitions, called *classes*, to give the specification of their *instance* methods,
   - the instantiation of one or more objects and
   - the specification of the activation of their methods.

3. Classes are taxonomically organized, in the sense that one can define a subclass as a specialization of one or more classes, from which it inherits the methods with the possibility of redefining them and adding new ones. Instances of a subclass are also instances of the superclass. The methods defined in a superclass are also available for instances of a subclass, if not redefined in the subclass. The inheritance mechanism is a defining characteristic of the object-oriented paradigm. These features provide several benefits:

    -   *Programming by stepwise refinement*: Programs are developed first for general cases, by defining methods for general classes, then these methods are refined by adding new subclasses.

    -   *Software economy*: Adding new subclasses, methods can be redefined only when strictly necessary.

    -   *Software reusability*: A method activation depends on the most specialized class to which an object belongs. Thus, new objects, each with their own methods, can be added with no further program modification.

The work of Cardelli [Card84] is an important step towards the inclusion of these capabilities in a strongly typed programming language: objects are represented as records with functional components, and a set of typing rules is given to define the formal semantics of multiple inheritance. This approach has been also adopted to define the type system of the conceptual language Galileo.

In this paper, to integrate the abstraction mechanisms for objects into the type system of a functional database programming language, objects are defined as another kind of denotable values of the language: in particular, they are instances of abstract tuple types. In this way, assertions can be used to specify objects constraints, and, since functions are first class values, objects can have functional attributes whose values are provided when the object is constructed, being possibly different from the corresponding value of other objects. Objects are here considered as passive entities, in the sense that they cannot run concurrently as processes. In addition to this, the following kinds of special attributes can be defined to model objects:

-   *modifiable attributes*, to specify values that can be updated: A modifiable attribute A with values of type T is defined as **mod** A: T. If O is an object with attribute A, the expression A **of** O gives the value of A, while the expression modA **of** O(NewValue) is the only way to modify this value, where modA is an automatically defined method to change the modifiable attribute A. In other words, the state of an object, if it is not specified otherwise (see hidden attributes), can be accessed from the outside, but it can be changed only by applying appropriate functions;

-   *default attributes*, to specify a value to be used if a value is not given when the object is created;

-   *derived attributes*, to specify a value obtained by evaluating the defining expression every time the attribute is selected; derived attributes must not be given when the object is created;

-   *hidden attributes*, to specify attributes which cannot be accessed outside the object.

Example

```
use rec type Employee <->
    (Name: string
    and mod Address: Address
    and mod Vacations := default 15
    and BirthYear : int
    and Age := derived
        Year of Today () - BirthYear of self
    and hide Password: string
    and hide TaxRate: real
    and hide mod GrossSalary: int
    and UpdateSalary := default
        fun (Password: string, NewSalary: int) is
            if Password = Password of self
            then modGrossSalary of self (NewSalary)
            else failwith "Permission denied"
        and NetSalary := derived
            GrossSalary of self -
            GrossSalary of self * TaxRate of self
    assert BirthYear of self > 1900
    elsefail "The employee would be too old"


and APoorEmployee :=
    mkEmployee
        (Name := "John Brown"
        and Address :=
            mkAddress (Street := "530 Park Avenue"
            and Town := "Scotch Plains")
        and BirthYear := 1950
        and Password := "Lucy"
        and TaxRate : 0.1
        and GrossSalary := 700)


and ARichEmployee :=
    mkEmployee
        (Name := "Ann Smith"
        and Address :=
            mkAddress (Street := "500 Fifth Avenue" and Town := "New
                York")
        and BirthYear := 1953
        and Password := "Bliss"
        and TaxRate : 0.5
        and GrossSalary := 1200);
```

This declaration introduces the object type Employee together with two objects, APoorEmployee and ARichEmployee, of type Employee, and the following considerations apply:

-   The expression Vacations of APoorEmployee denotes an integer value, initially 15, which can be updated with the operation modVacations of APoorEmployee(NewValue);

-   the attribute GrossSalary can neither be selected nor modified because it is defined hidden. To modify it, the explicitly defined UpdateSalary function must be used, which controls the access rights using another hidden attribute, Password;

- Age and NetSalary are defined as derived attributes because their values must be re-evaluated every time they are selected, to take into account possible modifications of values which occur in their definitions;
- default attributes, such as Vacations and UpdateSalary, may not appear as parameters in the object constructor mkEmployee;
- hidden attributes do not appear in the result of the representation function repEmployee;
- inside the attribute definitions, the identifier self is bound to the whole object;
- the values of the object attributes can be constrained by boolean expressions (*assertions*). Assertions on constant values are controlled when an object is constructed, like the BirthYear for objects of type Employee. Assertions on modifiable attributes are controlled when an object is constructed and by the mod functions when it is updated.

Object types can be specialized according to the following rule for abstract tuple type, which is an extension of those discussed in section 2. If r and s are abstract tuple types, and r is declared as subtype of s, then $s \supseteq r$ iff:

- the set of identifiers of r contains the set of identifiers of s.
- If r' and s' are the types of a common non modifiable identifier, including special attributes, then $s' \supseteq r'$.
- If r' and s' are the types of a common modifiable identifier, then r' is the same type as s'.
- If a common identifier is derived in r then it is derived also in s and vice versa.
- If a common identifier is hidden in r then it is hidden also in s and vice versa.

Finally, it is possible to constraint further the values of the subtype by adding new assertions.

An example of specialization of Employee is

use rec type Manager <->
    (**is** Employee
    and mod Projects: seq string
    and mod Vacations := **default** 20
    and NetSalary := **derived**
        GrossSalary **of** self -
        GrossSalaray **of** self *TaxRate **of** self + 500
    assert GrossSalary **of** self > 1500
    elsefail "Wrong value for GrossSalary".

Note that operations on objects can be defined in three ways:

- Through the definition of derived attributes, whose values are evaluated by expressions that are the same for all the instances of that type;
- through the definition of functional attributes, possibly default, whose values can be different for the instances of that type;
- through the definition of global functions that take objects as parameters.

The first possibility is the traditional one in object-oriented languages Smalltalk-like, while the other two result from the integration of the object paradigm in a functional language. In any case, the given subtype rules allow subtypes to inherit the operations defined on the supertype in a type safe way, that is without incurring in run time type errors.

4   Modeling Databases as Classes of Objects

In Galileo, the term *class* has a different meaning from that assumed in object-oriented languages like Smalltalk and Simula-67, because it is a mechanism to represent databases by means of sets of modifiable interrelated objects: A class is the collection of all the constructed objects of an abstract type, called the *member type* of the class. An element of a class is an object which is the computer representation of certain facts about an entity of the world that is being modeled. An object-oriented view of a database is characterized by the fact that there is a one-to-one correspondence between objects in the database and the modeled entities. Moreover, only objects that exist in the database can be used to model associations.

A class is characterized by a *name* and the *type* of its elements. The name of a class denotes the elements of the class currently present in the database (*class extension*), while the type, which must be an object type, gives the structure of the elements (*class intention*). The class extension varies in time: when an element is created with the mkType operator, it belongs automatically to the class, as long as it is not explicitly removed.

Each class can be either a *base class* or a *subclass*. A base class is defined independently of other classes, and it is used to model a primitive collection of entities. A subclass is defined in terms of other classes, and it is used to model alternative ways of looking at the same entities: A subclass extension is a subset of the superclass extension, while a subclass intention is a subtype of the superclass intention.

Example

```
use Employees class
    Employee <->
        (Name: string
        and mod Address: Address
        and mod Vacations := default 15
        and BirthYear : int
        and Age := derived
            Year of Today () - BirthYear of self
        and hide Password: string
        and hide mod GrossSalary: int
        and hide TaxRate: real
        and UpdateSalary := default
            fun (password: string, NewSalary: int) is
                if Password = Password of self
                then modGrossSalary of self (NewSalary)
                else failwith "Permission denied"
        and NetSalary := derived
            GrossSalary of self - GrossSalary of self * TaxRate of self
        assert BirthYear of self > 1900
        elsefail "The employee would be too old"
```

and Managers **subset of** Employees **class**
    Manager <->
        (**is** Employee
        and mod Projects: seq string
        and NetSalary := **derived**
            GrossSalary **of** self -
            GrossSalary **of** self *TaxRate **of** self + 500
        assert GrossSalary **of** self > 1500
        elsefail "Wrong value for GrossSalary"

and Department **class**
    Department <->
        (Name: string
        and mod Budget: int
        and mod Manager: Manager
        and mod Staff: **seq** Employee);

This definition introduces the class identifiers Employees, Managers, and Departments bound to modifiable sequences of Employee, Manager, and Department. Managers is a subclass of Employees and contains a subset of Employees.

Objects are used to model entities of the real world, and relationships among entities are modeled by the aggregation mechanism. For example, the association between Departments and Managers is modeled by the attribute Manager of Departments, whose values are objects of the class managers. In this way, to retrieve the Manager associated to a Department the tuple selection operator **of** can be used. In the same way, Staff is used to represent the multi-valued association between Departments and Employees.

When an object is constructed it is automatically inserted in the class and in all of its superclasses, moreover it is also possible to move an object of a superclass in one of its subclasses with the operator inSubClass, which has two parameters: the first one is the object present in the superclass, and the second one is a tuple containing the new attributes. To forbid the modification of the value of a redefined attribute when an object is inserted in a subclass, the inclusion operator checks that the value of the redefined attribute in the second parameter is a *subvalue* of the corresponding one of the first parameter, according to the following rules:

- v is subvalue of w if v = w.

- If v and w are tuples and v' and w' the values of a common identifier, then v is subvalue of w if v' is subvalue of w'.

- If v and w are two variants and v' and w' the values contained in the variants, then v is a subvalue of w if they have the same tag and v' is a subvalue of w'.

- If v and w are two sequences, then v is a subvalue of w if the sequences have the same number of elements and if v' and w' are the ith element in v and w respectively, then v' is a subvalue of w'.

When derived or functional attributes are redefined, the include operator is not available, since it is not possible to define a subvalue relations for this kind of values. Consequently, in these cases objects can be constructed only in the subclasses, and not moved from a superclass into a subclass.

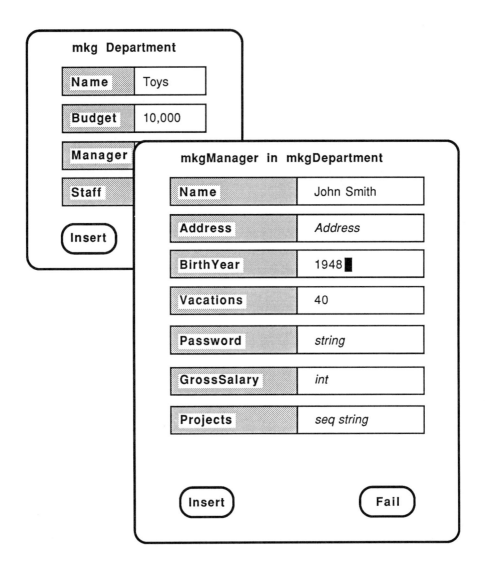

Fig. 1:   *Object graphical construction*

5   Interacting through Forms

The end-user can interact directly with the objects through a set of graphical primitives both for creating and for inspecting them. The system automatically generates the graphical primitives from the definition of abstract data types, and they can be used either directly from the system user or to define more sophisticated interfaces using auxiliary data types.

The definition of an abstract data type T introduces two additional functions, besides those to create and get the representation already discussed: the function mkgT to create a new value of type T, and the function editT to show a value on the screen with the possibility of modifying its mod attributes.

The evaluation of such primitives starts an interaction at the user's terminal. A two-dimensional structure is displayed with fields in which the user can insert values. Elementary types are represented with forms which have only one field, while structured types are represented with forms which have one field for any immediate component. If an attribute is structured, then its associated field can be expanded, on user demand, and a new form is shown which represents the attribute value. In every field, the user can choose between the insertion of a literal value, or the specification of a language expression, which is evaluated and its value is inserted in the field. An expression could also be a recursive call to the graphical interface.

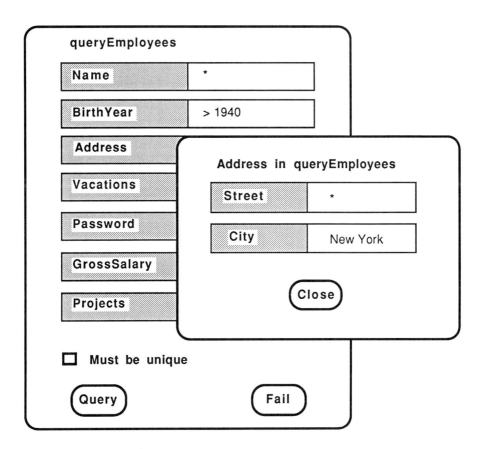

Fig. 2: *Graphical query for an object class*

In Fig. 1 is shown how the screen looks like during the creation of an object of type Department together with its Manager. Not yet expanded field have their types shown. The button Fail can be used to abort the insertion.

A new graphical primitive queryC is introduced for each defined class C. It is the graphical counterpart of the **all** operator of Galileo, which returns the sequence of all the elements of a class satisfying a certain condition. This primitive allows the user to specify a set of conditions in a bidimensional structure representing the class member type, to show graphically the sequence of objects satisfying the condition. A condition can be a boolean expression for simple values, a recursive activation of a query for class members, a condition on fields of an expanded form for structured values.

In Fig. 2 it is shown a graphical query on the Employee class, asking for employees living in NewYork with birth year greater than 1950. The system initially fills the fields with '*', which stands for any value. If Must be unique is chosen the result must be a single valued sequence.

6   Meta Database

Good data dictionary facilities are a common need for several application areas: Databases, Object-oriented Programming Systems, Knowledge Base Management Systems. The basic facilities required are a dictionary which the user can query to retrieve information about the definition of stored data. More sophisticated systems use the meta database as the system's kernel, upon which all the tools operate, even to modify the stored data.

In our proposal, a meta database can be queried and modifications are allowed only on descriptive information. The idea is that a set of predefined classes exists, which describes the principal information concerning classes, types and values of a data base. These classes are populated by the system, and the user can query them, either through the graphical interface or with the language expressions, and he can modify comment fields existing in all the metaclasses elements. The complete specification of the meta-schema is beyond the scope of the paper.

7   Values Persistence

Object-oriented languages are proposed for CAD Systems, Office Automation Systems, Knowledge Base Management Systems and DBMSs. For all these applications the information managed must be persistent. The problem of managing persistent data has both linguistic and implementative aspects. From the linguistic point of view, the fundamental decisions to be taken are:

-    For which categories of data to offer the capability of a persistent storage.

-    Which operators exist to make data persistent.

The assumption is made that every kind of data is potentially persistent, so that a procedure written to implement an algorithm on temporary data can work also on persistent data, and vice versa. Using different data types for persistent and temporary data is only a hindrance for the programmer, while a complete homogeneity between persistent and temporary data allows him to focus only on the algorithmic aspects of problems.

Since the persistence of data should be transparent to the programmer, there should not be any specific operator to make an object persistent. In an interactive system the transparence of persistence can be achieved making every object persistent as long as it is reachable from the top level environment. Control of the flush of data between temporary and persistent storage is completely accomplished by the system. This approach to data persistence is characterized by two key ideas:

- Every type of data can be persistent.

- The programmer can regard every data he can reach from the top level as persistent.

This point of view, together with the fact that the proposed language is functional and requires a high rate of dynamic allocation of memory, has a serious impact on the implementation of the system, as the control of the traffic of data between temporary work storage and persistent storage is moved from the programmer to the system.

The main problems which must be solved to implement data persistence for the proposed language are:

- The format problem.

- The addressing problem.

- The recovery of data after crashes.

- The deallocation of objects which become not accessible.

The format problem is the problem of choosing an internal representation for objects in temporary storage and for objects in persistent storage to optimize the use of the different devices underlying. When the persistent objects have a very regular structure, that is when they are only classes of homogeneus records, they can be stored in the persistent storage in some sophisticated way, grouping and splitting records to optimize the access time for some critical operation. Since objects of any type can be persistent, there is no simple persistent data storage schema which is efficient for highly heterogeneous and complex data structures. In this approach it seems a better solution to represent data in a similar way in persistent and temporary storage, to optimize, at least, transfer time.

The addressing problem arises because references to objects can not be coded through their work storage address, as they live mainly in persistent storage. On the other hand, to communicate with an object, its persistent address must be translated to get its current work storage address. In a persistent object-oriented system with a high granularity, address translation is the critical operation that affects the performance. Some caching scheme might be useful to lower the cost of the translation. However, it is impossible to store the translated address together with, or upon, the persistent identifier found in the calling object, because of the high cost of the management of work storage address for objects which can be swapped out. The problem is to find a translation schema which is efficient in terms of time and space, when a lot of small objects has to be managed. A persistent virtual memory schema is under investigation: data are transferred in the working memory a page at a time; every address will be translated every time it is used. This translation requires only a look-up in a direct access table. Data are loaded in working memory without any conversion. This schema seems simple, efficient and suitable to be supported by the hardware of existing machines.

The problem of recovery is well known in database systems, where persistent data must be safe against crashes. In a system where all objects are persistent, the popular technique of safely recording the updatings made to each data, to reapply them after a crash, is not suitable because of the amount of information to deal with. The shadow pages approach [Lori77] looks more promising. In this approach, each time a group of objects is modified, a new set of pages is allocated to contain their new version, and a new translation table is created to refer these new pages. When the operation is successfully completed, the atomic flipping of a persistent bit makes the new translation table, and the new pages, committed and persistent. If any trouble arises, the old versions will replace the new ones.

The problem of rescuing space used by no more accessible objects seems the most difficult to solve because every accessible object must be visited to find the space that can be freed. This operation must be made frequently because newly allocated objects tend to disappear quickly; if their space is not rescued, reachable data scatter and, when a page is brought in and out of working memory, lots of garbage is moved together with few useful data. On the other hand, the system manages also large quantities of old data which are stable and must not be visited, otherwise it would spend all its time looking for garbage. The solution is to divide data in different spaces exploiting their different characteristic, using big spaces, seldom collected, for old and stable data and little spaces, very frequently collected, for newly allocated and dynamic data [HeLi83]. This division should be made so that the collection of the smallest spaces can be made without visiting the bigger ones. We are experimenting a solution where the most recently allocated space is also the most efficiently accessed, and functions are handled efficiently, since functions are first class objects, and objects can contain functional components [AlGO88].

8   Conclusions

The point of view has been presented that a strongly typed object-oriented programming language should include the following features:
- A rich type system with concrete and abstract data types.
- Constraint definitions by assertions.
- The notion of object as the only kind of value which can be updated.
- Classes to support the abstraction mechanisms of semantic data models.
- Graphical interfaces automatically generated from objects definition.
- A meta database to store information about the definitions present in the system.
- Values persistence as an orthogonal property of the type system.

Other relevant features not discussed here are: a) a modularization mechanism, to structure complex applications as well as for separate compilation; b) a process mechanism to model active objects; c) transactions and concurrency control.

The notion of object here presented is similar to the one introduced in Smalltalk. The interesting aspect of the proposal is the use of objects in the framework of a strongly typed programming language with features to express declaratively abstract knowledge. Some of these features have already been implemented in a prototype of the conceptual language Galileo, which is a first important achievement of a long term project now underway at University of Pisa. The goal of the project is to design and implement an interactive integrated system to design and prototype database applications, and to experiment with advanced features of database programming languages. Among the other features, not described here, which will be implemented in the near future, there are high level graphical primitives which will be used to develop user interfaces as well as the standard interface as described in section 5.

9   References

[Alba83], [AlCO85], [AlGO88], [AlOO88], [BiNe78], [Brod80], [Card84], [CCA83], [DaNy66], [GoRo83], [HeLi83], [Lori77], [MyBW80], [OBBS86], [DiDB], [Rent81], [Schm78], [Sigp86], [StBo86], [Zani86].

8
An Object-Oriented Database for Trellis

Patrick O'Brien, Bruce Bullis, Craig Schaffert

Abstract

This paper discusses the design of an object-oriented database extension to Trellis, an object-based language with multiple inheritance and compile-time type-checking. The database, which we call an object-repository, *provides shared access to persistent objects in a multi-user environment. Furthermore, it provides the usual database amenities such as concurrency control, recovery, and authorization. The database is intended for applications, such as engineering data management, which have complex data structuring requirements and special data accessing needs.*

1   Introduction

The class of applications requiring database system support is quickly extending beyond the more traditional data processing applications into areas such as computer-aided design, office automation, programming environments, and artificial intelligence. These applications tend to have complex data structuring needs, significantly different data accessing patterns, and special performance requirements. Conventional database systems do not adequately support the special modeling and performance requirements of these applications. The object-oriented programming methodology, however, has proven to be particularly well suited for applications having complex data structuring needs. Furthermore, recent work in integrating object-oriented concepts with database technology has demonstrated the potential for satisfying their performance requirements [Maie86].

To address the needs of these applications, we are designing an object-oriented database extension to Trellis[1] [Scha86], an object-oriented language and programming environment developed at Digital. Trellis is currently a single-user system that provides automatic storage management and presents a one-level store model to the programmer. The expressive data modeling features of the Trellis language satisfy the complex data structuring requirements of these applications. The database's primary role is to provide shared access to persistent objects for multiple Trellis programs.

The database, which we are calling an *object repository*, is a container for all persistent objects. It provides a mechanism for classifying data by grouping objects within database collections. Collections are Trellis types which

---

[1]   Trellis is a trademark of Digital Equipment Corporation.

provide operations to access objects either through associative retrieval or by iterating over the collection's element. The repository also supports subset relationships between collections.

A Trellis program can store, retrieve, and replace objects in the repository. We have tried to make the interface between the programming language and the database as transparent as possible (i.e. maintain an illusion of a one level store). The relationships that exist between objects in local storage are preserved in the repository. The repository and the Trellis language support the same data structuring capabilities so there is no impedance mismatch. The repository also provides support for aggregate objects. For efficiency and performance reasons, the programmer can provide hints for retrieval and storage of aggregate objects.

Concurrency and recovery are also important issues. To allow programs to coordinate concurrent access to shared objects, we are looking at transactions, locking, and version control. Since versions play an important role in many of the application areas we are targeting, we would like to provide mechanisms to support version control.

Our goal is not to provide all of the capabilities that are required of a conventional database management system; for example, a system which is designed for online transaction processing. We are concentrating on the features essential to the class of applications described above. The role of the object repository is primarily for storing and retrieving relatively large complex objects and for providing sharing and recovery.

In the next section we give an overview of the Trellis language. In section 3 we discuss the motivation for our design of the object repository. Section 4 presents the programmer's view of database capability in Trellis. Section 5 discusses support for aggregate objects and their impact on performance. Section 6 describes our approach for handling sharing and concurrency. We conclude in section 7 with a discussion of future work.

2   The Trellis Language

The Trellis language combines a multiple-inheritance hierarchy with strict, compile-time type checking. It attempts to integrate the strengths of previous work in object-oriented programming. It uses the power of the "message passing" metaphor and inheritance hierarchies demonstrated by Smalltalk-80[2] [GoRo83]. It also builds upon the CLU [Lisk81] language which demonstrated that an object-oriented language can provide good performance, and, by providing type-abstraction and strict type-checking features, can actively support the programming goals of high reliability and maintainability.

In Trellis, objects with similar behavior are grouped into *types* (classes) and are known as *instances* of their types. A type characterizes the behavior of its instances by describing the operations that can manipulate those objects. *Type modules* are used to declare types and to group the operations and other definitions that define the behavior of the type.

Objects are manipulated by *operations*. To fully define an operation, the programmer must specify both an *interface* and an *implementation*. The interface describes how the operation is called. The implementation describes

---

2   Smalltalk-80 is a trademark of Xerox Corporation.

how the behavior of the operation is realized. The type of the first argument (*the controlling object*) to an operation determines the actual code to be invoked. There are two kinds of operations: *instance* operations and *class* operations. Instance operations apply to individual instances of a type. Class operations apply to a type as a whole, not to a particular instance of a type.

Objects encapsulate both state and behavior. In Trellis, state is captured in *fields*. The fields of an object, collected together, form the physical storage for the object. As with operations, there can be both *instance* fields and *class* fields. Trellis also provides a shorthand selector notation, called *components*, for accessing fields and defining operations that appear to be fields.

In Trellis, types can be related hierarchically through subtyping. Subtyping is based on behavior, not implementation. If a type S is a subtype of type T, then S objects must behave like T objects and may be used anywhere a T object may be used. Objects of type S can also have additional behavior defined by S. Moreover, a type can be a subtype of more than one type. If S is a subtype of both T and U, then S objects must behave like T objects and like U objects.

Trellis provides an *inheritance* mechanism that allows a subtype to share implementations with its supertypes. By default, a subtype inherits both the interfaces and the implementations of the definitions in its supertypes. Only the additions to the supertypes' behavior need be specified in the subtype. Inheritance of the supertypes' implementations, however, can be blocked by rewriting implementations in the subtype.

Sometimes several types are very similar. For instance, sets of integers and sets of strings have similar behavior. Trellis provides *type generators* which define a family of closely related types. For example, a Set type generator can be used to define the types Set[Integer], Set[String], and Set[Person]. The individual members of the family are known as *parameterized types* and can be used like any other type.

Trellis uses a conventional programming language syntax and employs standard procedure call notation to invoke operations on objects. There are a number of features in the language that significantly enhance its expressiveness. *Iterators*, for instance, provide the ability to access elements of a collection without revealing the implementation of the collection. Trellis supports an *exception handling* mechanism that allows for a more complete specification of the behavior of an operation. The language also provides additional support for encapsulation with *visibility* attributes for definitions.

More information on the Trellis language is available in the reference manual [ScCW85], the tutorial [OBri85], and in [Scha86].

3   Rationale for an Object Repository

In this section, we discuss why we have chosen to design a database-like object repository. We describe the particular needs of the applications we are targeting and justify why the object repository is better suited than conventional database models. Finally, we discuss the issue of integrating types and collections of objects into a coherent model.

The primary reason for adding database capability to Trellis is to enable programs to share objects. But there are some secondary reasons that we see as important benefits. For example, a database approach enables us to handle a larger amount of data than is practical using a virtual memory scheme. Adding transactions, coupled with the ability to deal with small chunks of data, provides a more practical finer-grained recovery scheme.

We first considered building the appropriate semantics for sharing by extending Trellis' one-level storage model so that all programs share a single address space. In a distributed system, programmers would not be forced to worry about whether objects were local or remote. Such a uniform distributed object system is the best generalization of a single node system because there is no change in programmer-visible semantics and is therefore simpler for the programmer to deal with.

Many questions arise in designing a uniform distributed system. For example, how does a programmer control the placement of objects? When an operation is applied to remote object, where does the computation actually occur? When should objects be copied or moved? Moreover, mechanisms are needed to permit atomic updating of multiple objects and to allow recovery from node crashes or communications failures.

The answers to these questions are not obvious. For example, simple transactions based on locking can provide for atomic update and recovery, but they tend to force a much more serial schedule than is logically necessary. Further mechanisms are required to get around this problem [WiLi85, ScSp84]. We believe that significant long term research is needed before such uniform distributed systems will be practical for day to day use.

In the meantime, we still want to share objects among users in a distributed system. A centralized object repository allows us to do this. Object repositories are easier to implement than global address spaces. We can use well-understood database technology to store and retrieve objects from a server, and there is no question about where computation occurs. Coordinating sharing is simpler in a more centralized system, and we do not have to invent an efficient distributed garbage collection algorithm.

There is of course a cost. An object repository may complicate the programmer's view by introducing a second level of storage. Some objects are temporary, others are persistent and shareable, and decisions must be made about when to update objects in the repository. Nevertheless, we believe this solution meets the requirements of our target application areas.

The specific needs of these application areas are somewhat different from conventional database applications such as transaction processing. The model of computation for conventional systems can be described as accessing lots of "small" records which are held for "short" periods of time. The emphasis is on throughput; there may be lots of contention for the same records; the volume of transactions is large; and response time is critical.

The applications we are targeting, such as programming environments and computer-aided design, have a different emphasis and somewhat different requirements. They tend to access "large" complex objects and hold on to them for "long" periods of time. The emphasis is on sharing of large objects; there is probably not a great deal of contention for the same objects; support for versions is desirable; objects have complex data structures which are not easily modeled using conventional database models; and quick retrieval of bulk data is required [BaKi85a, WoKL85].

These requirements are different but not necessarily incompatible with conventional database systems. There are tradeoffs, however, and we will be choosing mechanisms that support the model of computation we believe exists for these applications.

3.1 Data Modeling Power

The data structuring requirements of our target applications necessitate a different approach to satisfying their database needs. The data structuring capabilities of current database systems, with their sparsity of constructs and low-level primitives, do not adequately support the complexities and variations that occur in these applications. The object-oriented data model of Trellis, however, is well suited to handling these complexities. Therefore, we would like to extend the data modeling capabilities of Trellis to the object repository.

Perhaps one of the most fundamental problems of conventional database models is their lack of a notion of an abstract object [McKi81]. The correspondence between an object in the application environment and records in the database is indirect. In the relational model application objects are represented as record structures and are related indirectly through common attribute values. For example, a student and her advisor would typically be associated through an attribute which represents the advisor; the student record and the advisor record would each contain a copy of the attribute.

In the object-oriented model, objects represent themselves instead of using some identifier to stand for them, thus making it possible to directly reference an object from a related one. This *referential transparency* is just one of many advantages that the object-oriented data model provides. But it is very important since any change in an object's state is automatically seen by all other objects which refer to it - unlike relational systems, where a change in the key value of an entity is not propagated automatically to other tuples sharing that value. Moreover, restrictions that normalization enforces, such as flat fields, which further inhibit the notion of an abstract object, can be relaxed.

Since the repository and programming language support the same data types and structures, the usual *impedance mismatch* [Zani86] between programming language data structures and database data structures is alleviated. The impedance mismatch is exacerbated when object-oriented languages are interfaced to conventional databases, since objects correspond to real world entities and this one-to-one correspondence is not maintained with records or tuples in the database[3]. Thus, we allow programs to store and retrieve any type of object in the repository, without having to translate between different data structures.

3.2 Types and Collections

The concepts of types and type hierarchies in object-oriented programming languages, and classes and is-a hierarchies in semantic modeling languages, are important and somewhat related features. Our extension to Trellis to provide database capability has to integrate these related concepts in a consistent manner. We have decided to differentiate between the two concepts and provide separate mechanisms to model the different abstractions.

---

[3] Note that the reverse situation is probably equally undesirable. Interfacing a conventional language such as Pascal or C to an object-oriented database will present an impedance problem as well in the opposite direction.

A common complaint about conventional database systems is that they do not cleanly separate type definition from data declaration [CoMa84]. For example, in relational systems there is no distinction between a type `Employee` and a relation that contains `Employee` records. A single declaration defines both the record structure (tuple) and the container (set of tuples). Thus, redundant specification is necessary to declare several relations to hold `Employee` records.

Semantic modeling languages introduced *classification* [MyBW80], which is an abstraction mechanism used to group entities with similar properties into "classes". But classification also does not differentiate between the notion that an object has a type and the notion that we want to group objects into collections. Classification embodies these two distinct aspects: sometimes referred to as *intension* and *extension* [AlCO85]. The *intensional* aspect describes the behavior of objects in a class and is analogous to the type mechanism in object-based languages. The *extensional* aspect groups objects in a collection so they can be referred to as a single unit. It is more analogous to the concept of a set, rather than a type.

Similar to the problem with conventional database systems, classification does not allow one to have two collections of employees without having two distinct types. Trellis, however, cleanly separates type definition from type instantiation, and we also want to separate type definition from the definition of a collection of objects stored in the database.

Many semantic modeling languages provide a subtyping mechanism, sometimes referred to as an *is-a* hierarchy [MyBW80, McKi81]. Is-a hierarchies further confound the situation. For example, suppose we have an is-a relationship between a class `Part_time_employees` and a class `Employees`. This relationship introduces two constraints. First, the elements of `Part_time_employees` are always a subset of the elements of `Employees`: this is the extensional constraint. Second, the behavior of elements of `Part_time_employees` must be a specialization of the behavior of elements of `Employees`: this is the intensional constraint.

We believe that the reasons for subsetting collections of objects (extensional aspect) can be quite different from the reasons for constructing subtypes (intensional aspect). The subtype notion in programming languages has proven to be extremely useful. Subtyping and inheritance provide added flexibility for describing relationships between types and thus improve the structure of code. The subtype notion is usually a static aspect of the language - an object cannot change its type once it has been created. Subtypes are created to structure code for various reasons including specialization, implementation, and combination [HaOB87].

A collection of objects, on the other hand, might be divided into subsets for reasons quite different from subtyping criteria. For example, employees might be partitioned into subsets that reflect the department they currently belong to. Or we may restrict membership to certain collections based on some predicate involving the value of an attribute, for example an employee's salary. Unlike instances of a type, membership in a collection may change over time.

For these reasons, we have decided to distinguish between types and collections of objects, as well as their respective hierarchies. Types and the type hierarchy in Trellis deal with the intensional aspect, and the collection and sub-collection mechanism, which we will introduce in the next section, deal with the extensional aspect. This distinction increases the modeling capability of the language because it allows the use of the type and type hierarchy mechanism independently of the collection and subcollection mechanism.

4   Design of Database Features within Trellis

Our objective is to integrate database capability into the Trellis language using existing language features. This allows programs to access and manipulate database objects in the same manner as all other objects. We would like to adhere to the object-oriented and strongly typed nature of Trellis. Moreover, we do not want to separate the database manipulation language from the programming language. Initially we are concentrating on providing features that are essential to the application areas we are targeting. Therefore, some of the features of a conventional database management system, such as a sophisticated query facility or declarative integrity constraints, are not being considered.

Our design achieves a tight integration of database management concepts within the object-oriented style of Trellis. This contrasts with traditional language/database interfaces that rely upon a set of function calls or a separate data manipulation language which has little or no interaction with other language features. We use existing facilities for declaration of types and variables, along with existing control structures for iteration and exception handling. The database extension to Trellis is presented to the programmer as new types added to the library.

The most important type we introduce is the notion of a *database collection*, which groups objects to be stored in the database. Database collections are analogous to relations in the relational database model. The objects stored in a database collection are instances of Trellis types. Database collections can have sub-collection relationships: one collection can be a sub-collection of another collection with the implication that if B is a sub-collection of A then a member of B is also a member of A. We also define the notion of a *repository* which is a group of database collections.

4.1 Database Entities

The objects that are stored in a repository are instances of Trellis types. Types are defined using normal Trellis specifications and objects of any type can be stored in the repository. Employee is an example of a type whose instances might be stored in the database.

```
type_module Employee

component me.employee_no: Integer get_only;
component me.name: String;
component me.address: String;
component me.manager: Employee;
component me.salary: Integer;
component me.job_history: Set[Job];
```
    ! some operations defined on Employee, for example:
```
operation pay_raise (me, p: percent)
    signals (makes_too_much);

end type_module;
```
The component mechanism in Trellis enables programmers to view objects as having a record-like structure, similar to conventional database notation.

4.2 Database Collections

We define a new type generator, called `DB_Collection`, which generates database collection types. One can think of a database collection as a set of Trellis objects which reside in a repository. The database collection generator is very similar to the set generator. The set generator enables one to declare sets of some type. For example:

```
var my_set_of_strings: Set [String];
```

defines the variable my_set_of_strings as a set of strings. Similarly,

```
var my_employees: DB_Collection [Employee];
```

would define `my_employees` as a database collection of employees. The type specified with the generator, in this case `Employee`, defines the kind of objects which can be stored in the database collection.

If the type `Part_time_employee` was defined as a subtype of `Employee`, we could also insert `Part_time_employee` objects into the database collection `my_employees`. In fact, we can insert objects of any subtype of `Employee` into `my_employees`.

The database collection type is defined as

```
type_module DB_Collection [entity_type: Type]
```
! operations for DB_Collections go here
! we describe them below
```
end type_module;
```

The parameter `entity_type` determines the type of objects which will be stored in the collection. For example, if we have

```
var my_employees: DB_Collection [Employee];
```

then `entity_type` would refer to `Employee`.

A database collection has several operations that are defined on it; for example, "add an element", "remove an element", and "select a particular element". Another operation defined on the type `DB_Collection` is the `create` operation, which is used to generate a new instance of a database collection. The interface for the `create` operation is

```
operation create (Mytype,
                  name: String,
                  database: Repository,
                  indices: set [Component_Name],
                  super_collections: set [DB_Collection])
          returns (Mytype)
          signals (duplicate_name);
```

Several arguments are passed to `create` operations. The name of the collection is used to identify the collection at a later time. A collection has to exist in an object repository so the `create` operation takes the repository as an argument. The `indices` argument is a set of component names which are defined for the type `entity_type` and which should be regarded as indices for this collection. The `super_collections` argument specifies that this database collection is a sub-collection of the collections named in the set. The entity type of this collection will have to be the same type or a subtype of each super_collections' respective entity type (see Section 4.3).

The insert operation is used to add objects to a collection[4]. Its interface is

```
operation insert (me, entity: entity_type)
    signals (already_there);
```

If the object already exists in the collection the already_there exception will be raised.

The remove operation is used to delete objects from a collection. Its interface is

```
operation remove (me, entity: entity_type)
    signals (not_found);
```

The object entity is removed from the database collection. Note that this does not delete the object - it simply removes it from the collection.

There are two operations that can be used to retrieve objects from a collection. The elements operation is an iterator that returns all of the entities in the collection. Its interface is

```
operation elements (me)
    yields (entity_type);
```

To iterate over the elements in the employee collection mentioned earlier, we could write

```
for emp: Employee in elements (my_employees) do
    .
    .
    .
end for;
```

We also provide limited associative retrieval of objects within collections. The select iterator takes a predicate as an argument and will return the objects in the collection for which this predicate evaluates to true. It is defined as

```
operation select (me, p: DB_Predicate)
    yields (entity_type);
```

This mechanism will allow us to extract objects that satisfy a given condition from a database collection. We will also provide a select operation that return a new database collection and one that returns just a single object.

Since communication is expensive, we will want to use the DB_Predicate to filter the collection at the repository, and only transfer the objects that satisfy the predicate. This also enables the repository to use indices that may exist to speed up locating the desired objects. But evaluating a general programmer specified condition at the repository leads to some difficulties. For example, the condition might refer to non-shared objects that exist only on the client node.

Fully solving this problem requires a uniform distributed object system, and we decided earlier that this was too ambitious at this point. Our solution is to restrict the allowed conditions to those that the repository can safely evaluate. We will ensure at compile time that only proper conditions are presented to the repository.

---

[4] We do not have a key constraint on DB_Collections. The use of keys will be greatly diminished in an object-oriented database since uniqueness does not depend on data values. Moreover, programmers can always add an operation to the entity_type to check for uniqueness of some component attributes.

Programs will rely on transactions (see Section 6) to coordinate the updating of objects in the repository. After retrieving an object, a program can modify the object and the object will be automatically updated in the repository when the transaction completes. There is no explicit update or replace operation.

4.3 Sub-Collection Relationships

We allow programmers to define sub-collection relationships between database collections. Defining a collection `b` to be a sub-collection of a collection `a` means that the elements of `b` will be a subset of the elements of `a`. Therefore, if we iterate over the collection `a`, we will also return the elements of `b`. For this to work properly, there has to be a subtype relationship between the type of the elements of `b` and the type of the elements of `a`. In other words, `b`'s elements have to be a subtype (or the same type) of `a`'s elements.

Consider the following example:

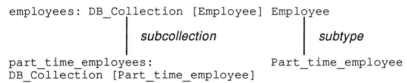

```
employees: DB_Collection [Employee]   Employee


            |  subcollection               |  subtype


part_time_employees:                  Part_time_employee
DB_Collection [Part_time_employee]
```

In this example, the collection `part_time_employees` is a sub-collection of `employees`, and the type `Part_time_employee` is a subtype of `Employee`. The collection `employees` includes the elements of the collection `part_time_employees`. Note that the type `Part_time_employee` must be a subtype (or the same type) of the type `Employee` for the sub-collection relationship to be valid.

4.4 Object Repositories

We introduce another type, `Repository`, which corresponds roughly to a database. An object repository is a collection of database collections.

The `create` operation will define a new object repository. Its interface is

```
operation create (Mytype, name: String)
     returns (Repository);
```

When creating an object repository, the programmer specifies a name for the repository.

The `locate` operation will find an existing object repository. Its interface is

```
operation locate (Mytype, name: String)
     returns (Repository)
     signals (not_found);
```

Programs would use this operation to access previously created repositories.

As an example, suppose we wanted to access an existing repository called the `company`, and iterate through the collections on the repository. We could do this in Trellis as follows

```
var company_db: Repository;
company_db := locate(Repository, "company");
for db: DB_Collection in db_collections (company_db) do
    .
    .
    .
end for;
```

The `db_collections` operation is an iterator which returns all of the database collections defined in the repository. Its interface is

```
db_collections (me)
     yields (DB_Collection);
```

We also provide an operation to return a particular database collection, given its name. Its interface is

```
operation find_db_collection (me, name: String)
     returns (DB_Collection)
     signals (not_found);
```

5   Support for Aggregate Objects

In an object-oriented system, a conceptual object, which represents some "real world" entity, is often made up of thousands of smaller objects. For example, a compound document object might consist of many objects, representing chapters, paragraphs, characters, and graphics. In some instances, the programmer will want to work with this group of objects, which constitute the document, as a single entity. Indeed, there is usually one object that acts as the root, and all other objects constituting this conceptual entity can be referenced through the root object. This conceptual entity is sometimes referred to as a complex or *aggregate* object.

The performance of an object-oriented database system is very dependent on how well it supports aggregate objects. Support for aggregate objects includes determining what gets transferred from the database when an aggregate object is referenced in a program. As well, the objects that constitute an aggregate object can be clustered together on disk. The clustering can be used to improve the performance to transfers.

The Trellis language permits arbitrary connectivity among objects. An object can be referenced by any number of objects including itself. Thus, from the programmer's view, aggregate objects can be modeled quite easily (i.e. any object can be thought of as an aggregate object). Since we want to make the use of repositories as transparent to the programmer as possible, we do not want to restrict the data modeling capabilities of Trellis by not allowing arbitrary references.

There is a tradeoff between expressiveness and efficiency, however. For example, allowing arbitrary references between objects can impact efficiency when storing objects in the repository. Suppose we have a compound document object (as described above) that references many other objects. If the language restricted connectivity, so that no other object could refer to any object referred to by the document, we could take advantage of this knowledge in the underlying storage scheme of the repository. We could cluster all of the objects in this document together on disk.

But in a compound document system the programmer might want to have different documents share a particular object, for example, an appendix. If arbitrary connectivity is allowed, using the same clustering strategy will not work. We can try to cluster objects together as much as possible, but some references to objects will inevitably get distributed across the disk. This is a price we are willing to pay to preserve the expressive and powerful data modeling capabilities of Trellis.

The ubiquitous reason that engineering design applications do not use commercially-oriented database management systems is poor performance. This poor performance is primarily caused by a lack of support for aggregate objects [Maie86, LoPl83]. Lorie illustrated this point by using a relational DBMS to store data from a CAD/CAM system. The relational schema consists of relations representing circuits, pins, connections, and so on. One of the examples used is a model of a 4-input AND circuit which is made up of three 2-input AND gates. To retrieve this circuit model from the DBMS required separate access to 22 tuples in five separate relations; if the database was local to the workstation, access was poor; if the data had to be requested across a LAN from a database server, the performance was intolerable.

Why is a relational database too slow? Associative access to disk is not the bottleneck - it is because each fetch or store on a part of the circuit model incurs the cost of a procedure call from the application program to the database. It is not the overhead associated with the procedure call that hurts performance, but rather the work that the database system performs on every call. A CAD tool would normally use record structures from the programming language to represent the circuit model. A procedure call to the database cannot compete with simple offset addressing for accessing a field of program memory[5].

To achieve sufficient performance to support design applications, such as CAD and compound documents, accessing an object will have to approach the speed of accessing a field in programming language record structures. If the repository has knowledge of aggregate objects, it can transfer the whole group of objects that constitute the aggregate object (in this case the circuit) in a single request, not dozens of individual requests. Thus, most references to objects will not require procedure calls to the database.

The system has to determine what actually gets transferred from the repository. Should it transfer a subset of what can be referenced or every object that can be referenced?

We would like to transfer only the objects that are actually used, especially when large aggregate objects are involved. One way to do this is to have the programmer give the system *transferring* hints by describing which objects are frequently used together, and, therefore, should be transferred together.

One place to describe transferring hints is in type declarations where the structure of objects is defined. But an object of a particular type may be used in many different ways, and one transferring strategy may not be optimal for all the different usages. For example, treating a compound document as an aggregate object and transferring all of its sub-objects when it is referenced might work well for a word processing application (i.e. you want to edit the document). But if an application was just displaying titles and authors of documents, transferring the whole document would be very inefficient. Therefore, allowing only one set of transferring hints to be defined with the document type declaration is probably insufficient.

Another place one could describe transferring hints is in the declarations of database collection or the operations that manipulate database collections.

---

[5] See [Maie86] for a more thorough explanation of this point.

When a collection is created the programmer already gives some usage hints by indicating the indices that can be used for associative retrieval of objects in the collection. The programmer could also give transferring hints for each collection. Therefore, a specific type would have more than one transferring strategy since instances of that type may reside in more than one collection. The objects in a particular collection may be used more uniformly than all instances of the type. Therefore, associating transferring hints with collections may result in more efficient groupings.

The repository will also require *clustering* hints to determine which objects should be clustered together in secondary storage. Objects that are clustered together may or may not want to be transferred together (the compound document example shown above also illustrates this point). Thus, we need a different mechanism to describe clustering hints.

Our initial approach is to associate default transferring and clustering hints with type declarations. But we allow the programmer to override these defaults and to specify alternative hints associated with database collections.

6   Sharing and Concurrency

One of the main reasons for having object repositories is to allow applications to share information. We must define what it means to share objects between applications and provide a synchronization mechanism for that sharing.

The object repositories provide a *sharing by copy* semantics. When an application retrieves an object from a repository, the application gets a copy of the object in its local storage. The application can modify the object locally as needed. These changes are not reflected back to the repository or to other applications until the changed object is written back to the repository. After the object has been updated in the repository, other applications may get the new version of the object when they ask the repository for the object. Applications will have to coordinate their changes when sharing objects.

We recognize the need for two kinds of "transaction-like" behavior to provide object consistency. Low level, "instantaneous", serializable transactions are needed to synchronize actions on the data in the repository. For example, if two applications want to read and write the same object, the low level transactions will ensure that the two applications will not interfere with each other (and possibly damage underlying data structures).

A number of applications also have "transaction-like" behavior. For example, a computer-aided design system may want to allow the design engineers to check out part of a design, work on the design, and then return the design. The semantics of this kind of "transaction" are application specific. Therefore, we want to provide a low level mechanism to allow application programmers to write these high level, application specific transactions easily.

Low level transactions can be implemented with locking, but we think that an optimistic approach will be more flexible. After considering some of the applications that we are trying to support, we believe that contention for objects will not be frequent, and, therefore, an optimistic approach will work well.

Initially, we are using timestamps and versions in our optimistic approach. If we assume that all objects are timestamped, the basic capabilities needed are

•   read an object at a particular time

- write a set of objects if another set of objects is unchanged since a particular time

These operations are sufficient but would be awkward for applications to use because of the bookkeeping associated with keeping track of read and write sets. Therefore, we are designing a *snapshot* mechanism to handle this bookkeeping for applications.

A snapshot of a repository is a view of the repository at a single instance in time. An application can create a snapshot, read objects from the snapshot, modify objects, and commit the changes to the repository. All objects that are read from the snapshot are "as they were" when the snapshot was created.

The snapshot mechanism keeps track of which objects have been read and which objects have been changed or created. When a snapshot is written back to the repository, the mechanism will verify that none of the objects in the read set have been modified by another transaction since the snapshot was created. If any of these objects have been changed, the write-back will be undone.

Our snapshot mechanism is designed to implement the low level, serializable transactions, but we think that applications will be able to use the mechanism to implement their own high level transactions. To provide some version support for the high level transactions, we will allow applications to use more than one snapshot at a time. We also provide a way of comparing objects from different snapshots.

7   Conclusion

We have presented a design of an object-oriented database extension to Trellis. The database is intended for applications, such as engineering data management, which have complex data structuring requirements and special data accessing needs. The primary purpose of the database is to provide shared access to persistent objects for multiple Trellis programs.

There are several areas which need further work. As mentioned in the previous section, we still have some design decisions to make for concurrency and recovery. The repository has to provide a mechanism for coordinating reliable updates to objects which are shared by several programs. We want to experiment with our optimistic approach to concurrency control which uses timestamps and snapshots. We also need a recovery scheme for handling failures (either client program failures or the failures of repository itself).

Support for aggregate objects is crucial if we want to provide adequate performance. Both the clustering of objects in the repository and the transferring of objects between the repository and local storage are important considerations. We will experiment with different strategies for clustering and transferring, as well as different mechanisms for allowing the programmer to describe hints for the system.

Providing limited but efficient associative retrieval of various objects from the repository is also an important capability. We have designed predicates which can be used to filter the objects that are retrieved from the repository. We will experiment with how comprehensive these predicates have to be - we hope that the repository will not need its own execution model.

Trellis provides a flexible scheme for handling program (schema) changes. The repository will have to support this scheme as well as provide support for versions of objects. For example, it will have to support multiple versions of objects of the same type and/or provide the ability to convert an object from an old version of a type to a newer version of that type.

We are currently implementing the system to test our design and ideas. As a yardstick for measuring whether our performance is suitable, we are using the Trellis programming environment. We believe that if the Trellis incremental compiler can run fast enough when its data structures are stored in the repository (by "fast enough" we mean achieve close to current levels of performance), then other applications such as CAD tools will be able to use the system productively. Furthermore, we believe that the combination of the Trellis language, programming environment, and object repository will result in a powerful system for application development.

8   References

[AlCO85], [BaKi85a], [CoMa84], [GoRo83], [HaOB87], [Lisk81], [LoPl83], [Maie86], [McKi81], [MyBW80], [OBri85], [ScCW85], [Scha86], [ScSp84], [WiLi85], [WoKL85], [Zani86].

9
Godal: An Object-Centered Database Language

Martin L. Kersten, Frans H. Schippers

Abstract

The central theme of this paper is the friction encountered when using a traditional object-oriented (O-O) language in the database arena. A series of (open) database issues is given for which the object-oriented paradigm does not provide an elegant solution. Following we describe a refinement of the O-O concepts which emphasizes the dynamic classification of objects through its evolving properties rather than the origine of its instantiation method. Such an approach is called object-centered *and is the basis for organizing the database in the programming language* Godal. *The complementary aspect explored is to organize the processing around active agents, called* guardians, *which are high-level declarative process descriptions which algorithmically react to states (changes) of the database.*

1   Introduction

The Object-Oriented paradigm represents one of the most successful paradigms in many areas of computer science. It has gained wide acceptance as a unifying paradigm for the design of database systems, programming languages, and artificial intelligence area over the last decade. Seminal is the role of Smalltalk [GoRo83] which shows that the concept is of particular importance when dealing with man-machine communication on a high-resolution graphics workstation.

Although the object-oriented paradigm has many different uses and therefore many different faces, the following aspects are being recognized as essential [Zani86]:

1. *Data abstraction and encapsulation,*

2. *Object identity independent of properties,*

3. *Messages,*

4. *Property inheritance,*

5. *Overloading,*

6. *Late binding,*

7. *Interactive interfaces with windows, menus and mice.*

As mentioned before, one of the areas where the object-oriented (O-O) programming paradigm has gained momentum is the database research area. The emphasis on the O-O aspects can best be illustrated by some of the ongoing projects in this area.

The first project to mention is the TAXIS in Toronto, where many aspects of the object-oriented programming paradigm has been explored. In particular, it has been used to model office environments and the design of conceptual data models [Nixo84].

A more direct approach to apply the O-O paradigm to the database arena has been taken by Maier et al [CoMa84]. They model the database management system directly after the Smalltalk language and its man-machine style [MaNG86, AnEM86b, MaSt86]. A conservative approach is explored in the POSTGRES project [Ston, Rowe]. An increasing stream of activities can also be recognized in the area of expert database systems. In particular, the design and implementation of knowledge base management systems. Example projects in this field are the constraint maintenance system PRISM [ShKe86] and the object-oriented database management system Sembase [King84a].

In this paper we review some of the problems which led to the increased interest in the object-oriented paradigm as exemplified by workable implementations of the language Smalltalk. We will argue that despite its desirable properties an object-oriented approach, as characterized above, leaves many database problems unresolved. As a step towards an adequate solution we suggest to switch focus to the characteristic properties of objects as they emerge during their life span and organize the processing around it. In contrast with the O-O approach this means that the class of an object becomes a dynamic property and that message passing between objects becomes more elaborated. We call such an approach *object-centered*, because it is the object representation of a real-world entity which determines its semantic properties rather than the class in which it happens to be created.

The rest of this paper is organized as follows. In section 2 some open database issues are formulated in an object-oriented context. Section 3 presents an overview of the object-centered database language Godal. In section 4 three examples are given to illustrate the effectiveness of our approach in dealing with cooperative processes, evolutionary databases and object class descriptions.

2   Database Problems in an Object-Oriented Language

In this section we review part of the open database problems and interpret them in an object-oriented context. In this discussion we limit ourselves to comparisons with Smalltalk (ST-80), because this language can be considered a prototypical example of an object-oriented language. The issues raised in this section have been discussed at various places and some predominant alternative approaches are described elsewhere in this volume.

An essential aspect of a database system is the data model it supports. The data model determines the data types, the operators applicable and the integrity constraints to be preserved. The three dimensions are used to illustrate some open problems and frictions with an object-oriented approach. A discussion of the architectural consequences of an O-O approach, such as persistency, sharing and performance, are beyond the scope of this paper.

2.1 Data Type

It is generally recognized that the relational model of data is insufficient to easily represent real-world semantics. In particular, the assumption that all objects can be represented as tuples in relations results in complex intra-relationship constraints. For example, CAD/CAM objects exhibit a hierarchical structure which are removed by the mapping to a relational scheme. The effect is that structure relationships among components should be regained by extensive use of (recursive) joins during query processing.

The prime advantage claimed of an object-oriented approach to database systems is precisely on this topic, because it provides the framework to define both the structure and the applicable operators of new objects in a consistent manner, hiding implementation details as much as possible. So far there is no friction with the O-O framework. Problems emerge if we consider the life cycle of an entity in the real-world as represented by an object in an O-O database system.

The first problem to consider is the need for multiple overlapping views of an entity, i.e. opaque data types. Two cases can be distinguished here. When the view is a re-ordering or a partial shielding of the properties then an object type hierarchy is sufficient, because inheritance and access is based on property name rather than by position. However, when the view represents the result of combining objects then we are faced with insurmountainable problems, such as view updates, renaming of methods to resolve ambiguous property definitions, and union (in)compatibility of composite object classes. For example, consider the two object classes representing departments (depnr, depname) and managers (name, depnr). Then the construction of the subclass representing the objects depmgr (depname, mgrname) should be defined as an evolving joins between two existing classes. This means that the new class should be automatically extended when either one of the super classes instance sets is changed. Moreover, method inheritance becomes ambiguous. In ST-80 such a class can not easily be defined. A solution to resolve ambiguous inheritance paths can be found in LOOPS [BoSt83].

The second issue deals with the classification of real-world entities over time. In current database systems an entity is classified once, during its creation. As soon as an entity changes category (=relation type) the old representation is removed and a new object is created. This way the object identity characteristic of an O-O might be violated.

Moving an instance to another class, assuming the representation is identical, is not possible in ST-80 either. This is a direct consequence of abstracting the behaviour of objects into hierarchical-structured class definitions and using initialization (and finalization) procedures.

In many cases the object class can be determined automatically from the attribute values of the object or can be explicitly administered as an instance variable. As an aside, a tagging of objects with the class names to which they belong provides a uniform solution to many view problems as well. For example, as soon as a person becomes older than 65 it should automatically be classified as a retired person. This requires that the database system contains a *daemon* watching for this event or a *triggering* mechanism such that as soon as the age is modified the entity is reclassified. A mechanism to describe this phenomenon within a class definition is conceivable, but requires a lot of programming effort.

2.2 Operations

In ST-80 implementations all objects are addressable, at the language level, by name. In database systems objects are primarily addressed by contents rather than by name. This means that the receiver of a message is a declaratively described collection of objects. Moreover, its effect on message passing is similar to selective broadcasting in operating systems. This means that more control is needed to assemble and manipulate the response set. Clearly, the simplistic message passing protocol in ST-80 is far from such an ideal situation.

The actions on a database take the form of transactions, units of work which preserve the integrity constraints. Moreover, the transaction concept is the unit of recovery from both system and user errors. The transaction concept is not available in most object-oriented languages; neither as recoverable unit, nor as mechanism for sharing the object base. Therefore, any database system built upon the ST-80 framework should use the built-in semaphore and process classes and re-implement the traditional database algorithms for transaction management.

As mentioned above, a desirable property of database systems nowadays is to be able to define a limited class of triggers. As soon as an update (or retrieval) action is applied to the database a procedure is automatically started to check for inconsistency etc.. Transferred to the ST-80 realm this would mean that one should be able to specify globally which message should be sent as a side-effect ofactual, user-activated messages.

The operators are passive in a ST-80 program. They are logically activated by an object receiving a message. Processes are provided as a separated built-in type. The gain from this approach is visibility of control. The disadvantage is that parallelism should be explicitly specified by the programmer. This is a pity, because the object-oriented paradigm suggests a way to avoid this by considering each object both as a static and a dynamic (process) entity.

2.3 Integrity Constraints

Real-world databases are protected against invalid data by integrity constraints. They come in many flavors, such as value range constraints, pattern constraints, ordering and functional constraints. Current database systems only support a limited set. In particular, value range constraints and referential constraints. In ST-80 all constraints should be described algorithmically by specialized (overloaded) operators. The effect is that constraint maintenance becomes 'visible' through the operator structure. However, the dispersed description of the integrity rules make them less amenable for formal analysis.

One of the interesting aspects in ST-80 is inheritance of properties through type hierarchies. This is convenient for specifying programs, but has some repercussions as well. One of its effects is that a tight link is established among the classes which make extension and modification of the class definition in the future cumbersome. Moreover, it ignores the fact that there are essential two different aspects of inheritance; structural and behavioural inheritance. Structural inheritance is the property that structural details of an object representation should be visible (under constraints) to the outside world, i.e. opaqueness of the representation. For example, when dealing with an aggregated object such as date then structural inheritance allows one to access and manipulate the individual date components, i.e. day, week, year fields.

Contrary, behavioural inheritance makes operational properties encapsulated in the type hierarchy to become part of the objects property list. These properties change dynamically as the object migrates between classes or when the class hierarchy is altered.

2.4 An Object-Centered Approach

The shortcomings reported above, (and elsewhere), indicate that strict adherence to the object-oriented language features is too restrictive. The prime cause of the friction is the static association of an object with its defining class, regardless the properties it exhibits over time. Moreover, the strict organization of classes into a hierarchy, and the dependencies introduced with it, complicate the manipulation of the semantic descriptions (class definitions). As a solution to the problems we propose an *object-centered* approach, which is characterized by the following features: (using the same framework as for O-O)

1) *Data abstraction and encapsulation*

   Every object comes with a set of characteristic properties which determine the set of operations used to operate upon and to change the object. Moreover, the object can hide its properties so as to support a private implementation of the applicable operations.

3) *Messages*

   Message passing is asynchronous. The receiver of the message is not (necessarily) known to the sender. The sender places several messages in the database upon which processes (objects) may react. The result of a message can only be determined by observing a particular database state.

4) *Property inheritance*

   The dichotomy of objects (static and dynamic) leads to supporting two kinds of inheritance as well; *structural inheritance* and *behavioural inheritance*. Structural inheritance makes properties of objects structurally associated with an object accessible. Dynamic inheritance makes the set of operations applicable to an object a dynamic property.

5) *Overloading*

   Operator definitions (methods) can be overloaded. Both the operator name, the argument types, and the state of the database determine the specific operator definition.

The object-oriented aspects 2), 6), and 7) introduced before remain valid. In the following section we illustrate how these aspects are reflected in the design of the programming language *Godal.*

3   A General Object-Centered Database Language

In this section we give a short description of the language *Godal.* The language has been designed to support the construction of knowledge based applications using an object-centered programming paradigm. A detailed description is given in [KeSc86a]. The language capitalize on experience in earlier object-oriented languages and addresses the database problems posed in the previous section. The prominent *Godal* design considerations are:

1. *Data base management*

    The language deals with a database of objects; integrity of the database is guaranteed through a generalized trigger mechanism; object selection is declarative, based on first-order logic; transaction processing primitives are included.

2. *Knowledge base management*

    Both simple facts (objects) and rules to derive facts are stored in the database in a uniform way. Facts can play roles in different interpretation domains concurrently. Both structural inheritance, i.e. using the value of an objects' subcomponent, and behavioural inheritance, i.e. using a value obtained from an objects' agent, are provided.

3. *Data flow driven computation*

    Operations are triggered when the operational constraints associated with processes become true in a particular state of the database or when an event is recognized.

4. *Modularity*

    Objects, functions and processes are logically grouped into modules, called worlds, with facilities to selectively export information.

The *Godal* design considerations influenced the choices of the particular language features, which are summarized below:

1. *Data paradigm*

    The structure of the data in a database is not static; rather it evolves over time to meet the changing information requirements of users. A declarative specification of the behavioural properties of data forms a proper basis to cope with database evolution. It allows both data and meta-data to be treated in a uniform fashion.

2. *Object-centered paradigm*

    The object-centered paradigm takes the object-oriented approach one step further by making class membership a dynamic property of objects. This way evolution of the knowledge base is accommodated without loosing the ability to safeguard its integrity.

3. *Rule-oriented paradigm*

    The rule-oriented paradigm allows for the description and use of procedural knowledge without specifying in advance all allowable control paths.

4. *Polymorphic typing*

    The language is basically typeless. Variables need not be declared before use. In essence, types are considered 'first class values' and thus may be the result of expressions. A dynamic typing system is easily included using the language primitives provided.

5. *Cooperative problem solving*

    Techniques for cooperative problem solving provide the means for distributed knowledge manipulation and forms a basis for contemplating parallel implementation architectures. The integrity of the database is guaranteed by the atomic behaviour of guardians which is implemented through data sharing.

3.1 The Object Base

The language contains three major building blocks: objects, guardians and functions. The objects are used to model the static aspects of entities. The guardians model processes and entity-classes. The functions define parameterized computations and provide refinements in processes description. In this subsection we discuss the structure object-base and its maintenance.

Objects represent entities in the real world, which are stored in a part of the Godal system called the object-base. Each object is (individually) described by a set of attributes. An attribute takes either a set of values (the singleton set is allowed) which denote primitive objects or object references. Alternatively an attribute value is assigned a (symbolic) description of how to compute the value, i.e.a deferred expression. Properties of an object can be added at any convenient time by inclusion of a new attribute. Similar, properties can be dropped by removing the attributes.

To simplify the construction of similar objects one can also encapsulate their description in an definition statement. A new instance is created by supplying the **new** operator with the name of the definition.

Below two object definitions and their instantiations are given.

```
new object artis
        address:= 'Plantage Parklaan'
        opened ::= clock>900 & clock <1730
end
new object hawk                      /* A new object called hawk. */
        isa_bird                     /* An attribute without value. */
        food := 'mice'               /* An attribute with string value. */
        location -> artis            /* artis is a component of tris object. */
end
```

The artis object describes the location of the Amsterdam zoo. The attribute opened is a deferred expression. Once its value is need the expression is evaluated. The hawk object has three attributes: isa_bird, food, and a reference to its habitat. The value of the isa_bird attribute is undefined. However, the object can still be recognized as a bird by checking the existence of the isa-birds attribute using the *has* operator, i.e. hawk:isa_bird = true.

This simple example also illustrates that objects may contain references to other objects in the object-base. In general, the structure of the Godal object-base is a directed graph and searching this graph is a prerequisite for finding objects of interest. To simplify the latter we provide search operators and use fingers, represented as variables, into this graph to remember locations.

The primitive search operator is the dot ('.'). It provides access to a component of an object given the component name. It is similar to the traditional record field denotation in other high-level programming languages. In the first expression below, the value of the food consumed by the hawk is retrieved. In this case its value is a singleton set, i.e {'mice'}. The field denotation can be applied recursively, accessing more detailed descriptions of the object. If the exact path is unknown then the dot-dot ('..') operator can be used. It recursively descends the graph looking for a reachable object with the proper name.

Both operators can be combined to form (partial) walks through the object graph. The starting point is either identified by a object name or a variable. If the starting point is an identifier then the search is context dependent. When used in a definition it is refers to an object described earlier in the same definition, the object under construction, or a global object. Otherwise the variable denotes the starting location.

Note that the dot and dot-dot mechanism is a form of structural inheritance, details are accessible to the outer levels through name navigation.

```
hawk.food              /* Denotes { 'honey' }. */
hawk.location          /* A zoo object. */
hawk..opened           /* value depends on actual time. */
hawk..address          /* Plantage Parklaan. */
```

The object graph can be modified with the assignment (:=), insert (->) and delete (/>) operator. They take the result of an expression and extend (or reduce) the attribute set of the object referenced. Thus, addition and deletion of attributes and values are conceptually identical.

```
hawk.food -> 'water'   /* Extend the value set. */
hawk /> food           /* The food-attribute is deleted. */
```

3.2 The Guardians

Guardians are high-level declaratively described processes which react to observed states and state changes in the object base. They are similar to daemons in the AI community, but differ in the way they are introduced and manipulated. A guardian has two distinctive components. First, like objects, it has a name and possibly a set of attributes. Second, it contains a list of rules. Each of which consists of a predicate (with free variables) and a statement block. The predicate is evaluated continuously against the current object base. As soon as a binding of the variables is found for which the predicate is true the statement block is executed.

Another distinctive property is that the statement blocks associated with guardian rules are interpreted as transactions. They move the object base from consistent state to consistent state. An undo operator is provided to the programmer to express recovery of user actions. The undo is automatically called when the statement block can not be executed with success. It is assumed that concurrent transactions are coordinated by a transaction manager using traditional database techniques.

The guardian shown below watches the database for birds. It ensures that the food attribute of birds is set. The domain limits the search space to objects with the isa-bird attribute and where i.e the food attribute set is empty.

```
guardian birdwatcher        /* Watches for birds */
    domain O:isa_bird & O.food = nil
        /*incomplete information has been localized */
        write 'What it the food of ', O.name, '\n'
        read O.food
end
```

4 Variables, Expressions and Statements

The lexical conventions in Godal are inspired by Prolog. Objects (attributes, guardians and functions) are named by identifiers (or string constants). Variables are recognized as identifiers starting with an upper case character. The variables are used in the same way as object names; they give access to objects. The lexical scope of the variable is limited to the lexical scope determined by the closest enclosing brackets.

Variables have two states; bounded and unbounded. The first occurrence of a variable defines it and turns it in an unbounded variable. Once a variable is assigned a reference to an object through an expression is becomes bounded. Automatic variable binding is also provided as a side-effect of rule evaluation (if-statement, do-statement, for-statement). When a variable is introduced in a rule then it is bound with an object in the object-base such that the factor (in which it occurs) does not denote the null object. For example, in the statements below the variable Bird is bound to *some* bird in the database. It is unknown which particular bird. Selective binding of variables can be obtained by specifying more distinctive properties.

During rule evaluation all possible variable bindings are explored to satisfy the constraint. The variables for which the rule is true remain bounded till the end of the associated statement block.

```
for Bird:isa_bird   /* successively binds with all birds */
        put 'bird=', Bird
od
```

In addition, some well-known control structures are introduced. A statement block is provided which enforces a sequential execution of the statements listed. The elements of the statement block are assignments, if-statements, repetitive statements, input/output statements and function calls. The assignment statement have been described before and need no further introduction.

If the conditional expression in an if-then-else statement does not contain new variables then it is identical to its counterpart in imperative languages. Otherwise the expression is interpreted as a rule and the new variables are temporary bound to an object such that the condition is true. Subsequently the statement block is executed. The do-statement is a repeated version of the if-statement, the block is executed as long as the conditional expression holds. The for-statement differs from the do-statement by collecting all possible variable bindings first.

Procedural abstraction is provided through function definitions. They consist of a sequence of domain descriptions, each domain is associated with the algorithmic action to be performed. If domains overlap then one is picked at random. The generality of this scheme allows all kinds of type-based and value-based function selections to be specified. Below a function is shown that returns the size of an object depending on the attributes associated with its argument.

```
function size(O)
        domain O:integer return (4)
        domain O:float return (8)
        domain O:string return (strlength(O))
        domain others write 'illegal function call\n'
end
```

5   Example Godal Programs

In this section we present three example Godal programs to illustrates the language features and their use. The examples illustrate cooperative problem solving, evolutionary database management, and object-class descriptions respectively.

5.1 The Card Game

This section presents an informal and intuitive introduction of the features of Godal by means of 'a card game'. Seated at the table are three players, called Shorty, Fat Boy, and Sue. A third person, the arbiter, shuffles a deck of cards and arrange them in a rectangle of 4 rows and 13 columns. When this is finished the arbiter takes three pieces of paper and writes down a task for each person.

The task for Shorty becomes:

For every two different cards in the same column exchange them such that the clubs occupy the first row, diamonds the second, hearts the third, and spades the fourth row.

The task for Fat Boy and Sue becomes:

For every card not in the proper column select a card from the proper column (and which is not at the correct column either) and exchange them.

As soon as the players receive their (private) goal the system is set into motion. All players move until no more actions are possible. The player who moves least recently is the winner.

This trivial game, of course, sorts all the cards by suites and value. The points of interest are that all players (processes) can work in parallel without knowledge of each others' task; the actual sequence of actions is determined by the state of the table (=database); the tasks are described by a high level declarative rule selecting the interested database states and a simple algorithm action; concurrent access is synchronized through an exclusive locking scheme. Below a sketch is given of the Godal description for this game.

```
new object card x := 1 y := 1 color := hearts number := 4 end
          /* 50 more cards */
new object card x := 13 y := 4 color := diamonds number := 1 end

function exchange (O,P)
domain O != nil & P != nil & P < > O
          V := O; O := P; P := V
end

new guardian shorty
domain C1.x = C2.x & C1 < > C2 & C2.color < > C1.color & C1.color = clubs C1.y<>1
               exchange (C1.y,C2.y)

domain C1.x = C2.x & C1 < > C2 & C2.color < > C1.color & C1.color = diamonds
        C1.y<>2
               exchange (C1.y,C2.y)

          /* the other two cases are similar. */
```

```
end

new guardian sue
domain R1.x < > R1.number & R2.x = R1.number & R2.number < > R1.number
        exchange (R1.x,R2.x)
        exchange (R1.y,R2.y)
end

new guardian fatBoy := sue end
```

5.2 A Small Relational Database

To illustrate the power of Godal some pieces of a relational database application are implemented below. The structure of the relational model is mapped onto objects tagged with the name of the relation they belong to. As the Godal user is free to construct such an object, it should be ensured that each object has the proper attributes. In the guardian *employee_class*, described below, omitted attributes are automatically introduced.

```
new object employee_prop
        employee; age; name; address; manager; birthyear
end

new guardian employee_class
domain O.employee
        /* find all superfluous employee attributes*/
        for O.A & !employee_prop:A
           put A, ' is an illegal employee attribute\n'
        rof
        /* add missing attributes */
        for employee_prop.A & !O:A
           O -> new A               /* extend attribute set */
        rof
end
```

Two integrity constraints are implied by the relational model. Namely, each tuple in a relation should be unique and each attribute name is unique within the tuple, and each attribute value is a singleton set. These constraints can be checked by a single guardian. To make it work we need some information to single out the tuples from other Godal object structures. One way to do this is to add the relation names as attributes to the constraint manager.

```
guardian relational_constraints
        schema->employee      /* watch the employee tuples *.

        domain Tuple.Relname & schema.Relname & Tuple.A1 & A1 != Tuple.A1
           put Tuple.A1, ' violates attribute uniqueness property '

        domain Tuple.Relname & schema.Relname & Tuple.A.V1 &
           Tuple.A.V2 & V1 != V2
           put Tuple.A, ' violates atomicity property '

        domain T1.Relname < > T2.Relname & equaltuple (T2,T1)
           put 'tuple ', T1, '['
           for T2.A write T2.A, ' ' rof
           write '] violates tuple uniqueness property \n'
end
```

Some application specific constraints can be implemented directly using operator overloading or by using a guardian to watch for undesirable situations. The latter approach is illustrated below which warns the user whenever the year of birth value becomes invalid.

```
function showtuple (T)
        domain T: employee
            /* display employee record */
        domain others
            /* display unrecognized object */
end

guardian retire_people
domain O : employee & O.age > 65
        showtuple (O)
        write 'Give this fellow a farewell party\n'
        forget O    /* deletes it from the database */
end

guardian semantic_constraints
domain T.Relname = employee & T.birthyear<1900 | T.birthyear >= 2000
        T.birthyear := nil
        showtuple (T)
        write ' violates year of birth constraint\n '
end
```

5.3 An Object Class Description

To illustrate how a Smalltalk-like class definition can be mapped to Godal we consider the concept of a Point and Rectangles. A Point represents an x-y pair of numbers usually designating a pixel in a Form. Points refer to pixel locations relative to the top left corner of the Form. By convention, x increases to the right and y downwards. In Smalltalk the class Point is predefined and provides facilities to create points, accessing the individual coordinates, point comparison, point arithmetic, and point functions (distance, transpose, etc.). The class Rectangle represent rectangular areas of pixels. Arithmetic operations take points as arguments and carry out scaling and translation to create new rectangles. Thus, the Rectangle class inherits the Points properties for manipulation of the rectangle corner and center points.

The mapping to Godal objects is straightforward. First we have to design an object structure to represent points and rectangles. Below a prototypical Point and Rectangle are presented. Note that this definition does not enforce rectangles to be initialized with points. The rest of the required functionality is obtained by defining a set of overloaded functions.

Unlike ST-80 the resulting class definitions are flat. That is, all overloaded functions are defined at the same level of abstraction. However, they are covered by different domain expressions, which particularize the instance to be taken in each case. The advantage of this approach is that new operator definitions can readily be included. In the case that function domains overlap one is picked at random.

```
object point (X,Y)
domain X: integer & Y: integer
        xcor := X
        ycor := Y
end

object rectangle (X,Y)
domain X: point & Y: point
        ltop := X
```

```
        rbot := Y
end

function less (X1, X2)
domain X1: point & X2: point
        return (X1.xcor < X2.xcor & X1.ycor < X2.ycor)

domain X1: rectangle & X2: rectangle
        /* left as an exercise */
end
```

6   Summary and Future Research

In this paper we have presented an overview of the object-centered programming language *Godal*. The rationale for its development has been partly motivated by presenting some current database problems. It shows that a more object-centered description of a data base results in greater flexibility of modelling the real world. In contrast with the traditional O-O approach this means that the class of an object becomes a dynamic property and that message passing between objects is more elaborated then suggested by Smalltalk implementations. Besides modelling flexibility the language features simplify the definition of evolutionary database systems [KeSc86b].

A functional prototype Godal processor has been implemented under BSD 4.3 in C. Our initial findings working with this implementation proves the validity of the language features. However, a more thorough symbolic analysis of the program is required to reduce the excessive overhead in finding qualifying objects for guardians. Parallel processor architectures are considered to further improved the execution speed.

The second area of attention is language functionality and the programming methods to be used. Programming in the Godal is complex because it is not always clear in advance what the combined, non-deterministic effect is of running the guardians in parallel. Wherever determinism is required it should be encoded in the application. A particular area where these aspects are being studied is the design of complex adaptable information systems, where the data model is changing rapidly and where rare information should be dealt with regularly. Initial investigations provide suggestive evidence that our language is particularly suited for this application area.

7   References

[AnEM86b], [BoSt83], [CoMa84], [GoRo83], [KeSc86a], [KeSc86b], [King84a], [MaNG86], [MaSt86], [Nixo84], [Rowe], [ShKe86], [Ston], [Zani86].

Part IV

Interfaces

10

PROTEUS: The DBMS User Interface as an Object

T. Lougenia Anderson, Earl F. Ecklund, Jr., David Maier[1]

Abstract

Our thesis is that the external representation of all components of a database system should be under programmer control: objects, schemes, commands, even the representation specifications themselves. Here we give the rationale and design for the PROTEUS interface system that sits atop an object-oriented DBMS. After introducing the model, TEDM, for the DBMS, we describe the classes of objects that model components of the database of interest to PROTEUS: type definitions, representation definitions, layouts, commands, and representation mappings. The advantage of "objectifying" everything is three-fold: the database itself can manage all the information of interest to PROTEUS, representation can be changed via database updates, and the representation mappings themselves can be expressed as database commands or rules. We conclude by showing how the pieces fit together, and outline some of our current research directions.

1   Introduction

The study of database systems has largely overlooked the display of data, even though database applications typically contain more code for data display and entry than for data manipulation. Relational technology provides a facile abstraction of secondary storage: there is no analogous abstraction for user interfaces. With the advent of object-oriented database systems that support complex objects and multiple connectivity, a fixed format for displaying the results of queries is no longer adequate. Also, a DBMS is

[1] D. Maier's work was partially supported by a contract from Tektronix Computer Research Laboratory and NSF grant IST 83 51730, co-sponsored by Tektronix Foundation, Intel, Digital Equipment, Servio Logic, Mentor Graphics, Xerox, IBM and the Beaverton Area Chamber of Commerce.

perceived as the system integrator in most applications. We fell that this integration role should provide both storage functions and the user interface functions, with the DBMS applications supplying only the application-specific computation.

The PROTEUS (for *Polymorphic Representation of Objects for Tailored End-User Systems*) project represents joint research between Tektronix and the Oregon Graduate Center. Its goal is to define tools to specify, store, and utilize object-oriented user interfaces in a DBMS. Thus, not only is the DBMS data to be stored as objects, but everything the user sees or manipulates is to be a database object, subject to external representation formats. In fact, the external representation formats are themselves database objects, as are DBMS DML objects such as queries, updates, and commands. Of course, schema and meta-schema data are also stored in object form.

A second goal is to support interactive user interfaces, which means that PROTEUS must support both visual specifications (what the user sees) as well as behavioral specifications (how the user interacts with the interface). These specifications of the visual and behavioral aspects of the user interface should be given declaratively rather than procedurally, as can now be done for DBMS data definition and manipulation. We feel declarative specification makes construction and reuse of interfaces easier, allows tuning and minor modification without disproportionate amounts of programmer time, and allows optimization and physical independence of interfaces. Also, customization (often cited as one of the most important features of a successful user interface) should be accomplished through the DBMS language by changing the underlying user-interface-defining objects.

Because of our commitment to interactivity, PROTEUS will also support what Morgenstern describes as dynamic user interfaces [Morg83]. That is, if an update is made to the underlying data (by the user or by anyone else), then any views being displayed that depend on the update will be changed and redisplayed automatically. A view displayed to the user will be a window that, at any point in time, reflects the most current, up-to-date information available in the database (unless the user explicitly requests a snapshot instead - we call this a static user interface).

In PROTEUS, a representation is a mapping between an internal database object, such as `Person` or `Department`, and some displayable form for the object (we call these displayable forms *layout objects*). Each internal object will have many different representations, in order to satisfy the needs of different applications. For example, one representation for `Person` might display only a person's name and social security number in reverse video, while another representation might display all the fields defined for a person in a specified order. Each representation mapping is itself an object that can be reused in defining new user interfaces. Also, new representations can be added to the database to meet the demands of evolving applications. Of course, representations are "two way streets", since the user must also be able to update an internal object through its representation.

Finally, since everything the user sees is an object, it is natural to require that a query be an object also. Thus, a query will have an internal form and many different representations (e.g., a relational calculus representation, a forms-based representation, a semantic data model representation, etc.).

Why should a complete, declarative specification of the user interface be stored in the database? It seems to be an obvious extension of the existing database view mechanisms that provides more services to more applications and users from a central location. This centralization avoids duplication of effort, duplication of database features from application to application, and inconsistency in the user interface for groups of related applications. Also, since the DBMS already provides for the evaluation of a declarative language, this extension should fit in naturally.

2   Previous Work

PROTEUS represents the confluence of three existing currents of conceptual development: visual (graphical) interfaces, display specifications, and representation mappings. Visual database interfaces [BrHu86], [GGKZ85], [HeRo85], [KiMe84], [Rowe85], [StKa82], [WoKu82], [Zloo77] involve displaying information in or about a database in such a manner that the user can refer to both the values and the structure of the data. Display specifications [Born81], [Born85], [BrCr85], [FrBK82], [Lieb85], [MaNG86], [Morg83] describe the display media for an application, with both layout and behavioral aspects being represented in the description. Representation mappings [AnCl85], [BCPB84], [BaRa85], [Cout84], [Pilo83a], [Pilo83b], [Tsic82] address format independence between stored representation of data and the display presentation of the same data (which may depend on the context of the application). This section reviews selected examples of each of these three currents. We have also published a bibliography on the subject [AnEM86a].

The seminal work on visual interfaces to a relational database is Query-By-Example [Zloo77]. QBE derives its representation for the structure of a relation from a scheme of the relation (stored in the database). The user is able to enter a query in the forms presented and invoke execution of the query, whose result is returned in the same forms (i.e. structure) as used for the expression of the query. QBE has been generalized in two directions: visual interfaces with extended functionality (e.g. updates, accessing metadata) and visual interfaces to other data models. Rowe's Fill-in-the-Form [Rowe85] provides a toolkit for the user to specify the behavioral interpretation to be placed on different forms used in the interface. Fill-in-the-Form also enables the user to provide a full function interface to the database including update actions as well as queries.

Visual database interfaces are more common in richer data models, as linear, lexical syntax is less satisfactory for representing data items in those models. Wong and Kuo (GUIDE [WoKu82]) queried the Entity/Relationship data model, Heiler and Rosenthal (G-WHIZ [HeRo85]) queried the functional data model using DAPLEX, and King and Melville (SKI [KiMe84]) queried a semantic data model. Bryce and Hull (SNAP [BrHu86]) browse the scheme of a semantic data model and derive selection queries as a restriction on the scheme structure. Goldman, Goldman, Kanellakis, Zdonik's ISIS system [GGKZ85] offers a sophisticated graph-oriented user interface to a DBMS using a semantic model. ISIS provides for scheme construction, browsing, and querying of the database.

Three factors involved in the specification of the display for a user interface are: the dynamic nature of the interface, the layout of objects on the display, and the behavior of the display and the database when certain events occur. Much of the prior work in this area focused on one or two of these factors. Morgenstern [Morg83] defined dynamic views in which the data displayed is the most current data available to the database. Thus updates to a viewed object instantaneously cause the display to be updated to view the new value. Friedell, Barnett, and Kramlich [FrBK82] describe a system in which updates to the database trigger an incremental update to the view cache (the portion of the view visible on the display). Their system determines the placement of icons (representations for objects) using heuristics based on ordering of attribute values, data types, and data distributions.

Lieberman [Lieb85] defines the EZwin, and object whose attributes include a window, a process, state, and behavior. When the mouse enters an EZwin window, the state of the EZwin determines the sensitivity to the event and the associated behavior. In Maier, Nordquist, and Grossman's SIG system [MaNG86] each display specification consists of a list of *recipes*, one of which is selected based on the displayed object's current state. Each recipe is composed of a list of *ingredients*, which specify templates for sub-displays and their arrangements. Those templates correspond either to system-supplied views of common data types (such as text and list) or an *abstract view* on a sub-object, which defers display decisions on that object to another display specification. Display specifications contain some declarative description of behavior, such as menus and levels, to which to propagate changes, but particular update actions must be given procedurally. At a higher level Borning's ThingLab [Born81], [Born85] enables one to build a toolkit which can then be used to specify an interface.

Representation mappings allows an object to be mapped into a representation format that may depend on the access path or query through which the object is viewed, on the profile of the user viewing the object, or on the semantics of the application task accessing the data. Anderson and Claghorn's ADE system [AnCl85] allows multiple printable representation mappings for each object in an object-oriented database where the mappings are stored in the database, and each object has a default mapping that is dependent on the path taken to access the object. Barbic, et al. [BCPB84], [BaRa85] use mappings to give representations of office information system data formated to produce particular forms. Coutaz's Box system [Cout84] composes a *formatter* mapping with a *compositor* mapping in order to map a box description into a box, which is in turn mapped into a screen view. A box may be composed of sub-boxes (boxes for sub-objects). Multiple mappings of a box are possible by restricting the compositor to a selected set of sub-boxes of the box.

Pilote's INTERPRET system [Pilo83a], [Pilo83b] supports declarations for the conceptual structure, the lexical structure, and the dialogue structure of an interface. INTERPRET uses mappings to associates natural language representations (ascii strings) with objects stored in the database. Tsichritzis' Form Management system [Tsic82] uses templates to specify a media-oriented representation of an (office) form. A template represents a mapping from a form to an expression suitable for the medium (text, voice, or display). Multiple templates may provide representations of a form in different media or multiple mappings into the same medium from one form.

3   TEDM Overview

For our examples, we use TEDM (Tektronix Engineering Data Model), currently under development at Tektronix Computer Research Laboratory and the Oregon Graduate Center. TEDM is designed to meet the needs of engineering database applications for entity identity, complex objects with shared subparts, an inheritance hierarchy to organize the database scheme, and a data language with declarative capabilities [MaPr84]. The model described here is a simplified form of the full model.

TEDM supports *simple* and *complex* objects. Simple objects are taken from a fixed set of base types, which for our examples will be `String`, `Integer` and `Boolean`. (String literals appear in single quotes; integers are prefixed with #.) Complex objects are collections of *fields*, each of which has the form

```
fieldname -> value
```

where the value is a simple object or another complex object. These complex objects are similar to the Ψ-terms of Ait-Kaci [AitK84]. The following object describes a department.

```
(deptName -> 'engineering',
 budget -> #1253500,
 deptChair ->
    (name -> (first -> 'William',
              last -> 'Porter')),
 building -> 'C51',
 building -> 'C52')
```

Note that we may have multiple occurrences of a fieldname in an object.

A single object may be the value in multiple fields. To capture multiple references in a linear syntax, TEDM uses *object tags* prefixing objects. For example, if we want the chair of the department to reference the department of which he is a member, we can use a tag D:

```
:D (deptName -> 'engineering',
        budget -> #1253500,
        deptChair ->
            (name -> (first -> 'William',
                      last -> 'Porter'),
                      facultyIn -> :D),
        building -> 'C51',
        building -> 'C52')
```

TEDM supports types for objects. A type definition looks much like an object description, but with type names for values.

```
PersonName = (first -> String:,
              last -> String:)

Person = (name -> PersonName:)

Department = (deptName -> String:,
              deptChair -> Person:,
              building => String:)
```

The type that is the value of a field in a type definition is called the *range type* of the field. For example, `Person` is the range type of the `deptChair` field. The double arrow indicates a field that may have multiple occurrences. We will usually write object descriptions with type names inserted, except for simple values.

```
Department:D
    (deptName -> 'engineering',
     budget -> #1253500,
     deptChair ->
        Person: (name ->
                      PersonName:
                          (first -> 'William',
                           last -> 'Porter'),
                      facultyIn -> Department:D),
     building -> 'C51',
     building -> 'C52')
```

Each type has a corresponding *type set* of objects that conform to the type description. An object may belong to several type sets, and need not belong to every typeset to which it conforms. Furthermore, types in TEDM are *prescriptive*, not *proscriptive*: an object may have more fields than required by a type. In the example above, there is a budget field that is not required by the Department type. Types are organized into a hierarchy, where a subtype inherits all the fields and restrictions of the supertype, but can add other fields and restrictions. Thus, we could define

```
FacultyMember = (name -> PersonName:,
                 age -> Integer:,
                 salary -> Integer:)
```

as a subtype of Person. The top of the hierarchy is the type All, whose typeset contains all objects known to the system.

Types are represented within TEDM by objects, called *type-defining objects* (TDOs). Fig. 1 shows a simplified version of a TDO for the type FacultyMember above. Actual TDOs can associate types with paths, not only single field names, and can also impose coreference constraints. The TDOs shown in the superClass and fieldType fields above are incompletely specified. Their values are really other complete TDO objects.

```
TypeDef:(typeName -> 'FacultyMember',
         superClass -> TypeDef: (typeName -> 'Person'),
         hasField ->
          FieldDef:(fieldName -> 'name',
           fieldType -> typeDef: (typeName -> 'PersonName'),
           multiple -> false),

         hasField ->
          FieldDef: (fieldName -> 'age',
           fieldType -> TypeDef: (typeName -> 'Integer'),
           multiple -> false),

         hasField ->
          FieldDef: (fieldName -> 'salary',
           fieldType -> TypeDef: (typeName -> 'Integer'),
           multiple -> false))
```

Fig.1:   *An Example Type-Defining Object*

The data language for TEDM is influenced by logic languages, and consists of *commands*, which handle update and I/O, and *rules*, which define virtual fields and objects. Both constructs have the basic form

    <head> <arrow> <pattern>

where <arrow> is <= for a command and <- for a rule. The <pattern> is a sequence of *terms*, which are templates for matching objects in the database, and look like partial object descriptions. However, what were tags before are now *object variables*. The <head> for a command is a term indicating an update operation, such as changing a field value, adding an object of a type set, or creating an object. It may also be a View [ ] operation. The View [ ] operation has two forms. In the first, only one argument is given:

    View[:F] <= FacultyMember:F(age -> #26)

The representation function for the viewed object is determined from the object's class. We explain how the information for selecting the representation function is stored in Section 7. The second form of the `View` command gives the representation function explicitly: `View[:F, :R]`. The head for a rule looks like the term for an update operation in a command, but denotes demand, rather than immediate, evaluation.

Variables are shared between the <head> and <pattern> parts. The semantics of a command is that for every binding of the variables to database objects that fulfills the <pattern>, perform the update (or other operation) given in the <head>. (Full TEDM allows also a single match or user selection of the number of matches for a pattern, as well as certain forms of negation.)

Examples: Add a salary field to the person named William Porter.

```
:P (salary -> #63000) <=
    Person:P
    (name -> PersonName:
                   (first -> 'William',
                    last -> 'Porter'))
```

Add that person to the `FacultyMember` typeset.

```
FacultyMember:P <=
    Person:P
       (name -> PersonName:
                      (first -> 'William',
                       last -> 'Porter'))
```

Change that person's name.

```
:P (name ->
    PersonName: *
        (first -> 'O',
         last -> 'Henry')) <=
    Person:P
        (name ->
             PersonName:(first -> 'William',
                         last -> 'Porter'))
```

The * in the head term indicate the creation of a new object. Rules look much the same as commands. The rule

```
:P(chairs -> :D) <-
    Department:D(deptChair -> Person:P)
```

defines a virtual field `chairs` for persons who chair departments.

A few remarks on commands in TEDM: Constructing an answer to a query is a separate operation from viewing the constructed object. For example, we can create pairs consisting of a department's budget and its chair's salary with

```
Ans: * (bud -> :B, sal -> :S) <-
    Department:
        (budget -> :B,
         deptChair ->
             Person: (salary -> :S))
```

Note that `Ans` objects will have existing database objects as field values. A viewing command can then be used to look at objects in the `Ans` type set.

The multiple matching aspect of patterns admits several kinds of viewing. Suppose we want to see department chairs along with buildings that their departments occupy. Since `building` is a multiply occurring field in `Department`, we could get multiple matches of B for each binding of P with the pattern

```
Department:
     (deptChair -> :P, building -> :B)
```

One way to handle the multiple answers is to view such pairs one at a time:

```
View[:P], View[:B] <=
     Department:
          (deptChair -> :P,
           building -> :B)
```

(We allow multiple operations in the head of a command.) Here the user would be offered P-B bindings as separate views. However, a more natural presentation would show all the buildings for a department chair at once. To define a representation for a collection of buildings, we want to aggregate the B bindings associated with a given P binding into a single object. We can do so in TEDM by first creating an answer object for each department chair, then inserting all the buildings.

```
CBAnswer: *
     (dChair -> :P,
      buildingSet -> :*) <=
               Department:(deptChair -> Person:P)

:A(buildingSet -> (element -> :B)) <=
               Department:
                    (deptChair -> Person:P,
                     building -> B),
          CBAnswer: A(dChair -> :P)
```

An object with a single, multiply occurring, field models a set in TEDM:

```
Set = (element => All:)
```

Once we form such aggregates, we can also use them as arguments to functions that compute over whole sets, such as counts and averages.

Few joins are necessary in TEDM queries, as they are not needed to overcome the decomposition of objects forced by normalization in the relational model. Most semantic connections can be made by following paths. When a join is necessary, it can be on object identity, rather than just on simple values.

```
SameChair: *
     (dept1 -> :D1, dept2 -> :D2) <=
          Department: D1 (deptChair -> Person:P),
          Department: D2 (deptChair -> :P)
```

The TEDM command language has been prototyped in Prolog using a storage structure based on binary and ternary relations [Zhu86].

4   Representation Defining Objects

If a user asks a DBMS for a particular person's birthdate, the DBMS must retrieve the answer, and then either figure out how to display it or pass the information on to some application for display. For example, if the person's birthdate is the first day of April, 1950, then possible display forms might be "*4/1/50*", "**4-1-50**", "April 1, 1950", "50Apr1", and so on. Thus the date is either displayed as it is stored in the database, or the display information is in the application program that sits between the user and the DBMS. For important data types such as date, conventional DBMSs sometimes provide several "hardwired" displays. However, it is usually not possible to add any new displays.

In PROTEUS, display information is stored in *Representation Defining Objects* or RDO's. Since an RDO is an object, it can have fields. Each RDO has a `name`, which can be used externally to refer to the underlying representation mapping. An RDO has a `repType` field, which stores the set of internal types for which it is a representation. Finally, an RDO has a `repFunction` field, which stores a declarative specification (i.e., query) that will perform the mapping between an internal database object whose type is contained in `repType`, and a layout defining object. This mapping is shown graphically in Fig. 2.

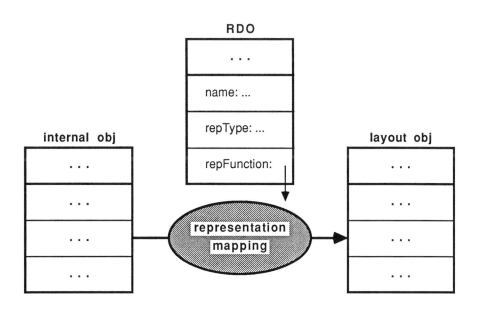

Fig. 2:   *The Representation Mapping*

Obviously, the query defining a `repFunction` will frequently be quite complex. This query must specify those fields of `repType` that are to appear (or may conditionally appear) in the representation, and the ordering and composition of those fields. Envisioned composition operators include list, nest, stack, merge, and so on. Also, ordering predicates for any multi-valued fields of the type must be given. Finally, emphasis attributes (flash, reverse, shade, embolden, outline, underline, overline, font, point size) must be specified for each field of the `repType` type. Note that an RDO for a type may contain (i.e., call on) other RDO's. For example, an RDO for a `Date` type may call on the RDO's for the range types of its fields `month`, `day`, and `year`.

Each type also has a default representation, which is the one used to display objects in the type if the users does not (or cannot) specify otherwise. For example, if the user wants to see all persons, and the TEDM command

```
View [:P] <= Person:P
```

is given, then the default representation for the `Person` type would be used to display the objects requested.

A particular field in a type can also have a default representation that overrides the default representation for the range type of the field. This makes the representation used to display an object dependent on the context from which the object is accessed, which should result in a more appropriate display for a given query. If the user requests the value of a field without specifying the representation for the field value, then the default representation associated with the field will take over. (Note that the default representation for a field must be one of the possible representations for the range type of the field.) For example, if the user wants to see all people who are spouses, and the TEDM query

```
View [:P] <= Person (spouseOf -> :P)
```

is given, then the default representation associated with the `spouseOf` field will be used (instead of the default representation for the `Person` type). However, the default representation for the `spouseOf` field must be one of the possible representations for `Person`, which is the range type of `spouseOf`. For a more complete discussion of default representations for types and fields as well as recursion in RDO's, see Anderson and Claghorn [AnCl85].

The storing of RDO's in the database has some interesting implications. Browsing has become an acceptable, often preferred method of interacting with a database. The usual scenario is that the user navigates between sets of objects by following field links and, when an interesting set is found, browses through the objects in the set. In PROTEUS, another form of browsing will be possible. Instead of browsing through the objects in a set, it will be possible to browse through the set of representations for a particular object (perhaps to select one to use in creating a new user interface). For example, given a particular `Person` object, it will be possible to flip through several representations for the object, or to simultaneously display several representations of the object for comparison. Browsing through different representations for an object will also enable the user to interactively select the one that contains the attributes the user knows, if the representation is to be used as a template for a query.

If a user wants to view the objects belonging to a type and doesn't know any specific fields of the type (or doesn't want to type them in!), then the default representation for the type can be used to display the objects. (Note that the current, conventional DBMSs sometimes incorporate a default representation for each type, consisting of the entire list of fields for the type. For a typical type, the number of fields and subfields may run into the hundreds, and objects of the type may contain many shared values. A default display that showed all fields of the object at all levels would likely overwhelm the user.) Alternatively, the system can show examples of the representations possible, allowing the user to make a selection from those displayed.

5   Layout Objects

A *layout object* (LO) is a tree-structured object that can be efficiently interpreted by a rendering process to create and maintain a display. An LO results from applying a representation mapping to an internal database object. The non-leaf nodes in an LO describe the composition of the display, while the leaf nodes describe the contents of the display. Fig. 3 shows a very simple LO for displaying a person's name and social security number, as well as the resultant display.

The non-leaf nodes `Stack` and `Series` describe the vertical and horizontal composition of the display elements in the resulting two-dimensional display. Both of these object types can have an arbitrary number of components; in this example, the `Stack` node and the two `Series` nodes all have two components each. Each of these composition-describing nodes themselves have fields, such as `scroll` (a Boolean value indicating if the components are scrollable as a whole), and `viewedObj` (the optional pointer to an internal database object whose fields are being displayed by the sub-tree). The `viewedObj` field will be described in more detail in the next section.

The leaf nodes in this example are of two types, `fixedText` and `varText`. The `fixedText` nodes contain the strings "NAME" and "SOCIAL SEC#", which appear as headers in the resulting display. The `varText` nodes contain the current values "Mike Smith" and "574-48-6077" to be displayed in the data portions of the resulting display. The first data field is scrollable, as indicated by the field attached to the corresponding `varText` node. The `displayVal` field contains the actual text to be displayed. The `onField` field contains the name of the `Person` field from which `displayVal` was derived. The value of that field is itself passed through a representation mapping, from an RDO whose name is stored in the `useRep` field. That RDO presumedly concatenates first and last names into a single string. (At the lowest level, some representation mappings, such as for concatenating strings, will be supplied with the system.) This pointer to the `Person` field is necessary to support dynamic displays, as will be discussed further in the next section. Other display fields shown in Fig. 3 include `emphasis`, `font`, etc.

Scrolling is not the only aspect of behavior that may be specified for a display object. One can specify what happens when the cursor enters a field (called the *entering behavior*), when the cursor leaves a field (the *exit behavior*), the editing capability within a field, the action given to indicate that an update is to be accepted and that an internal object is to be modified (corresponding to a sub-tree or a leaf node within an LO), and so on.

It is also possible, for `Series` and `Stack` objects, to specify the alignment behavior for components. If a `Series` object contains a list of `Stacks` as its components, then alignment of the `Series` object would mean that the rows formed by the `stack` objects would always have the same internal boundaries, and that scrolling of one the `Stack` objects would result in scrolling all the other stack objects. Alignment for a `Stack` object that contains a list of `Series` objects as its components would mean that the columns always have the same internal boundaries, and that scrolling of one of the `Series` objects would result in scrolling all the other `Series` objects. Finally, a `Grid` object is one in which all row and column boundaries are the same, and scrolling in any direction causes the entire `Grid` to be scrolled. (A `Grid` is the usual report or table form of display). We are considering constraint satisfaction as a method of implementing this alignment behavior (e.g., constrain a display to maintain a particular relationship between field sizes).

Ordering for items in a `Series` or `Stack` object is specified in the representation mapping. However, the layout object is responsible for maintaining sort order.

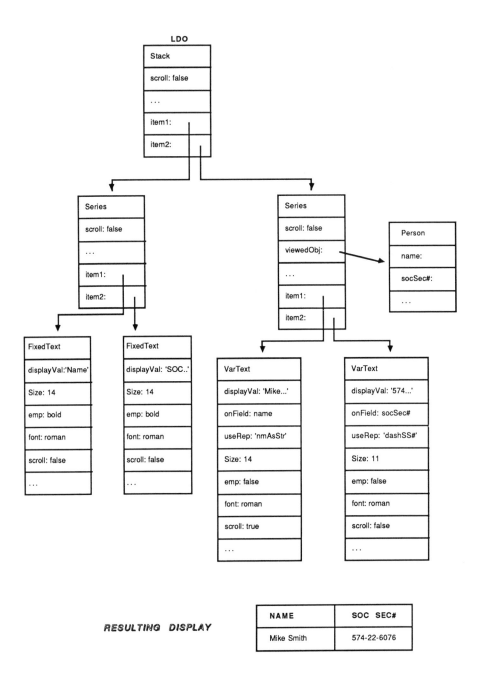

Fig. 3:   *An Example Layout Object*

An LO is typically created each time the display needs to be redrawn. However, the components of the LO could be constructed either lazily or eagerly, depending on the display requirements. Pieces of an LO can be reused if the sub-objects they represent haven't changed. Also, an LO is typically destroyed after it is no longer of use in the current display. However, it is possible that an LO might stay around after this time if the application requires caching for efficiency purposes (e.g., for flipping through images quickly, for fast undo functionality, etc.).

6 Commands as Objects

Our position, that all entities connected with a database be objects with programmer control over representation, implies that commands and rules in the data language should be objects. Also, we intend to use commands and rules as representation mappings, and therefore need a way to store them as values in an RDO. Thus, we may consider the description of commands given in Section 3 as simply one particular concrete syntax for an abstract data language constructed from objects. We assume the database command processor accepts certain types of objects as its input.

A command object has a field for the head and for the pattern.

```
Command = (head => QueryTerm:,
           pattern => QueryTerm:)
```

We need to explain the type `QueryTerm`. `QueryTerm` has a subclass for every regular type in the database. So, for our example, we would have `PersonTerm`, `DepartmentTerm`, `FacultyMemberTerm`, and so forth, arranged in a hierarchy that follows the hierarchy of regular classes. Thus, `PersonTerm` is a superclass of `FacultyMemberTerm`. Each such subtype of `QueryTerm` has the corresponding regular type as a subtype, plus a subtype for templates. The following shows an example of this.

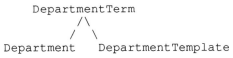

The template subtype is generated from the sibling regular type by changing the range type `C` of each field to `CTerm`:

```
DepartmentTemplate =
    (deptName -> StringTerm:,
     deptChair -> PersonTerm:,
     building -> StringTerm:)
```

(Observe that we could generate the TDO for `DepartmentTemplate` as a representation of the TDO for `Department`. Kinky.) In a pattern involving a `Department`, not all fields need be constrained. We provide a special object `any` that belongs to `QueryTerm` and matches any object. (A more succinct notation could be obtained by allowing fields to be omitted in a template object. Supporting that alternative would require modifying the TEDM typing system to allow optional fields whose values are typed when present.) A `DepartmentTemplate` object where every field has the value `any` is equivalent to a typed variable: `Department:D`. Variable names are not needed in `QueryTerms`; a duplicated variable is captured by multiple references to a `QueryTerm`.

Example: The command

```
Ans:* (bud -> :B, sal -> :S) <=
    Department:
         (budget -> :B,
          deptChair -> Person: (salary -> :S))
```

is represented by the command object

```
Command:
    (head ->
        AnswerTemplate:(for -> new,
                        bud -> :T1,
                        sal -> :T2),
     pattern ->
        DepartmentTemplate:
             (budget -> StringTemplate:T1,
              deptChair ->
                  PersonTemplate:
                      (salary ->
                          IntegerTemplate:T2,
                       name -> any),
              deptName -> any))
```

For the head of a command, we use a template object as well, but include a `for` field to indicate which object is being updated. The `for` field can reference a `QueryTerm` in the pattern, a regular object, or the special value `new` that indicates a new object should be created rather than an existing object modified.

Example: For the command

```
:P (salary -> #63000) <=
    Person:P
         (name -> PersonName:
                     (first -> 'William',
                      last -> 'Porter')
```

we have the command object

```
Command:
    (head ->
        PersonTemplate:
             (for -> :T1,
              salary -> #63000,
              name -> any),
     pattern ->
        PersonTemplate:T1
             (name ->
              PersonNameTemplate:
                     (first -> 'William',
                      last -> 'Porter')))
```

The `any` in the head field means the `name` field will not be updated. We could not use `T1` directly as the template for the head, because of possible conflict between an existing `salary` field and the new value for `salary`.

Command objects are much more than simply parse trees of the linear syntax given before. For one, they can reference actual database objects, rather than just templates (which is why `Department` is a subtype of `DepartmentTerm`). Thus, we can specialize a rule to apply to a single object if we want.

Example: The following *command* creates a *rule* that defines the virtual field `chairs` for just the person named William Porter.

```
Rule:*
   (head ->
     PersonTemplate:*
       (for -> :P,
        name -> any,
        chairs -> :T1),
    pattern ->
     DepartmentTemplate:*T1
       (deptName -> any,
        deptChair -> Person:P,
        building -> any)) <=
   Person:P
     (name -> PersonName:
                  (first -> 'William',
                   last -> 'Porter'))
```

Note that we combine * with an object variable when we want to create a new object that is referenced in two places.

7 System Architecture and Example Query

In previous sections, the components of the PROTEUS system (command objects, representation defining objects, and layout defining objects) were discussed. This section puts the pieces together and summarizes their interaction.

Suppose the user wishes to pose the query "Give me a faculty member from the math department". The corresponding TEDM command is as follows.

```
View [:F] <=
   Department:D
     (name -> 'math',
      hasFaculty -> :F)
```

The user has not specified how the faculty member object `:F` is to be displayed, but rather is depending on the system to determine an appropriate display. In order to see how this is done, it is necessary to delve into the meta-schema information for the type objects `Department` and `FacultyMember`. A sketch of the necessary additions to the TDOs is shown in Fig. 4.

The `TypeDef` specifies the type name (e.g., `Department`), the fields (e.g., `hasFaculty`), the set of all possible representations for the type (e.g., `Name-n-SS#`, `AllFields`, `SS#`), and the default representation for the type (e.g., `SS#` for `FacultyMember`). Each field definition may also include a default representation, which indicates how information from the range type of the field is to be displayed if it is accessed through the field. For example, the field `hasFaculty` has a default representation of `Name-n-SS#`. Since the `View` command above uses the field `hasFaculty`, the `Name-n-SS#` representation will be the one used to display the `FacultyMember` object requested by the command.

PROTEUS uses the default representations given in the TDO's to expand the `View` command above into the form shown in Fig. 5. The dashed line in Fig. 5 separates the original command with one addition, `:R`, from the new display information derived from the defaults stored in the TDOs. The first `TypeDef` finds the name of the default representation for the `hasFaculty` field. The second `TypeDef` finds the representation function `:R` used by the `View` command to display the `FacultyMember`.

```
TypeDef: (typeName -> 'Department',
          hasField -> FieldDef:(fieldName -> 'hasFaculty',
                                defaultRep -> 'Name-n-SS#'),
          hasField -> FieldDef: (...), ...)
TypeDef: (typeName -> 'FacultyMember',
          hasField -> FieldDef: (...),
          defaultRep -> RDO: (name -> 'SS#'),

          rep -> RDO: (repName -> 'Name-n-SS#',
                       repType -> TypeDef: (...),
                       repFunction -> Stack:?Show ...),

          rep -> RDO: (repName -> 'AllFields',
                       repType -> typeDef: (...),
                       repFunction -> ...),

          rep -> RDO: (repName -> 'SS#',
                       repType -> typeDef:(...),
                       repFunction -> ...),

          rep -> RDO: (...)...)
```

Fig. 4: *Type Defining Objects*

A sketch of the representation function, `:R`, is given in Fig. 6. It is this representation function that produces the LO shown in Fig. 3.

```
View [:F,:R] <= Department:D (name->'math',hasFaculty->:F),
-----------------------------------------------------------
TypeDef: (className -> 'Department',
          hasField ->
              FieldDef:(fieldName -> 'hasFaculty',
                        defaultRep -> :N)),
TypeDef: (className -> 'FacultyMember',
          rep -> RDO: (repName -> :N,
                       repFunction -> :R))
```

Fig. 5: *The Expanded Command*

In the `View` command above, processing for the static case (i.e., when the display is a snapshot of the underlying database), proceeds as follows. The command is expanded, as shown in Fig. 5, to incorporate the default representation mapping for the field `hasFaculty`. The command is translated, via an inverse representation mapping, to a command object (Section 6). The command processor matches the pattern part of the command object against the existing internal `FacultyMember` and `Department` objects. The representation function shown in Fig. 6 is then evaluated. It sets the global variable `?Show` (maintained in the user's workspace) to point to the layout object. The display process (we call it the *renderer*), senses the change in the `?Show` variable, and displays the new layout object.

The pattern in the `View` command above can generate many different faculty members. In order to display another faculty member, the user closes the current display, which causes the matching process and representation mapping to create a new LO for the renderer to display.

```
Stack:?Show <=
   (scroll -> false,
    ...
   item1 -> Series:*
              (scroll -> false,
               ...
               item1 -> FixedText:*
                           (displayVal -> 'Name',
                            size -> 14,
                            emp -> 'bold',
                            font -> 'roman',
                            scroll -> false,
                               ... ),
               item2 -> Fixedtext:* (...)),
   item2 -> Series:*
              (scroll -> false,
               viewedObj -> :F,
               item1 -> VarText:*
                           (size -> #14,
                            scroll -> true,
                            font -> 'roman',
                            onField -> 'name',
                            useRep -> 'NameAsString',
                            displayVal -> ''
                               ... ),
               item2 -> VarText:* (...)))
```

Fig. 6:   *An Example Representation Function*

Now consider the case where the user can update an internal object from the external display. (We assume the updatable external display is produced as in the static case above.) The node in the LO corresponding to the part of the display to be updated contains a `dynamicRule` field, as sketched in Fig. 7. The value of this field is a `Command` object that can be evaluated to update the internal database object underlying the modified portion of the display. (Note that the command has been specialized to point to just that underlying database object.) The renderer evaluates this rule to make the update to the database object, which in turn causes the whole cycle of the representation mapping to begin again. A new LO is produced, and the renderer senses a change in the ?Show variable as in the static case above.

8   Future Work

Dynamic Displays

In the last section, we sketched the PROTEUS architecture for the static display case and for the dynamic case in which the display is to reflect changes the user makes to the database. We did not cover the dynamic case where the display is to reflect changes made by any user to the database, such as another display on the same internal object.

In this last case, there are several architectural alternatives which will solve the dynamic display problem. One alternative is for the renderer to refresh the display sufficiently often so that it is as current as it can be, given the time required to refresh. Another alternative is for the renderer to monitor all internal objects for which it is the display. This would require backward pointers from the LO to all updatable internal objects. The final alternative is to require that all internal objects maintain pointers to the LO's of which they are a part, and to send alerts to the corresponding renderers should an update be made. We have yet to decide which alternative is best in PROTEUS.

Composing RDOs

RDOs are currently recursive, in that one RDO may contain other RDOs. We would also like to make them serially composable, in that the output of one RDO's repFunction could be the input of another repFunction. This would enable us to build complex representation mappings from simplier ones. One possibility that we are investigating is the use of unification of TEDM terms to achieve this composition of representation mappings.

Information Suppression in Displays

For table-style displays, it is sometimes desirable to be able to suppress the display of fields in a row if the same information is contained in the preceding row of the table. A good example of this is the tabular display of flight schedules between two cities. Assume the first row in the table contains fields for the two cities, followed by fields containing a departure and an arrival time. Then the succeeding rows should contain only the remaining departure and arrival time pairs, with the two city fields blank.

The general case of information suppression may require some notion of the display history, since suppression in the current display seems to depend on the information in past display. Also, a marking scheme could be employed whereby components of the current display are marked as redundant (and therefore ignored by the renderer) if they are the same as in the last display.

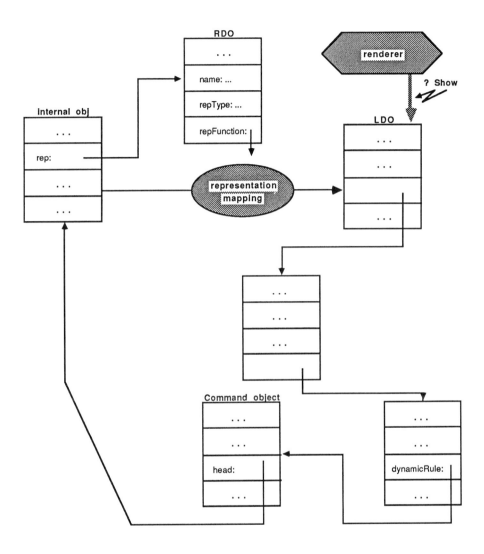

Fig. 7:   *Representation Mapping with Dynamic Updating*

Ambiguity in the Default Representation

If the display variable appears in more than one type or in more than one field, then the default representation can be ambiguous. For example, in the command

```
View[:F] <=
     FacultyMember:F, Student:F
```

there are two possible default representations, one for the `FacultyMember` type and one for the `Student` type. Resolving this ambiguity could be handled in several ways. The system could arbitrarily pick one of the default representations or use the default corresponding to the first type mentioned in the command (in this example, `FacultyMember`). Alternatively, the system could present the `:F` object as mapped through the two default representations, allowing the user to interactively pick the one desired. With the object orientation of PROTEUS, these and other policies for handling ambiguity should be straightforward to implement.

9 References

[AitK84], [AnCl85], [AnEM86a], [BaRa85], [BCPB84], [Born81], [Born85], [BrCr85], [BrHu86], [Cout84], [FrBK82], [GGKZ85], [HeRo85], [KiMe84], [Lieb85], [MaNG86], [MaPr84], [Morg83], [Pilo83a], [Pilo83b], [Rowe85], [StKa82], [Tsic82], [WoKu82], [Zhu86], [Zloo77].

11

An Object-Oriented Interface to a Relational Database

T. Learmont, R.G.G. Cattell

Abstract

We require a database system that is efficient for operations on individual data objects without losing the functionality provided by a relational DBMS. Typically, our database operations cannot be expressed as a single query in SQL or another high-level relational language, and must be decomposed into many simple "object-oriented" queries. The queries are invoked by programs rather than directly by an end-user; response time must be at least an order of magnitude faster than conventional DBMSs. An SQL processor, even with parameterized compilation, is not usually optimized for fast response for such trivial queries. We might get the performance we require from an "object-oriented" database system such as Maier et al [MSOP86], but then we would lose the powerful relational facilities. Instead of using either an object-oriented language or the high-level SQL language, we chose to use an efficient object-level interface to a relational DBMS, called ERIC (Entity-Relationship Interface Convention), to give us the best characteristics of both kinds of database in one system. In this paper, we describe ERIC and its implementation, and explain how the relational and object-oriented viewpoints on databases may be combined.

Keywords: *Object-Oriented, SQL, Database System, Response Time, Engineering Databases*

1   Introduction

We need to support engineering applications requiring fast response times. These applications include CAD (Computer Aided Design), CASE (Computer Aided Software Engineering), and a variety of real-time or network service programs that perform relatively simple queries but require a response in a small number of milliseconds. For example, imagine an application displaying

---

a computer circuit layout or building architecture on a graphical display, in which information about the individual components and their interconnectivity is stored in a database. These programs may execute between 10 and 1000 simple queries to complete the drawing. Such applications typically require response times better than 10 milliseconds in order to provide reasonable response to the user.

In addition to specific engineering applications, we wish to support general-purpose database tools that use the mouse and bitmap graphics to allow a user to browse through databases quickly, or to see databases graphically [Catt83, Sun86]. These tools also require fast response times to provide a reasonable interface to the user.

There is a tremendous gap between the performance provided by in-memory programming language data structures versus disk-based structures in a relational database management system. A relational system typically may respond to queries in a few tenths of a second. Simple lookups in in-memory structures can be performed in microseconds. This factor of 100,000 difference in response time is the result of a number of factors, only one of which is the disk reads required by a database system.

We believe there is a place for a database system with 10 to 100 times the response time performance of a conventional relational database system, to fill the gap between such systems and specialized or in-memory data structures. There are a number of changes we propose to make to achieve this performance, but the first is to propose a different kind of interface between the programmer and database system, ERIC, that deals with individual operations on objects as opposed to the aggregates of objects addressed by a high-level query language. In this paper, we describe ERIC and its implementation in a relational database system.

2   Data Model

For the purposes of this paper, we are using the term "object-oriented" to refer to programs that operate on one object at a time, as contrasted to relational queries on aggregates of objects. Our purpose is to focus attention on the need for functionality and performance using object-by-object operations in engineering applications as *well* as providing a higher-level data manipulation language. The term "object-oriented" hase elsewhere been used to mean encapsulation of the data structure of an object, so that an object's data is visible only through procedures associated with the object. We do not *want* to encapsulate the structure, we want a high-level query language to be able to refer to the fields of an object. (Fields may still be "virtual", i.e. defined procedurally, if necessary to provide data independence.)

In short, we want two different views of the same database. As an example, we will consider the database shown in Fig. 1, from both an object-oriented and a relational perspective. Fig. 1 is an entity-relationship diagram of our example database, in which the entities are shown as rectangles, and relationships as ovals. The entity tables (person, document, organization) each have a unique identifier (name or title), while relationship tables do not.

Each arrow in the diagram represents a many-to-one relationship. For example, we allow each person to have many [number, area code] pairs in the "phone" relationship. The relationship between persons and organizations is many-to-many, as it is composed of two one-to-many relationships. There is also a "role" associated with each member relationship instance, to indicate the title or role of the person in the organization they belong to. The organization entity type has only one field, the name, which is a key. The person and document entity types have a second field in addition to their key (birthday for person, pubdate for document).

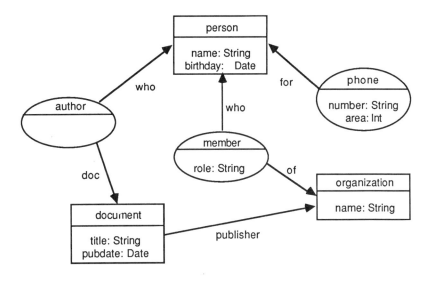

Fig. 1:   *Entity-Relationship Perspective on Database*

Now, consider how this database would be stored in a relational DBMS, in Fig. 2. We create six tables, one for each entity-type record, and one for each relationship-type record. In relational database systems that implement referential integrity, we could define reference constraints: in the author table, "who" references a person, and "doc" a document; in the member table, "who" references a person, and "of" an organization; in the phone table, "for" references a person; and, in the document table, "publisher" references an organization. The other attributes would be simple strings, dates, and integers.

In relational database systems that do not incorporate referential integrity in the data schema definition, note that information is lost in a relational representation of this database: applications must be written knowing which attributes are references to which [entity] relation keys.

In an object-oriented database system, we might represent the same database a shown in Fig. 3. We define three object types, one for each of the entity types in Fig. 1 (person, organization, and document). Simple date and string fields of the entities are represented similarly as fields of the object. The one-to-many relationships between entities may be represented as list-valued fields of the objects, on the "one" side of the one-to-many relationship, or as a pointer field on the "many" side of the relationship, or both. A many-to-many relationship may be represented as list-valued fields on both ends.

We show the documents that a person authored as a list-valued field of person, "pubs". Note that we also show the authors of each document as a list-valued field of the document, "authors". In an object-oriented database system in which references are represented by pointers, we may require such a representation (with pointers in both directions) for efficiency. However, note that the same information is represented in two different places: the "author" table of the relational model is encoded in both the person and document objects in the object-oriented model. This could lead to update anomalies in the object-oriented representation. We could store a relationship between entities in only one object, as we have done for the "member" relationship, stored as the "members" field of the organization type, but as we just noted, there may then be performance implications for getting from a person object to the organization objects they belong to.

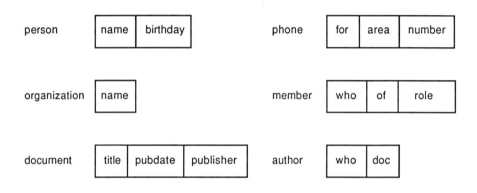

Fig. 2: *Relational Perspective on Database (Field Types omitted)*

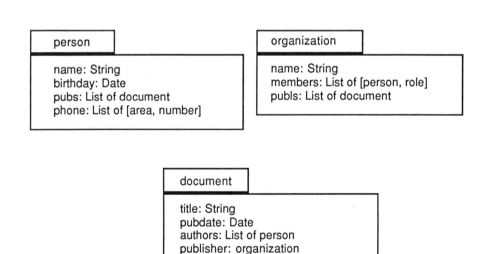

Fig. 3: *Object-Oriented Perspective on Database*

For simplicity, we have shown only the minimum database to illustrate the points we wish to make in this paper. In an object-oriented database system, we might have a variety of other features such as the ability to associate operations with each object type as well as data fields, or allowing a hierarchy of object types, so that the fields and operations of a more general object (e.g., "person") could automatically be inherited by a subtype (e.g., "professor"). These features can be added in a relational or entity-relationship DBMS, as well, but we do not need to deal with them for the purposes of this paper.

3   Interface Architecture

The goal of the ERIC interface is to provide both a relational and an object-oriented interface to the same database. Both objects and relational tuples will dually be represented by records in an ERIC database. The actually ERIC interface is a set of procedure definitions, separated into four groups:

1. The ERIC/Query procedures provide an SQL interface to a database.

2. The ERIC/Object procedures provide object-oriented operations.

3. The ERIC/Schema procedures allow access and update of database type definitions.

4. The ERIC/Access procedures provide an "access method" physical interface, on which both the ERIC/Query and ERIC/Object procedures can be implemented.

To understand the use of the ERIC procedures, some background is necessary on the primitives that they use.

We will use the term "record" to refer to something that can equivalently be an object or a row in a relation. The ERIC interface provides a unique identifier for records that is used to refer to the record in all the ERIC procedures. The unique record identifier internally encodes both the type of the record and a unique identifier within that type.[1]

In order to fetch records from a database, we will use the concept of a *scan*. A scan is a list of records that satisfy a database request, together with a current position in the list, initially set to the beginning of the list when the scan is "opened". Scans are referred to by a *scan handle*, returned to a client program when the scan is opened.

For the purposes of this paper, it will be necessary to describe only the ERIC/Object procedures. The ERIC/Query procedures are quite straightforward: an SQL query may be sent to a database, and the records satisfying the query may sequentially be fetched into the client program's variables. SQL insert and update statements may also be executed. The commercially available version of the ERIC/Query and ERIC/Access procedures are described in [Sun86]. This product also contains an earlier read-only version of the ERIC/Schema procedures; a complete discussion ERIC/Schema is deferred to a future paper.

---

[1] Not all relational databases provide unique identifiers. See discussion of functional database requirements.

4   ERIC/Object

ERIC provides the following operations on objects (records).

object_insert (type, field1, value1, field2, value2, ...) --> id

> creates a new object of the given type, with the given field values. Each of the values may be a simple data item, such as a string, integer, or date, or it may be a reference to another object (an id).

object_delete (id)

> deletes the object with the given identifier.

field_get (id, field) --> value

> fetches the value of a single field of an object.

field_put (id, field, value)

> stores a new value into a field of an object.

While these operations do not provide the "syntactic sugar" of an object-oriented language, it is easy to see how operations on objects could be composed into these procedure calls.

5   ERIC/Object Scans

Scans are provided to fetch objects that satisfy specific constraints.

object_open (type, field1, value1/range1, field2, value2/range2,..) -> scan_handle

> creates a scan satisfying the conjunction of the field constraints specified. Each of the field value/ranges may be a simple value (as in the operations in the previous section), or a range of values that the field must lie between.

object_next (scan_handle) --> id

> fetches the next object that satisfies the constraints of a scan, returning its unique identifier.

We could, for convenience, provide an object_fetchlist operation that replaces object_open and object_next by returning a single list; we use a scan handle underneath for efficiency, as the entire list need not be generated.

We also provide an abbreviated form of the object_open and object_next procedures for a common case of looking up a single object by its key field, or to find an object referenced by a particular field:

object_fetch (type, field, value) --> id

> fetches the object of the given type with the given field value, returns an error if not unique or does not exist.

In our implementation of reference fields, references may be followed equally efficiently in both directions; thus in Fig. 3, for example, the publisher in the document object and the publs list of documents in the organization object are actually the same underlying relationship. Thus, the object_fetch operation may be used to fetch a document's publisher (the many-to-one direction), and the object_open (or object_fetchlist) operation may be used to fetch an organization's publications (the one-to-many direction).

6   Functional Database Requirements

In order to implement ERIC/Object efficiently, a DBMS needs the following:

*   unique ids for each record,
*   some form of transactions or locking which guarantees that an id is valid for a length of time, and
*   some way to translate ids to valid database values when storing a reference.

    Each of these points is described below.

6.1 Unique Ids

Our ERIC interface requires that the underlying database provide us with some sort of unique ids on which to build ERIC/Object. The id must uniquely specify one record in the database. Theoretically, these ids could be composed of field values (as opposed to tuple-ids) and built on top of a conventional relational query language. In our typical application, however, the performance of ids built from "field values" would not be adequate for accessing relationship (non-keyed) records - the DBMS would be forced to *search* for the desired record before performing an object_delete() or field_put(). Using tuple-ids as the basis for ERIC/Object ids, however, allows the DBMS to perform the delete or modify *without searching* for the record. The ERIC/Access procedures described in [Sun86] provide the kind of *ids* required for ERIC/Object. Note that it may also be possible to build the ERIC/Object routines on top of SQL cursors, since the cursor position provides a way to quickly access a specific record.

6.2 Guarantee that an Id Remains Valid

The DBMS must support some form of transactions or locking to guarantee that the *ids* remain valid during the course of a logical transaction. In order to change a phone number, for example, the program must first obtain an *id* for the desired record (possibly by using the object_open() and object_next() routines), and then modify the phone number by using the field_put() routine. The id must not become invalid between the time that it is first returned by object_next() and when it is used as an argument to the field_put() routine. The DBMS may provide some form of automatic transactions which remain open as long as the program uses the *id*, some form of *transaction_open* and *transaction_close* routines to explicitly open and close a transaction, or it may provide explicit locking routines (*object_lock* and *object_unlock*) which allow the program to determine how long the *id* remains valid. The id need not remain valid across "transactions" - it only needs to be valid *during* a single transaction.

6.3 Translate Ids to Valid Database Values when Storing a Reference

As mentioned above, ERIC/Object uses *ids* to specify records during a transaction. Any use of an id to specify a *reference* field value in an object_insert() or field_put() call[2], however, must be translated by the database system into a database reference that will remain valid across transactions. This does not cause problems for object-oriented databases where every record is an object with a unique identifier and may be *referenced* by another record. In most relational databases, however, only those records with keys can be uniquely specified and thus referenced. If we wish to be able to translate an object-oriented database into a relational one and vice versa, this reference incompatibility leaves us with two choices:

1. require that database designers define keys for objects that will be referenced elsewhere in the database, so that an equivalent relational database can be constructed, or

2. automatically generate keys for those tables that are referenced elsewhere and do not have keys.

In practice, we feel that the constraints imposed by (1) are not overly restrictive, as it is generally necessary to have some identifier external to the computer for objects that are referenced in multiple places anyway. However, our implementation of ERIC/Access provides primitives to automatically generate unique identifiers for records, and this could be used automatically in *object_insert* calls to generate a key when none is specified for records that could be referenced elsewhere.

7 Implementation

An "object-oriented" interface entails not only a database interface with an object-oriented perspective, but one that is *efficient* for operations on objects. We believe this is obtained by building the object-oriented interface ERIC/Object on a DBMS that supports object-oriented operations at the access-method level rather than on top of a relational query language as proposed in POSTGRES [Ston].

In our implementation of ERIC (based on the UNIFY relational DBMS), we have achieved very good response time performance[3] for object-oriented operations [RuCa87]. On a Sun workstation, operations such as field_get and object_open can be executed in a few milliseconds when much of a database is cached in memory, and in a single disk access in most other cases.

---

[2] In our sample database, a new *author* record would be created by first getting the ids for the desired *person* and *document* records and then calling *object_insert*:

    person_id = object_fetch (person, name, "John Smith");
    doc_id = object-fetch (document, title, "Kauai: Paradise on Earth");
    author_id = object_insert (author, who, person_id, doc, doc_id);

[3] Because our typical application is highly interactive, the most important measurement is response time - how long a user must wait for the database operations before continuing with his or her work.

Based on our experience, we believe that a DBMS must have the following kinds of features to provide the necessary response time:

- low (or no) query overhead,
- the ability to process related queries efficiently,
- internal, object-oriented performance enhancements, and
- caching of information in local memory to reduce the number of disk accesses.

These points are described below.

7.1 No Query Overhead

The DBMS should provide a way to retrieve or modify information with a minimum of overhead. As mentioned in the introduction, an example of a typical application is one that displays a computer circuit layout and requires between 10 and 1000 simple queries to obtain the necessary information. Compare this to a typical "forms-based" application which will only do one or two queries as part of the display. The sheer number of queries requires that the overhead be reduced as much as possible; any unnecessary query overhead (such as from a query optimizer) may reduce the response time to unacceptable levels. A DBMS that supports ERIC/Access (which has virtually no query overhead) or compiled queries (with no parsing *or* optimizer overhead) is more likely to provide adequate response time than one that requires parsing of embedded queries.

7.2 Process Related Queries Efficiently

The DBMS should provide a way to use the relationships between queries to improve performance. In typical ERIC/Object applications, there are two places where the relationship between queries can be exploited:

- when doing a search for all objects that are related to a given object, and
- when modifying the value of a database field which was recently retrieved for display.

Typical ERIC/Object applications will retrieve all the information from the database associated with a given object. Thus, the application will retrieve a specific *person* record, the *author* records that are associated with that person, the *member* records that are associated with that person, and the *phone* records that are associated with that person. A conventional relational database system can not take advantage of the fact that each of these queries is related - they each deal with the same *person*. A DBMS that supports ERIC/Access, however, provides the ability to *remember* the results of one query and avoid re-calculating that information for subsequent queries.

Another operation that is common in ERIC/Object applications is to retrieve values from the database, display them, and let the user edit the values. The application must then store those changed values in the database. Again, a conventional relational database can not take advantage of the fact that it just retrieved that information to speed up storing the information. ERIC/Access (and the databases it is implemented on) allow the application to quickly modify the field value of a record that was recently displayed - without the overhead of doing any searching to find the desired record.[4]

7.3 Internal Object-Oriented Performance Enhancements

There are DBMS enhancements that will greatly improve performance for object-oriented operations. These enhancements can also improve performance for relational queries, but are geared more to an object-oriented model. Two such enhancements are *reference pointers* (or pre-joins) and intelligent read-ahead.

The UNIFY DBMS provides *pointers* for reference fields. Basically, all the records that reference a given record are linked together in a doubly-linked list. Because the related records are "pre-joined", it is very efficient to retrieve reference records. In fact, the reference records can be retrieved in a constant time regardless of the number of records in the table because retrieving them amounts to walking through a linked list. No unnecessary records are accessed, and thus the records are retrieved in a minimum of time. The reader should note that simple clustering is not as effective for object-oriented access because it is difficult to cluster records around two differing fields. In the database in Fig. 1, for example, *member* records could be clustered around the "who" field or the "of" field, but not both. In an object-oriented world, it might be equally likely to retrieve the member records based on the person as to retrieve the member records based on the organization.

Intelligent read-ahead can also be used to improve DBMS object-oriented performance. Because the database knows which objects are related to which other objects, this information can be used to intelligently fetch data before it is requested, thus improving response time.

7.4 Caching Information in Local Memory

The DBMS can cache data in local memory to improve performance. Although important for improving performance for relational queries in general, caching data is particularly effective for improving object-oriented performance because the queries tend to be related and hence access the same file pages. Caching data *locally* requires a different "distributed database" strategy than that proposed for most relational databases [HaFe86]. Rather than the typical client - server model of remote database access where the client workstation makes one or more remote procedure calls to the database server for each query, we believe that as much of the database as possible should be resident on the client workstation. Not only will this reduce the load on the centralized server, it will also provide the best interactive response time by minimizing the network traffic.

---

4 ERIC/Access provides two routines, *rec_addr* and *rec_byaddr*, which allow a program to save and restore a "record address" (essentially tuple-ids, or *tids*). While retrieving the information from the database, the application can easily save the record address. In order to store a changed value, the saved address is made *current* and the field value can be changed. There is no searching involved.

8   Summary

For the purposes of this paper, we have used the term "object-oriented" to refer to simple database operations, as opposed to all that can be expressed in a relational language such as SQL. We have deferred other connotations of "object-oriented" (the ability to associate procedures with objects, and allow a hierarchy of types of objects) to our future work.

We have proposed that both object-oriented and relational operations be permitted on the same database, as many applications require both kinds of interfaces depending on the type of operation required for a particular use. We have shown how both perspectives may be supported in a single data model. Our approach provides referential integrity and higher efficiency for object operations than a relational DBMS, and provides a normalized structure and higher-level query language than an object-oriented language.

We have implemented our proposal in a particular relational database system, UNIFY, achieving good performance for both the relational and object-oriented interfaces. We are exploring its implementation in other relational systems.

9   References

[Catt83], [HaFe86], [MSOP86], [RuCa87], [Ston], [Sun86].

Part V

Application Support

12
A Shared Object Hierarchy

Lawrence A. Rowe

Abstract

This paper describes the design and proposed implementation of a shared object hierarchy. The object hierarchy is stored in a relational database and objects referenced by an application program are cached in the program's address space. The paper describes the database representation for the object hierarchy and the use of POSTGRES, a next-generation relational database management system, to implement object referencing efficiently. The shared object hierarchy system will be used to implement OBJFADS, an object-oriented programming environment for interactive multimedia database applications, that will be the programming interface to POSTGRES.

1 Introduction

Object-oriented programming has received much attention recently as a new way to develop and structure programs [GoRo83, StBo86]. This new programming paradigm, when coupled with a sophisticated interactive programming environment executing on a workstation with a bit-mapped display and mouse, improves programmer productivity and the quality of programs they produce.

A program written in an object-oriented language is composed of a collection of objects that contain data and procedures. These objects are organized into an *object hierarchy*. Previous implementations of object-oriented languages have required each user to have his or her own private object hierarchy. In other words, the object hierarchy is not shared. Moreover, the object hierarchy is usually restricted to main memory. The LOOM system stored object hierarchies in secondary memory [KaKr83], but it did not allow object sharing. These restrictions limit the applications to which this new programming technology can be applied.

There are two approaches to building a shared object hierarchy capable of storing a large number of objects. The first approach is to build an object data manager [AMKP85, CoMa84, DaSm86, Derr86, KhVa87, MSOP86, That]. In

This research was supported by the National Science Foundation under Grant DCR-8507256 and the Defense Advanced Research Projects Agency (DoD), Arpa Order No. 4871, monitored by Space and Naval Warfare Systems Command under Contract N00039-84-C-0089.

this approach, the data manager stores objects that a program can fetch and store. The disadvantage of this approach is that a complete database management system (DBMS) must be written. A query optimizer is needed to support object queries (e.g., "fetch all *foo* objects where field *bar* is *bas*"). Moreover, the optimizer must support the equivalent of relational joins because objects can include references to other objects. A transaction management system is needed to support shared access and to maintain data integrity should the software or hardware crash. Finally, protection and integrity systems are required to control access to objects and to maintain data consistency. These modules taken together account for a large fraction of the code in a DBMS. Some proponents of this approach argue that some of this functionality can be avoided. However, we believe that eventually all of this functionality will be required for the same reasons that it is required in a conventional database management system.

The second approach, and the one we are taking, is to store the object hierarchy in a relational database. The advantage of this approach is that we do not have to write a DBMS. A beneficial side-effect is that programs written in a conventional programming language can simultaneously access the data stored in the object hierarchy. The main objection to this approach has been that the performance of existing relational DBMS's has been inadequate. We believe this problem will be solved by using POSTGRES as the DBMS on which to implement the shared hierarchy. POSTGRES is a next-generation DBMS currently being implemented at the University of California, Berkeley [StRo86]. It has a number of features, including data of type procedure, alerters, precomputed procedures and rules, that can be used to implement the shared object hierarchy efficiently.

Fig. 1 shows the architecture of the proposed system. Each application process is connected to a database process that manages the shared database. The application program is presented a conventional view of the object hierarchy. As objects are referenced by the program, a run-time system retrieves them from the database. Objects retrieved from the database are stored in an object cache in the application process so that subsequent references to the object will not require another database retrieval. Object updates by the application are propagated to the database and to other processes that have cached the object.

Other research groups are also investigating this approach [AbWi86, AnEM86b, KeSn86, Mary87, Meyr86, Skar88a]. The main difference between our work and the work of these other groups is the object cache in the application process. They have not addressed the problem of maintaining cache consistency when more than one application process is using an object. Research groups that are addressing the object cache problem are using different implementation strategies that will have different performance characteristics [KhVa87, Krab85, MSOP86].

This paper describes how the OBJFADS shared object hierarchy will be implemented using POSTGRES. The remainder of the paper is organized as follows. Section 2 presents the object model. Section 3 describes the database representation for the shared object hierarchy. Section 4 describes the design of the object cache including strategies for improving the performance of fetching objects from the database. Section 5 discusses object updating and transactions. Section 6 describes the support for selecting and executing methods. And lastly, section 7 summarizes the paper.

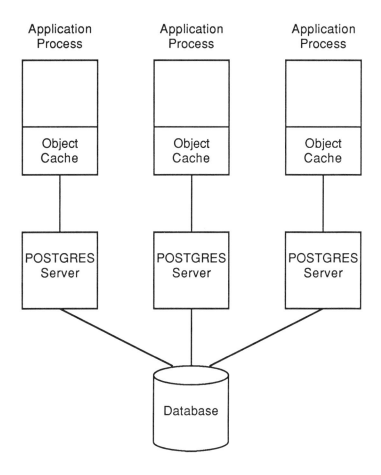

Fig. 1:   *Process Architecture*

2   Object Hierarchy Model

This section describes the object hierarchy model. The model is based on the Common Lisp Object System (CLOS) [BoKi87] because OBJFADS is being implemented in Common Lisp [Stee84].

An *object* can be thought of as a record with named *slots*. Each slot has a data type and a default value. The data type can be a primitive type (e.g., *Integer*) or a reference to another object.[1] The type of an object is called the *class* of the object. Class information (e.g., slot definitions) is represented by

---

1 An object reference is represented by an *object identifier (objid)* that uniquely identifies the object.

another object called the *class object*.[2] A particular object is also called an instance and object slots are also called *instance variables*.

A class inherits data definitions (i.e., slots) from another class, called a *superclass*, unless a slot with the same name is defined in the class. Fig. 2 shows a class hierarchy (i.e., type hierarchy) that defines equipment in an integrated circuit (IC) computer integrated manufacturing database [RoWi87]. Each class is represented by a labelled node (e.g., *Object*, *Equipment*, *Furnace*, etc.). The superclass of each class is indicated by the dark line with an arrowhead. By convention, the top of the hierarchy is class named *Object*. In this example, the class *Tylan*, which represents a furnace produced by a particular vendor, inherits slots from *Object*, *Equipment*, and *Furnace*.

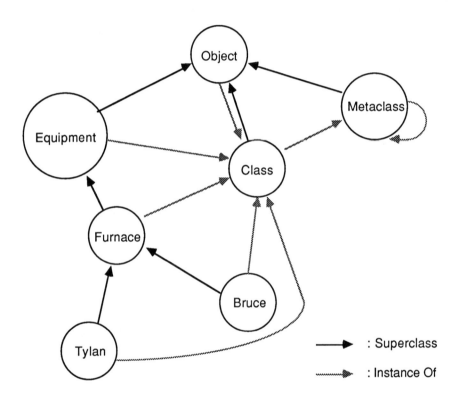

Fig. 2:   *Equipment Class Hierarchy*

As mentioned above, the class is represented by an object. The type of these class objects is represented by the class named *Class*. In other words, they are instances of the class *Class*. The *InstanceOf* relationship is represented by light lines in the figure. For example, the class object *Equipment* is an instance of the class *Class*. Given an object, it is possible to determine the class of which it is an instance. Consequently, slot definitions and, as described below, procedures that operate on the object can be looked-up in the class object. For completeness, the type of the class named *Class* is a class named *MetaClass*.

Fig. 3 shows class definitions for *Equipment*, *Furnace*, and *Tylan*. The definition of a class specifies the name of the class, the metaclass, the superclass, and the slots. The metaclass is specified explicitly because a different metaclass is used when the objects in the class are to be stored in the database. In the example, the class *Tylan* inherits all slots in *Furnace* and *Equipment* (i.e., *Location*, *Picture*, *DateAcquired*, *NumberOfTubes*, and *MaxTemperature*).

Variables can be defined that are global to all instances of a class. These variables, called *class variables*, hold data that represents information about the entire class. For example, a class variable *NumberOfFurnaces* can be defined for the class *Furnace* to keep track of the number of furnaces. Class variables are inherited just like instance variables except that inherited class variables refer to the same memory location. For example, the slot named *NumberOfFurnaces* inherited by *Tylan* and *Bruce* refer to the same variable as the class variable in *Furnace*.

Class *Equipment*
MetaClass *Class*
Superclass *Object*
Slots
      Location   *Point*
      Picture   *Bitmap*
      Date Acquired   *Date*

Class *Furnace*
MetaClass *Class*
Superclass *Equipment*
Slots
      NumberOfTubes   *Integer*
      MaxTemperature *DegreesCelcius*

Class *Tylan*
MetaClass *Class*
Superclass *Furnace*
Slots

Fig. 3:   *Class Definitions for Equipment.*

Procedures that manipulate objects, called *methods*, take arguments of a specific class (i.e., type). Methods with the same name can be defined for different classes. For example, two methods named *area* can be defined: one that computes the area of a *box* object and one that computes the area of a *circle* object. The method executed when a program makes a call on *area* is determined by the class of the argument object. For example, area(x)

calls the area method for *box* if *x* is a *box* object or the *area* method for *circle* if it is a *circle* object. The selection of the method to execute is called *method determination*.

Methods are also inherited from the superclass of a class unless the method name is redefined. Given a function call "*f(x)*", the method invoked is determined by the following algorithm. Follow the *InstanceOf* relationship from *x* to determine the class of the argument. Invoke the method named *f* defined for the class, if it exists. Otherwise, look for the method in the superclass of the class object. This search up the superclass hierarchy continues until the method is found or the top of the hierarchy is reached in which case an error is reported.

Fig. 4 shows some method definitions for *Furnace* and *Tylan*. Furnaces in an IC fabrication facility are potentially dangerous, so they are locked when they are not in use. The methods *Lock* and *UnLock* disable and enable the equipment. These methods are defined for the class *Furnace* so that all furnaces will have this behavior. The argument to these methods is an object representing a furnace.[3] The methods *CompileRecipe* and *LoadRecipe* compile and load into the furnace code that, when executed by the furnace, will process the semiconductor wafers as specified by the recipe text. These methods are defined on the *Tylan* class because they are different for each vendor's furnace. With these definitions, the class *Tylan* has four methods because it inherits the methods from *Furnace*.

method Lock(self: *Furnace*)
. . .
method UnLock(self: *Furnace*)
. . .
method CompileRecipe(self: *Tylan*, recipe: *Text*)
. . .
method LoadRecipe(self: *Tylan*, recipe: *Code*)
. . .

Fig. 4: *Example Method Definitions*

Slot and method definitions can be inherited from more than one superclass. For example, the *Tylan* class can inherit slots and methods that indicate how to communicate with the equipment through a network connection by including the *NetworkMixin* class in the list of superclasses.[4] Fig. 5 shows the definition of *NetworkMixin* and the modified definition of *Tylan*. With this definition, *Tylan* inherits the slots and methods from *NetworkMixin* and *Furnace*.

A name conflict arises if two superclasses define slots or methods with the same name (e.g., *Furnace* and *NetworkMixin* might both have a slot named *Status*). A name conflict is resolved by inheriting the definition from the first

---

3 The argument name *self* was chosen because it indicates which argument is the object.

4 The use of the suffix *Mixin* indicates that this object defines behavior that is added to or mixed into other objects. This suffix is used by convention to make it easier to read and understand an object hierarchy.

class that has a definition for the name in the superclass list. Inheriting definitions from multiple classes is called *multiple inheritance*.

Class *NetworkMixin*
MetaClass *Class*
Superclass *Object*
Instance Variables
      HostName   *Text*
      Device   *Text*
Methods
        SendMessage(self: *NetworkMixin*; msg: *Message*)
        ReceiveMessage(self: *NetworkMixin*) **returns** *Message*

Class *Tylan*
MetaClass *Class*
Superclass *Furnace NetworkMixin*
   . . .

Fig. 5:   *Multiple Inheritance Example*

3   Shared Object Hierarchy Database Design

The view of the object hierarchy presented to an application program is one consistent hierarchy. However, a portion of the hierarchy is actually shared among all concurrent users of the database. This section describes how the shared portion of the hierarchy will be stored in the database.

Shared objects are created by defining a class with metaclass *DBClass*. All instances of these classes, called *shared classes*, are stored in the database. A predefined shared class, named *DBObject*, is created at the top of the shared object hierarchy. The relationship between this class and the other predefined classes is shown in Fig. 6. All superclasses of a shared class must be shared classes except *DBObject*. This restriction is required so that all definitions inherited by a shared class will be stored in the database.

The POSTGRES data model supports attribute inheritance, user-defined data types, data of type procedure, and rules [RoSh79, StRo86] which are used by OBJFADS to create the database representation for shared objects. System catalogs are defined that maintain information about shared objects. In addition, a relation is defined for each class that contains a tuple that represents each class instance. This relation is called the *instance relation*.

OBJFADS maintains four system catalogs to represent shared class information: *DBObject*, *DBClass*, *SUPERCLASS*, and *METHODS*. The *DBObject* relation identifies objects in the database:

     CREATE DBObject(Instance, Class)

where

     Instance   is the *objid* of the object.

     Class   is the *objid* of the class object of this instance.

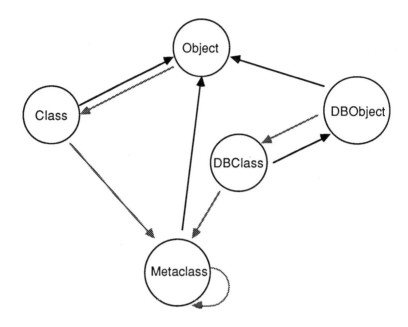

Fig. 6: *Predefined Classes*

This catalog defines attributes that are inherited by all instance relations. No
tuples are inserted into this relation (i.e., it represents an abstract class).
However, all shared objects can be accessed through it by using transitive
closure queries. For example, the following query retrieves the *objid* of all
instances:

        RETRIEVE (X.Instance)
        FROM X in DBObject*

The asterisk indicates closure over the relation *DBObject* and all other
relations that inherit attributes from it.

    POSTGRES maintains a unique identifier for every tuple in the database.
Each relation has a predefined attribute that contains the unique identifier.
While these identifiers are unique across all relations, the relation that
contains the tuple cannot be determined from the identifier. Consequently, we
created our own object identifier (i.e., an *objid*) that specifies the relation and
tuple. A POSTGRES user-defined data type, named *objid*, that represents this
object identifier will be implemented. *Objid* values are represented by an
identifier for the instance relation (*relid*) and the tuple (*oid*). *Relid* is the unique
identifier for the tuple in the POSTGRES catalog that stores information about
database relations (i.e., the *RELATION* relation). Given an *objid*, the following
query will fetch the specified tuple:

        RETRIEVE (o.all)
        FROM o IN *relid*
        WHERE o.oid = *oid*

This query will be optimized so that fetching an object instance will be very fast.

The *DBClass* relation contains a tuple for each shared class:

CREATE DBClass(Name,Owner) INHERITS (DBObject)

This relation has an attribute for the class name (*Name*) and the user that created the class (*Owner*). Notice that it inherits the attributes in *DBObject* (i.e., *Instance* and *Class*) because DBClass is itself a shared class.

The superclass list for a class is represented in the SUPERCLASS relation:

CREATE SUPERCLASS(Class, Superclass, SeqNum)

where

Class	is the name of the class object.
Superclass	is the name of the parent class object.
SeqNum	is a sequence number that specifies the inheritance order in the case that a class has more than one superclass.

The superclass relationship is stored in a separate relation because a class can inherit variables and methods from more than one parent (i.e., multiple inheritance). The sequence number is required to implement the name conflict resolution rule.

Methods are represented in the METHODS relation:

CREATE METHODS(Class, Name, Source, Binary)

where

Class	is the *objid* of the class that defines the method
Name	is the name of the method.
Source	is the source code for the method.
Binary	is the relocatable binary code for the method.

Method code is dynamically loaded into the application program as needed. Method determination and caching are discussed below.

Object instances are represented by tuples in the instance relation that has an attribute for each instance variable. For example, if the classes *Equipment*, *Furnace*, and *Tylan* shown in Fig. 3 were defined with metaclass *DBClass*, the relations shown in Fig. 7 would be created in the database. When an OBJFADS application creates an instance of one of these classes a tuple is automatically appended to the appropriate instance relation.

CREATE Equipment(Location, Picture, DateAcquired)
INHERITS(DBObject)

CREATE Furnace(NumberOfTubes, MaxTemperature)
INHERITS(Equipment)

CREATE Tylan()
INHERITS (Furnace)

Fig. 7: Shared object relations

The POSTGRES data model uses the same inheritance conflict rules for attributes that CLOS uses so attribute inheritance can be implemented in the database system. If the rules were different, OBJFADS would have to simulate data inheritance in the database or POSTGRES would have to be changed to allow user-defined inheritance rules as in CLOS.

Thus far, we have not described how OBJFADS data types (i.e., Common Lisp data types) are mapped to POSTGRES data types. Data types will be mapped between the two environments as specified by type conversion catalogs. Most programming language interfaces to database systems do not store type mapping information in the database [AlCO85, AlHS78, Atki83, Mylo85, RoSh79, Schm77]. We are maintaining this information in catalogs so that user-defined data types in the database can be mapped to the appropriate Common Lisp data type.

The type mapping information is stored in three catalogs: *TYPEMAP*, *OFTOPG*, and *PGTOOF*. The *TYPEMAP* catalog specifies a type mapping and procedures to convert between the types:

CREATE TYPEMAP(OFType, PGType, ToPG, ToOF)

where

OFType   is an OBJFADS type.

PGType   is a POSTGRES type.

ToPG   is a procedure that converts from the OBJFADS type to the POSTGRES type.

ToOF   is a procedure that converts from the POSTGRES type to the OBJFADS type.

The table in Fig. 8 shows the mapping for selected Common Lisp types. Where possible, Common Lisp values are converted to equivalent POSTGRES types (e.g., *fixnum* to *int4*). In other cases, the values are converted to a print representation when they are stored in the database and recreated by evaluating the print representation when they are fetched into the program (e.g., symbols and functions). We expect over time to build-up a set of user-defined POSTGRES types that will represent the commonly used Common Lisp types (e.g., *list*, *random-state*, etc.). However, we also expect application data structures to be designed to take advantage of the natural database representation. For example, it makes more sense to store a list as a separate relation with a common attribute (e.g., a *PO#* that joins a purchase order with the line items it contains) than as an array of *objid's* in the database.

Class variables are more difficult to represent than class information and instances variables. The straightforward approach is to define a relation *CVARS* that contains a tuple for each class variable:

CREATE CVARS(Class, Variable, Value)

where *Class* and *Variable* uniquely determine the class variable and *Value* represents the current value of the variable. This solution requires a union type mechanism because the attribute values in different tuples may have different types. POSTGRES does not support union types because they violate the relational tenet that all attribute values must have the same type.

Two other representations for class variables are possible with POSTGRES. First, a separate relation can be defined for each class that contains a single tuple that holds the current values of all class variables. For example, the following relation could be defined for the *Furnace* class:

FurnaceCVARS(NumberOfFurnaces)

Common Lisp	POSTGRES	Description
fixnum	int4	4 byte integer.
float	float	4 byte floating point number.
(simple-array string-char)	char []	Variable length character string.
symbol	char []	A string that represents the symbol (e.g., "'x'" for the symbol x).
(local) object	char []	A string that contains a function call that will recreate the object when executed.

Fig. 8:   *Data Type Mapping Examples*

Unfortunately, this solution introduces representational overhead (the extra relation) and requires another join to fetch the slots in an object. Moreover, it does not take advantage of POSTGRES features that can be used to update the count automatically.

The second alternative uses POSTGRES rules. A rule can be used to define an attribute value that appears to the application as if it was stored [StHH87]. For example, the following command defines a rule that computes the number of furnaces:

REPLACE ALWAYS Furnace*(
                NumberOfFurnaces = COUNT{Furnace*.Instance})

A reference to *Furnace.NumberOfFurnaces* will execute the COUNT aggregate to compute the current number of furnaces. The relation variable *Furnace** in the aggregate specifies that tuples in *Furnace* and all relations that inherit data from *Furnace* (e.g., *Tylan* and *Bruce*) are to be counted. With this representation, the database maintains the correct count. Notice that the command replaces this value in *Furnace** which causes the rule to be inherited by all relations that inherit data from *Furnace*. The disadvantage of this approach is that the COUNT aggregate is executed every time the class variable is referenced.

POSTGRES provides another mechanism that can be used to cache the answer to this query so that it does not have to be recomputed each time the variable is referenced. This mechanism allows the application designer to request that a rule be evaluated early (i.e., precomputed) and cached in the appropriate relation. In other words, the furnace count will be cached in the relations *Furnace*, *Tylan*, and *Bruce* so that references to the variable will avoid recomputation. Updates to *Furnace* or subclasses of *Furnace* will cause the precomputed value to be invalidated. POSTGRES will recompute the rule off-line or when the class variable is next referenced whichever comes first.

Class variables that are not computable from the database can be represented by a rule that is assigned the current value as illustrated in the following command:

REPLACE ALWAYS Furnace(x = *current value*)

Given this definition, a reference to *Furnace.x* in a query will return the current value of the class variable. The variable is updated by redefining the rule. We plan to experiment with both the single tuple relation and rule approaches to determine which provides better performance.

This section described the object hierarchy model and a database design for storing it in a relational database. The next section describes the application process object cache and optimizations to improve the time required to fetch an object from the database.

4   Object Cache Design

The object cache must support three functions: object fetching, object updating, and method determination. This section describes the design for efficiently accessing objects. The next section describes the support for object updating and the section following that describes the support for method determination.

The major problem with implementing an object hierarchy on a relational database system is the time required to fetch an object. This problem arises because queries must be executed to fetch and update objects and because objects are decomposed and stored in several relations that must be joined to retrieve it from the database. Three strategies will be used to speed-up object fetch time: caching, precomputation, and prefetching. This section describes how these strategies will be implemented.

The application process will cache objects fetched from the database. The cache will be similar to a conventional Smalltalk run-time system [Kaeh81]. An object index will be maintained in main memory to allow the run-time system to determine quickly if a referenced object is in the cache. Each index entry will contain an object identifier and the main memory address of the object. All object references, even instance variables that reference other objects, will use the object identifier assigned by the database (i.e., the *Instance* attribute). These indirect pointers may slow the system down but they avoid the problem of mapping addresses when objects are moved between main memory and the database.[5] The object index will be hashed to speed-up object referencing.

Object caching can speed-up references to objects that have already been fetched from the database but it cannot speed-up the time required to fetch the object the first time it is referenced. The implementation strategy we will use to solve this problem is to precompute the memory representation of an object and to cache it in an OBJFADS catalog:

CREATE PRECOMPUTED(Objid, ObjRep)

where

---

5 Most Smalltalk implementations use a similar scheme and it does not appear to be a bottleneck.

Objid   is the object identifier.

ObjRep   is the main memory object representation.

Suppose we are given the function *RepObject* that takes an object identifier and returns the memory representation of the object. Notice that the memory representation includes class variables and data type conversions. An application process could execute *RepObject* and store the result back in the *PRECOMPUTED* relation. This approach does not work because the precomputed representation must be changed if another process updates the object either through an operation on the object or an operation on the relation that contains the object. For example, a user could run the following query to update the values of *MaxTemperature* in all *Furnace* objects:

REPLACE Furnace*(MaxTemperature = *newvalue*)

This update would cause all *Furnace* objects in *PRECOMPUTED* to be changed.[6]

A better approach is to have the DBMS process execute *RepObject* and invalidate the cached result when necessary. POSTGRES supports precomputed procedure values that can be used to implement this approach. Query language commands can be stored as the value of a relation attribute. A query that calls *RepObject* to compute the memory representation for the object can be stored in *PRECOMPUTED.Objrep*:

RETRIEVE (MemRep = RepObject(*$.Objid*))

$.Objid refers to the object identifier of the tuple in which this query is stored (i.e., *PRECOMPUTED.Objid*). To retrieve the memory representation for the object with objid "Furnace-123", the following query is executed:

RETRIEVE (object = PRECOMPUTED.ObjRep.MemRep)
WHERE PRECOMPUTED.objid = "Furnace-123"

The nested dot notation (*PRECOMPUTED.Objrep.MemRep*) accesses values from the result tuples of the query stored in *ObjRep* [Zani83]. The constant "Furnace-123" is an external representation for the *objid* (i.e., the *Furnace* object with *oid* 123). Executing this query causes *RepObject* to be called which returns the main memory representation of the object.

This representation by itself does not alter the performance of fetching an object. The performance can be changed by instructing the DBMS to precompute the query in *ObjRep* (i.e., to cache the memory representation of the object in the *PRECOMPUTED* tuple). If this optimization is performed, fetching an object turns into a single relation, restriction query that can be efficiently implemented. POSTGRES supports precomputation of query language command values similar to the early evaluation of rules described above.[7] Database values retrieved by the commands will be marked so that if they are updated, the cached result can be invalidated. This mechanism is described in greater detail elsewhere [Ston,Ston87].

The last implementation strategy to speed-up object referencing is prefetching. The basic idea is to fetch an object into the cache before it is referenced. The *HINTS* relation maintains a list of objects that should be prefetched when a particular object is fetched:

---

6   *Furnace* objects cached in an application process must also be invalidated. Object updating, cache consistency, and update propagation are discussed in the next section.

7   The POSTGRES server checks that the command does not update the database and that any procedures called in the command do not update the database so that precomputing the command will not introduce side-effects.

CREATE HINTS(FetchObject, HintObject, Application)

When an object is fetched from the database by an application (*Application*), all *HintObject's* for the *FetchObject* will be fetched at the same time. For example, after fetching an object, the following query can be run to prefetch other objects:

RETRIEVE (obj = p.ObjRep.MemRep)
FROM p IN PRECOMPUTED, h IN HINTS
   WHERE p.Objid = h.HintObject
         AND h.FetchObject = *fetched-object-identifier*
         AND h.Application = *application-name*

This query fetches objects one-at-a-time. We will also investigate precomputing collections of objects, so called *composite objects* [StBo86]. The idea is to precompute a memory representation for a composite object (e.g., a form or procedure definition that is composed of several objects) and retrieve all objects into the cache in one request. This strategy may speed-up fetching large complex objects with many subobjects.

We believe that with these three strategies object retrieval from the database can be implemented efficiently. Our attention thus far has been focussed on speeding up object fetching from the database. We will also have to manage the limited memory space in the object cache. An LRU replacement algorithm will be used to select infrequently accessed objects to remove from the cache. We will also have to implement a mechanism to "pin down" objects that are not accessed frequently but which are critical to the execution of the system or are time consuming to retrieve.

5   Object Updating and Transactions

This section describes the run-time support for updating objects. Two aspects of object updating are discussed: how the database representation of an object is updated (database concurrency and transaction management) and how the update is propagated to other application processes that have cached the object.

The run-time system in the application process specifies the desired update mode for an object when it is fetched from the database into the object cache. The system supports four update modes: local-copy, direct-update, deferred-update, and object-update. Local-copy mode makes a copy of the object in the cache. Updates to the object are not propagated to the database and updates by other processes are not propagated to the local copy. This mode is provided so that changes are valid only for the current session.

Direct-update mode treats the object as though it were actually in the database. Each update to the object is propagated immediately to the database. In other words, updating an instance variable in an object causes an update query to be run on the relation that represents instances of the object. A conventional database transaction model is used for these updates. Write locks are acquired when the update query is executed and they are released when it finishes (i.e., the update is a single statement transaction). Note that read locks are not acquired when an object is fetched into the cache. Updates to the object made by other processes are propagated to the cached object when the run-time system is notified that an update has occurred. The notification mechanism is described below. Direct-update mode is provided so that the application can view "live data".

Deferred-update mode saves object updates until the application explicitly requests that they be propagated to the database. A conventional transaction model is used to specify the update boundaries. A begin transaction operation can be executed for a specific object. Subsequent variable accesses will set the appropriate read and write locks to ensure transaction atomicity and recoverability. The transaction is committed when an end transaction operation is executed on the object. Deferred-update mode is provided so that the application can make several updates atomic.

The last update mode supported by the system is object-update. This mode treats all accesses to the object as a single transaction. An intention-write lock is acquired on the object when it is first retrieved from the database. Other processes can read the object, but they cannot update it. Object updates are propagated to the database when the object is released from the cache. This mode is provided so that transactions can be expressed in terms of the object, not the database representation. However, note that this mode may reduce concurrency because the entire object is locked while it is in the object cache.

Thus far, we have only addressed the issue of propagating updates to the database. The remainder of this section will describe how updates are propagated to other processes that have cached the updated object. The basic idea is to propagate updates through the shared database. When a process retrieves an object, a database alerter [BuCl79] is set on the object that will notify the process when it is updated by another process. When the alerter is trigger by another process, the process that set the alerter is notified. The value returned by the alerter to the process that set it is the updated value of the object. Note that the precomputed value of the object memory representation will be invalidated by the update so that it will have to be recomputed by the POSTGRES server. The advantage of this approach is that the process that updates an object does not have to know which processes want to be notified when a particular object is updated.

The disadvantages of this approach are that the database must be prepared to handle thousands of alerters and the time and resources required to propagate an update may be prohibitive. Thousands of alerters are required because each process will define an alerter for every object in its cache that uses direct-, deferred-, or object-update mode. An alerter is not required for local-copy mode because database updates by others are not propagated to the local copy. POSTGRES is being designed to support large database of rules so this problem is being addressed.

The second disadvantage is the update propagation overhead. The remainder of this section describes two propagated update protocols, an alerter protocol and a distributed cache update protocol, and compares them. Fig. 9 shows the process structure for the alerter approach. Each application process (AP) has a database process called its POSTGRES server (PS). The POSTMASTER process (PM) controls all POSTGRES servers. Suppose that AP_i updates an object in the database on which $M \leq N$ AP's have set an alerter. Fig. 10 shows the protocol that is executed to propagate the updates to the other AP's. The cost of this propagated update is:

2M+1	process-to-process messages
1	database update
1	catalog query
1	object fetch

The object fetch is avoidable if the alerter returns the changed value. This optimization works for small objects but may not be reasonable for large objects.

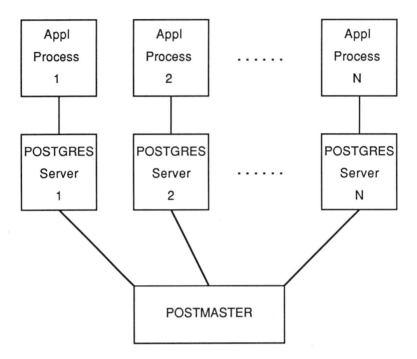

Fig. 9:   *Process Structure for the Alerter Approach*

1. AP_i updates the database.
2. PS_i sends a message to PM indicating which alerters were tripped.
3.   PM queries the alerter catalog to determine which PS's set the alerters.
4.   PM sends a message to PS_j for each alerter.
5.   Each PS_j sends a message to AP_j indicating that the alerter has been tripped.
6.   each PS_j refetched the object.

Fig. 10: *Propagated Update Protocol for the Alerter Approach*

The alternative approach to propagate updates is to have the user processes signal each other that an update has occurred. We call this approach the *distributed cache update* approach. The process structure is similar to that shown in Fig. 9, except that each AP must be able to broadcast a message to all other AP's. Fig. 11 shows the distributed cache update protocol. This protocol uses a primary site update protocol. If AP_i does not have the update token signifying that it is the primary site for the object, it sends a broadcast message to all AP's requesting the token. The AP that has the token sends it to AP_i. Assuming that AP_i does not have the update token, the cost of this protocol is:

- 2   broadcast messages
- 1   process-to-process message
- 1   database update
- 1   object fetch

One broadcast message and the process-to-process message are eliminated if AP_i already has the update token. The advantage of this protocol is that a multicast protocol can be used to implement the broadcast messages in a way that is more efficient than sending N process-to-process messages. Of course, the disadvantage is that AP's have to examine all update signals to determine whether the updated object is in its cache.

1. AP_i acquires the update token for the object.

2. AP_i updates the database.

3. AP_i broadcasts to all AP's that the object has been updated.

4.   Each AP_j that has the object in its cache refetches it.

Fig. 11: *Propagated Update Protocol for the Distributed Cache Approach*

Assume that the database update and object fetch take the same resources in both approaches and that the alerter catalog is cached in main memory so the catalog query does not have to read the disk in the alerter approach. With these assumptions, the comparison of these two approaches comes down to the cost of 2 broadcast messages versus 2M process-to-process messages. If objects are cached in relatively few AP's (i.e., M < < N) and broadcast messages are efficient, the distributed cache update appears better. On the other hand, if M is larger, so the probability of doing 2 broadcasts goes up, and broadcasts are inefficient, the alerter approach appears better. We have chosen the alerter approach because an efficient multicast protocol does not exist but the alerter mechanism will exist in POSTGRES. If this approach is too slow, we will have to tune the alerter code or implement the multicast protocol.

6   Method Determination

Method determination is the action taken to select the method to be executed when a procedure is called with an object as an argument. Conventional object-oriented systems implement a cache of recently called methods to speed-up method determination [GoRo83]. The cache is typically a hash table that maps an object identifier of the receiving object and a method name to the entry address of the method to be executed. If the desired object and method name is not in the table, the standard look-up algorithm is invoked. In memory resident Smalltalk systems, this strategy has proven to be very good because high hit ratios have been achieved with modest cache sizes (e.g., 95% with 2K entries in the cache) [Kras83].

We will adapt the method cache idea to a database environment. A method index relation will be computed that indicates which method should be called for each object class and method name. The data will be stored in the *DM* relation defined as follows:

CREATE DM(Class, Name, DefClass)

where

Class   is the class of the argument object.

Name   is the name of the method called.

DefClass is the class in which the method is defined.

Given this relation, the binary code for the method to be executed can be retrieved from the database by the following query:

RETRIEVE (m.Binary)
FROM m IN METHODS, d IN DM
WHERE m.Class = d.DefClass
         AND d.Class = *argument-class-objid*
         AND d.Name = *method name*

The DM relation can be precomputed for all classes in the shared object hierarchy and incrementally updated as the hierarchy is modified.

Method code will be cached in the application process so that the database will not have to be queried for every procedure call. Procedures in the cache will have to be invalidated if another process modifies the method definition or the inheritance hierarchy. Database alerters will be used to signal object changes that require invalidating cache entries. We will also support a check-in/check-out protocol for objects so that production programs can isolate their object hierarchy from changes being made by application developers [Katz83].

7   Summary

This paper described a proposed implementation of a shared object hierarchy in a POSTGRES database. Objects accessed by an application program are cached in the application process. Precomputation and prefetching are used to reduce the time to retrieve objects from the database. Several update modes were defined that can be used to control concurrency. Database alerters are used to propagate updates to copies of objects in other caches. A number of features in POSTGRES will be exploited to implement the system, including: rules, POSTQUEL data types, precomputed queries and rules, and database alerters.

8   References

[AbWi86], [AICO85], [AIHS78], [AMKP85], [AnEM86b], [Atki83], [BoKi87], [BuCl79], [CoMa84], [DaSm86], [Derr86], [GoRo83], [Kaeh81], [KaKr83], [Katz83], [KeSn86], [KhVa87], [Krab85], [Kras83], [Mary87], [Meyr86], [MSOP86], [Mylo85], [RoSh79], [RoSt87], [RoWi87], [Schm77], [Skar], [StBo86], [Stee84], [StHH87], [Ston87], [Ston], [StRo86], [That], [Zani83].

13
Towards an Object-Oriented Data Model for a Mechanical CAD Database System

David L. Spooner

Abstract

This paper discusses an ongoing research project to design and implement an object-oriented data management system for a mechanical CAD environment. This system will manage hierarchically structured objects stored in main memory and secondary storage. Recent work has been devoted to a requirements analysis for the data model of this system. To aid in identifying these requirements, an object-oriented solid modeling system was developed. We give a brief overview of this system, discuss requirements for the data model, and present the first version of this data model.

1 Introduction

If a database management system (DBMS) is to effectively manage design data and provide an integrated environment for design, it must have some knowledge of the intended use of the data it manages. In other words, the DBMS must have some knowledge of the semantics of the data it is storing. At present, most of this knowledge is contained in application programs and the database designer's head since few DBMSs are capable of dealing with it.

This observation leads to the idea of using data abstraction and object-oriented techniques for modeling and integrating the various types of data encountered in a mechanical CAD environment. Abstract data types provide a means for defining complex data structures, while at the same time providing semantic information about the data through the set of operations defined for the types. Furthermore, by formalizing application programs as operators on high-level abstract data types, additional semantic control over manipulation of the data is possible. Object-oriented programming techniques enhance the semantic content of the data by defining relationships, with inheritance of properties and operators, between the abstract data types. These two data organizational methodologies seem particularly appropriate for CAD because the fundamental principles behind them are creation and manipulation of objects (abstract data types), and these are exactly the activities done during

This work was supported by National Science Foundation, Grant Number DMC-8600930, and by the Industrial Associates Program of the Rensselaer Polytechnic Institute Center for Interactive Computer Graphics. Any opinions implied or expressed are those of the author.

the design process. Other advantages of these techniques over more traditional forms of data management for mechanical CAD are discussed in [Camm86] and [SpMF86].

These ideas are being used in an ongoing research project to design and implement an object-oriented data management system for mechanical CAD. This paper focuses on the requirements of the data model for this system. In the next section we provide background material on the conceptual design of the data model. This is followed by a discussion of an experimental object-oriented solid modeling system developed to evaluate these concepts and identify requirements. A list of requirements for the data model, and the first version of the data model developed from these requirements, are then presented.

2   Background

Two forms of abstraction are particularly useful for modeling mechanical CAD data. The first is aggregation which treats a related collection of objects as a higher level object. For example, an *edge* in a boundary representation of a mechanical part can be viewed as an aggregation of two *vertexes* and a *curve*. In general, an aggregation may collect together individual objects, or sets of objects. This form of abstraction is useful for modeling part-component hierarchies.

The second form of abstraction is generalization which allows members of a class of similar objects to be viewed generically as instances of a higher level object type. For example, *solid model* can be considered as a generalization of *Constructive Solid Geometry Tree*, and *Boundary Representation* [ReVo83]. This form of abstraction is useful for modeling design alternatives.

Both aggregation and generalization can be used to build hierarchies of abstractions [SmSm77a, SmSm77b]. These hierarchies can be combined into a hierarchy of hierarchies by having each object participate simultaneously in both aggregation and generalization abstractions. Thus, for example, an object representing a part in a generalization hierarchy can define the basic components of the part as an aggregation hierarchy. This aggregation hierarchy can then be inherited by all the specializations of the part in the generalization hierarchy, and further refined to describe the details of each alternative of the part. This provides a powerful tool for modeling the data in a CAD environment. (For more details, see [SpMF86].

This is where object-oriented techniques become useful. The generalization hierarchies discussed above are very similar to the object class hierarchies found in Smalltalk [GoRo83] and other object-oriented environments. Indeed, the notion of inheritance of properties and operators exhibited by these environments corresponds almost exactly to the notion of inheritance mentioned in the preceding paragraph. In other words, each edge in an object's class (generalization) hierarchy represents an "is a" relationship. The objects are therefore logically organized by these explicitly stated semantic relationships, rather than being a collection of independent abstractions.

To validate these concepts and identify requirements for an object-oriented data model for a mechanical CAD database system, it was necessary to study a substantial CAD application. An object-oriented solid modeling system was developed for this evaluation. Smalltalk was chosen for the implementation because it provides a programming environment that includes many of these concepts, and, those that it does not, can be simulated with Smalltalk constructs.

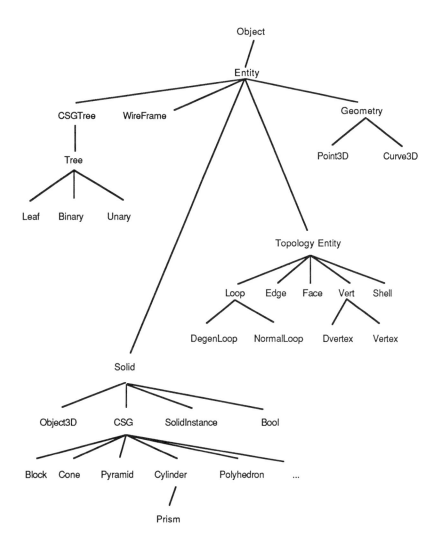

Fig. 1:   *Solid Modeler Object Hierarchy*

3   Object-Oriented Solid Modeling System

Mapping from the aggregation and generalization hierarchies to object class hierarchies in Smalltalk is straightforward. Generalization is handled automatically by the object class hierarchy of the language. Aggregation is handled by defining instance variables within the instances of a class to contain the components of the aggregation. When a component of an aggregation is a set of objects, its corresponding instance variable is assigned a *Collection* object to contain the set.

A 3-D graphics system for Smalltalk was implemented, and the first version of the object hierarchies for solids. The modeling system supports creation, editing and display of boundary representations and constructive solid geometry (CSG) models of solids [ReVo83]. These models are based on the IGES Experimental Solids Proposal [IGES84]. Drawings are done as wire-frame representations of a solid. Fig. 1 shows the object class hierarchy used in the system. The solid modeling system consists of about 3000 lines of Smalltalk object class definitions, and the 3-D graphics system consists of another 1000 lines. Future work will build interfaces from the solid modeler to application programs to further our understanding of the way objects are manipulated by complex CAD applications, and to give preliminary estimates of the performance requirements needed from an object-oriented data manager for CAD.

4   Data Model Requirements

The solid modeling project identified many requirements and issues that must be addressed in designing a data model for mechanical CAD. On the negative side was the limited use that could be made of inheritance within models for solids. For modeling solids, aggregation and other relationships were more important than generalization which allows inheritance. On the positive side, the data semantics expressed in the object hierarchies and operations defined for objects proved to be a major advantage of the object-oriented data modeling approach, leading to the ability to express and enforce more sophisticated integrity constraints within the data model.

Based on what was learned during development of the system, many data model requirements were identified. These are listed below. This list can also be viewed as a critique of the strengths and weaknesses of the Smalltalk paradigm for use as a data model for mechanical CAD data. A survey of other proposed data models for CAD [Atwo85, Daya85, BuCe85, Camm86, HaSi86] has also influenced this list of requirements.

1. Data must be modeled as objects organized into aggregation (part-component) hierarchies and generalization (design alternative) hierarchies.

    This is viewed as a fundamental concept in our data management approach and is included as the principal requirement for the data model.

2. The data model must support definition of object intentions as well as extensions.

    The data model must allow prototypical objects to be defined representing the intention for the database. It must be possible to create instances of these prototypical objects each with a unique identity. The set of all instances of a prototypical object is the extension of the object.

3. It must be possible to define properties of objects.

    It must be possible to define properties for the intention of an object, and for all instances in the object's extension to have values for these properties. It must be possible in the intention of an object to specify constraints on the values for properties.

4.   The data model must allow definition of operations (methods) for objects.

The ability to define operations for an object is necessary to allow the semantics of the object to be fully specified. Operations for an object will typically not be executed while the object is in the database. They will be applied to the object when it has been extracted from the database and placed in main memory under control of an application. Nevertheless, they are an important part of the definition of the object.

5.   The data model must support inheritance of properties and operations.

To achieve the full benefits of the semantic modeling capabilities of the object-oriented paradigm, it is necessary to allow inheritance of both properties and operations. While this capability is used extensively in an object-oriented programming environment, it will be used primarily for integrity constraint enforcement within the data manager.

6.   It must be possible to represent relationships between objects.

Aggregation and generalization represent two specific types of relationships between objects; however, it is necessary to represent arbitrary relationships. It must be possible to represent the intention as well as the extension of these relationships, and it must be possible for relationships to have properties and for constraints to be imposed on relationships.

Smalltalk has a class, *Association*, for establishing relationships between two objects. More generally, a relationship between objects can be represented as an aggregation of the participating objects by defining a new class to represent the relationship with an instance variable to record each participating object. As discussed in [HaSp87], it is important to be able to distinguish between relationships among components of one object and relationships between distinct objects. Therefore, since aggregation is used in the data model to represent the components of an object, it should not also be used to represent relationships between distinct objects. The *Association* class must be suitable extended to serve this purpose.

7.   The data model must allow the intentions and extensions of objects to be modified (dynamic schemas).

By its nature, design is a dynamic activity. It is not reasonable to assume that the intentions of all objects can be defined before the design process begins. Smalltalk modifies all instances of a class whose definition is edited, assigning null values to new instance variables for existing objects, and deleting values for deleted instance variables. An alternative proposed in [Camm86] is for changes in a class definition to affect future instances of the class only. This has the advantage of not destroying data in existing instances. For archival reasons, this data may be important. A compromise solution is to apply versioning methods to class definitions.

8.   Strong typing in the data model.

One of the major problems with Smalltalk for data management is the lack of type checking for variables. Instance variables in objects have no declared type, and parameters in messages to methods have no declared types. Types in Smalltalk are associated with values rather than variables. While this approach has some advantages for a programming language, it creates significant problems for a data manager [MSOP86].

Integrity checking, a potential advantage of an object-oriented data manager, is weakened, and query processing and optimization are more difficult [MSOP86]. Therefore, we conclude that strong typing of variables (instance variables and parameters in messages) is required for our data model ([Stro86] and [Scha86]).

9.   Full support for recursive object structures.

Recursive object structures appear frequently in mechanical CAD. Two examples are assembly hierarchies and CSG trees. Therefore, any data model to support mechanical CAD must allow recursive object structures.

10.   Equivalent support for aggregation and generalization.

Generalization/specialization is supported in Smalltalk by the class hierarchy. Thus, all generalization abstractions are clearly stated and defined. Aggregation, on the other hand, is supported weakly, at best, in Smalltalk. Aggregation is implemented using instance variables in a class. These instance variables are not typed so that violations of the aggregate definition are possible. Since both forms of abstraction are important in modeling CAD data (indeed, aggregation was more important in the solid modeling system), stronger support is needed for aggregation.

11.   Efficient and flexible update capabilities for objects.

The design process is an iterative process often requiring redesign of a part. Thus, data must be updated easily and efficiently with minimal loss of performance after numerous updates. It is also likely that some types of data (e.g., edge files) produced in a mechanical CAD environment will be represented as one large object for performance reasons. Thus, it is necessary to be able to efficiently edit and manipulate large objects as well as small.

12.   Multiple inheritance, a convenience, but not a necessity.

The need for multiple inheritance is a controversial issue. We have found in implementing the modeling system that while multiple inheritance would have been convenient in a few instances, it was never necessary. There was always an acceptable way to model data without multiple inheritance. Thus, we do not make multiple inheritance an absolute requirement for the data model.

13.   Support for methods and procedures.

One problem discovered in the solid modeling system project is that many times a method operates on several objects and produces several other objects as a result. In these cases, it is not clear which class should contain the method. Conceptually, it is not associated with any single class. Thus, a "procedure" concept distinct from class methods is needed for these situations. A technique for registering procedures in the data manager similar to that used by Stonebraker for registering operations for abstract data types [Ston86] may be appropriate.

14.   Specification and enforcement of data integrity constraints.

Part of the specification of the semantics of an object is the definition of the integrity constraints on the value of the object, on the properties of the object, and on the relationships in which the object participates. Thus, the full definition of the intention of an object type must include the specification of these integrity constraints.

It is not reasonable to expect a data manager to enforce arbitrary application specific integrity constraints. For example, in a solid modeling application, the data manager should not be responsible for verifying the correctness (integrity) of a solid model. This is something that the solid modeler application must do. On the other hand, one can expect a data manager to enforce less complex integrity constraints on the values and structure of data and relationships for the objects in the database. This amounts to guaranteeing that the extension of the database satisfies the intention of the database as defined for the data manager.

5   Design Decisions for the Data Model

Knowledge gained from the solid modeler project also allowed us to make several decisions in designing a data model to satisfy these requirements. The first such decision concerns the basic data modeling paradigm to use. There are many variations to the object paradigm. At one extreme, exemplified by Smalltalk [GoRo83], object classes are rigorously defined and each object is an instance of exactly one class and has its behavior determined by this class. At the other extreme, exemplified by systems such as COOLE [Brem86] and Object Logo [Schm86], are systems which have no notion of class. In these systems there is no distinction made between an object and a class.

The second extreme offers a very flexible environment for object-oriented programming. This flexibility is less appropriate for a database environment, however. The notions of classes and instances of classes are analogous to domain and domain values in traditional database systems. It will be more difficult to exploit current technology using the second paradigm. Another argument against the second paradigm is that it does not support our requirement of representation for both database intentions and extensions as well.

We found the class/instance paradigm of Smalltalk sufficient for our solid modeling system and most other applications we have developed. This paradigm also includes the notion of an abstract class that exists only to describe the common properties and operations of its subclasses. We found this concept to be extremely useful in developing the solid modeling system. Therefore, we choose the class/instance paradigm as our basic data modeling paradigm.

One of the requirements demands the ability to handle recursive object structures. Recursive data models complicate the problems of query processing as discussed in [Rose86] and [HaSS87]. We plan to adopt the techniques in [HaSS87] and [SpHS87] to query recursive object structures using extended projection and transitive closure functions. Our experience indicates that these techniques work well for the applications we have tried.

As indicated in the requirements above, multiple inheritance, while convenient, has not proven to be necessary for the solid modeling system. The place where multiple inheritance may be more useful is in design of the data manager itself [BuCe85]. One can envision an object data manager implemented so that basic services provided by the data manager (e.g., concurrency control, security, and integrity checking) are implemented as objects whose services are inherited by all data objects. This type of multiple inheritance has been called "mix ins" in some systems [Symb85]. Since we have not found a strong need for multiple inheritance, and since an efficient implementation of it is likely to be non-trivial, we choose not to include it in our data model at this time. Instead, we will investigate the use of "mix ins" in developing the system.

Requirement Number	Data Model Layer			
	Entity	Storage	Semantic	Programming
1.	X			
2.	X			
3.	X			
4.			X	X
5.			X	X
6.		X	X	
7.	X		X	
8.	X		X	
9.	X		X	
10.	X			
11.	X	X	X	X
12.			X	
13.			X	X
14.			X	

Table 1: Data Model Layers Responsible for Each Requirement

6   The Data Model

In the preceding sections, the object-oriented programming language view of the requirements for a data manager was presented. As a result, some of the requirements contain aspects that, while appropriate in a programming language environment, are not as appropriate in a data management environment. Thus, a second view of the requirements is needed; namely the database view.

The database view of the data model consists of four layers. At the inner-most layer is the Entity Model that deals with the structure of object extensions. At the outer-most layer is the Programming Model that deals with objects as presented to an application program. Between these layers are two layers containing a Storage Model and Semantic Model. The Storage Model deals with relationships between disjoint objects and the way these objects and relationships are mapped to storage. The Semantic Model is concerned with the integrity constraints that are defined for the objects and relationships in the database.

Given this view of the data model, many of the requirements from the preceding sections belong more in the outer layers of the data model. The goal becomes to identify the basic underlying concepts that must be included in the Entity Model; and then to build upon this layer to produce the Storage, Semantic and Programming Models so that the layers collectively satisfy the requirements identified above. The advantage of this organization is that inner layers of the data model concentrate on efficient data management, while outer layers add capability as needed to produce a flexible object-oriented data model.

Table 1 shows which layers are primarily responsible for each of the requirements. As can be seen, many of the requirements are handled by multiple layers. In general, the implementation of a requirement in a particular layer affects the functionality of all outer layers.

6.1 Entity Model

The Entity Model and the Storage Model are based on ideas originally developed by Hardwick as part of the ROSE object-oriented data manager [HaSi86, HaSS87]. The Entity Model uses AND/OR trees to describe the structure of objects. This satisfies the requirement for strong support of both aggregation and generalization as described below.

A recursive data structure suitable for a variety of CAD objects is shown in Fig. 2. The structure is a template that can be used in a mechanical assembly database to describe nested assemblies. A similar data structure with suitable name changes can be used in a Constructive Solid Geometry (CSG) database to describe nested CSG trees and in other applications that require data with a similar structure. It is used here to demonstrate the major ideas in the Entity Model. The role of an Ibit (Instantiation bit) is to define an origin for each part or sub-assembly contained in the assembly. The role of an Rbit (Recursive bit) is to allow an assembly to contain primitive parts and sub-assemblies.

In the figure, a tree of aggregation and generalization abstractions is represented as a tree of AND nodes and OR nodes [SmSm77a, McNR83]. AND nodes are used to describe aggregation abstractions, and OR nodes are used to describe generalization abstractions. For example, an Assembly object is an aggregation of an Ibit sub-object and a Rbit sub-object, and an Rbit object is a generalization of a part sub-object and an assembly sub-object. In the figure, AND nodes have an arc directly below their origin, and OR nodes do not.

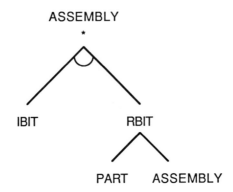

Fig. 2:   *Generic Form for a Recursive CAD Object*

The star immediately below the root of the assembly object in Fig. 2 represents an association abstraction [BrRi84]. It shows that an assembly object can contain a variable length list of aggregations instead of just one. An association can be applied to an aggregation, a generalization, or an object with only one sub-object. The latter case is a degenerate form of the first two, and, in effect, allows associations to be defined independently of aggregations and generalizations.

```
(ASSEMBLY
        (IBIT (X 10.0) (Y 5.0))
        (RBIT (ASSEMBLY
                        (IBIT (X 1.0) (Y 2.0))
                        (RBIT (PART (DESC nut)
                                        (WEIGHT 1.0)
                                        (GEOMETRY nut.dat)))
                        (IBIT (X 3.0) (Y 2.0))
                        (RBIT (PART (DESC bolt)
                                        (WEIGHT 2.0)
                                        (GEOMETRY bolt.dat)))))
        (IBIT (X 0.0) (Y 0.0))
        (RBIT (PART (DESC plate)
                        (WEIGHT 3.0)
                        (GEOMETRY plate.dat))))
```

Fig. 3:   *A Mechanical Assembly*

Fig. 3 describes an object that can be modeled using this data model. The object represents an assembly containing a *nut*, a *bolt*, and a *plate*, and it is described using a modified LISP notation. This notation describes the object as a left parenthesis, an attribute, a value, and a right parenthesis. The value is made up of simpler sub-objects that are described recursively using the same notation. The assembly in the figure contains a sub-assembly and a primitive part (the plate) at the next lower level of abstraction.

Fig. 4 describes a specific data structure for the object given in Fig. 3. In this figure, the data structure has been expanded to include definitions for Parts and Ibits, and to demonstrate the concepts of domains and attributes. Domains correspond to object types. All objects, whether the root of a distinct object hierarchy, or a sub-object in one of these hierarchies, must have a domain. An attribute defines a role for a domain in an abstraction. Both concepts are needed when a domain plays more than one role in an abstraction. For example, the domain real has two roles in the Ibit abstraction.

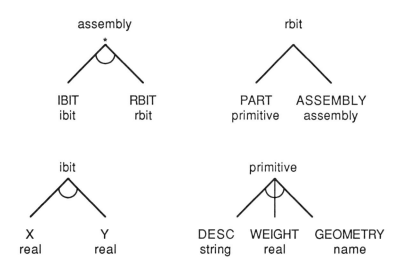

Fig. 4:   *Entity Model for Mechanical Assemblies*

This representation for objects is used in the ROSE data manager, and has proven to work well for a variety of CAD/CAM applications. It assumes that objects will be composed of deeply nested hierarchical structures of sub-objects, and that an entire hierarchy will be stored and retrieved together. An application program will load an object hierarchy into main memory, and then decompose and manipulate the object there. These assumptions are valid in the type of environment for which the data model is intended because CAD/CAM applications will require an entire design or an entire segment of a design at once. It is rarely the case that an application will require a single weight, for example, from a large design without also requiring the rest of the design.

6.2 Storage Model

While the Entity Model describes the structure of an object, it does not include any notion of relationships between objects. This is the job of the Storage Model. The Storage Model is based on a modified Entity-Relationship Model [Chen76]. The object types defined by the Entity Model form the "entities" for the Storage Model. The Storage Model is then used to define relationships between these object types.

Entity-Relationship (ER) diagrams can be used to illustrate the Storage Model for a particular application. Rectangles are used to represent object types, and diamonds are used to represent relationships, as in standard ER diagrams. However, unlike standard ER diagrams, rounded rectangles are used only to define the key of an object type. The attributes of the object type are defined in the Entity Model by an AND/OR tree.

A second deviation from the standard Entity-Relationship Model is that there are two categories of object types (entities) in the Storage Model -- *independent* objects and *dependent* objects. An independent object is an object that forms the root of an object hierarchy defined by the AND/OR trees in the Entity Model. Dependent objects are sub-objects of independent objects. Independent objects can be written to secondary storage as part of the permanent database, while dependent objects cannot. They must first be integrated into higher level objects which are independent objects, and then stored as part of the independent object. The AND/OR trees in the Entity Model define how to do this integration. This allows the database designer to control how the objects defined in the Entity Model are clustered when mapped to permanent storage.

Another way of looking at this aspect of the Storage Model is that it defines the boundary of a logical cluster of data as viewed by application systems. This allows flexibility so that complex objects with many sub-objects in the database can be reorganized into collections of smaller objects when extracted from the database for use. It also gives guidance to the data manager in the physical clustering of objects in secondary storage to optimize performance, and it allows greater data independence for the objects defined by the Entity Model from changes in the physical database design. As discussed by Wiederhold [Wied], it is not necessary that objects be mapped to secondary storage in exactly the form they will be used in main memory. In fact, some leeway here is necessary to allow the organization of objects to change as requirements change throughout the design process.

As an example, consider a simple mechanical CAD application dealing with assemblies of parts. A complete assembly defines a *model* object which is an aggregation of an *assembly* object and a *specification* object. The Entity Model for *assembly* objects is defined in Fig. 4, and it is assumed that an appropriate Entity Model for *specification* objects has been defined. Finally, assume that the geometric definition of a part is defined by a *CSG* object with an appropriate AND/OR tree definition in the Entity Model.

A Storage Model for this application is shown in Fig. 5. *Model* objects, *specification* objects, and *CSG* objects are independent objects (indicated by the presense of a blackened corner for these object types in the Storage Model diagram). All other objects are dependent objects (indicated by the absence of a blackened corner for these objects types, or by omission of the object type from the diagram). Thus, the complete definition of an assembly, including all sub-assemblies and parts, must be packaged into a *model* object before it can be stored into secondary storage as part of the permanent database. Note that this design for the Entity and Storage models is only one of many that a database designer may choose.

Fig. 5 also contains definitions of relationships between object types. In this case, the relationship between a part and its geometry is the only relationship not directly implied by the AND/OR trees in the Entity Model. Again, this was a design decision for the database designer.

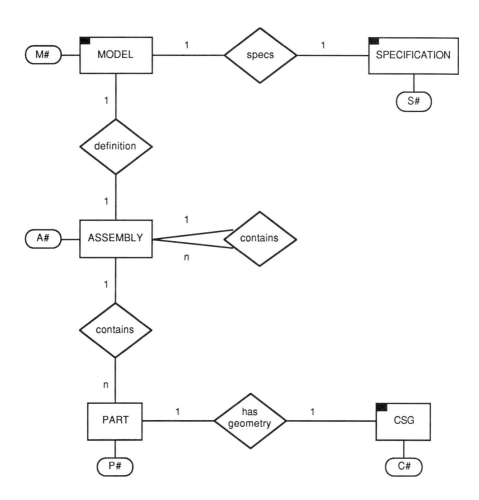

Fig. 5:   *Storage Model for a Mechanical CAD Application*

6.3 Semantic Model

As yet, the data model includes no notion of operations (methods) defined for specific object types. This is because we feel that associating operations with objects in a data manager is primarily useful for definition of semantics and integrity constraints. In a programming language, a wide range of operations can be associated with objects and used to manipulate the objects in main memory. In the data manager, however, the operations that are applied to objects are such generic things as retrieve, store, create and delete. Thus, specific operations (methods) for objects are useful primarily as a means for defining constraints on these generic operations.

Inheritance of operations, an important feature of object-oriented systems, will also be important here. Integrity constraints defined for one object must be inherited by all specializations of that object in an inheritance hierarchy. This not only simplifies the definition of integrity constraints, but also helps to define some of the semantics of the data being modeled by the objects in the database.

For example, the generic delete operation may be written to invoke pre-delete and post-delete operations immediately before and after it deletes an object. Default predelete and post-delete operations may be defined for the root object in the object class hierarchy. Object classes that require special integrity checks before and/or after a delete operation can define their own specialized pre-delete and post-delete operations. When an object of one of these types is deleted, the inheritance and dynamic binding facilities of the object-oriented paradigm cause the appropriate pre- and post-delete operations to be invoked. The default pre-and post-delete operations are invoked only if no others have been defined for the object and its ancestors. A similar approach can be used for the other generic data manager operations.

These ideas are discussed in more detail in [LaSJ86]. This work is only a beginning, however. Semantic and integrity constraint enforcement with exception handling is one of the major areas where object-oriented data models are superior to traditional data models for mechanical CAD data [BuCV86]. Our future work will concentrate heavily in this area.

6.4 Programming Model

The final layer in the data model is the Programming Model. It is debatable whether the Programming Model should be considered part of the data model since it concerns interfaces to applications. In traditional database technology, it is the data definition language and data manipulation languages of a system. However, we feel that the Programming Model is an integral part of our data modeling approach, and include it as the outer layer of the data model.

A typical mechanical CAD computing environment consists of application programs that create and analyze designs, render images, produce NC programs, and do many other related things. This software provides the major functionality of the engineering environment. Most of it is written using traditional procedural programming languages such as C and FORTRAN. The use of object-oriented languages to develop software to replace existing systems will be a slow evolutionary process, if it occurs at all. Thus, an object-oriented database system for an engineering environment must provide programming language interfaces designed for procedural as well as object-oriented programming languages.

The Programming Layer currently supports two programming language interfaces that differ primarily in the degree of coupling between the database and the programming language. The first is a low-level interface closely tied to the data model and the types of abstractions it supports. It allows a user to travers an object structure using a set of operations that return "semantic-pointers" into an object's structure. These "semantic-pointers" contain attribute and abstraction type information to allow the semantics of the data model to be maintained. The second interface supports a higher level of abstraction with looser coupling. Application programs request objects that are loaded into application program data structures. To make this efficient, a preprocessor uses an object's Entity Model from the database and the declaration of an application program's data structures to generate a programming language function to translate an object of that type into the program's data structures. As a result, the translation is done with compiled code at run-time to as large an extent as possible.

Neither interface preserves the message passing paradigm for invocation of methods. This is motivated by two factors. First, performance may be improved if application programs are able to manipulate an object directly rather than going through a message passing paradigm to invoke methods to do this, especially when objects are in secondary storage. Second, existing CAD software is not designed for a message passing type of interaction and would have to be substantially rewritten to use this type of interface. Our experiences with attempting this type of modification have been very negative [SpMi84]. Of course, allowing application programs to directly manipulate an object rather than using predefined methods can lead to integrity problems. Thus, a compromise is needed that combines the advantages of both approaches. The result is an interface that exploits the integrity enforcement advantages of the object paradigm, while retaining the performance, usability, and flexibility required by existing engineering application software. This interface also provides a migration path for new software developed with a programming language that supports a richer object-oriented environment. This is a second focus of our future work.

Finally, an interactive query language is needed in the data model for specification of searches and extraction of objects from the database. Since SQL is a standard for relational database query languages, the query language is being developed as an extension to it. We are exploring extended projection and transitive closure functions to do this [SpHS87].

7   Implementation Approach

In a mechanical CAD environment as we envision it, most independent objects will be large and composed of many smaller objects organized in a hierarchy as defined by the Entity Model. Thus, each independent object is analogous in size to a file that typically is managed by the file system of an operating system. In fact, operating systems such as Unix and VMS are set up to manage directories of files of this size, and code management systems such as SCCS [Unix83] and CMS [VMS82] have been developed to handle versioning and configuration of these files.

In our initial data manager, we would like to take advantage of this existing software to manage the physical storage of objects. Therefore, we will map independent objects as defined by the Storage Model to files - one object per file. All objects of a particular type will be in one subdirectory of the operating system. The name of the file containing an object is the key for the object from the Storage Model. This is the technique used in the ROSE system, and a similar technique has been proposed for the GORDION system [EgEl87]. This will allow us to take advantage of existing capabilities in operating systems, and, if the operating system supports remote network file access, we can take advantage of this to form the rudiments of a distributed data management system.

The initial prototype implementation is taking advantage of the ROSE system to implement the Entity and Storage Models. The Semantic Model is being developed as a layer on top of the ROSE system which implements an object paradigm with methods, messages and inheritance. The Programming Model also takes advantage of the ROSE system, where possible.

8   Conclusions

In this paper we have presented some of the requirements for a data model to support mechanical CAD applications. These requirements were identified during the development of a solid modeling application, and were used to guide the development of a four layer data model. This data model was also presented.

The data model differs from other object-oriented data models in several ways. Most importantly is the interaction between the Entity and Storage Models. These models allow data to be organized into deeply nested hierarchical data structures for storage in the database, but also allow this data to be exploded easily into smaller objects when the data is extracted from the database for use. The desirability of this is a direct consequence of the way mechanical CAD applications access data. It also solves the problem in some object-oriented systems of knowing what objects to migrate to secondary storage when the user requests that a particular object be stored. In those systems, there is no clear definition of the logical clustering of objects. The Semantic and Programming Models have also been defined specifically with mechanical CAD applications in mind. While the need for strong support for aggregation is now becoming apparent and is being included in many object-oriented data models, when this project began, few such data models included adequate support for this type of abstraction. Finally, the data model has been kept as simple as possible, including only those ideas that were felt to be truly useful to mechanical CAD applications. It is hoped that this will lead to an easy to use system with the high performance demanded by interactive design and engineering systems. Initial implementation experiences indicate that there is reason to be optimistic [Hard87].

9   Acknowledgement

I would like to thank Martin Hardwick whose close collaboration has helped develop many of the ideas presented here. I would also like to thank the referees whose comments helped to improve an earlier version of this paper.

10 References

[Atwo85], [Brem86], [BrRi84], [BuCe85], [BuCV86], [Camm86], [Chen76], [Dada86], [Daya85], [EgEl87], [GoRo83], [Hard87], [HaSi86], [HaSp87], [HaSS87], [IGES84], [LaSJ86], [McNR83], [MSOP86], [ReVo83], [RoKB85],

[Rose86], [Scha86], [Schm86], [SmSm77a], [SmSm77b], [SpHS87], [SpMF86], [SpMi84], [Ston86], [Stro86], [Symb85], [Unix83], [VMS82], [Wied].

14

A Data Modeling Methodology for the Design and Implementation of Information Systems

Peter Lyngbaek, William Kent

Abstract

Formal specifications that precisely and correctly define the semantics of software systems become increasingly important as the complexity of such systems increases. The emerging set of semantic data models which support both structural and operational abstractions are excellent tools for formal specifications. In this paper we introduce a methodology, based on an object-oriented data model, for the design and development of large software systems. The methodology is demonstrated by applying the object-oriented data model to the specification of a database system which implements the given model. The specification serves several purposes: it formally defines the precise semantics of the database commands, it provides a basis from which the corresponding database system software can be systematically derived, and it tests and demonstrates the adequacy of such a model for defining software systems in general. The design methodology introduced combines techniques from data modeling, formal specifications, and software engineering.

1   Introduction

The importance of formal semantic definitions of large, complex software systems has been widely recognized over the past years. A formal semantic definition is a precise specification of the semantics of a given system. It serves as a basis for the development of implementations of the system and can be used to verify correctness of the implementations. A formal definition can be thought of as a contract between users and developers of the system being defined.

Operational and denotational semantics [BjJo78, Gord79] have been demonstrated to be useful tools for programming language design and compiler development [Beki74, BjOe80, Donz80], and there is a growing acceptance of such techniques for data model and database system designs [BjLo82]. A formal definition of a database system expresses the semantics of the database commands and it may be used by the implementors of the database system, technical manual writers, database designers and database end-users.

Data models are becoming increasingly powerful. Their semantic expressiveness and high levels of data abstractions make the differences between semantic data models [Abri74, Chen76, MyBW80, HaMc81, Ship81] and modern object-oriented programming languages [GoRo83] vanish. Data models that support both static (structural) and dynamic (operational) modeling constructs can be used as formal specification tools suitable for semantic definitions of complex software systems such as information systems.

In this paper, we show how to use an object-oriented data model as a tool for specifying large software systems. The approach, which supports a data-driven methodology for the design and development of software systems, is an extension of the fact-based data analysis and design described in [Kent83b]. The methodology is demonstrated by defining an object-oriented database system in terms of the the data model it implements. The static modeling constructs of the data model, e.g., objects, types, and relationships, can be used to define the semantic domains of the corresponding information system. The dynamic modeling constructs, e.g., the database operations, can be used to define the semantics of the commands of the information system. The definition is based on a procedural programming language similar to the ones a database designer might use for writing database operations.

The advantages of using a data model as a tool for the definition of its own semantics are twofold. Firstly, a user of the formal definition only has to deal with one formalism, namely the data model itself. An application developer learns the capabilities of the database system in the same formalism he will use to define his own applications. An understanding of the data model is required anyway by the system implementors, manual writers, database designers, and database users in order for them to do their jobs. The fact that the user of the formal definition does not have to understand an additional specification language is an important one because the major objections to formal specification languages are their complexity and difficulty of use and understanding. The second reason for using a data model as a formal specification tool is to demonstrate the power of the model. This is similar to implementing a compiler for a given programming language in its own language.

To a limited extent, data models have previously been used to specify themselves. Metadata that describe the structure of a database can be modeled by the same model as the one used to model the content of the database. Various implementations of the relational model, for example, store the meta-data in pre-defined relations [Cham76, Zloo77]. These relations, often called the system tables, describe all the relations of a database, including themselves, by their names, attributes, and access rights. A number of semantic data models have also been used to describe their own meta-data [Codd79, Catt80, LyMc84b]. In the object-oriented data model supported by the Personal Data Manager [LyMc84b], for example, a type is modeled as an object with pre-defined attributes such as Name, Instances, Supertype, and Subtypes. Self-describing database systems [Mark85] introduce an intension-extension dimension of data description which allows changes of user-data explicitly to be controlled in the corresponding schema. That way, the same data manipulation language can be used to manipulate both meta-data and user-data.

Even though it has been successfully demonstrated that the structure of a database can be defined in terms of its own structural modeling constructs, little work has been done to demonstrate how the semantics of the data definition and manipulation commands of a database system can be defined in terms of the primitive operations of the database system. In [BjLo82], it is shown how the structure of an IMS database as well as the semantics of the

IMS database commands can be modeled using the VDL notation [BjJo78]. The goal of this paper is to illustrate the same thing for an object-oriented database system, but instead of using VDL as a formal specification language we will use the structural and operational modeling constructs of the underlying object-oriented data model.

The rest of this paper is organized as follows. Section 2 describes the object-oriented data model, called the Iris Data Model, which provides the framework for the formal specification methodology. Section 3 outlines the design methodology and illustrates how it can be applied to the specification of the Iris database management system [Derr86, Fish87]. Finally, Section 4 contains some concluding remarks.

2 Iris Data Model Overview

The notion of object or entity is central to most semantic data models [Abri74, Chen76, MyBW80, HaMc81, Ship81]. Object-oriented data models introduce a semantically rich set of structuring primitives that support abstractions such as classification, generalization, and aggregation [SmSm77a]. Objects, which represent things or concepts from an application environment, are unique entities in the database with their own identity and existence. They can be referred to regardless of their attribute values. Therefore, referential integrity [Date81] can be supported. This is a major advantage over record-oriented data models in which the objects, represented as records, can be referred to only in terms of their attribute values.

Semantic models that support the modeling of database operations, i.e., procedural abstractions [MyBW80, BeFe83, LyMc84a, DeKL85] introduce a high degree of data independence. In such models, objects can be accessed and manipulated in terms of pre-defined operations and functions only.

The Iris Data Model falls into the general category of semantic data models. The Iris Data Model is based on only two primitive constructs - *objects* and *functions*. These primitives, which support the modeling of state and behavior, encompass many other modeling constructs such as attributes, instance variables, relationships, types, and operations. The roots of the model can be found in previous work on Daplex [Ship81] and its extensions [Kulk83] and the Taxis language [MyBW80]. A subset of the Iris model, which has been implemented at Hewlett-Packard Laboratories, is briefly described below. It is beyond the scope of this paper to further compare the model with related work on semantic data modeling.

2.1 Objects and Types

Objects represent entities and concepts from the application domain being modeled. They have the following characteristics:

1. Objects are classified by type. Objects that share common properties belong to the same type.

2. Objects may serve as arguments to functions and may be returned as results of functions.

The model distinguishes between *literal objects* and *non-literal objects*. Literal objects are immutable and include Integer, Real, Boolean, and String objects. They are directly representable. Literal objects are system-defined and are always known to the database. I.e., there are no operations to explicitly create or destroy them. Non-literal objects are not directly representable in external form, but they can be referenced in terms of their property values, i.e., their relationships to other objects. Internally, non-literal objects are represented by surrogates which are unique object identifiers.

The database command *NewObject* introduces a new object and adds it to the extension of a specified user-defined type and all its supertypes. The database command *DeleteObject* deletes a specified user-defined object from the database.

Types, which have unique names, are collections of objects. Objects belonging to the same type share common properties. For example, all the objects belonging to the Person type have a Name and an Age property. Objects are constrained by their types to be applicable to only those functions that are defined on the types.

Types are organized in a type structure that supports generalization and specialization. A type may be declared to be the subtype of another type. Functions defined on a supertype are also defined on the subtype. We say that such functions are *inherited* by the subtype. The Iris type structure is a directed acyclic graph. A given type may have multiple subtypes and multiple supertypes. The type Object is the supertype of all other types and therefore contains every object. Types are objects themselves, and their relationships to subtypes, supertypes, and instances are expressed as functions in the system [Kent78].

For each type in the database there is an associated predicate function, called a *typing function*, which has the same name as the type. The typing function maps objects onto the Boolean objects True and False. A given object is mapped to True if it is an instance of the type with which the typing function is associated; otherwise it is mapped to False.

In order to support graceful database evolution, the Iris type graph can be changed dynamically. The database command *NewType* introduces a new type as a subtype of specified suptertypes. An existing user-defined type is deleted from the database by the database command *DeleteType*. Objects may gain and lose types throughout their existence. The command *AddInstance* adds a specified user-defined object to the extension of a specified user-defined type and all its supertypes. A user-defined object is removed from the extension of a specified user-defined type and all its subtypes by the database command *RemoveInstance*. New subtype/supertype relationships among existing types cannot be created in the current Iris version.

2.2 Functions

Properties of objects, relationships among objects, and computations on objects are expressed in terms of functions. Functions are defined over types and they may be multivalued and have side-effects. For example, DepartmentOf is a function defined on Employee objects:

```
DepartmentOf:  Employee -> Department
```

DepartmentOf(Smith) will return the department to which Smith is assigned, e.g., Sales.

A type can be characterized by the collection of functions defined on it. The Employee type might have the functions EmployeeNumber, Name, DepartmentOf, and Birthdate defined over it:

```
EmployeeNumber:  Employee -> Integer

Name:  Employee -> String

DepartmentOf:  Employee -> Department

Birthdate:  Employee -> Date
```

Functions can also express properties of several objects. For example, the function AssignmentDate defined on employees and departments will return the date an employee was assigned to a department:

```
AssignmentDate:  Employee x Department -> Date
```

If Smith was assigned to the Sales department on 1/1/84 then

```
AssignmentDate(Smith, Sales) = 1/1/84
```

Functions may have complex values. The function AssignedOn defined on Date objects returns pairs of Employee and Department objects:

```
AssignedOn:  Date -> Employee x Department
```

If two assignments were made on 6/1/82, e.g., Wong was assigned to the Research department and Jones to the Marketing department then

```
AssignedOn(6/1/82) = {<Wong, Research>,<Jones, Marketing>}
```

The AssignedOn function illustrates a multi-valued function.

The specification of an Iris function consists of two parts: a *declaration* and an *implementation*. The database command *NewFunction* declares a new function by specifying its name together with its argument and result types. The implementation of a function specifies how the values of the function are obtained. Function implementation is described below. The command *DeleteFunction* deletes a specified function from the database.

2.3 Function Implementation

Function values may be explicitly stored in the database or they may be computed. In general, Iris will support four ways to specify a function implementation: Stored Functions, Derived Functions, Procedural Functions, and Foreign Functions.

Stored Functions. A function may be explicitly stored in a table, i.e., corresponding argument and result values (the graph of the function) are maintained in a single table. Several functions may be stored in the same table in order to improve performance (Section 2.7). Stored functions may be updated, that is, the mappings from argument values to result values can be explicitly specified (Section 2.6). The actions of retrieval and updates are implicitly defined in terms of relational operations on the tables.

Derived Functions. A function may be derived from other functions regardless of their implementation. A derived function is defined by a derivation expression which is an Iris query (Section 2.4). It can be thought of as a view of the stored data. The update semantics of derived functions are not always well-defined. For example, if the derivation expression of a given function requires joining several tables, the function cannot be directly updated. However, the actions of updates are implicitly defined by Iris in those cases where it can solve the "view update" problem. Functions that are defined as inverses of stored functions are examples of updatable derived functions.

Procedural Functions. A function may be specified as a general-purpose operation with flow control, conditionals, and side-effects. Such functions are written in an extended Iris language and have the potential of being optimized by the Iris System. Procedural functions can be viewed as a generalization of derived functions in the sense that they might not return results, their results (if any) are not necessarily obtained from stored tables, and they may have side-effects. Computed functions with side-effects may serve to define the update semantics of other derived functions. For example, the definer of a derived function may explicitly specify how an update is mapped into updates of the underlying stored tables by writing a procedural function that is to be executed when the derived function is updated.

Foreign Functions. A program written in some foreign programming language and compiled outside of Iris may be bound to an Iris function. When the function is invoked the program is dynamically loaded and executed. Foreign functions cannot be optimized by the Iris system. However, they provide extensibility and a flexible way of implementing database operations.

The various implementations of functions described above allow functions to represent attributes, relationships, views, and computations. A user invoking a given function does not have to know whether the function returns a stored fact, a derived fact, or a computed value. Therefore, high levels of data abstraction and data independence are supported.

Four kinds of actions can be performed on an Iris function - one for the retrieval command *Find* and one for each of the update commands *Set*, *Add* and *Remove*. In the case of a stored function or a simple derived function, the implementation of the update actions are deduced by the system. For complex functions, such as a function involving a join, it is necessary for the function definer explicitly to specify the implementations.

The current Iris implementation supports stored, derived, and foreign functions. Section 2.7 describes how functions are stored. Derived functions are described in Section 2.4. Foreign functions are described in [CoLy88]. Procedural functions are currently being implemented.

2.4 Derived Functions and Rules

Some functions are semantically interdependent, in the sense that an update to one should be reflected by a change in the other. Inverse functions constitute the most common example. Consider the properties of a department:

```
Name:  Department -> String

Manager:  Department -> Employee

Employee:  Department -> Employee
```

At present, we expect the value of Employees(Sales) to include Smith. But suppose we perform the update:

```
set DepartmentOf(Smith) = Purchasing
```

Such an update should automatically update the Employees function so that Smith will appear among the employees of Purchasing rather than Sales.

Sometimes more than two functions are so inter-related. All of the following functions are semantically interrelated:

```
AssignmentDate:  Employee x Department -> Date

AssignedOn:  Date ->  Employee x Department

DeptHist:  Department ->  Employee x Date

EmpHist:  Employee -> Department x Date
```

The function DeptHist returns for a given department its past and current employees and their assignment dates. Similarly, EmpHist returns for a given employee his employment history.

The interdependence among such functions is expressed by deriving them from a common underlying base predicate. Predicates are Boolean-valued functions that express relationships among the objects involved. For example, an Assignment predicate expresses a relationship among employees, departments, and dates:

```
Assignment:  Employee x Department x Date ->  Boolean
```

If Smith was assigned to the Sales department on 1/1/84 then

```
Assignment(Smith, Sales, 1/1/84) = True
```

The functions AssignmentDate, AssignedOn, EmpHist, and DeptHist can then be defined by the derivations shown below. The derivation expression is a *Find* command (Section 2.6).

```
AssignmentDate(e, d) ::=
    find date/Date where Assignment(e,d,date)

AssignedOn(date) ::=
    find e/Employee, d/Department
        where Assignment(e,d,date)

DeptHist(d) ::=
    find e/Employee, date/Date
        where Assignment(e,d,date)

EmpHist(e) ::=
    find d/Department, date/Date
        where Assignment(e,d,date)
```

In effect, an update to one of these functions implies an update to the underlying predicate, which in turn propagates into all the other functions derived from that predicate. Notice that a function derivation, which is introduced by the database command *Define*, provides an implementation for a function previously declared by a *NewFunction* command.

Derived functions can be thought of as rules. For example, given a *Parent* function, a *Grandparent* function can be defined as follows:

```
Grandparent(p/Person)  ::=
    find gp/Person where gp = Parent(Parent(p))
```

A more complex rule definition might look like this:

```
Oldercousin(p/Person)   ::= find c/Person
    where c = Child(Sibling(Parent(p)))
    and Age(c) > Age(p)
```

Notice that the nested-function notation in Iris function definitions dispenses with the variables needed in Prolog [ClMe81] to carry results from one function call to the next. Variables can, however, be used in Iris function bodies if required.

Prolog rules return a stream of results. Similarly, Iris functions can return multiple results. In nested function calls, the results of the inner function serve as arguments to the outer function which returns all the results corresponding to these arguments. For example, the function call:

```
Nameofperson(Children(Member(Deptwithname("Sales"))))
```

returns all of the names of all of the children of all of the members of all of the departments with name "Sales".

Like Prolog, Iris makes the closed-world assumption - any fact which is not deducible from the data in the database is assumed to be false.

The current Iris prototype does not support recursive function definitions. Furthermore, universal quantification, nested quantifiers, and negation are not supported at the time.

2.5 Object Participation Constraints

Functions of one argument are generally characterized as being either single-valued or multi-valued, and either required or optional (total or partial). "Participations" express such constraints in a more generalized fashion, applicable to functions of multiple arguments, including predicate functions.

Functions have specifications for each of their argument and result parameters which indicates a minimum object participation (MINP) and a maximum object participation (MAXP). The object participation specifications, which are required by every stored Iris function, are constraints. As an example, consider the CurrentAssignment predicate in which both MINP and MAXP of Employee objects are one, and MINP and MAXP of Department objects are zero and many, respectively:

```
CurrentAssignment:
    Employee [1,1] x Department [0,m] -> Boolean
```

The constraint MINP = 1 on the Employee argument specifies that each employee must participate at least once, i.e., each employee must have a department.

The constraint MAXP = 1 on the Employee argument specifies that each employee may participate at most once, i.e., each employee has at most one department.

It is useful to note that any parameter having MAXP = 1 can serve as a unique key in the underlying tables in which the data is stored. This applies to employees in this case, since no employee can occur here more than once.

The constraint MINP = 0 on the Department argument specifies that a department need not participate at all, i.e., a department may have no employees.

The constraint MAXP = m on the Department argument specifies that each department may participate many times, i.e., a department may have many employees.

The minimum and maximum object participation constraints for a stored predicate implicitly determine the object participation constraints for all the derived functions whose derivations depend on the predicate.

For ordinary functions of one argument, participations correspond to simpler constraints. Consider the DepartmentOf function:

```
DepartmentOf:
     Employee [1, 1] -> Department [0, m]
```

The constraint MINP = 1 on the Employee argument specifies that each employee must participate at least once, hence this function is "required". An argument with MINP = 0 would indicate an optional function.

The constraint MAXP = 1 on the Employee argument specifies that each employee may participate at most once, hence this function is single-valued. An argument with MAXP = m would indicate a multi-valued function.

Object participation constraints are further described in [LyVi87]. In the future, participations will be specifiable for sets of arguments, expressing constraints on combinations of argument values.

2.6 Database Updates and Queries

Properties of objects can be modified by changing the values of functions. For example, the command:

set Salary(Smith) = $30000.00

will cause the Salary function to return the value $ 30000.00 in a future invocation with the parameter Smith.

The values of multi-valued functions can also be modified by *Add* and *Remove* commands. Thus, the command:

add Friend(John) = Susan

adds Susan to the set of John's friends. Similarly, Ron is removed from the set of Helen's friends by the following Remove command:

remove Friend(Helen) = Ron

Updates to sets of objects can also be specified. An example of such an update would be to increase the salary of all engineers by 10 percent:

set Salary(e/Engineer) = s/Integer
    where s = Salary(e) * 1.1

The database can be queried by specifying predicates on objects and function values. The following Find command retrieves all the employees assigned to Sales on 3/1/83:

find e/Employee
    where AssignmentDate(e, Sales) = 3/1/83

and the command

find d/Department **for some** e/Employee
    where AssignmentDate(e, d) = 3/1/83

returns all the departments to which employees were assigned on 3/1/83.

A Find command without a list of return variables returns a Boolean value. The value returned is True if there exists a binding of the existentially quantified variables such that the Boolean expression is True. For example, the Find command:

find for some d/Department **where** DepartmentOf(Jones) = d

returns the value True if Jones is assigned to a department. If Jones is not employed by any department the value False is returned.

2.7 Physical Database Design

A particular implementation of the Iris Data Model may support a number of
database design commands that allow physical storage structures and access
methods for functions to be defined. The current Iris prototype supports two
database design commands, *Store* and *Index*, described below.

2.7.1 Store

The store command specifies how to materialize one or more predicate
functions. Store implements base predicate functions using tables, i.e., the
graphs of the functions are stored in tables. That way, the database
commands Set, Add, Remove, and Find are mapped by the database system
to table operations.

In order to illustrate the Store command, consider the three predicates:

```
Employee: Object [1, 1] -> Boolean
Project:  Employee [0, 1] x Project [0, m] -> Boolean
Manager:  Subordinate/Employee [0, 1] x
          Supervisor/Employee [0, m] -> Boolean
```

The command:

> **store** Project

causes a single table to be created and used to materialize the Project
predicate function. The table has one column for each of the argument
parameters Employee and Project. The table will only contain employees who
are assigned to projects and projects to which employees are assigned.

If several predicates are specified by the same Store command, they will all
be clustered together in a single table. The command:

> **store** Project **on** Employee, Manager **on** Subordinate

causes the two predicates Project and Manager to be implemented using the
same table. The table has three columns. One column, called the clustering
column, is shared by the parameters Employee of Project and Subordinate of
Manager. These clustering parameters are specified by the **on** clauses of the
Store command. All the clustering parameters must have the same object type
and they must be "keys", i.e., their upper object participation must be one. In
addition to the clustering column, the table has one column corresponding to
each of the other parameters of the specified predicates. The clustering
column will only contain employees who are assigned to projects or have
managers. If an employee is assigned to a project, but has no manager, the
manager value will be null. Correspondingly, if an employee has a manager,
but is not assigned to a project, the project value will be null.

It is possible to cluster the typing function of a given type with other
predicates if the type coincides with the clustering parameters. Thus, the
command:

> **store** Employee, Project **on** Employee, Manager **on** Subordinate

causes the instances of the Employee type, the Project predicate, and the
Manager predicate to be stored together in the same table. The table has
three columns, one corresponding to Employee objects, one to Project
objects, and one to Supervisor (also employee) objects. Now the clustering

column will contain all employees, with unassigned employees having a null project and a null supervisor.

When a function stored with an **on** clause is a unary predicate, a column is generated to contain the Boolean value of the predicate. Consider, for example, the predicate:

```
Exempt: Employee [1, 1] -> Boolean
```

The following Store command will create a table with two columns:

```
store Employee, Exempt on Employee
```

The clustering column is of type Employee. The other column, which corresponds to the predicate Exempt, is of type Boolean.

2.7.2 Index

The Index command creates search indexes for the tables created by the Store command. The command:

```
index Project on Employee
```

causes an index to be created for the table used to implement the Project predicate. The index is defined on the column which corresponds to the Employee parameter of Project.

2.8 Future Directions

The model presented above is a subset of a full Iris Data Model which has not yet been finalized; being a research prototype, it is subject to change.

The full Iris Data Model will eventually support a modularization mechanism that allows related functions to be grouped together in modules. Functions visible within a module can then be specified to be invisible outside the module or visible only in certain other modules. That way, data encapsulation will be supported.

The full model will also support the specification of semantic integrity constraints that are more general than the object participation constraints currently supported.

3   Design Methodology

The design methodology supported by the Iris Data Model is a data-driven approach to software design and development. The methodology applies both to vendor systems and to user applications. It is an extension of the fact-based data analysis and design described in [Kent83b]. The principal steps of designing a given application are:

1.   Definition of the application's object (entity) types (3.1).

2.   Definition of the type structure (3.1).

3.   Definition of the fundamental relationships among the objects. These relationships correspond to "facts" in [Kent83b] (3.2).

4.   Definition of the properties of the objects (3.3).

5.   Definition of the dependencies among properties (3.3).

6.   Definition of semantic integrity constraints (3.4).

7.   Definition of application-oriented operations (3.5).

8.   Definition of modules for data encapsulation and protection (3.7).

9.   Specification of the physical realization of types and properties (3.6).

Definition of the object types and the type structure is supported by Iris type definitions (Section 3.1). The fundamental relationships among the types are supported by Iris predicates (Section 3.2). Properties of objects and their interdependencies are supported by Iris functions and function derivations (Section 3.3). The specification of general integrity constraints is currently not supported by the Iris prototype (Section 3.4). The definition of operations will be supported by procedurally defined Iris functions. These functions are defined in terms of other functions that are either stored, derived, or procedurally defined (Section 3.5). Modules are currently not supported by the Iris prototype (Section 3.6). The specification of a physical realization is supported by the materialization of Iris functions as stored data.

Below, the Iris database system is itself defined in such terms. Users will define their own applications in similar terms. When they are finished, the system will contain a combination of system-defined and user-defined objects, types, functions, constraints, operations, and modules. It is beyond the scope of this paper to give guidelines for finding the "best" design of a given application.

3.1 System-Defined Types

The semantics of the database commands are defined by functions on objects of system-defined types. Some of these types are defined below:

Object   The type Object is the root of the type structure. It contains every object including itself, and it is the supertype of every type except itself.

Function   The type Function contains every function. It is an immediate subtype of Object.

Type   The type Type contains every type, including itself. It is an immediate subtype of Object.

UserType   The type UserType contains every user-defined type, i.e., types created by the NewType command. System-defined types are not contained in UserType. UserType is an immediate subtype of Type.

UserTypeObject   The type UsertypeObject contains all user-defined objects, i.e., objects created by the NewObject command. It is the supertype of every user-defined type, and it is an immediate subtype of Object.

The Iris meta-data is represented by objects that are instances of some of the system-defined types. An instance of the system-defined type Function, for example, represents an Iris function; an object which belongs to the system-defined type UserType represents a user-defined type.

Fig. 1 shows part of the Iris type structure. Not all the system-defined types are shown in the figure. User-defined types appear in the type graph as direct or indirect subtypes of UserTypeObject.

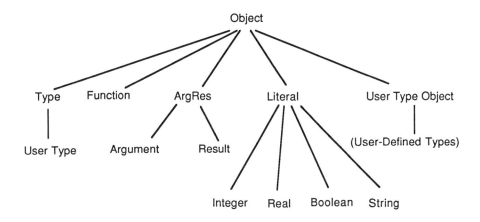

Fig. 1:   *Type Structure*

The system-defined types also have associated typing functions. For example, the typing function associated with the type UserTypeObject:

```
UserTypeObject: Object [1, 1] -> Boolean
```

maps an object to True if the object is an instance of a user-defined type. The typing function associated with the type UserType:

```
UserType:  Object [1, 1] -> Boolean
```

maps a type object to True if the type is user-defined, and the typing function Integer:

```
Integer:  Object [1, 1] -> Boolean
```

maps an object to True if the object is an integer.

3.2 System-Defined Predicate Functions

The objects representing meta-data are interrelated to one another by a number of system-defined predicates. For example, the object representing a given type must be related, via appropriate predicates, to other objects representing the type's name, subtypes and supertypes, typing function, and instances.

TypeName is an example of a system-defined predicate. It expresses the fact that every type must have a unique name. TypeName is defined as follows:

```
TypeName:   Type [1, 1] x String [0, 1] -> Boolean
```

Since the minimum object participation of the Type parameter is 1, every Type instance must be related to a String object by the TypeName predicate, since the maximum object participation of the Type parameter is 1, a given Type instance can be related only to a single String object. Furthermore, since the maximum object participation of the String Parameter is 1, a given String object can be related to at most one Type instance by the TypeName predicate.

The predicate TypeName is one of many system-defined predicates. Additional predicates are defined below:

```
TypingFunction: Type [1, 1] x Function [0, 1] -> Boolean
```

Each type has an associated typing function. The typing function maintains the instances of the type.

```
SubSuper:   Subtype/Type [0, m] x Supertype/Type [0, m] ->
            Boolean
```

Each type has zero or more subtypes and zero or more supertypes. As illustrated in Section 3.4 in a constraint, all types except "Object" have at least one supertype.

```
UserType:   Type [1, 1]  -> Boolean
```

A type is either user-defined or system-defined. A system-defined type cannot be deleted and instances cannot be added to it directly by the user.

The system-defined predicates introduced so far all describe Type objects. There are many more predicates describing functions, and argument and result parameters. Functions, for example, are described by their names, argument and result counts, function bodies, and dependent functions (in case of function derivations). Argument and result parameters are described by their names, types, functions, minimum and maximum object participations, and positions in the argument or result lists of their functions.

3.3 Derived System Functions

Various uses of the system-defined base predicates can be expressed more conveniently in terms of functions derived from the base predicates. Some of these system-defined derived functions, which are used to define the semantics of the database commands, are introduced below:

```
NameOfType:  Type -> String
NameOfType(t)  ::=  find s/String where TypeName(t, s)

TypingFunctionOf:  Type -> Function
TypingFunctionOf(t)  ::=
        find f/Function where TypingFunction(t,f)

Supertypes: Subtype/Type -> Supertype/Type
Supertypes(sub)  ::=  find sup/Type where SubSuper(sub,sup)
```

The function TypeInstance, defined below, is a derived predicate. An object is an instance of a type if the corresponding typing function is true for the object:

```
TypeInstance:  Type x Object  ->  Boolean
TypeInstance(t,o)  ::= find where TypingFunctionOf(t)(o)
```

Some of the object-oriented aspects of the data model are expressed by derived functions that are defined on a single type. Such functions can be grouped together according to the types of their arguments. That way, a grouping of a set of functions define the "properties" of a type.

The properties of Type objects, for example, may include Supertypes, Subtypes, Instances, and NameOfType:

```
Type
      NameOfType
      Instances
      Supertypes
      Subtypes
```

Supertypes and NameOfType are derived above. The functions Instances and Subtypes can be derived in a similar manner from the predicates Type Instance (which is derived from TypingFunction) and SubSuper, respectively.

3.4 System Constraints

Constraint enforcement is not included in the subset of the Iris model currently implemented. For illustrative purposes, we show some constraints applicable to the functions defined above.

The type Object is the one and only type having no supertype:

```
NameOfType(t) =
         'Object' <=> not for some s/Type SubSuper(t,s)
```

There is no closed loop of subtypes:

```
not for some t/Type,s/Type SubSuper(t,s) and SubSuper(s,t)
```

The type UserTypeObject contains all user-defined objects:

```
UserTypeObject(o) <=>
            for some t/Type TypeInstance(t,o) and UserType(t)
```

(UserTypeObject could actually be defined this way.)

The database commands must guarantee that those constraints are satisfied.

3.5 Semantics of the Iris Database Commands

In this section we illustrate how the abstract semantics of the database commands AddInstance, NewObject, and Newtype can be formally defined.

The semantics of the Iris database commands are defined by a collection of Iris operations. In future versions of the prototype, Iris operations will be supported by procedurally defined functions. The operations manipulate the system-defined types and predicates, and they may call other operations that define parts of the semantics. In this paper, a Pascal-like language serves as our procedural language and only four Iris primitives are used:

NEW   Introduces a new object of type Object to the database.

DELETE   Deletes an existing object from the database.

SET   Assigns a new value to a single-valued function.

FIND   Returns the objects that satisfy a given Boolean expression.

In order to be able to distinguish between the database commands being defined and the primitives used to define them, the primitives are all written in upper case letters. The keywords of the host programming language are written in boldface.

3.5.1 AddInstance

The AddInstance command adds a user-defined object to the extension of a user-defined type and all its supertypes:

```
1.         AddInstance(o: UsertypeObject, t: UserType)
2.         {
3.             AddToType(o,t);
4.         }
```

1.   AddInstance is a database command. It takes as parameters a user-defined object and a user-defined type.

3.   The semantics of adding an object to a type are defined by the AddToType operation (see below). By introducing the operation AddToType, several other operations, such as NewObject and NewType, can share the definition of adding an object to a type.

```
5.         AddToType(o: Object, t: Type)
6.         {
7.             var s: Type;
8.             SET TypingFunctionOf(t)(o) = True;
9.             foreach s in Supertypes(t)
10.                SET TypingFunctionOf(s)(o) = True;
11.        }
```

5.   AddToType defines the semantics of adding an object to a type. The operation, which is not constrained to user-defined objects and user-defined types, is not directly available to users (an example of modularization).

8.   Add the object as an instance of the type by setting the value of the associated typing function to True.

9.-10.   Add the object as an instance of all the supertypes.

3.5.2 NewObject

The NewObject command creates a new user-defined object and adds it to a user-defined type and all its supertypes. The semantics of NewObject are defined in terms of AddToType:

```
1.         NewObject (t: UserType): UserTypeObject
2.         {
3.             var o: Object;
4.             o:= NEW();
```

```
5.            AddToType(o,t);
6.            return (o);
7.        }
```

1.   NewObject is a database command. It takes a user-defined type as a parameter and returns a user-defined object.

4.   Create the new object using the NEW primitive.

5.   Add the new object as an instance of the type and all its supertypes.

6.   Return the object.

3.5.3 NewType

The NewType command creates a new user-defined type of a specified name and makes it a subtype of specified supertypes. If the set of user-types is empty the new type becomes an immediate subtype of User Type Object. The semantics of NewType are defined in terms of AddToType:

```
1.        NewType (name:String,super:set of UserType):UserType
2.        {
3.            var t, s1, s2: Type;
4.            t:= NEW();
5.            AddToType (t, UserType);
6.            SET NameOfType(t) = name;
7.            NewTypingFct (name);
8.            foreach s1 in super do
9.            {
10.               SET SubSuper(t,s1) = True;
11.               foreach s2 in Supertypes(s1)
12.               SET SubSuper(t,s2) = True;
13.           }
14.           SET SubSuper(t, UserTypeObject);
15.           Return(t);
16.       }
```

1.   NewType is a database command. It takes as parameters a string object and a possibly empty set of user-defined types, and it returns a user-defined type.

4.   Create a new object using the NEW primitive.

5.   Add the new object as an instance of the type UserType.

6.   Set the name of the type. The object participations of the system-defined predicate TypeName will cause the SET operation to fail if the specified type name is not unique with respect to other type names.

7.   Create the associated typing function. It is beyond the scope of this paper to define the operation NewTypingFct. In general, NewTypingFct is a specialization of the NewFunction database command.

8.   For each specified supertype ...

10.   Make the new type its subtype.

11.-12.   The new type is also a subtype of all the supertype's supertypes.

14.   Make the new type a subtype of the type UserTypeObject. This must
            be done explicitly in case the set of supertypes is empty.

15.   Return the new type.

3.6 Modularization

As mentioned before, modularization is not part of the subset of the Iris model
currently implemented. However, if a module construct were available one
can imagine a grouping of the functions and operations introduced above into
two kinds of modules, system modules and user modules.

The system modules would contain functions and operations that are not
made available to the end-user of the system. The operation AddToType is an
example of an operation that belongs to a system module. The user modules
would contain all the database commands, e.g., AddInstance, NewObject,
NewType, that are available to the end-user.

3.7 Implementing the Model

The abstract semantics defined in the previous two sections can be turned into
an implementation of the specified system. The idea is to implement the
operations as programs that manipulate a system catalog. The system catalog
is an implementation of the system-defined types and predicates.

In order to define the system catalog, we must specify its data structures
and show how the predicates can be mapped onto these data structures. The
system catalog can be automatically generated by applying the database
design commands Store and Index to the system-defined predicates. That
way, the system catalog designer does not have to deal with the details of
building the catalog. Rather, he must understand the semantics of the
database design commands used to create the catalog.

We will now show how the Store and Index commands can be used to
define an implementation of the system-defined predicates. In this particular
implementation, the predicates describing Type objects will be represented by
two tables in the system catalog. The two tables are called Type Table and
SubSuper Table, and they maintain information about the types and the
subtype/supertype relationships, respectively.

The Type Table is described by the following Store and Index commands:

```
store Type, TypeName on Type, TypingFunction on Type,
UserType on Type
index Type on Object, TypeName on String
```

When predicates are stored in a table, each argument parameter of a
predicate corresponds to a column in a table. In describing a column of the
table, there are three things to be identified:

1.   The predicate whose parameter maps to the column.

2.   The particular parameter of the predicate which is mapping to the
      column.

3. The object type of that parameter. Data entries in this column are constrained to objects of that type.

Fig. 2 illustrates these three specification items for the Type Table. A special convention is used for the first column. Since this is the clustering column (corresponding to the **on** parameters of the Store command), all the predicates have one argument which maps to this column. In truth, all four predicates are supported by the first column, not just the Type predicate.

The Type Table has four columns. The first column, the clustering column, contains the type objects. The second column contains the type names, the third the typing function objects, and the fourth column, which corresponds to the unary predicate function UserType, contains Boolean values.

Fig. 2 shows the types of the four columns and the names of the parameters of the predicate functions to which the columns correspond.

	Column	Column 2	Column3	Column 4
Column Type:	Type	String	Function	Boolean
Predicate:	Type	TypeName	TypingFunction	UserType
Parameter:	Object	String	Function	Boolean

Fig. 2: *Type Table Specification*

The Type Table has an index on column 1 and column 2.

The data entries for an example Type Table are illustrated in Fig. 3. The Type Table describes four types, one of which is system-defined (e.g., Function) and three of which are user-defined. Notice how the unary predicate function UserType is implemented by a Boolean-valued column (e.g., column 4) of Type Table.

Column 1	Column 2	Column 3	Column 4
type 1	Function	func7	False
type 2	Person	func88	True
type 3	Employee	func108	True
type 4	Department	func112	True

Fig. 3: *An Example Type Table*

When functions are derived from predicates whose values are stored in a table, the values of those functions are simultaneously being maintained in the table. For example, the arguments to NameOfType (Section 3.3) are looked up in the first column of the Type Table, and the results are taken from the second column.

The SubSuper Table is described by the following store and Index commands:

store SubSuper

index SubSuper **on** Subtype, Supertype

The SubSuper Table has two columns. The types of the columns and the names of the parameters of the predicate functions to which the columns correspond are illustrated in Fig. 4.

	Column 1	Column2
Column Type:	Type	Type
Predicate:	SubSuper	SubSuper
Parameter:	SubType	SuperType

Fig. 4:   *SubSuper Table Specification*

The SubSuper Table has an index on column 1 and column 2.

Now, given a system catalog consisting of a collection of tables like the ones described above, the operations on the system-defined predicates and derived functions can be implemented by programs that query and manipulate the tables.

4   Conclusions

In this paper we have described a tool and a methodology for the design and implementation of information systems. The methodology can be applied to other kinds of software development as well. The methodology, which is data driven, suggests the use of a semantically powerful object-oriented data model as a tool for formal specifications of the abstract semantics of software systems. An abstract specification precisely defines the semantics of the operations of the system under consideration and it is a basis on which an actual implementation of the system can be built.

The methodology was applied to the specification of the semantics of the object-oriented data model supporting the methodology and it was shown how database design commands, e.g., the Store and Index commands, might be used to refine the abstract specification to an actual implementation of an object-oriented database system.

The proposed methodology is an attempt to close the gap between the fields of semantic data modeling, formal specification languages, and software engineering. Instead of using different techniques and tools for the various tasks that occur during the life cycle of an information system, i.e., formal definitions, software development, maintenance, and use, we suggest collecting all of these tasks under one umbrella: the data model.

5   Acknowledgements

The object-oriented data model and the methodology for software design proposed in this paper are parts of the Iris Database Project at Hewlett-Packard Laboratories.

The authors would like to thank Nigel Derrett, Tom Ryan, and Arun Swami for their helpful comments on earlier versions of this paper.

6   References

[Abri74], [BeFe83], [Beki74], [BjJo78], [BjLo82], [BjOe80], [Catt80], [Cham76], [Chen76], [ClMe81], [Codd79], [CoLy88], [Date81], [DeKL85], [Derr86], [Donz80], [Fish87], [Gord79], [GoRo83], [HaMc81], [Kent78], [Kent83b], [Kulk83], [LyMc84a], [LyMc84b], [LyVi87], [Mark85], [MyBW80], [Ship81], [SmSm77a], [Zloo77].

Part VI

Architecture

15

The Architecture of the EXODUS Extensible DBMS

Michael J. Carey, David J. DeWitt, Daniel Frank, Goetz Graefe,

Joel E. Richardson, Eugene J. Shekita, M. Muralikrishna

Abstract

With non-traditional application areas such as engineering design, image/voice data management, scientific/statistical applications, and artificial intelligence systems all clamoring for ways to store and efficiently process larger and larger volumes of data, it is clear that traditional database technology has been pushed to its limits. It also seems clear that no single database system will be capable of simultaneously meeting the functionality and performance requirements of such a diverse set of applications. In this paper we describe the initial design of EXODUS, an extensible database system that will facilitate the fast development of high-performance, application-specific database systems. EXODUS provides certain kernel facilities, including a versatile storage manager and a type manager. In addition, it provides an architectural framework for building application-specific database systems, tools to partially automate the generation of such systems, and libraries of software components (e.g., access methods) that are likely to be useful for many application domains.

1 Introduction

Until recently, research and development efforts in the database management systems area have focused on supporting traditional business applications. The design of database systems capable of supporting non-traditional application areas, including engineering applications for CAD/CAM and VLSI data, scientific and statistical applications, expert database systems, and image/voice applications, has emerged as an important new research direction. These new applications differ from conventional applications such as transaction processing and from each other in a number of important ways. First, each requires a different set of data modeling tools. The types of entities

This research was partially supported by the Defense Advanced Research Projects Agency under contract N00014-85-K0788, by the Department of Energy under contract #DE-AC02-81ER10920, by the National Science Foundation under grants MCS82-01870 and DCR-8402818, and by an IBM Faculty Development Award.

and relationships that must be described for a VLSI circuit design are quite different from those of a banking application. Second, each new application area has a specialized set of operations that must be efficiently supported by the database system. It makes little sense to talk about doing joins between satellite images. Efficient support for the specialized operations of each new application area is likely to require new types of storage structures and access methods as well. For example, R-Trees [Gutt84] are a useful access method for storing and manipulating VLSI data. For managing image data, the database system needs to support large multidimensional arrays as a basic data type; storing images as tuples in a relational database system is generally either impossible or terribly inefficient. Finally, a number of new application areas require support for multiple versions of entities [DaSm86, KaCB86].

Recently, a number of new database system research projects have been initiated to address the needs of this emerging class of applications: EXODUS[1] at the University of Wisconsin [CaDe85, CDRS86], PROBE at CCA [DaSm86, MaDa86], POSTGRES [StRo86, Ston] at Berkeley, GEMSTONE at Servio Logic Corporation [CoMa84, MSOP86], STARBURST at IBM Almaden Research Center [Schw86], and GENESIS [Bato86] at the University of Texas-Austin. Although the goals of these projects are similar, and each uses some of the same mechanisms to provide extensibility, the overall approach of each project is quite different. For example, POSTGRES will be a more "complete" database management system, with a query language (POSTQUEL), a predefined way of supporting complex objects (through the use of POSTQUEL and procedures as a data type), support for "active" databases via triggers and alerters, and inferencing. Extensibility will be provided via new data types, operators, access methods, and a simplified recovery mechanism. A stated goal is to "make as few changes as possible to the relational model". The objective of the PROBE project, on the other hand, is to develop an advanced DBMS with support for complex objects and operations on them, dimensional data (in both space and time dimensions), and a capability for intelligent query processing. Unlike POSTGRES, PROBE will provide a mechanism for directly representing complex objects. Like EXODUS, PROBE will use a rule-based approach to query optimization so that the query optimizer may be extended to handle new database operators, new methods for existing operators, and new data types. An extended version for DAPLEX [Ship81] is to be used as the query language for PROBE. GEMSTONE, with its query language OPAL, is a complete object-oriented database system that encapsulates a variety of ideas from the areas of knowledge representation, object-oriented and non-procedural programming, set-theoretic data models, and temporal data modeling. STARBURST is an architecture for an extensible DBMS based on the relational data model, and its design is intended to allow knowledgable programmers to add extensions "on the side" in the form of abstract data types, access methods, and external storage structures.

In contrast to these efforts, and like GENESIS, EXODUS is being designed as a modular (and modifiable) system rather than as a "complete" database system intended to handle all new application areas. In some sense, EXODUS is a software engineering project - the goal is to provide a collection of kernel DBMS facilities plus software tools to facilitate the semi-automatic generation of high-performance, application-specific DBMSs for new applications. In this paper we describe the overall architecture of EXODUS. Section 2 presents an overview of the components of EXODUS. Section 3 describes the lowest level of th system, the Storage Object Manager,

---

[1] EXODUS: A departure, in this case, from the ways of the past. Also an EXtensible Object-oriented Database System.

summarizing material from [CDRS86]. Section 4 describes the EXODUS Type Manager, which provides (among other things) a general schema management facility that can be extended with application-specific abstract data types. Section 5 addresses a difficult task in extending a database system: the addition of new access methods. EXODUS simplifies this task by hiding most of the storage, concurrency control, and recovery issues from the access method implementor via a new programming language, E; E is an extension of C that includes support for persistent objects via the Storage Object Manager of EXODUS. Section 6 discusses how application-specific database operations are implemented in EXODUS, and Section 7 describes the rule-based approach to query optimization employed in EXODUS. Section 8 outlines some of the user interface issues that lie ahead, and Section 9 briefly summarizes the paper and discusses our implementation plans.

2   An Overview of the EXODUS Architecture

In this section we describe the architecture of the EXODUS database system. Since one of the principal goals of the EXODUS project is to construct an extensible yet high-performance database system, the design reflects a careful balance between what EXODUS provides the user[2] and what the user must explicitly provide. Unlike POSTGRES and PROBE, EXODUS is not intended to be a complete system with provisions for user-added extensions. Rather, it is intended more as a toolbox that can be easily adapted to satisfy the needs of new application areas. Two basic mechanisms are employed to help achieve this goal: where feasible, we furnish a generic solution that should be applicable to any application-specific database system. As an example, EXODUS supplies at its lowest level a layer of software termed the Storage Object Manager which provides support for concurrent and recoverable operations on arbitrary size storage objects. Our feeling is that this level provides sufficient capabilities such that user-added extensions will most probably be unnecessary. However, due to both generality and efficiency considerations, a single generic solution is not possible for every component of a database system.

In cases where one generic solution is inappropriate, EXODUS instead provides either a **generator** or a **library** to aid the user in generating the appropriate software. As an example, we expect EXODUS to be used for a wide variety of applications, each with a potentially different query language. As a result, it is not possible for EXODUS to furnish a single generic query language, and it is accordingly impossible for a single query optimizer to suffice for all applications. Instead, we provide a generator for producing query optimizers for algebraic languages. The EXODUS query optimizer generator takes as input a collection of rules regarding the operators of the query language, the transformations that can be legally applied to these operators (e.g., pushing selections before joins), and a description of the methods that can be used to execute each operator (including their costs and side effects); as output, it produces an optimizer for the application's query language in the form of C source code.

In a conventional database system environment it is customary to consider the roles of two different classes of individuals: the database administrator and the user. In EXODUS, a third type of individual is required to customize EXODUS into an application-specific database system. While we referred to

---

[2] Our use of the word *user* will be more carefully explained in the following paragraphs.

this individual as a "user" in the preceding paragraphs, he or she is not a user in the normal sense (i.e., an end user, such as a bank teller or a cartographer). Internally, we refer to this "user" of the EXODUS facilities as a "database implementor" or DBI. While the Jim Grays of the world would clearly make outstanding DBIs, our goal is to engineer EXODUS so that only a moderate amount of expertise is required to architect a new system using its tools. Once EXODUS has been customized into an application-specific database system, the DBI's role is completed and the role of the database administrator begins.

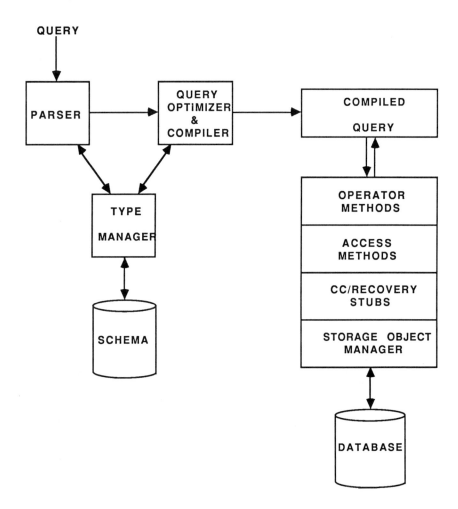

Fig. 1:   *EXODUS System Architecture*

We present an overview of the design of EXODUS in the remainder of this section. While EXODUS is a toolkit and not a complete DBMS, we find that it is clearer to describe the system from the viewpoint of an application-specific database system that was constructed using it. In doing so, we hope to make it clear which pieces of the system are provided without modification, which must be produced using one of the EXODUS generators, and which must be directly implemented by the DBI using the E programming language.

2.1 EXODUS System Architecture

Fig. 1 presents the structure of an application-specific database management system implemented using EXODUS. The following tools are provided to aid the DBI in the task of generating such a system:

1. The Storage Object Manager.

2. The E programming language and its compiler for writing database system software.

3. A generalized Type Manager for defining and maintaining schema information.

4. A library of type independent access methods which can be used to associatively access storage objects.

5. Lock manager and recovery protocol stubs to simplify the task of writing new access methods and other database operators.

6. A rule-based query optimizer and compiler.

7. Tools for constructing user front ends.

At the bottom level of the system is the Storage Object Manager. The basic abstraction at this level is the storage object, an untyped, uninterpreted variable-length byte sequence of arbitrary size. The Storage Object Manager provides capabilities for reading, writing, and updating storage objects (or pieces of them) without regard for their size. To further enhance the functionality provided by this level, buffer management, concurrency control, and recovery mechanisms for operations on shared storage objects are also provided. Finally, a versioning mechanism that can be used to implement a variety of application-specific versioning schemes is supported. A more detailed description of the Storage Object Manager and its capabilities is presented in Section 3.

Although not shown in Fig. 1, which depicts the runtime structure of an EXODUS-based DBMS, the next major component is the E programming language and compiler. E is the implementation language for all components of the system for which the DBI must provide code. E extends C by adding abstract data types and a notion of persistent object pointers to the language's type definition repertoire. For the most part, references to persistent objects look just like references to other C structures; the DBI's index code can thus deal with index nodes as arrays of key-pointer pairs, for example. Whenever persistent objects are referenced, the E translator is responsible for adding the appropriate calls to fix/unfix buffers, read/write the appropriate piece of the underlying storage object, lock/unlock objects, log images and events, etc. Thus, the DBI is freed from having to worry about the internal structure of persistent objects. For buffering, concurrency control and recovery, the E language includes statements for associating locking, buffering, and recovery protocols with variables that reference persistent objects. Thus, the DBI is provided with a mechanism by which he or she can exercise control (declaratively) - insuring that the appropriate mechanisms are employed. E should not be confused with either database programming languages such as RIGEL [RoSh79], Pascal/R [Schm77], Theseus [Shop79], or PLAIN [KeWa81], as these languages were intended to simplify the development of database applications code through a closer integration of database and programming language constructs, or with object-oriented query languages such as OPAL [CoMa84, MSOP86] - the objective of E is to simplify the development of **internal** systems software for a DBMS.

Layered above the Storage Object Manager is a collection of access methods that provide associative access to files of storage objects and further support for versioning (if desired). For access methods, EXODUS will provide a library of type-independent index structures including B+ trees, Grid files [NiHS84], and linear hashing [Litw80]. These access methods will be implemented using the "type parameter" capability provided by the E language (as described in Section 5). This capability enables existing access methods to be used with DBI-defined abstract data types without modification - as long as the capabilities provided by the data type satisfy the requirements of the access methods. In addition, a DBI may wish to implement new types of access methods in the process of developing an application-specific database system. EXODUS provides two mechanisms to greatly simplify this task. First, since new access methods are written in E, the DBI is shielded from having to map main memory data structures onto storage objects and from having to write code to deal with locking, buffering, and recovery protocols. EXODUS also simplifies the task of handling concurrency control and recovery for new access methods using a form of layered transactions, as discussed in Section 5.

While the capabilities provided by the Storage Object Manager and Access Methods Layer are general purpose and are intended to be utilized in each application-specific DBMS constructed using EXODUS, the third layer in the design, the Operator Methods Layer, contains a mix of DBI-supplied code and EXODUS-supplied code. As implied by its name, this layer contains a collection of methods that can be combined with one another in order to operate on (typed) storage objects. EXODUS will provide a library of methods for a number of operators that operate on a single type of storage object (e.g., selection), but it will not provide application or data model specific methods. For example, it cannot provide methods for implementing the relational join operator or for examining an object containing satellite image data for the signature of a particular crop disease. In general, the DBI will need to implement one or more methods for each operator in the query language associated with the target application. E will again serve as the implementation language for this task.

At the center of EXODUS architecture is the Type Manager. The EXODUS Type Manager is designed to provide schema support for a wide variety of application-specific database systems. The data modeling facilities provided by EXODUS are those of the type system of the E programming language, with the Type Manager acting as a repository (or "persistent symbol table") for E type definitions. The type system of E includes a set of primitive, built-in types (e.g., int, float, char), a set of type constructors (record, union, variant, fixed-length array, and insertable array or variable-length sequence), and an abstract data type (ADT) facility which allows the DBI to define new data types and operations. In addition, the Type Manager maintains the associations between EXODUS files and the E types of the objects that they contain; it also keeps track of type-related dependencies that arise between types and other types, files and types, stored queries and types, etc. In designing the type facilities of EXODUS, our goal was to provide a set of facilities that would allow the capabilities of the Storage Object Manager to be exploited, and that would allow the modeling needs of a wide range of applications to be handled with little or no loss of efficiency[3]. Section 4 presents a more detailed overview of the capabilities provided by the Type Manager, including a discussion of its dependency-maintenance role.

Execution of a query in EXODUS follows a set of transformations similar to that of a relational query in System R [Astr76]. After parsing, the query is optimized, and then compiled into an executable form. The parser is responsible for transforming the query from its initial form into an initial tree of database operators. During the parsing and optimization phases, the Type Manager is invoked to extract the necessary schema information. The executable form produced by the query compiler consists of a rearranged tree of operator methods (i.e., particular instances of each operator) to which query specific information such as selection predicates (e.g., name = "Mike" and salary > $200,000) will be passed as parameters. As mentioned earlier, EXODUS provides a generator for producing the optimization portion of the query compiler. To produce an optimizer for an application-specific database system, the DBI must supply a description of the operators of the target query language, a list of the methods that can be used to implement each operator, a cost formula for each operator method, and a collection of transformation rules. The optimizer generator will transform these description files into C source code for an optimizer for the target query language. At query execution time, this optimizer behaves as we have just described, taking a query expressed as a tree of operators and transforming it into an optimized execution plan expressed as a tree of methods.

Finally, the organization of the top level of a database system generated using EXODUS will depend on whether the goal is to support some sort of interactive interface, an embedded query interface such as EQUEL [AlHS76], or an altogether different form of interface. We plan to provide a generator to facilitate the creation of interactive interfaces, and we are exploring the use of the Cornell Program Synthesizer Generator [ReTe84] as a user interface generator for EXODUS[4]. This tool provides the facilities needed for implementing structured editors for a wide variety of programming languages, the goal of such editors being to help programmers formulate syntactically and semantically correct programs. Since the syntax and semantics of typical query languages are much simpler than that of most modern programming languages, it is clear that we will be able to apply the tool in this way; it remains to be seen whether or not it is really "too powerful" (i.e., overkill) for our needs. As for supporting queries that are embedded programs, two options exist. First, if the program simply contains calls to operator methods, bypassing the parser and optimizer, then a linker can be used to bind the program with the necessary methods (which can be viewed as a library of procedures). The second option, which will be a difficult task, is to provide a generalized tool to handle programs with embedded queries (ala EQUEL). It will be relatively easy to provide a generic preprocessor which will extract queries and replace them with calls to object modules produced by the parser, optimizer, and compiler; however, it is unclear how to make the underlying interface between the application program and database system independent of the (application-specific) data model. For example, in the relational model a tuple-at-a-time or portal [StRo84] interface is commonly used, whereas with the Codasyl data model, the database system and application program

---

3 While we initially considered providing a generalized class hierarchy, such a facility can be efficiently supported on top of the type facilities that we provide. We also felt that different applications would be likely to want very different things from such a hierarchy.

4 We have experimented with the idea of generating a QUEL-like interface using this tool.

exchange currency indicators as well as record occurrences. These issues
will be explored further in the future.

3   The Storage Object Manager

In this section we summarize the key features of the design of the EXODUS
Storage Object Manager. We begin by discussing the interface that the
Storage Object Manager provides to higher levels of the system, and then we
describe how arbitrarily large storage objects are handled efficiently. We
discuss the techniques employed for versioning, concurrency control,
recovery, and buffer management for storage objects, and we close with a
brief discussion about files of storage objects (known as file objects). A more
detailed discussion of these issues can be found in [CDRS86].

3.1 The Storage Object Manager Interface

The Storage Object Manager provides a procedural interface. This interface
includes procedures to create and destroy file objects and to open and close
file objects for file scans. For scanning purposes, the Storage Object Manager
provides a call to get the object ID of the next object within a file object. It also
provides procedures for creating and destroying storage objects within a file.
For reading storage objects, the Storage Object Manager provides a call to
get a pointer to a range of bytes within a given storage object; the desired byte
range is read into the buffers, and a pointer to the bytes there are returned to
the caller. Another call is provided to inform EXODUS that these bytes are no
longer needed, which "unpins" them in the buffer pool. For writing storage
objects, a call is provided to tell EXODUS that a subrange of the bytes that
were read have been modified (information that is needed for recovery to take
place). for shrinking/growing storage objects, calls to insert bytes into and
delete bytes from a specified offset in a storage object are provided, as is a
call to append bytes to the end of an object. Finally, for transaction
management, the Storage Object Manager provides begin, commit, and abort
transaction calls; additional hooks are provided to aid the access methods
layer in implementing concurrent and recoverable operations for new access
methods efficiently (as discussed in Section 5).

   In addition to the functionality outlined above, the Storage Object Manager
is designed to accept a variety of performance-related hints. For example, the
object creation routine mentioned above accepts hints about where to place a
new object (i.e., "place the new object near the object with id X") and about
how large the object is expected to be (on the average, if it varies); it is also
possible to hint that an object should be alone on a disk page and the same
size as the page (which will be useful for the access methods level). The
buffer manager accepts hints about the size and number of buffers to use and
what replacement policy to employ. These hints will be supported by allowing
a *scan group* to be specified with each object access, and then having the
buffer manager accept these hints on a per-scan-group basis, allowing easy
support of buffer management policies like DBMIN [ChDe85].

3.2 Storage Objects and Operations

As described earlier, the storage object is the basic unit of data in the Storage Object Manager. Storage objects can be either small or large, a distinction that is hidden from higher layers of EXODUS software. Small storage objects reside on a single disk page, whereas large storage objects occupy potentially many disk pages. In either case, the object identifier (OID) of a storage object is an address of the form (*page #, slot #*). The OID of a small storage object points to the object on disk; for a large storage object, the OID points to its *large object header*. A large object header can reside on a slotted page with other large object headers and small storage objects, and it contains pointers to other pages involved in the representation of the large object. Other pages in large storage objects are private rather than being shared with other objects (although pages are shared between versions of a storage object). When a small storage object grows to the point where it can no longer be accomodated on a single page, the Storage Object Manager will automatically convert it into a large storage object, leaving its object header in place of the original small object. We considered the alternative of using logical surrogates for OID's rather than physical addresses, as in other recent proposals [CoMa84, StRo86], but efficiency considerations led us to opt for a "physical surrogate" scheme - with logical surrogates, it would always be necessary to access objects via a dense surrogate index[5].

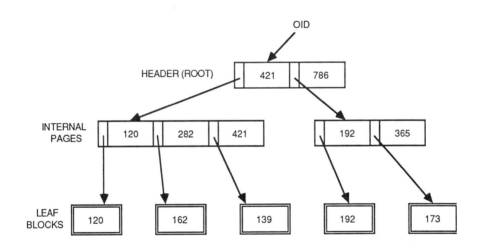

Fig. 2:   *An Example of a largestorage object*

Fig. 2 shows an example of our large object data structure; it was inspired by Stonebraker's ordered relations structure [Ston83a], but there are a number of significant differences [CDRS86]. Conceptually, a large object is an

---

[5] This is true unless the objects are kept sorted on surrogate ID. In this case, a non-dense surrogate index can be used.

uninterpreted byte sequence; physically, it is represented as a B+ tree like index on byte position within the object plus a collection of leaf blocks (with all data bytes residing in the leaves). The large object header contains a number of (*count, page #*) pairs, one for each child of the root. The count value associated with each child pointer gives the maximum byte number stored in the subtree rooted at that child, and the rightmost child pointer's count is therefore also the size of the object. Internal nodes are similar, being recursively defined as the root of another object contained within its parent node, so an absolute byte offset within a child translates to a relative offset within its parent node. The left child of the root in Fig. 2 contains bytes 1-421, and the right child contains the rest of the object (bytes 422-786). The rightmost leaf node in the figure contains 173 bytes of data. Byte 100 within this leaf node is byte 192 + 100 = 292 within the right child of the root, and it is byte 421 + 292 = 713 within the object as a whole. Searching is accomplished by computing overall offset information while descending the tree to the desired byte position. As described in [CDRS86], object sizes up to 1 GB or so can be supported with only three tree levels (header and leaf levels included).

Associated with the large storage object data structure are algorithms to *search* for a range of bytes (and perhaps update them), to *insert* a sequence of bytes at a given point in the object, to *append* a sequence of bytes to the end of the object, and to *delete* a sequence of bytes from a given point in the object. The insert, append, and delete operations are novel because inserting or deleting an arbitrary number of bytes (as opposed to a single byte) into a large storage object poses some unique problems compared to inserting or deleting a single record from an ordered relation. Algorithms for these operations are described in detail in [CDRS86] along with results from an experimental evaluation of their storage utilization and performance characteristics. The evaluation showed that the EXODUS storage object mechanism can provide operations on very large dynamic objects at relatively low cost, and at a reasonable level of storage utilization (typically 80% or higher).

3.3   Versions of Storage Objects

The Storage Object Manager provides primitive support for versions of storage objects. One version of each storage object is retained as the current version, and all of the preceding versions are simply marked (in their object headers) as being old versions. The reasons for only providing a primitive level of version support is that different EXODUS applications may have widely different notions of how versions should be supported [Ston81a, DaLW84, KaLe84, BaKi85b, ClTa85, KSUW85, SnAh85, KaCB86]. We do not omit version management altogether for efficiency reasons - it would be prohibitively expensive, both in terms of storage space and I/O cost, to maintain versions of large objects by maintaining entire copies of objects.

Versions of large storage objects are maintained by copying and updating the pages that differ from version to version. Fig. 3 illustrates this by an example. The figure shows two versions of the large storage object of Fig. 2, the original version, V_1, and a newer version, V_2. In this example, V_2 was created by deleting the last 36 bytes from V_1. Note that V_2 shares all nodes of V_1 that are unchanged, and it has its own copies of each modified node. A new version of a large storage object will always contain a new copy of the path from the root to the new leaf (or leaves); it may also contain copies of other internal nodes if the change affects a large fraction of the object. Since the length of the path will usually be two or three, however, and the number of internal pages is small relative to the number of pages of actual data (due to high fanout for internal nodes), the overhead for versioning large objects in this scheme is small - for a given fixed tree height, it is basically proportional to the difference between adjacent versions, and not to the size of the objects.

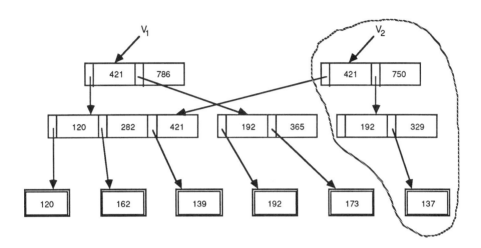

Fig. 3.:   *Two versions of a large storage object*

Besides allowing for the creation of new versions of large storage objects, which is supported by allowing the insert, append, delete, and write (i.e., read and modify a byte range) operations to be invoked with versioning turned on, the Storage Object Manager also supports deletion of versions. This is necessary for efficiency as well as to maintain the clean abstraction. The problem is that when deleting a version of a large object, we must avoid discarding any of the object's pages that are shared (and thus needed) by other versions of the same object. [CDRS86] describes an efficient version deletion algorithm that addresses this problem, providing a way to delete one version with respect to a set of other versions that are to be retained.

3.4 Concurrency Control and Recovery

The Storage Object Manager provides concurrency control and recovery services for storage objects. Two-phase locking [Gray79] of byte ranges within storage objects is used for concurrency control, with a "lock entire object" option being provided for cases where object level locking will suffice. To ensure the integrity of the internal pages of large storage objects while insert, append, and delete operations are operating on them (e.g., changing their counts and pointers), non-two-phase B+ tree locking protocols [BaSc77] are employed. For recovery, small storage objects are handled using before/after-image logging and in-place updating at the object level [Gray79]. Recovery for large storage objects is handled using a combination of shadowing and logging - updated internal pages and leaf blocks are shadowed up to the root level, with updates being installed atomically by overwriting the old object header with the new header [Verh78]. The name and parameters of the operation that caused the update are logged, and a log sequence number [Gray79] is maintained on each large object's root page; this is done to ensure that operations on large storage objects can be logically undone or redone as needed. A similar scheme is used for versioned objects, but the before-image of the updated large object header (or entire small object) is retained as an old version of the object.

3.5 Buffer Management for Storage Objects

An objective of the EXODUS Storage Object Manager design is to minimize the amount of copying from buffer space that is required. A second (related) objective is to allow sizable portions of large storage objects to be scanned directly in the buffer pool by higher levels of EXODUS software. To accomodate these needs, buffer space is allocated in variable-length *buffer blocks*, which are integral numbers of contiguous pages, rather than in single-page units. When an EXODUS client requests that a sequence of N bytes be read from an object X, the non-empty portions of the leaf blocks of X containing the desired byte range will be read into one contiguous buffer block by obtaining a buffer block of the appropriate size from the buffer space manager and then reading the pages into the buffer block in (strict) byte sequence order, placing the first data byte from a leaf page in the position immediately following the last data byte from the previous page. (Recall that leaf pages of large storage objects are usually not entirely full.) A scan descriptor will be maintained for the current region of X being scanned, including such information as the OID of X, a pointer to its buffer block, the length of the actual portion of the buffer block containing the bytes requested by the client, a pointer to the first such byte, and information about where the contents of the buffer block came from. The client will receive a pointer to the scan descriptor through which the buffer contents may be accessed[6]. Free space for the buffer pool will be managed using standard dynamic storage allocation techniques, and buffer block allocation and replacement will be guided by the Storage Object Manager's hint mechanism.

3.6 File Objects

File objects are collections of storage objects, and they are useful for grouping objects together for several purposes. First, the EXODUS Storage Object Manager provides a mechanism for sequencing through all of the objects in a file, so that related objects can be placed in a common file for sequential scanning purposes. Second, objects within a given file are placed on disk pages allocated to the file, so file objects provide support for objects that need to be co-located on disk. Like large storage objects, a file object is identified by an OID which points to its root (i.e., an object header); storage objects and file objects are distinguished by a header bit. Like large storage objects, file objects are represented by an index structure similar to a B+ tree, but the key for the index is different in this case - a file object index uses *disk page number* as its key. Each leaf page of the file object index contains a collection of page numbers for slotted pages contained in the file. (The pages

---

6   As is discussed in Section 5, the E language actually hides this structure from the DBI.

themselves are managed separately using standard disk allocation techniques.) The file object index thus serves as a mechanism to gather the pages of a file together, but it also has several other nice properties - it facilitates the scanning of all of objects within a given file object *in physical order* for efficiency, and it allows fast deletion of an object with a given OID from a file object (since the OID includes a page number, which is the key for the file object index). Note that since all of the objects in a file are directly accessible via their OIDs, a file object is *not* comparable to a surrogate index - any indices on the objects within a given file will contain entries that point directly to the objects being indexed, a feature important for performance. Further discussion of file object representation, operations, concurrency control, and recovery may be found in [CDRS86].

4   Types and the Type Manager

4.1 EXODUS Type Definition Facilities

Files in EXODUS contain what we refer to as typed objects, which are storage objects as viewed by the E programming language through its type system. Files are constrained to contain objects of only one type; this is not as restrictive as it may sound, however, because E includes union and variant as type constructors. Thus, if Employee and Department records should be stored together on disk for efficiency reasons, for example, an Emp-Dept variant type could be defined to serve as the type of file for storing the records.

The EXODUS type system allows types for typed objects to be defined by combining base types via type constructors. Base types are types that are accessible only through the set of operations defined on them; they correspond to the abstract data types of ADT INGRES [Ston86] or of conventional programming languages. The primitive EXODUS base types include int, float, char, and enumerations. In addition, EXODUS provides support for the addition of new base types (e.g., rectangle, complex number, or even a large base type such as image) and their operations via a flexible ADT facility (described further in Section 5). The definition of such ADTs is one of the tasks of the DBI. The type constructors provided by E include pointers, fixed length arrays, insertable arrays (i.e., variable length sequences), records, unions, and variants. Type constructors may be used in a nested fashion (e.g., and array of records is permissible). Whenever possible, such as for arrays of fixed length records, the E compiler will produce code which minimizes the amount of run time interpretation incurred in accessing an instance of a constructed type.

As a final note, observe that the presence of pointers (which are physically realized as object IDs) together with the other type constructors makes it possible to model more complex recursive types (i.e., typed objects within other typed objects) at a higher level of an application-specific DBMS. We expect this extensible type system to be sufficiently powerful to serve most applications satisfactorily.

4.2 The Role of the Type Manager

The Type Manager provides a facility for the storage of all persistent type information. In addition to E type definitions, it maintains information about all of the pieces (called fragments[7]) that go into making up a compiled query, as well as information about the relationship of these pieces to each other. It also keeps track of the correspondence of files to their types. In short, the Type Manager keeps track of type information and most everything else that is related to or dependent upon such information.

Since the fragments of a query include the types of the objects stored in the files that it references, there is a close relationship between what the Type Manager does and what traditional schema facilities do. The Type Manager does not, however, provide a complete schema facility for end users, as it does not store information about things such as cardinalities or protection and security. Requirements for such non-type-related schema information are expected to vary from application to application, so maintaining this sort of information is left to each application-specific DBMS. The DBI is expected to maintain a set of catalogs for storing such information, presumably defined in terms of the end-user data model that the target system is designed to support.

4.2.1 Fragments

EXODUS is based on a late *binding model* of database architecture. That is, database systems built using EXODUS tools compile information on the database structure and operations into fragments that are stored by the Type Manager. Compiled query plans are the last fragments bound, and they are compiled and linked (sometime prior to the execution of the query) to fragments that were compiled earlier. This process requires that the Type Manager maintains dependency information between the fragments. As described in the next section, maintaining this ordering information is an important part of the Type Manager's job.

Files are treated like fragments, but they slightly different in that they do not exist as code. To the Type Manager, a file is a triple of the form *<fname, ftype, fid>*, where *fname* is the character string naming the file, *ftype* is the name of the type of the file, and *fid* is its file id as defined by the Storage Manager.

4.2.2 Dependencies

As indicated above, certain time ordering constraints must hold between all fragments constituting a complete query, including files. For example, a compiled and linked query plan must have been created more recently than the program text for any of the methods or ADT operations that it employs; otherwise, out-of-date code will have been used in its creation. In addition, we observe that a given type or set of operations is likely to have several representations: the E source code, perhaps an intermediate, parsed representation, a linkable object, and, for queries, an executable binary.

---

[7] The type definitions themselves are also referred to as fragments, just like all other pieces of query-related information.

Similar time ordering constraints must also hold between these representations.

This is not unlike the problem of determining whether or not the constituent parts of a large software system are all up to date, and in fact the functionality of the Type Manager should not be unfamiliar to users of the Unix™ **make** facility [Feld79]. However, unlike **make**, which only examines dependencies and timestamps when it is started up, the Type Manager maintains a graph of inter-fragment dependencies at all times; this graph may change as fragments and dependencies are added to and subtracted from the database.

The Type Manager also plays a role in maintaining data abstraction that distinguishes it from **make**. In particular, a type used by a query plan is likely to in turn use other types to constitute its internal representation. The first type is not, strictly speaking, *dependent* upon the linkable object code of these constituent types; that is, while it must be eventually be linked with their code, it is not necessary that their object code be up to date, or even compiled, until link time. We call fragments of this sort *companions*; **make** has no facilities for specifying and using companions. The Type Manager, however, requires such a facility, as otherwise it would be unable to provide a complete list of objects constituting a query, which is necessary when a query is to be linked.

4.2.3 Rules and Actions

The Type Manager maintains the correct time ordering of fragments via two mechanisms: *rules* and *actions*. The set of fragments constitutes the nodes of an acyclic directed graph; rules generate the arcs of this graph. When a fragment is found to be older than those fragments upon which it depends (with the dependencies being determined from the rules), a search is made for an appropriate action that can be performed to bring the fragment up to date. Both rules and actions are defined using a syntax based on regular expressions so as to allow a wide range of default fragment dependencies to be specified with a minimum of actual rule text. Disambiguating heuristics exist to deal with possible action conflicts (such as when two regular expressions match the same fragment name).

5   Access Methods in EXODUS

Application-specific database systems will undoubtedly vary from one another in the access methods that they employ. For example, while B+ trees and an index type based on some form of dynamic hashing are usually sufficient for conventional business database systems (e.g., a relational DBMS), a database system for storing and manipulating spatial data is likely to need a spatial index structure such as the KDB tree [Robi81], R tree [Gutt84], or Grid file [NiHS84] structures. We plan to provide a library of available access methods in EXODUS, but we expect this library to grow - new, specialized index structures will undoubtedly continue to be developed as emerging database applications seek higher and higher performance. A complication is that a given index structure is expected to be able to handle data of a variety of types (e.g., integers, reals, character strings, and even newly-defined types) as long as the data type meets the prerequisites for correct operation of the index structure (e.g., a B+ tree requires the existence of a total ordering operator for its key type) [Ston86]; this includes operating on data types that are not defined by the DBI until after the index code has been completely written and debugged.

As described in Section 2, access methods reside on top of the Storage Object Manager of EXODUS in the architecture of application-specific database systems. In addition, type information missing at compile time must be somehow provided to the access method code at run time. One of the goals of the EXODUS project is to simplify the task of adding new access methods to a new or existing application-specific database system. The major sources of complexity in adding a new access method seem to be (i) programming (and verifying) the access method algorithms, (ii) mapping the access method data structure onto the primitive objects provided by the storage system, (iii) making the access method code interact properly with the buffer manager, and (iv) ensuring that concurrency control and recovery are handled correctly and efficiently. Although the access method designer is probably only interested in item (i), this can comprise as little as 30% of the actual code that he or she must write in order to add an access method to a typical commercial DBMS, with items (ii) - (iv) comprising the remaining 70% [Ston85b]. To improve this situation - dramatically, we hope - EXODUS provides a programming language for the DBI to use when implementing new access methods (and other operations). This language, E, effectively shields the DBI from items (ii) - (iv) - the E translator produces code to handle these details based on the DBI's index code plus a few declarative "hints".

In the remainder of this section, we outline the way in which new access methods are added to EXODUS, including how the programming constructs chosen for E simplify the writing of access method code, and how buffering, concurrency control, and recovery issues are handled "under the covers" in a nearly transparent fashion. We should note that many important details of the design of E are necessarily omitted from the following discussion; it is intended only to give the reader the general introduction to the ideas. For more detail, see [RiCa86].

5.1 The E Implementation Language

The E language is a derivative of C [KeRi78] with the addition of a set of programming constructs carefully chosen to provide high leverage to the DBI. A number of these constructs were inspired by developments in programming languages over the last 10 years, most notably, from CLU [LSAS77] and Pascal [JeWi75]. Its major features include the ability to bind a pointer variable to an object in a file, and to declare abstract data types in the spirit of CLU clusters. Program structure is fully modular, with separate compilation possible for all modules (including parameterized modules, which have a certain amount of missing type information). In addition there are several new type constructors and control abstractions.

By providing these facilities, E allows the DBI to define and then to manipulate the internal structure of storage objects for an access method (e.g., a B+ tree node) in a more natural way than by making direct calls to the Storage Object Manager and explicitly *coding structure overlays and offset computations. In particular, E allows the DBI to ignore the fact that storage objects can be arbitrarily large; the E translator will insert appropriate calls to get the storage object byte ranges needed by the DBI. The output of the E language translator is C source code with EXODUS-specific constructs replaced by collections of appropriate lower-level C constructs, additional routine parameters, and calls to the Storage Object Manager. In other words, the Storage Object Manager is effectively the E translator's "target machine", and the resulting C source code will be linked with the Storage Object Manager.

In addition to these facilities, the E language provides the DBI with declarative access to the Storage Object Manager's hint facilities (which were described in Section 3). Associated with each file-bound pointer variable in an E source program is a scan descriptor as described in Section 3; such a variable inherits the hints associated with its type definition. In the absence of hints, E will provide reasonable default assumptions, but hints make it possible for a knowledgeable DBI to tune the performance of his or her code by recommending the appropriate lock protocol, buffer replacement strategy, storage object size, etc., to be associated with a persistent object (scan) variable. E will also provide a hint mechanism that will permit the DBI to influence the way that E types are laid out on secondary storage (providing the dual of a buffering hint, in a sense).

5.2 Writing Access Methods in E

To demonstrate the usefulness of the E implementation language and to further explain its features, let us consider how the DBI might go about implementing B+ trees. We define B+ trees as an abstract data type, that is, as a type whose operations are available to users of the type, but whose internal representation is hidden. In this case, the operations probably include *create_index*, *destroy_index*, *lookup*, *insert*, and *delete*. To describe the internal structure of a B+ tree node, the DBI would define a C-like structure to represent its contents. Within an ADT module, there may be many typedefs; the one which has the same name as the ADT is the representation type. The ADT module *BTree* defined in Fig. 4 is an example of such a definition; the variant typedef BTree is the representation type for the ADT.

Note that the module has several parameters representing the "unknowns" at the time the DBI is writing the code. These include the type of the key over which the index is built, the ordering operators on those keys, and the type of entity being indexed; within the module, these parameters are used freely as type and procedure names. The implementation of parameterized types such as BTree is such that the unknown quantities are compiled into extra, hidden parameters to the routines that form the ADT's interface.

BTree's definition also hints[8] to the E translator that new B+ tree nodes should be one page in size, that hierarchical locking should be used in B+ tree operations, and that a LIFO buffer management policy with three buffer blocks should be used for the scan. (Buffers and locks are allocated on a per scan basis.)

Given these definitions, the DBI can proceed to access and manipulate storage objects as though they were standard in-memory structures. Fig. 4 also gives an example code fragment from a B+ tree search routine. In this routine, the parameter node is a pointer to a BTree. Each time the E translator encounters a statement in which *node* is dereferenced, it will translate this reference into a sequence of several C statements - at runtime this sequence will check to see if the appropriate bytes of the objects are already in the buffer pool by inspecting *node's* scan descriptor, calling the Storage Object Manager to read the desired bytes (and perhaps subsequent bytes) into the

---

[8] The hint facilities are currently being designed, so the hint syntax used in our example is preliminary; our intent is simply to convey the flavor of the hint facilities that E will provide.

buffer pool if not; then the actual reference will take place in memory. Since *key_type* is unknown when this code is compiled, the E translator will compile code such that the needed information (e.g. its size) is passed in under the covers; the resulting offset calculations which index into the key-pointer-pair arrays will make use of these parameters.

```
adt Btree [ entity_type, key_type, equal, less]
type entity_type;
type key_type has int equal(), int less();
{
      typedef enum { INTERNAL, LEAF} NodeType;

      typedef struct { key_type value; BTree *child; } key_ptr_pair;

      typedef struct { key_type value; entity_type *ptr[ ? ]; } key_ptr_list;

      typedef variant { NodeType nodetype;
            INTERNAL:     { int height; key_ptr_pair data[ ? ]; };
            LEAF:         { key_ptr_list data[ ? ]; };
      } BTree # obj(PAGESIZE); lock(HIERARCHICAL); buffer(LIFO,3) #;

      /*figure out which pointer to follow */

      private int search_node( node, key )
      BTree *node;
      key_type key;
      {
            /*simple binary search over node */
            int   min, max, middle;
            min = 0;
            max = lengthof( node->data ) - 1;
            while (min <= max)
                  {
                  middle = (min + max)/2
                  if(equal   (key,node->data[middle].value)) return
(middle);
                        else if(less(key,node->data[middle].value)) max =
                                                            middle-1;
                        else min = middle + 1;
                        }
            return(-1);
      }     /*search_node*/

      /*find first entity with specified key*/

      public entity_type *BT_lookup (key)
      key_type key;
      {
            ...
      }     /*BT_lookup*/

      ...

}     /*BTree*/
```

Fig. 4:   A Partial B+ Tree Example

E provides other operations on pointers into files as well. For example, the call *new(n)* creates a new object in the file to which *n* is bound and sets *n* to point at it; *free(n)* disposes of the object to which *n* is pointing. Other calls will also be provided, including calls to create and destroy files. The E translator will recognize these calls and replace them with appropriate lower-level Storage Object Manager calls.

5.3 Transparent Transaction Management

We have described how the E language simplifies the DBI's job by allowing access method structures and algorithms to be expressed in a natural way, and we have indicated how the E translator adds Storage Object Manager calls when producing C code. In this section we describe how concurrency control and recovery fit into the picture; the problem is complicated by the fact that access methods often require non-two-phase locking protocols and have specialized recovery requirements for performance reasons [Ston86]. These functions will be handled by the E translator through a combination of *layered transactions* and *protocol stubs*[9]

5.3.1 Layered Transactions

Transaction management for access methods in EXODUS is looseley based on the layered transaction model proposed by Weikum [WeSc84]. Weikum's model is based on the notion of architectural layers of a database system, with each layer presenting a set of objects and associated operations to its client layers. Each operation is a "mini-transaction" (or nested transaction) in its own right, and thus a transaction in a client layer can be realized as a series of mini-transactions in one or more of its servant layers. Concurrency control is enforced using two-phase locking on objects within a given layer of the system. Objects in a servant layer are locked on behalf of the transaction in its client layer, and these locks are held until the client transaction completes. Recovery is layered in a similar manner. As a mini-transaction executes, it writes level-specific recovery information to the log; when it completes, its log information is removed and replaced by a simpler client-level representation of the entire operation. To undo the effects of an incomplete layered transaction at a given level, the effects of a number of completed mini-transactions plus one in-progress mini-transaction must be undone; we must first undo the incomplete mini-transaction (recursively, in general) using its log information, then run the inverse of each completed mini-transaction. Weikum proposes what amounts to a per-transaction stack-based log for recovery.

While we draw much inspiration from Weikum, our access method transaction management facilities differ in some respects. First, EXODUS is not strictly hierarchical in nature, instead being a collection of interacting modules. (This does not invalidate the notion of a layered transaction, however.) Also, we provide more general locking than the strict two-phase model in Weikum's proposal, allowing locks set by a servant to be either explicitly released or passed to its client. This is particularly important for

---

[9] Currently, we are focusing our efforts on the difficult problem of automatically buffering pieces of large objects; our thoughts on how to deal with concurrency control and recovery are still in preliminary state.

access methods, as two-phase locking (even within a single index operation) is often considered to be unacceptable [BaSc77]. Lock passing is also needed to prevent phantoms when a new key-pointer pair is inserted into an index - unless the client retains a lock on the index leaf page, other transactions may run into consistency problems due to incorrect existence information. Lastly, efficient log management is essential to overall performance, and we view Weikum's per-transaction stack-based log as too unwieldy. Instead, we employ standard circular log management techniques, ignoring entries for completed mini-transactions during recovery processing.

Returning to our discussion of access methods, note that the access methods layer presents objects (e.g., indices) and operations (e.g., insert, delete, search, etc.) to its clients. If a client transaction executes a series of inserts, its effects can be undone via a series of corresponding deletes. The access methods layer, in turn, is a client of the Storage Object Manager, which presents storage objects and such operations as create object, insert bytes, append bytes, etc.

5.3.2 Protocol Stubs

Layered transactions will simplify the task of writing access methods because calls to other layers can be viewed as primitive, atomic operations. However, this is just a transaction model; the task of actually implementing the model still remains. For example, someone must still write the code to handle B+ tree locking and recovery, and getting this correct can be quite difficult. EXODUS will provide a collection of protocol stubs, managed by the E compiler, to shield the DBI from the details of this problem as much as possible. Briefly, a protocol stub is an abstraction of a particular locking protocol, implemented as a collection of code fragments (which the E translator inserts at appropriate points during the compilation of an E program) plus related data structures. The code fragments consist of locking/logging calls to the EXODUS transaction manager (a component of the Storage Object Manager). The data structures describe information on lock modes (and their compatibility) which is passed to and used by the lock manager. We currently expect that the generation of new protocol stubs will be a complicated task, and that stubs will be considered by the average DBI as being a non-extensible part of the basic EXODUS system. The use of existing stubs will be easy, on the other hand, and EXODUS will provide a collection of stubs for two-phase locking and for the hierarchical locking (or lock chaining) protocol of [BaSc77]. A DBI writing a new access method will only need to (1) select the desired protocol at compile time via E's declarative hints, as mentioned earlier; (2) bracket each access method operation with begin and end transaction keywords in E; and then maybe (3) include one or two stub-specific routine calls in the access method operation code (an example of which is given below).

As a concrete example, we briefly sketch a protocol suitable for concurrent and recoverable access to most sorts of hierarchical index structures. The basic idea is to use the B+ tree lock-chaining protocol of [BaSc77] for concurrency control, and to use shadowing for operation-atomicity [Verh78]. Consider a B+ tree insert operation: Using lock chaining as we descend the tree, we can release locks on all ancestors of a safe node once we have locked that node. To realize this protocol, the hierarchical locking protocol stub will implicitly set locks on nodes as they are referenced, keeping track of the path of locked nodes. When the DBI's code determines that a "safe" node has been reached, it can call a lock stub routine called *top-of-scope* to announce that previously accessed nodes (excluding the current one) are no longer in the tree scope of interest to the insert operation. The appropriate lock release operations can then be transparently handled by the lock stub routine. As for recovery, the insert operation will cause node splitting to occur up to the last *top-of-scope*. If changed nodes below this level are automatically shadowed, then the insert can be atomically installed at end-of-operation by overwriting the *top-of-scope* node after its descendent pages have been safely written to disk [CaDS85]. (While the Storage Object Manager does not directly support shadow-based recovery, the E translator can generate C code which uses the versioning mechanism of the Storage Object Manager to accomplish this task.)

5.4 Other Uses of E

We have described briefly how the E language provides the DBI with a facility for writing access method operations without worrying about such issues as the size of objects, making calls to the Storage Object Manager, or access method specific concerns of concurrency control and recovery. E is actually more than just an implementation language for access methods. The E compiler is really at the heart of an EXODUS system. For example, if some application needs a specialized fundamental type then the new type and its operations are written in E by the DBI. Since such operations may need to deal with arbitrarily large portions of objects - for example, the DBI might wish to add an ADT called "matrix" and then provide a matrix multiplication operator - the DBI's job will be significantly simpler if he or she can write the desired code without regard for the size of the underlying storage objects. Finally, the operators which implement the application's data model are also written in E.

6   Operator Methods

The Operator Methods Layer contains the E procedures used to implement the operators provided to the user of the database system. For each operator, one or more procedures (or methods) may exist. For example, in a relational DBMS this layer might contain both nested-loops and sort-merge implementations of the relational join operation. In general, the operators associated with a data model are *schema independent*. That is, the operators (and their corresponding implementations) are defined independently of any conceptual schema information - the join operator, for example, will join any two relations as long as the corresponding join attributes are compatible with one another (even if the result happens to be semantically meaningless).

There are two strategies for implementing such generic operators. First, the procedures implementing the operators could request the necessary schema information at run-time from the Type-Manager. The second strategy is to have the query optimizer and compiler compile the necessary schema information into code fragments that the compiled query can pass to the operator method at run-time. For example, in the case of the join, the optimizer would produce four code fragments: two to extract the source relation join attributes (with one procedure for each source relation), one to compare the two join attributes, and one to compose a result tuple from the two source tuples. Again, the solution for this layer is the use of parameterized modules; it is the types of the tuples being joined (or projected, or ...) which are unknown in this case.

Instead of providing generic (and, hence, semantics-free) operators to the database users, a number of researchers [Webe78, RoSh79, Derr86, LyKe86] have proposed to provide only "schema dependent" operations to the user. For example, in a database of employees and departments, the type of operations supported would be of the form hire-employee, change-job, etc. When the hire-employee operation is invoked, the necessary base entities are updated in such a fashion as to insure that the database remains consistent. Given the capabilities of EXODUS, implementing this style of operators is quite obviously feasible. The DBI could implement the operators directly using the functionality provided by the Access Methods and Storage Object Manager. Alternatively, they could be implemented using more generic operators. It appears that the database administrator of an IRIS database [Derr86, LyKe86] is expected to implement the schema-specific operators using an underlying database system that is basically relational in nature.

As is the case for access methods, we anticipate providing some level of operator support via a library of operator methods. For example, most data models are likely to want methods for performing associative accesses (i.e., selection) and for scanning through all of the objects contained in a particular file object.

7   Rule Based Query Optimization and Compilation

Given the unforeseeably wide variety of data models we hope to support with EXODUS, each with its own operators (and corresponding methods), EXODUS includes an optimizer *generator* that produces an application-specific query optimizer from an input specification. The generated optimizer repeatedly applies algebraic transformations to a query and selects access paths for each operation in the transformed query. This transformational approach is outlined by Ullman for relational DBMSs [Ullm82], and it has been used in the Microbe database project [Nyug82] with rules coded as Pascal procedures. We initially considered using a rule-based AI language to implement a general-purpose optimizer, and then to augment it with data model specific rules. Prolog [WaPP77, ClMe81], OPS5 [Forg81], and LOOPS [BoSt83] seemed like interesting candidates, as each provides a built-in "inference engine" or search mechanism. However, this convenience also limits their use, as their search algorithms are rather fixed and hard to augment with search heuristics (which are very important for query optimization). Based on this limitation, and also on further considerations such as call compatibility with other EXODUS components and optimizer execution speed, we decided instead to provide an optimizer generator [GrDe86] which produces an optimization procedure in the programming language C [KeRi78].

The generated optimization procedure takes a query as its input, producing an access plan as its output. A query in this context is a tree-like expression with logical operators as internal nodes (e.g., a join in a relational DBMS) and sets of objects (e.g., relations) as leaves. We do not regard it as part of the optimizer's task to produce an initial algebraic query tree from a non-procedural expression; this will be done by the user interface and parser. An access plan is a tree with operator methods as internal nodes (e.g., a hash join method) and with files or indices as leaves. Once an access plan is obtained, it will then be transformed into an iterative program using techniques due to Freytag [Frey85, FrGo86].

There are four key elements which must be given to the optimizer generator (in a description file) in order for it to generate an optimizer. (1) the operators, (2) the methods, (3) the transformation rules, and (4) the implementation rules. Operators and their methods are characterized by their name and arity.

Transformation rules specify legal (equivalence-preserving) transformations of query trees, and consist of two expressions and an optional condition. The expressions contain place holders for lower parts of the query which will not be affected by the transformation, and the condition is a C code fragment which is inserted into the optimizer at the appropriate place. Finally, an implementation rule consists of a method, an expression that the method implements, and an optional condition. As an example, here is an excerpt from the description file for a relational DBMS:

```
%operator 2 join
%method 2 hash-join merge-join
join(R,S) <-> join (S,R);
join(R,S) by hash-join(R,S);
```

Both the operator and method declarations specify the number of inputs. The symbol "<->" denotes equivalence, and "by" is a keyword for implementation rules. If merge-join is only useful for joining sorted relations, then a rule for merge-join would have to include a condition to test whether each input relation is sorted.

In addition to this declarative description of the data model, the optimizer requires the DBI to supply a collection of procedures. First, for each method, a cost function must be supplied that calculates the method's cost given the characteristics of the method's input. The cost of an access plan is defined as the sum of the costs of the methods involved. Second, a property function is needed for each operator and each method. Operator property functions determine logical properties of intermediate results, such as their cardinalities and record widths. Method property functions determine physical properties (i.e., side effects), such as sort order in the example above.

The generated optimization procedure operates by maintaining two principal data structures, MESH and OPEN. MESH is a directed acyclic graph containing all the alternative operator trees and access plans that have been explored so far. A rather complex pointer structure is employed to ensure that equal subexpressions are stored and optimized only once, and also that accesses and transformations can be performed quickly. OPEN is a priority queue containing the set of applicable transformations; these are ordered by the cost decrease which would be expected from applying the transformations.

MESH is initialized to contain a tree with the same structure as the original query. The method with the lowest cost estimate is selected for each node using the implementation rules, and then possible transformations are determined and inserted into OPEN using the transformation rules. The optimizer then repeats the following transformation cycle until OPEN is empty: the most promising transformation is selected from OPEN and applied to MESH. For all nodes generated by the transformation, the optimizer tries to find an equal node in MESH to avoid optimizing the same expression twice. (Two nodes are equal if they have the same operator, the same argument, and the same inputs.) If an equal node is found, it is used to replace the new node. The remaining new codes are matched against the transformation rules and analyzed, and methods with lowest cost estimates are selected.

This algorithm has several parameters which serve to improve its efficiency. First, the *promise* of each transformation is calculated as the product of the top node's total cost and the *expected cost factor* associated with the transformation rule. A matching transformation with a low expected cost factor will be applied first. Expected cost factors provide an easy way to ensure that restrictive operators such as join and transitive closure have less input data. Second, while it seems to be wasted effort to perform an equivalence transformation if it does not yield a cheaper solution, sometimes such a transformation is necessary as an intermediate step to an even less expensive access plan. Such transformations represent hill climbing, and we limit their application through the use of a *hill climbing factor*. Third, when a transformation results in a lower cost, the parent nodes of the old expression must be reanalyzed to propagate cost advantages. It appears to be a difficult problem to select values for each of these parameters which will guarantee both optimal access plans and good optimizer performance. Thus, it would be nice if they could be determined and adjusted automatically. Our current prototype initializes all expected cost factors to 1, the neutral value, and then adjusts them using sliding geometric averages. This has turned out to be very effective in our preliminary experiments. We are currently experimenting with the hill climbing and reanalyzing factors to determine the best method of adjustment.

8 EXODUS User Interfaces

As discussed in Section 2, a database system must provide facilities for both ad hoc and embedded queries. While tuple-at-a-time and portal [StRo84] interfaces look appropriate for record-oriented database systems, we have only just begun thinking about how to provide a more general technique for handling embedded queries in programs. Certainly, given the goals of the EXODUS project, we will need to develop data model independent techniques to interface programs to application specific database systems, but this may prove to be quite difficult. For example, it is hard to envision a generic interface tool that could satisfactorily interface a VLSI layout tool to a VLSI database system; in such an environment, it may be that the only sensible approach is to treat the application program and its procedures as operators in the database system, thus enabling the program to directly access typed objects in the buffer pool. Alternatively, it may be possible to provide a library of interface tools: portals for browsing sets of objects, graphical interfaces for other applications, etc. We intend to explore alternative solutions to this problem in the future.

For ad hoc query interfaces, tools based on attribute grammars appear promising. Unlike the grammars used by generators like YACC, which can be used for little besides parsing the syntax of an input query, grammars which allow complex sets of attributes and attribution functions may capture the semantics of a query, incorporating knowledge of schema information to guide query construction, detect errors, and generate appropriate structures for transmission to the optimizer. To test these ideas we are constructing a QUEL interface using the Cornell Program Synthesizer Generator [ReTe84]. The Generator takes a formal input specification, producing as its output an interactive, syntax- and semantics-driven editor similar in flavor to Emacs. For a query language, the editor will guide the user step-by-step in creating properly formed queries and will transform this calculus representation of the query into a syntax tree in the operator language recognized by the optimizer. During the process of producing this syntax tree, the editor will be responsible for translating from a calculus representation to an initial algebraic representation of the query. The editor will call on the Type Manager to provide access to schema information, as schema information determines a large part of the underlying semantics of the query. Since the concrete syntax of the query language, its abstract syntax, and the translation between the abstract syntax and the database operator language are all generated automatically from a formal specification, it should be a straightforward process to change or enhance the language recognized by the user interface.

9 Summary and Current Status

In this paper we described the design of EXODUS, an extensible database system intended to simplify the development of high-performance, application-specific database systems. As we explained, the EXODUS model of the world includes three classes of database experts - ourselves, the designers and implementors of EXODUS; the database implementors, or DBIs, who are responsible for using EXODUS to produce various application-specific DBMSs; and the database administrators, or DBAs, who are the managers of the systems produced by the DBIs. In addition, of course, there must be users of application-specific DBMSs, namely the engineers, scientists, office workers, computer-aided designers, and other groups that the resulting systems will support. The focus of this paper has been the overall architecture of EXODUS and the tools available to aid the DBI in his or her task.

As we described, EXODUS includes two components that require little or no change from application to application - the Storage Object Manager, a flexible storage manager that provides concurrent and recoverable access to storage objects of arbitrary size, and the Type Manager, a repository for type information and such related information as file types, dependencies of types and code on other types, etc. In addition, EXODUS provides libraries of database system components that are likely to be widely applicable, including components for access methods, version management, and simple operations. The corresponding system layers are constructed by the DBI through a combination of borrowing components from the libraries and writing new components. To make writing new components as painless as possible, EXODUS provides the E database implementation language to largely shield the DBI from the details of internal object formats, buffer management, concurrency control, and recovery protocols. E is also the vehicle provided for defining new ADTs, which makes it easy for the DBI to write operations on ADTs even when they are very large (e.g., and image ADT). At the upper level of the system EXODUS provides a generator that produces a query optimizer and compiler from a description of the available operations and methods, and tools for generating application-specific front-end software are also planned.

The initial design of EXODUS is now basically complete, including all of the components that have been described here, and implementation of several of the components has begun. Some preliminary prototyping work was done in order to validate the Storage Object Manager's algorithms for operating on large storage objects [CDRS86], and over half of the Storage Object Manager has been implemented since that time. A first implementation of the rule-based query optimizer generator is basically complete, and it has been used to generate most of a full relational query optimizer. The Type Manager and the E programming language translator implementation efforts are getting underway now, and we hope to have initial implementations of most of the key components of EXODUS by the middle of 1987. Soon thereafter we expect to bring a relational DBMS up on top of EXODUS as a test of our tools, and we will then begin looking for more challenging applications with which to test the flexibility of our approach.

10 References

[AiNa86], [AlHS76], [Astr76], [BaKi85b], [BaSc77], [Bato86], [BoSt83], [CaDe85], [CaDS85], [CDRS86], [ChDe85], [ClMe81], [ClTa85], [CoMa84],

[DaLW84], [DaSm86], [Derr86], [Feld79], [Forg81], [Frey85], [FrGo86], [Gray79], [GrDe86], [Gutt84], [JeWi75], [KaCB86], [KaLe84], [KeRi78], [KeWa81], [KSUW85], [Litw80], [LSAS77], [LyKe86], [MaDa86], [MSOP86], [NgFG82], [NiHS84], [ReTe84], [RiCa86], [Robi81], [RoSh79], [Schm77], [Schw86], [Ship81], [Shop79], [SnAh85], [Ston81a], [Ston83a], [Ston85b], [Ston86], [Ston], [StRo84], [StRo86], [Ullm82], [Verh78], [WaPP77], [Webe78], [WeSc84].

16

Persistent Memory: A Storage System for Object-Oriented Databases

Satish M. Thatte

Abstract

Object-oriented databases are needed to support database objects with a wide variety of types and structures. Object-oriented techniques, such as abstraction and inheritance mechanisms, which are widely used in symbolic processing, can be very useful in object-oriented databases. The advent of automatically managed, garbage-collected virtual memory was crucial to the development of today's symbolic processing. No analogous capability has yet been developed in the domain of persistent objects managed by a file or database system. A persistent memory provides a storage system for long-term, reliable retention of objects with rich types and structures in virtual memory itself. Because no separate file system is assumed for long-term, reliable storage of objects, the system requires a crash recovery scheme at the level of virtual memory, which is a major contribution of the paper.

The persistent memory system is based on a uniform memory abstraction, which eliminates the distinction between transient objects (data structures) and persistent objects (files and databases), and therefore, allows the same set of powerful and flexible operations to be applied with equal efficiency on both transient and persistent objects from a programming language such as Lisp or Prolog. A persistent object manager implemented on top of the persistent memory manages named persistent objects with rich structure. It is expected that the persistent memory system will lead to significant simplifications in implementing applications such as object-oriented databases.

1 Introduction

Many new applications, such as computer-aided design (CAD) in engineering disciplines, multi-media information systems, and expert database systems require databases that can support objects of a wide variety of *types* with the ability to express *complex relationships* among objects [HaMa85]. The type of an object refers to a template used for creating instances of that type. The structures of objects reflect the relationships among objects. Object-oriented programming and object-oriented systems have much to offer to develop databases with an "object-oriented" view [Loch86]. Object-oriented databases can greatly benefit from object-oriented programming systems, such as the Flavors system on Lisp machines and the Smalltalk system, widely used in the symbolic processing and artificial intelligence community. These systems provide sophisticated and rich abstraction mechanisms to define abstract types and to hide the implementation details of objects. Objects have a well-defined operational interface to its users. Powerful inheritance mechanisms are available to build higher levels of abstractions, i.e., higher-level objects can inherit the properties of other objects. Large systems can be divided naturally into coherent parts, which can be developed and maintained separately. Also, specifying redundant information can be eliminated.

The advent of automatically managed, garbage-collected virtual memory storage organization was crucial to the development of today's object-oriented systems based on object-oriented programming languages. Such a storage system removes the burden of storage management (storage allocation and deallocation, garbage collection, compaction, paging) from the programmer. In addition the storage system allows efficient representation and sharing of objects with a wide variety of types and structures via sophisticated pointer structures. No analogous storage organization has yet been developed in the domain of *persistent* objects managed by a file system or database. As a consequence, the programmer is forced to flatten rich structures of objects resident in virtual memory before the objects can be stored in a file system or conventional database. This task puts a great burden on the programmer and adversely affects system performance.

We believe that the architecture of a storage system will play a crucial role in the ease and efficiency with which object-oriented database systems can be developed and used. The storage architecture required by persistent memory ties the notion of object *persistence* to the garbage collection process; an object persists independent of its type or the storage medium on which it resides, so long as it cannot be garbage collected. Thus, persistent memory extends the concept of automatically managed, garbage collected virtual memory to a storage architecture that also includes database objects. In a persistent memory, both transient and persistent objects reside in a single address space, and for a given type of object, have identical representations.

Outline of the paper: Section 2 presents a critique of existing approaches to implementing object-oriented databases. Section 3 briefly describes our approach based on persistent memory. The persistent memory system is based on a *uniform memory abstraction*, which eliminates the distinction between transient and persistent objects, and therefore allows the same set of powerful and flexible operations to be applied with equal efficiency on both transient and persistent objects from a programming language such as Lisp or Prolog, without requiring a special-purpose database language. The uniform memory abstraction is presented in Section 4. The storage architecture, as presented by persistent memory, supports long-term, reliable retention of richly structured objects in the virtual memory itself, without resorting to a file system. Therefore, implementation of the architecture requires a crash recovery scheme at the level of virtual memory. A crash recovery scheme for the persistent memory is presented in Section 5. It is based on an efficient check-pointing and roll back scheme. Resilient objects are persistent objects that survive system crashes and shutdowns, even if they are created or updated after the last checkpoint operation. Section 6 describes the management of resilient objects. A persistent object manager is implemented on top of the persistent memory to name and manage persistent objects. Section 7 briefly describes the functions of such a manager.

As the title of this paper reflects, the paper concentrated on the storage system for object-oriented databases, not on the database manager itself. It provides only a brief description of a database manager that can be implemented on top of the persistent memory. Section 8 presents our thoughts on extending the persistent memory system in a network-based distributed computing environment so that multiple users can share persistent objects on multiple machines. Section 9 concludes the paper.

2 Critique of Existing Approaches to Object-Oriented Databases

Conventional database systems (network, hierarchical, or relational models) are not adequate to support the needs of object-oriented databases because they do not have the necessary diversity and richness of type and structure of objects. Realizing these shortcomings of conventional databases, the research community has followed a number of different approaches to develop databases to support a richer variety of object types and structures. These efforts can be classified into two broad classes and are briefly reviewed below.

1. **Extension of conventional database models:** The database community has extended conventional database models with richer data types. The INGRES relational database has been extended to enhance its applicability to engineering problems [StGu84]. Support for pictorial databases has been implemented on top of and by extending relational and hierarchical databases in the SDMS [Hero80] and VGQF [McMc81] systems. The MAPS system is a cartographic data manager with explicit support for the display of spatial knowledge [McKe84].

    Although these systems have contributed to the understanding of the problems associated with supporting a diversity of data types, they all have involved grafting additional functionality on top of an existing model. Therefore, many capabilities, such as recursive procedures, or functions as true first-class objects [AbSu85], are awkward, difficult, or inefficient (due to interpretive overhead) to implement in these extended databases. As a consequence, the applicability of the resultant systems has been limited [HaMa85].

2. **Persistent object systems:** Recently many researchers [Atki83, Atki84, Cock84, Mish84, Butl86] have followed the approach of making objects created and manipulated by programs *persistent*. Butler has developed a scheme to make Lisp objects persistent on top of a conventional database (INGRES) [Butl86]. The programmer must declare that the value of a variable is persistent and all the fetching and updating is handled automatically. The low-level Lisp functions that manipulate lists (e.g. CAR, CDR, ...) have been altered to examine their arguments to check for persistence. To partially overcome the retrieval costs of fetching persistent objects from the INGRES database, objects are buffered in virtual memory.

    Persistent Object Management system [Cock84] is an ongoing research effort to produce an extension of Algol that provides automatic access to a database system. OM, extends a dialect of Lisp, called Scheme, to encompass persistent Lisp objects. The designers of these systems rejected the use of conventional databases for their limited repertoire of data types and structures, and built new database systems to handle data types needed by their programming languages and extended the heap facilities of their respective programming languages to provide access to heaps that reside in their databases. They also build new database primitives that are appropriate to operate on the data structures in persistent heaps. The advantage of this approach is that the system can provide only the facilities needed by the particular language. No overhead is paid for features not useful to the language.

In all these persistent object schemes, persistent and transient objects still reside in two different storage organizations; transient objects reside in the virtual memory, and persistent objects in a general-purpose database [Butl86], or in a special-purpose database [Mish84, Atki84, Cock84]. Therefore, operations on persistent objects are invariably slower than on transient objects. There is a large overhead to access persistent objects because their pointers must be dereferenced by software, taking several machine cycles. In addition, buffer management is necessary to reduce the cost of fetching persistent objects.

3   Our Approach to Persistent Objects

Symbolic computers, such as the TI Explorer[1] and Symbolics 3670 are perhaps the best tools available today to implement applications that need a rich variety of object types and structures because of their support for rich knowledge representation and inference techniques, object-oriented programming languages, and integrated program development environments. In these computers, objects representing knowledge exhibit a *structure* defined by pointers connecting objects. This structure is usually complex and dynamic, i.e., it changes rapidly. All processes and objects share a single virtual address space [Texa85b]. Sharing of objects via pointer structures allows efficient and flexible representation of knowledge. The representation is also processed most efficiently by the machine because it is defined in the machine architecture, and hence is directly interpreted by hardware or microcode. The pointers to objects serve as *names* that can be passed as procedure parameters, returned as procedure results, and stored in other objects as components. A high proportion of data is pointers to other data and structures. This storage model requires automatically garbage collected memory - a feature supported by Lisp machines.

Our approach to object persistence in a symbolic computing environment is based on a fundamentally different paradigm [That85, That86]. We would like to make objects persistent in the virtual memory itself. The literature on persistent[2] memory dates back to 1962, when Kilburn [Kilb62] proposed *single-level* storage, in which all programs and data are named in a single context. Saltzer [Salt78] proposed a *direct-access* storage architecture, where there is only a *single* context to bind and interpret all objects. Traiger [Trai82] proposed mapping databases into virtual address space. It seems that simple data modeling requirements of computer applications of that time discouraged productization of these proposals partly because they are much more difficult to implement than the conventional virtual memory and database systems. We strongly believe that these proposals must be revived and adapted to the needs of object-oriented databases if we are to support their demanding requirements of data modeling and long-term storage of objects with rich types and structures.

---

[1] **Explorer** is a trademark of Texas Instruments Incorporated.

[2] In the literature, terms such as *permanent, stable, direct-access*, or *single-level* storage are also used.

The MIT MULTICS system [BeCD69] and the IBM System/38 [IBM80] have attempted to reduce the storage dichotomy. However, both have major shortcomings for symbolic computing. Unlike Lisp machines, each process has its own address space. All persistent information is in files. A file mapped into the address space of a process cannot hold a machine pointer to a file mapped in the address space of a different process. Thus, sharing of information among different processes is more difficult than with Lisp machines. Furthermore, there is no automatic garbage collection, which is essential for supporting symbolic languages.

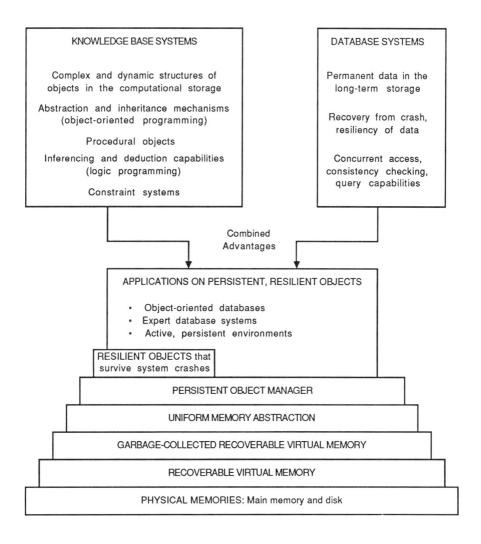

Fig. 1: *Persistent Memory: Storage System for Object-Oriented Data Bases*

The persistent memory is based on a *uniform memory abstraction*. In this abstraction, an object persists as long as it can be prevented from being garbage collected. The abstraction is implemented on a single, large virtual address space to support large knowledge-based applications. The concept of persistent memory, however, does not depend on the address space size. A major contribution of this paper is a recovery scheme at the level of virtual memory itself, i.e., a *recoverable* virtual memory. A recoverable virtual memory is essential because no separate file system is assumed for the purpose of recovering permanent data. The implementation of recoverable virtual memory is based on an efficient checkpointing scheme that incrementally captures the entire state of the machine, and roll back scheme that rolls back the machine state to the last checkpoint following a system crash.

Our approach is illustrated in Fig. 1. Successively more powerful abstractions are created on top of the physical memory resources. The first layer of abstraction is a recoverable virtual memory. A garbage collector runs on top of it to reclaim space occupied by inaccessible or garbage objects. Discussion on garbage collection is outside the scope of this paper. A good treatment can be found in [Moon84, McEn86].

Persistent objects created after the last checkpoint will not survive a system crash. Similarly, the checkpointed state will not reflect changes made to persistent objects after the checkpoint but before the crash. We define a resilient object as one which can not only survive beyond the lifetime of a program that created it, but can also survive system crashes. Resilient objects require the notion of atomic actions or transactions for their implementation. Thus, resilience is a stronger property than persistence. Not all applications require resilient objects.

Thus, as shown in Fig. 1, the persistent memory defines a storage architecture to support applications that combine the strengths of AI and database technologies. It should be mentioned that the proposed system is *not* intended to completely eliminate the need for a file system. A file system will be used as an archival medium to store objects for which there is no space in persistent memory. A file system will also be needed to support dismountable or removable storage media.

4   Uniform Memory Abstraction

The uniform memory abstraction is an *abstraction* of a persistent memory system, i.e., it defines the *architecture* of a storage system that manages both transient and persistent memory objects *uniformly*. As an abstraction it defines only *what* the external characteristics of the persistent memory should be, and *not how* to implement a system with these characteristics. As shown in Fig. 2, in the uniform memory abstraction a processor views memory as a set of variable-sized blocks or objects interconnected by pointers. Each memory object consists of one or more memory words, which are stored in *consecutive* virtual addresses. Pointers are typically implemented as virtual addresses. The notion of memory objects in the uniform memory abstraction corresponds to objects used in high-level programming languages, such as numbers, booleans, characters, strings, Lisp CONS cells, arrays, vectors, records, procedures, or environments. These language-level objects can be implemented using one or more memory objects interconnected by pointers. Application-level objects are constructed by combining language-level objects.

The abstraction has the notion of *persistent root*, which is a distinguished object located at a fixed virtual address and disk location. All objects that are in the *transitive closure* of the persistent root, i.e., reachable from the persistent root by following pointers, are persistent. The persistent root survives system shutdowns or crashes. Typically, the persistent root may contain a pointer to a table that points to other tables or structures of persistent objects and so on. Thus, the persistent root anchors all persistent objects. Its role is similar to the root of a directory hierarchy in a file system.

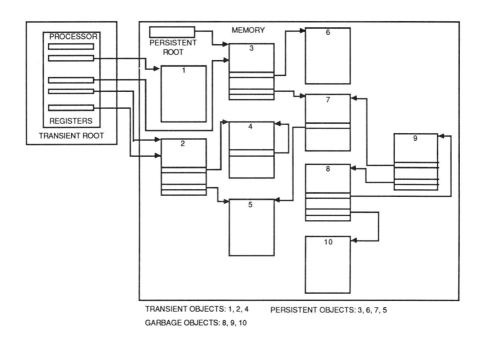

TRANSIENT OBJECTS: 1, 2, 4   PERSISTENT OBJECTS: 3, 6, 7, 5
GARBAGE OBJECTS: 8, 9, 10

Fig. 2:   *Uniform Memory Abstraction*

The persistence attribute of an object depends solely on whether that object can be prevented from being garbage collected even after the program that created it has terminated; this can be easily arranged by making that object a member of the set of objects in the transitive closure of the persistence root. Persistence based solely on the persistent root rather than the properties of the storage medium allows a complete separation of the persistence attribute of an object from its type or relationship with other objects. Numbers, characters, lists, procedures, environments, etc., can be persistent objects while they exist in virtual memory. Therefore, an invocation of a procedure as a persistent object is as easy and efficient as its invocation as a transient object.

The processor contains a number of "registers"[3]. The processor can access a memory object, i.e., read and write its individual words, if any of its registers holds a pointer to the object. The processor can access memory objects only via *logical* addresses; a logical address consists of a pair (i,j), where "i" is the id of a processor register, and "j" indicates the *j*-th word of an object being pointed at by processor register "i". Each memory reference can be checked for bounds, i.e., "j" in a logical address (i,j) should not exceed the size of the object pointed to by processor register "i". Registers in the processor define the *transient root* of the memory system. They do not survive a system shutdown or crash. All objects that are in the transitive closure of the transient root, but *not* in the transitive closure of the persistent root, are called transient. All the remaining objects are garbage and are reclaimed by a garbage collector. In Fig. 2, objects 1, 2 and 4 are transient; objects 3, 5, 6 and 7 are persistent; and objects 8, 9 and 10 are garbage.

From the machine point of view, transient and persistent objects are indistinguishable. From the user point of view, there is no need to treat transient and persistent objects differently - hence, the name *uniform* memory abstraction; all the user needs to know is that to make an object persistent, he has to place it in the transitive closure of the persistent root. The pointers to objects serve as *names* that can be passed as procedure parameters, returned as procedure results, and stored in other objects as components. The uniform memory abstraction requires automatically *garbage collected* memory - a feature supported by Lisp machines. Thus, the abstraction provides an appropriate storage model to store both transient and persistent objects.

The persistent object manager is implemented on the uniform memory abstraction. The interface between the persistent object manager and the uniform memory abstraction defines *how* the persistent root should be accessed, i.e., both read and modified. A well-controlled *procedural interface* to the persistent root is desired instead of an interface that allows direct manipulation of the persistent root, because accidental or malicious destruction of the persistent root can destroy the entire persistent memory which may be used as a repository that can be shared among several processes and applications. Providing application routines with direct access to the persistent root would make the interface at too low a level, since applications would be in contention for use of the root and there would be no way to keep track of persistent objects, which are often not related or user readable.

The integrity of the structure of the memory system is essential to guarantee that a roll-back process following a system crash to the last checkpointed state would be able to recover the system. Otherwise, the checkpointing operation may capture a state whose integrity has already been violated, and no recovery would be possible by rolling back the system to the corrupted checkpointed state following a system crash. The notion of the integrity of memory system refers to the integrity of the *structure* of the graph of memory objects interconnected by pointers.

The key features of the uniform memory abstraction, which forms the foundation for the integritiy of the memory system, are discussed below:

1.   Memory accesses only via logical addresses.

2.   Unforgeability of pointers.

3.   Bounds checking.

---

[3] The word *register* is used in a generic sense; it may be a hardware register or a scratch-pad memory in the processor.

4.   Automatic garbage collection.

5.   No run-away memory allocation.

It is assumed that most user software will be written in a high-level language (such as Lisp or language embedded in Lisp) and not in an assembly language. The integrity of the memory system is preserved because using a high-level language, it is impossible to forge a pointer, no information outside the bounds of an object can be accessed, and objects are accessed only via logical addresses. Therefore, the graph of memory objects undergoes transition only from one consistent state to another, ensuring its structural integrity (unless there is an undetected hardware failure that violates the integrity).

In addition, the integrity of the memory system requires that it should be automatically garbage collected, and there is no "run-away" memory allocation problem. Automatic garbage collection is essential to be able to make computational progress in a finite amount of memory space. Without the reclamation and reuse of memory space occupied by an object proven to be garbage (i.e., no outstanding pointers to the object from non-garbage objects), the system would eventually come to a halt as it would run out of memory, and at this point it could be restarted if and only if more memory resource were made available via garbage collection. Similarly, a runaway process that requests memory beyond its assigned quota must be halted and reset; otherwise, the system would eventually come to a halt as it would run out of memory.

5   Recoverable Virtual Memory

The uniform memory abstraction is implemented on top of the garbage-collected virtual memory system of a host computer. In the absence of system crashes and shutdowns, it is a straightforward matter to implement the abstraction. However, in real systems both events do occur, and sometimes rather too frequently. It must be emphasized that the problem will not disappear by making the processor's hardware and memory free of failures because software failures may still crash the system, and crashes caused by software failures are far more common than hardware failures. In today's computers, the storage dichotomy comes to the "rescue"; after a system crash, the contents of virtual memory are assumed to be lost, and the system is booted from a file system or a boot device. All the persistent information is usually safe in a file system and survives system crashes.

Therefore, the most challenging problem in implementing the storage architecture of persistent memory is to develop a crash recovery scheme to maintain object consistency in the presence of system crashes. In fact, at least one project (Intel iMAX-432 object filing system) decided to live with the storage dichotomy due to a lack of crash recovery schemes [PoKW81]. Recovery becomes even more challenging in memory systems of symbolic computers: a page may contain multiple objects, and an object may span multiple pages. An object can point to any other object, and other objects can hold pointers to it. Writing a single object to stable storage cannot maintain object consistency with respect to other objects, unless the entire system state is captured on disk.

Failures dealt with by a recovery scheme can be classified as *system crashes* and *disk crashes*. A system crash can occur due to power failure, hardware failure, or software error. It is signalled by a power failure interrupt, or hardware checking circuits, or software error handling routines when they cannot handle a software error or an exception condition. The rate of system crashes in a single-user machine is expected to be a few crashes per month, and the recovery time of several minutes is acceptable, assuming no permanent hardware failures. System crashes due to software errors are expected to be much more common than those due to hardware failures. The recovery scheme for system crashes is described first, followed by the treatment of disk crashes.

Our recovery scheme is inspired from the study of recovery schemes known in the conventional database community [Lori77, Reut80]. However, the key difference between our recovery scheme and database recovery schemes is that our scheme is at the level of virtual memory itself. To our knowledge no existing computers have a recovery capability at this level. Our recovery scheme is based on an efficient checkpointing technique that captures the entire system state and stores it on disk in an *incremental* fashion. Changes in the memory system following the last checkpoint are incrementally accumulated on disk in *sibling* pages. The correct sibling to be fetched on a page fault and the disk block on which it is to be written are identified by means of timestamps. The scheme keeps the entire machine state valid within the last few minutes on disk. After a system crash, recovery is achieved by *rolling back* the system state to the last checkpointed state. The recovery scheme is *application-independent* and *user-transparent*.

Our recovery scheme is quite different from the Disk-save or Sysout operations on today's Lisp machines. The disk-save operation is used to save the entire virtual address space of a TI Explorer Lisp machine into a disk band [Texa85a] by *copying* the contents of the entire address space; similarly the Sysout operation is used to copy the entire virtual address space of a Xerox 1100 Lisp machine into a file [Xero83]. Consequently, these operations are very slow (10 to 15 minutes) on today's moderate size address spaces of about 100 M bytes. The primary use of these operations is to create a customized Lisp world by loading Lisp functions from a file system and then saving the Lisp world using the disk-save or sysout operation. The user can boot the machine using such a Lisp world. These operations are not adequate to construct a recoverable virtual memory in the sense presented in this paper. Moreover, these operations cannot be scaled up for the future bigger address spaces of several gigabytes due to unacceptable time and space overheads. In contrast, our recovery scheme is based on an efficient checkpointing operation that captures the state of machine in few seconds in an incremental fashion with modest disk space overhead as explained below. For lack of space, the paper presents only the high-level salient features of the recovery scheme. Details can be found in [That85].

Page and timestamp management: A virtual page is materialized on disk in either *sibling* or *singleton* form. In sibling form, two disk blocks are allocated to a virtual page. These sibling blocks are only logical siblings and need not be physically adjacent on disk. In singleton form, a single disk block is allocated. A page is materialized in sibling form if it is expected to contain data that is likely to be modified. To reduce the disk space requirement, a page is materialized in singleton form if it is unlikely to be modified in the future (for example, a page containing instructions). Pages in sibling form may be converted to singleton form, whenever appropriate, to save disk space as explained later in this section. However, as in a conventional virtual memory system, a virtual page occupies only a single page frame when resident in main memory.

When a page is written to disk, a timestamp that records the time of the disk write operation is generated. The page header may be used to record the timestamp. Alternatively, the page table that maps virtual addresses to disk addresses may be used to record the timestamps. Timestamps are derived from a timer that runs reliably even in the presence of system shutdowns and crashes. The granularity of timestamps need only be moderately smaller than the time for a disk write operation because pages cannot be written faster than the disk write speed. With a 10 milliseconds granularity, a 64-bit timer can generate unique timestamps for over 5.8 billion years! Therefore, a 64-bit wide field for timestamps is more than adequate.

When a page is materialized in sibling form, its siblings are assigned initial timestamps of -1 and -2, indicating that both are yet to be written[4]. When a page is materialized in singleton form, it is assigned a timestamp of -1. All disk blocks that are modified since their initial materialization on disk will have unique timestamps within a machine.

The siblings are denoted as x and x'. $TS\,(x)$ and $TS\,(x')$ denote the timestamps of x and x', respectively. As will soon become clear, siblings x and x' may exchange their roles when they are written to disk. A singleton page is denoted as s and its timestamp as $TS\,(s)$. The time of the last checkpoint operation is denoted as T_{chk}. It is stored in a reliable fashion at a known disk location.

For a singleton page s, if $TS\,(s) < T_{chk}$, then s belongs to the checkpointed state; if $T_{chk} < TS(s)$, s is outside the checkpointed state. For sibling pages x and x', if $TS\,(x) < TS(x') < T_{chk}$ or $TS\,(x') < TS\,(x) < T_{chk}$, the sibling with the smaller timestamp contains outdated information, and the sibling with the larger timestamp belongs to the checkpointed state; if $TS\,(x) < T_{chk} < TS\,(x')$ or $TS\,(x') < T_{chk} < TS\,(x)$, the sibling with the smaller timestamp belongs to the checkpointed state, and the sibling with the larger timestamp is outside the checkpointed state. Because of the way the timestamps are initialized and updated, "$T_{chk} < TS\,(x) < TS\,(x')$" or "$T_{chk} < TS\,(x') < TS\,(x)$" case is not possible.

Four cases arise on a page fault depending on whether the page is in sibling or singleton form and its timestamp

Case 1. Page fault on a sibling page, and $TS\,(x) < TS(x') < T_{chk}$ or $TS\,(x') < TS\,(x) < T_{chk}$: "$TS\,(x) < TS\,(x') < T_{chk}$" case is described here. The treatment of "$TS\,(x') < TS\,(x) < T_{chk}$" is analogous. The sibling with the larger timestamp, x', is kept in main memory, and the other sibling, x, is discarded. When the page is written to disk, it is written over the disk space of the discarded sibling x, because x contains useless information. Disk space of x' must not be written over because it would destroy the checkpointed state. The timestamp relationship now becomes $TS\,(x') < T_{chk} < TS\,(x)$, i.e., case 2 below. Thus, x and x' exchange their roles.

Case 2. Page fault on a sibling page, and $TS\,(x) < T_{chk} < TS\,(x')$ or $TS\,(x') < T_{chk} < TS\,(x)$: "$TS\,(x) < T_{chk} < TS\,(x')$" case is described here. The treatment of "$TS\,(x') < T_{chk} < TS\,(x)$" is analogous. The sibling with the larger timestamp, x', is kept in main memory, and the other sibling, x, is discarded. Unlike case 1, however, the page is written over its own disk space, i.e., over disk space of x', because x' is *not* part of the last checkpointed state and can be written over, while disk space of x belongs to the checkpointed state and must not be destroyed. The timestamp relationship remains $TS\,(x) < T_{chk} < TS\,(x')$, i.e, case 2.

Case 3. Page fault on a singleton page and $TS\,(s) < T_{chk}$: If the singleton page is modified, at page-out time it must be converted to a sibling form because the checkpointed state must not be overwritten. Sibling x retains the contents and timestamp of the original singleton, and sibling x' contains the

---

[4] This initialization scheme is not unique. Other schemes are possible.

modified contents and the timestamp of page-out time. The timestamp relationship becomes $TS(x) < T_{chk} < TS(x')$, i.e., case 2. The disk space for s is reclaimed.

Case 4. Page fault on a singleton page and $T_{chk} < TS(s)$: At page out time, no conversion to sibling form is needed because singleton s does not belong to the checkpointed state and can be written over its own disk space. Time timestamp relationship remains $T_{chk} < TS(s)$:, i.e., case 4.

Sibling to singleton conversion: To reduce the disk space requirement, a sibling page may be converted back to singleton form when both siblings remain inactive for a long period, defined by a *threshold* parameter. The disk space manager hunts for such inactive sibling page; if $TS(x) < TS(x') < T_{chk}$ and $T_{chk} - TS(x') < threshold$, then the disk space for both siblings x and x' is reclaimed by converting them into singleton form. Singleton s contains the original contents and timestamp of sibling x'. The treatment for "$TS(x') < TS(x) < T_{chk}$ and $T_{chk} - TS(x) < threshold$" is analogous.

Checkpoint process: The checkpoint process may be initiated by an application or the system. At checkpoint time, the checkpoint process saves all processor registers, i.e., the transient root into a *snapshot* object. The snapshot object is part of virtual memory. The page containing the snapshot object is written to disk. The snapshot object may be incorporated in the transitive closure of the persistent root to make it persistent. All dirty pages in main memory are then written to disk. Finally, T_{chk} is updated on disk to the current time, completing the checkpoint process. This update operation must be implemented as an *atomic* operation; T_{chk} is either successfully updated or it does not change at all. Right after the checkpoint completion, for all sibling pages, $TS(x) < TS(x') < T_{chk}$ or $TS(x') < TS(x) < T_{chk}$, and for all singleton pages, $TS(s) < T_{chk}$.

It is highly desirable to reduce the time required for the checkpoint operation so that the user processes are not suspended too long. This is achieved by keeping the fraction of dirty pages in main memory at the checkpoint time reasonably small with a background write process that continually cleans up dirty pages between successive checkpoints. Normally this process is scheduled as a low-priority process so that user processes are not adversely affected. When the checkpoint operation is initiated, the priority of this process is increased to complete the cleaning of all the remaining dirty pages without any preemption by the scheduler.

Dirty page clean-up requires disk bandwidth in addition to that needed for the normal paging activity. Our calculations show that for typical processors (speed: 1 to 4 million instructions per second), typical disk systems (access time: 30 to 50 milliseconds), and a moderate page fault rate (page fault period: 500K to 1 M machine instructions per page fault), 50% to 80% disk bandwidth is available to clean-up dirty pages, and convert siblings to singletons and singletons to siblings. This bandwidth is judged to be adequate to support a recoverable virtual memory on a workstation such as the TI Explorer Lisp machine.

Modifications to the garbage collector: In a persistent memory system, the garbage collector needs to be modified; the garbage collector reclaims the disk space occupied by pages that contain garbage objects. In the persistent memory, the underlying disk space for a garbage page cannot be immediately reclaimed if it belongs to the checkpointed state. If the disk space were to be reclaimed, it will disturb the checkpointed state. For the persistent memory, reclamation of the disk space for a garbage page is postponed until the next checkpoint; after the completion of the next checkpoint, the disk space corresponding to the garbage page does not belong to the checkpointed state, and can be safely reclaimed. Note that it is the *disk space* of garbage virtual pages whose reclamation needs to be postponed, and not the reclamation of *garbage virtual pages* themselves. Garbage virtual pages can be reclaimed and made available to the memory allocator immediately.

Post-crash recovery: It is assumed that after a system crash diagnostics are run to detect permanent hardware failures and faulty hardware, if any, is already replaced. Fig. 3 indicates the post-crash recovery process described below.

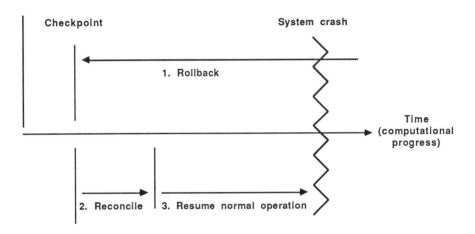

Fig. 3:   *Post-crash Recovery*

1.   Rollback the system to the last checkpointed state by restoring the processor registers from the snapshot object on disk.

2.   Reconcile with the external world. Part of the restored checkpointed state is related to the system configuration and I/O interfaces specific to the checkpoint time. This state must now be reconciled with the current time and configuration.[5]

3.   Resume the normal system operation.

Disk crashes: Disk crashes arise from disk head crashes, deterioration of the magnetic media itself, or bugs in the disk driver software. On a single-user workstation, the disk crash rate is expected to be a few failures per year, with the recovery time of a few hours. Disk crashes are treated differently from system crashes because they may corrupt the checkpointed state on disk; therefore, the roll-back technique used for recovery from system crash may not work. To deal with disk crashes, the last checkpointed state on disk needs to be archived on another media, such as a streaming tape. This operation is

---

[5] For example, part of the restored checkpointed state may contain a timer variable, which reflects the time of the last checkpoint. The timer variable must be adjusted to reflect the current time. The state of I/O device registers and device control blocks may need to be adjusted so that the I/O devices become ready for normal operation.

expected to be performed a few times a week, preferably as an overnight operation - a scenario consistent with the expected disk crash rate of few failures per year, with the recovery time of a few hours. After a disk crash, a failed disk needs to be replaced with a new one, which is then initialized from the last archived checkpointed state.

6   Resilient Objects

If checkpoints are taken frequently, say every ten minutes, the user may lose at most the last ten minutes of work due to a system crash. This may be quite acceptable for interactive program development and many applications on a personal machine. However, for some applications, such as graphics or text editing, loss of work may be an irritating annoyance, if not a calamity. What these applications need is object resilience.

A persistent memory system can support resilient objects with the help of a transaction[6] management package that keeps *undo* and *redo* logs to advance the state of the machine beyond the last checkpoint. When a client process initiates a transaction, the transaction manager executes it by following a protocol similar to the two-phase locking protocol [EGLT76] to allow concurrent transactions. A transaction management system implemented directly on top of persistent memory is briefly described below. The undo and redo logs are persistent objects.

1.   Acquire all locks on the required objects from the lock manager.

2.   For every *write* operation, create appropriate entries in the undo and redo logs for the transaction. Apply consistency checks to decide whether the transaction should be committed or aborted. If it is to be committed, go to step 3. If it is to be aborted, use the undo log to undo changes; release all locks; discard the undo and redo logs, and exit.

3.   Write information in the redo log in persistent memory to the *external* redo log kept on disk *outside* virtual memory[7]. The redo log in persistent memory may now be discarded.

4.   Notify the client process of successful completion of the transaction, and release all locks acquired in step 1. The undo log in persistent memory may now be discarded.

The post-crash recovery process for resilient objects consists of the following additional steps after step 2 of Fig. 3. These steps re-establish applications to a state consistent with committed transactions.

•   Apply the undo log found in the checkpointed state in the *reverse time order*. If a checkpointed state contains changes made by an uncommitted transaction, it will also contain the corresponding undo log entries required to undo the changes.

•   Apply the external redo log maintained outside virtual memory in the *forward time order*. Now the normal system operation can be resumed.

---

6   The notion of transactions is due to Eswaran et. al. [EGLT76].

7   This operation is necessary for the survival of the redo information of committed transactions from system crashes. The external redo log survives system crashes because it is kept *outside* virtual memory.

Database systems can be constructed as applications on top of resilient objects. Since the persistent memory can support complex object types and structures, resilient objects also enjoy the same benefits. Therefore, a database object can contain pointers to arbitrary objects, such as procedures, lists, and other arbitrary structures. Complex structures of objects including *cyclical* structures, which are quite common in symbolic computing, can be supported.

Our approach of constructing a database system on top of resilient objects has great flexibility and representational power, and it should be contrasted with the current approach of implementing resilient objects on top of a conventional file system or database. The current approach is quite rigid; it can support neither arbitrary types of objects nor complex structures. In addition, our approach is expected to be easier to implement than conventional database systems: No file or database buffers or explicit I/O operations are needed. If the transaction commits before a crash, then as presented above, its redo information is already written to the external redo log and the undo information is discarded. Therefore, there is no need to maintain an external undo log.

7   Persistent Object Manager

As shown in Fig. 4, the persistent object manager provides client application programs with an interface to persistent memory. The client interface provides two main services to client applications: the first service is a *namespace service* which supports operations for creating and managing a namespace of mappings of user-supplied names into Lisp objects; and the second service provides the undo and redo log primitives for implementing atomic transactions required for resilient objects, as described in Section 6. The persistent object manager does *not* itself implement any existing database data model, such as the relational data model; instead, it provides one step above the persistent memory on which to interface to application programs directly or to support higher level data managers.

It is desirable to provide a namespace facility in the persistent object manager. The idea of providing a namespace facility is not new in itself. The Xerox Clearinghouse [OpDa81] provides a namespace for naming and locating various objects, such as machines, workstations, file users, and people in a distributed environment. The namespace facility planned within the persistent object manager provides a mapping of user-supplied names into persistent objects within a single machine. What is new is that the namespace names and their related objects are themselves persistent since they are accessible from the system's persistent root. Namespace names are intended to serve as application-specific persistent roots available to applications as needed and providing access paths to persistent Lisp objects. Deleting a name-object association from a namespace deletes an access path to an object and does not necessarily affect the object itself.

Names in a namespace provide convenient hooks for associating with an object application-specific data type information, import-export functions for archiving or retrieving an object in the file system, archiving reasons, protection and locking information, usage statistics (date last used, "by whom" information, ect.), version or timestamp information, and human- or machine-readable documentation. Namespace names divide the persistent space into shared or disjoint persistent spaces. An access control scheme (using passwords, for instance) can be built that gives users access to only part of the namespace, making it possible to guarantee that transitive closures of some roots are disjoint from transitive closures of others.

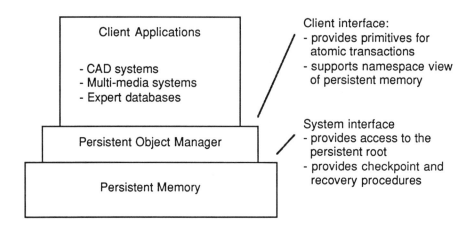

Fig. 4:   *Persistent Object Manager and its Interfaces*

8   Future Work

We are investigating the extensions of persistent memory in a network-based distributed system. The motivation of this effort is to be able to share objects in a distributed environment. The distributed computing environment envisioned consists of several symbolic workstations connected among themselves and with one or more file servers via a local-area network. Each workstation's virtual address space is divided into *persistent areas*. An area is the unit of garbage collection like Bishop's areas [Bish77]. It is called "persistent" area because it is also a unit of recovery, and persists across system crashes. Our approach is expected to solve the two very difficult problems in this type of computing environment, viz., network-wide garbage collection, and network-wide recovery. Since a persistent area is the unit of garbage collection as well as recovery, it can be garbage-collected independent of any other areas. Similarly, it can be independently recovered from crashes. There is neither any dependence on nor any coorporation required from other workstations to complete garbage collection or recovery of an area.

9   Conclusion

We strongly believe that the storage dichotomy in today's computers will be a serious impediment in the development object-oriented database systems. The storage dichotomy puts a heavy burden of storage management on the programmer, and causes a space and time penalty due to the translation and transfer of information between virtual memory and databases. Our approach to object-oriented databases is based on persistent memory that eliminates the distinction between transient and persistent objects. Implementation of persistent memory requires a recovery capability at the level of virtual memory itself. Our recovery scheme is based on timestamp and sibling page techniques, and has low space and time overheads. Resilient objects can be implemented on top of a persistent memory. Many applications that include CAD systems, multi-media systems, expert database systems, and object-oriented databases are expected to be implemented with greater ease, flexibility and performance on persistent, resilient objects than on a file system or on a conventional database.

10 References

[ABLN85], [AbSu85], [Atki83], [Atki84], [BeCD69], [Bish77], [Butl86], [Cock84],

[EGLT76], [HaMa85], [Hero80], [IBM80], [Kilb62], [Lamp81], [Loch86], [Lori77],

[McEn86], [McKe84], [McMc81], [Mish84], [Moon84], [Myer82], [Nier85a],

[OpDa81], [PoKW81], [Reut80], [Salt78], [StGu84], [Ston81b], [Texa85a],

[Texa85b], [That85], [That86], [Trai82], [Weis85], [Xero83].

17

ObServer: An Object Server for an Object-Oriented Database System

Andrea H. Skarra, Stanley B. Zdonik, Steven P. Reiss

Abstract

ObServer is a server process that manages persistent objects in an object-oriented database system. The system is implemented under UNIX[1] 4.3 BSD on a network of workstations with the server and its data residing on a single node. Clients communicate asynchronously with ObServer from possibly remote and dissimilar machines by messages sent according to interprocess communication (IPC) protocols. ObServer manages secondary storage, transactions, and concurrent access to objects in a multiuser environment in which transactions are interactive and probably long. The implementation emphasizes efficiency in the transfer of objects through the potential bottlenecks of IPC and file access. ObServer needs minimal semantic knowledge of the objects it manages, and thus can support application programs built on arbitrary type systems.

The paper describes the model, interface, and implementation of Observer and discusses some of the more interesting issues that were encountered during its design. ObServer is currently in use as an object server for two different systems: ENCORE, an object-oriented database system with multiple inheritance, and GARDEN, a graphical programming environment. An extended example of GARDEN as an ObServer client is presented.

1 Overview

ObServer is a resource for any system whose function includes the allocation of memory units from a shared and persistent space. ObServer packages the

---

This research was supported in part by the National Science Foundation under grants DCR8605567 and SER8004974, by International Business Machines Corporation under contract 55916 with amendment contract 643513, by the Office of Naval Research under contract N00014-86-K-0621, by the Defense Advanced Research Projects Agency under the Office of Naval Research contract N00014-83-K-0146, ARPA order 4786, by a grant from the AT&T Foundation, and by a contract with the Digital Equipment Corporation. Partial equipment support was provided by Apollo Computer, Inc.

1   UNIX is a trademark of AT&T Bell Laboratories.

units as named objects and manages their persistent storage within the memory space. In addition, it manages transaction processing and concurrency control. The system's habitat is a network of workstations (i.e., nodes) each running independent processes. The server process and its data reside on a single node, while its clients run on possibly remote and dissimilar machines in the network as separate processes. Clients concurrently access the shared memory managed by the server via asynchronous interprocess communication (IPC) protocols. A client's interaction with ObServer is framed by a *session* and within a session by *transactions*. A transaction consists of a series of messages between the client and server and is non-nested.

ObServer was designed as an object server for two distinct object-oriented systems: ENCORE, a database system with multiple inheritance [ZdWe85b, ZdWe86], and GARDEN, an interactive programming environment [Reis86]. Further, we were interested in using ObServer to better understand issues in the area of database systems for design applications. As a result, we identified several requirements for the model and implementation. First, transaction processing had to be flexible enough to handle long, interactive transactions as well as the shorter, more traditional kind. Next, efficiency had to be optimized, particularly in file access and interprocess transfer of objects. Finally, ObServer had to be able to manage objects of arbitrary types, since ENCORE and GARDEN are based on different type structures.

1.1 Transaction Management

The system's transaction management scheme was designed for potentially long, interactive process controlled by a user at a workstation. Conventional schemes are designed for relatively short transactions that are controlled by the execution of a program. The nature of our transaction model is reflected in the types of locks provided by the system, the method used for deadlock resolution, the correctness criteria for concurrency control, and the support of an explicit undo capability. The undo facility allows an interactive user to return to a former state of his current transaction. The user sets marks at arbitrary points within the transaction to which he may wish to return later. Undoing to a particular mark removes the effect of the transaction (i.e., writes and locks) from the database system.

In accordance with more traditional schemes, ObServer also supports transactions that are single-level and atomic. Transactions cannot be nested; a client must terminate its current transaction before beginning a new on. If a client crashes before committing a transaction, the effect of the transaction is removed from the database. If the server crashes, the effect of all transactions that have not been committed or are in the process of being committed is removed from the database upon re-initializing the server.

1.1.1 Data Consistency

Our concurrency control mechanism was designed with the rationale that applications have individualized requirements for data consistency. We wanted to provide a set of primitives flexible enough for users to implement concurrency schemes that best suit their environments. For example, it is possible for the system to ensure serializable and atomic execution of concurrent transactions. Alternatively, an application might use the concurrency primitives in a way that does not yield such a strong guarantee about data consistency.

The serializable execution of concurrent transactions is typically achieved in a database system through the use of a two-phase locking or an optimistic control scheme [Ullm82]. Neither method of concurrency control, however, is well suited to an interactive environment in which transactions may be long. If locking is used, objects may be unavailable for prolonged periods. On the other hand, optimistic schemes necessitate aborting transactions when timestamp conflicts occur, so that large amounts of work can be lost. Moreover, the design process may be more aptly modelled as a set of parallel and interrelated activities rather than isolated, serial ones (e.g., the components of a design are generally designed in parallel by cooperating teams). The concurrent accessibility of objects may be more important in collaborative design environments than strict serializability.

ObServer offers two concurrency models: *serializable* or *cached*. An application that always requests the serializable model produces a database with degree three consistency [GLPT76]. Serializability is achieved by a standard two-phase locking implementation with read and write locks. In the cached model two-phase locking is also implemented, but read locks are not required for a read. Instead, two novel lock types (notify and writekeep) are provided that increase the availability of shared objects and decrease the IPC cost associated with committing a transaction. The cached model results in degree two data consistency and shifts some responsibility for maintaining transaction atomicity to the client.

1.1.2 Locks

The lock types supported by ObServer are implemented with an object-level granularity and provide a concurrency control scheme that can be tailored by an application to its own requirements for data consistency and resiliency. Clients use objects by copying them from the server process into the virtual memory space of their own process via IPC protocols. The objects are manipulated locally and are explicitly saved when a client writes them back to the server by IPC. A new version of an object is visible to all clients only when that version is the product of a committed transaction.

The system provides a two-phase locking protocol with standard *read* and *write* locks for applications requiring serializable execution of concurrent transactions. Clients request a lock before reading an object from the database and a write lock before modifying the object and returning it. Since clients are interactive in our transaction model, lock requests that cannot be granted immediately are merely queued by the server; communication with the client is not suspended.

Alternatively, an application may opt for the cached model of concurrency control in which objects are transferred between processes only when they have been modified by one client and are needed by another. The cached model is implemented by the addition of two lock types, *notify* and *writekeep*. Moreover, read locks are not required for a client to read an object. Instead, a client can request a notify lock on each object that it reads. Subsequently, the server sends the client a notify message every time one of the objects is modified by a committed transaction. The client may then request a new copy of the modified object from the server.

Writekeep locks allow a client to keep written objects beyond the point of transaction commit rather than incur IPC overhead by returning them to the server when they are not in demand by any other client. A client wishing to modify an object initially obtains a write lock on the object within a transaction. When the client commits the transaction, it can request the conversion of the write lock to a writekeep lock; it then keeps the object instead of returning it to the server. The client may continue to modify the object in subsequent transactions. Later, the server may send the client a message to return the object (i.e., a committed version of the object), because another client has requested either a copy of or a lock on the object.

The cached model of concurrency control supports an environment optimized for data sharing and performance through the cooperative use of notify and writekeep locks. The model is especially appropriate for situations in which collaborative designers are working on separate but related components. Each designer modifies only certain of the components, but frequently requires the current design status of the others. Thus, a designer acquires write/writekeep locks on the components he is to modify and notify locks on the others. As the designer commits a transaction, the server sends messages to other designers who hold notify locks on components modified by the transaction. The notify holders may then request new copies of the components. If the designer has kept modified components with writekeep locks, he must return only those requested by the server for other designers needing a copy or a write lock. The notify lock allows for wider sharing of data since multiple designers can maintain copies of a component simultaneously during its modification. The use of writekeep locks enhances performance since a designer never has to return a component to the server unless he has finished with the component or another designer needs it.

The risk in using the cached model is that serializability and atomicity are not guaranteed in the execution of concurrent transactions. A client may read an object o with a notify lock, make modifications in other objects that depend on values in o, and commit before receiving notification from the server that another committed transaction has already modified o. A client who keeps objects with writekeep locks becomes the custodian of the most recently committed versions and thus assumes the responsibility for maintaining stable copies of the objects. Moreover, partitioning of the network may isolate the server from those committed database objects with writekeep locks. As a result, the objects are rendered unavailable, and the database becomes fragmented.

1.1.3 Deadlock

Deadlock is defined and resolved in ObServer in a manner consistent with our transaction model. The interactive nature of the model discouraged the use of any mechanism in the locking scheme that could result in suspending or aborting clients. Consequently, clients are not aborted in order to resolve deadlock. Instead, their lock requests are dequeued. A user whose lock request was denied because of deadlock may choose to resubmit the request, commit the current state of his transaction, or continue by manipulating other objects in his work space.

In our definition of deadlock we do not consider the order in which lock requests are queued. Assume that transaction T1 holds write locks on objects o1 and o2, and that T2 and T3 are each queued for both o1 and o2. Even if T2 precedes T3 in the o1 queue and T3 precedes T2 in the o2 queue, deadlock does not exist in our system. Neither T2 nor T3 is suspended by being queued, and one of them may choose to abort or commit their results thus far rather than wait for T1 to complete. If both are still queued when T1 terminates,

T2 will receive a lock on o1, T3 will receive a lock on o2, and deadlock will be present. Consequently, the waiting lock request of either T2 or T3 will be dequeued.

1.2 Communication

Communication between ObServer and its clients follows a mailbox model. A client sends a request to the server and is not suspended while the server processes the request. The server sends reply messages to clients, and is not suspended while each client receives the messages from its mailbox and reads them. The server may send its messages soon after a request has been made or after some delay. For example, lock requests may be granted immediately, or they may wait in a queue to be granted or denied later. Also a client holding a notify lock on an object may receive messages from the server periodically when the object is changed by other clients.

An asynchronous model of communication was chosen for two reasons. First, the relationship between client requests and server replies is not necessarily one-to-one. A client holding a notify lock on an object may receive any number of messages regarding the object at arbitrary intervals. A client holding a writekeep lock on an object may or may not receive a message to return the object as a result of another client's request. In short, both the server and client can act as message initiator and recipient during the processing of a given client request. Thus, the pattern of communication better fits an asynchronous model than a synchronous one (e.g., remote procedure call).

Second, clients of ObServer are predominantly interactive. As a result, suspending clients during the synchronous processing of a request is not an attractive option. Delays in processing may occur due to flushing of message buffers, server overload, or queuing in the case of lock requests. Asynchronous communication allows an interactive client to continue to do other useful work while waiting for the server to respond to a particular request.

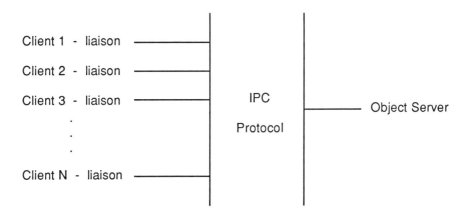

Fig. 1:   Clients communicate with the object server by linking to a liason. The server is connected to each liason by an IPC protokol

For applications requiring synchronous communication, an interface to the system may be written that suspends clients until the server completely processes each request and polls for messages initiated by the server. For example, a client requesting locks would be suspended until all requests had been granted or denied because of error or deadlock. If any of the requests were for notify locks, the application would then poll periodically for notify messages from the server.

Requests made by a client may concern a session (e.g., open, close), a transaction (e.g., begin, abort, commit) or objects (e.g., lock, remove, read, write). Replies made by the server include reports of success/error and notification (e.g., locks granted, deadlock, notify lock activation). The interface between ObServer and its clients is provided by a module called the liaison that is loaded with each client (Fig. 1). The communication primitives supported by the liaison are more completely described in the Appendix.

1.3 File Access / Interprocess Transfer

ObServer manages object creation and manipulation with mechanisms that emphasize efficiency during file access and interprocess transfer of data. For example, objects are read and written in blocks. That is, an application can request that an aggregate of objects be read or written in a single interaction with the server, generating only one IPC transfer and allowing the server to optimize its interaction with the file system.

When an application creates an object, it assigns to the object a unique identifier (UID) that was allocated by ObServer for the application. UIDs are requested and allocated independently of the size of the objects that will eventually receive the UIDs; UID allocation is separate from storage allocation. Thus, an application can receive in advance an arbitrarily large number of UIDs from ObServer in a single request and assign them to objects without waiting for ObServer to reserve space in the database. Space in the database files is allocated only when the objects are eventually written to ObServer.

1.4 Applications

ObServer currently supports two applications: ENCORE, an object-oriented database system with multiple inheritance, and GARDEN, a graphical programming environment. Other applications that we envision include blackboard and mail systems. The flexibility in ObServer to support arbitrary applications is a result of its not requiring semantic information about any object it stores other than the object's name (i.e., its UID). ObServer can therefore manage the persistent storage of shared objects of any type system, since it imposes no type structure of its own.

ENCORE [ZdWe85b, ZdWe86] represents a data model in the tradition of other high-level semantic data models [Chen76, Codd79, HaMc81, MyBW80, Ship81, SmFL83, SmSm77b]. The model is based on a type system that implements the notions of operation and property, version control, and associative retrieval. It is possible to create an instance of a type as a new version of an older object, to relate the object to other objects, to invoke operations on the object that are defined by its type, or to locate a set of objects that meets some condition. Type objects provide the interpretation of non-type objects. Types, operations, and properties are all persistent objects in ENCORE that are stored in the database via the services of ObServer.

The ENCORE system is controlled by a single process that implements the type mechanism. The initiation of an ENCORE process by a user involves executing a relatively small piece of code that retrieves a necessary set of system objects from the ObServer database. Since types, operations, and properties are all persistent objects in ENCORE, its system code is contained primarily within database objects and is retrieved only when needed. Users of ENCORE thus share system code in the same way as they share other database objects.

The GARDEN system has its own type structure and requirements of the object server. An extended example that describes GARDEN and illustrates the use of ObServer by an application follows.

2   Implementation

ObServer runs under the UNIX 4.3 BSD operating system and is implemented in the C programming language. The structure of the server reflects its function, and its operation is driven by requests from its clients.

2.1 Operation

ObServer operates in the following five states:
- *initialize* - create/open files and initialize data structures
- *memory* - compact database files
- *passive* - await requests from new or existing clients
- *active* - respond to client requests
- *termination* - close database in consistent state

ObServer is started in *initialize* and passes through *memory* to *passive*. After client requests have been processed in *active*, the server returns to *passive* unless clients are no longer in session with the server. When there are no clients the server returns to *memory* before *passive*. An error or an interrupt occurring in any of the first four states causes the server to enter *termination*.

2.2 Structure

ObServer consists of six components: *switchboard, manager, undo, locks, files,* and *uids*. In addition, a *liaison* is provided that clients use in communicating with the server (Fig. 1, 2).

The *manager* receives client requests through the *switchboard* and translates them into tasks for execution by *uids, files, undo,* and *locks*. The manager then translates the information returned from the tasks into a list of replies for clients. Clients other than the one initiating the request may receive replies. For example, a request to commit a transaction generates replies for clients holding notify locks on objects written by the transaction and for clients queued for locks held by the transaction. The list of replies is passed to the *switchboard* for delivery to each client's *liaison*.

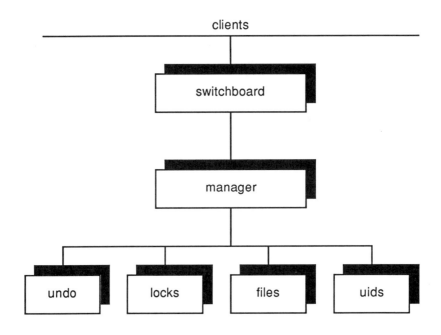

Fig. 2:   *The six modules of the object server and their paths of communication*

The liaison provides a functional interface to the server that hides the details of communication protocols and implementation from the view of the client. Moreover, the liaison assists the server and client by preparing requests from the client (e.g., prepending headers, grouping written objects into a block) and replies from the server (e.g., removing headers).

2.2.1 UIDs

Each object in the database has a unique identifier (UID). UIDs are 32-bit quantities that are allocated sequentially from a free-list by ObServer upon request from a client creating objects. UIDs allocated by the server but not assigned to any objects by the client are returned to the free-list. The UIDs of deleted objects are not reused, however, since references to the objects may remain in the database.

2.2.2 Files

The files managed by ObServer (i.e., the *entity* file, the *index* file, and the *log* file) provide stable storage for objects. The level of consistency in the database files is a function of the concurrency primitives that have been chosen by applications. Applications that always request the serializable model of concurrency, for example, produce a database with degree three consistency.

The entity file contains the database objects; the index file contains an entry for each object in the entity file that was written by a committed transaction. Index entries are organized sequentially by object UID, and each is comprised of the entity file location and size of the object. Thus, only one file access is required to find the location of an object and another to obtain the object itself. We can use a simple and efficient indexing scheme because the server controls UID allocation, and the UID of an object is its key; objects do not have arbitrary, user-defined names. If the object has been removed, the index entry contains a special symbol, a *tombstone*, to resolve references to the object. The possibility of sparseness in the index file is lessened by the sequential method used by the server to allocate UIDs. Moreover, the UNIX file system doesn't use space on the disk for unwritten pages of a file, so that a logical gap in the index does not necessarily correspond to physical disk space.

All objects received from clients are written to the entity file; objects are not maintained within the virtual image of the server process. Objects are always written to a free space in the file by a first-fit algorithm rather than to the same locations as their prior versions. Consequently, objects grouped into a block by the liaison can be written as a unit to the file in a single access. Versions of objects written by a transaction prior to commit are referenced by a temporary index residing in main memory that allows uncommitted writes to be undone. The permanent index file is updated only when a transaction that wrote objects commits or when a client returns objects on which it held writekeep locks. Thus, all uncommitted transactions are effectively aborted in the event of a server crash. When the server is not in session with any clients the entity file is compacted: each block of objects is completely copied to a target free space (possibly by way of a temporary free space) before the index entry for each object is modified and the former space freed. If the server crashes during compaction, objects may be caught in the temporary location but their integrity will remain intact.

Objects to be read from the database are sorted by location before being read from the entity file to take advantage of cases in which objects written together are read together. The location used for an object is that found in the index file, except when the reader is an uncommitted transaction that has written to the object; then the location in the temporary index is used. Versions of objects referenced by the temporary index are not visible to any transaction except the writer.

The log file is used to protect consistency in the database during the commit of a transaction. A server crash during a commit may interrupt the incremental modification of the index file. Therefore, the original of each index entry changed by a commit is written to the log file. When the commit is completed, the log file is cleared. If the log file contains entries when the server is initialized, consistency can be reinstated by resetting entries in the index file to those listed in the log file.

2.2.3 Locks

Four lock types are supported by ObServer: *read, write, writekeep,* and *notify*. Read and write locks are implemented with their usual semantics in a two-phase locking protocol and are used by applications requiring serializable execution of concurrent transactions. Writekeep and notify locks offer an alternative concurrency model in which sharing and performance are enhanced. The latter two lock types belong to a session rather than to a transaction and persist without regard to transaction boundaries. Notify locks may be requested at any time during a session and act like triggers; they do not conflict with any lock type. Writekeep locks are essentially write locks that survive beyond the commit of the transaction that was granted them. A client that is modifying objects initially obtains write locks on them within a transaction. If the client plans further modification, it can convert the write locks to writekeep locks at transaction commit instead of returning the objects to the server. Write locks expire at transaction end; a writekeep lock expires upon return of the committed object or at session end.

The lock protocol involving notify and writekeep locks is message-mediated and insures fairness among cooperative users. The server sends a message to a client holding a notify lock on an object when the object is modified by the committed transaction of another client. The object is considered modified if the transaction either returns the object at commit or doesn't return the object but requests a writekeep lock on it. The notify holder may then send a request to the server for a new copy of the object.

If a client has kept an object with a writekeep lock, the server sends it a request to return the object when there are read requests or lock requests pending for the object. When a client returns a committed object, the server removes the writekeep lock and services any pending requests. The protocol insures fairness because the writekeep lock is released upon return of the object. Other clients wanting to modify the object can then be granted a write lock in turn.

The lock table is implemented as a hash table and contains an entry for every object on which a current client holds a lock. When a client requests a lock, the request may be granted, queued, or denied because of an error (e.g., object deleted or nonexistent). A request is queued when the desired lock conflicts with any lock held on the object by another client; queued requests are later granted or denied in order to resolve deadlock. An algorithm to detect deadlock executes periodically[2], and any lock requests involved in a circular wait are dequeued; clients are not aborted.

2.2.4 Undo

The undo facility of ObServer allows a client to return to a former state of the current transaction. The state is indicated by a mark previously laid down by the client. The server undoes a transaction to a mark by removing the effect of actions, such as lock requests or written objects, from the database. *Redo* is not supported primarily because locks given up during an undo are granted to waiting transactions. Consequently, it may not be possible to return immediately to a previous lock state by a redo; it may be necessary to queue the transaction for a previously held lock rather than immediately granting it. Similarly, the request *unlock* is not supported; it may not be possible to return immediately to a previous lock state by undoing an unlock (i.e., re-locking).

---

2 The algorithm is currently run after every *potential deadlock occurrence* (PDO), where a PDO is defined as either the queuing of a client's lock request when at least one other client has queued requests or the granting of locks to a client during an abort, commit, or undo_lock by another client. It is possible to run the algorithm after some number of PDOs or after some period of time when the number of PDOs is greater than zero.

2.2.5 Switchboard and Liaison

The communication scheme between ObServer and its clients is bidirectional and asynchronous and is implemented on UNIX stream sockets, so that message delivery is reliable, sequenced, and unduplicated. A communication buffer is implemented within the liaison and the server process so that transmission of interrupted and thus incomplete messages can be resumed without confusion.

A round-robin schedule is used by the server in receiving requests (i.e., one request at a time from each client with submitted requests in turn). In contrast, a queue of pending replies is maintained for each client. For each client in turn, replies are sent until its queue is empty or until its socket can accept no more. An error condition resulting from an attempted send or receive indicates a problem in socket patency and/or client robustness. In either case, the client's current transaction is aborted, and its session is closed.

Objects sent between the server and its clients are each prefixed by a UID and byte size; requests and replies also contain headers. Because the server and its clients may exist on different machines, a common representation for header values must be chosen for transfer of data. Thus, the server converts headers to net byte order before sending replies to clients, and host byte order after receiving requests. Similarly, the liaison converts requests to net byte order and converts replies to host byte order.

3   The GARDEN Example

One of the applications using the object server is the GARDEN system. GARDEN is a programming environment designed to support a wide variety of visual languages in a consistent framework. It is based on an object-oriented programming system and uses an object-oriented database to transform this system into an environment.

GARDEN uses an object-oriented programming system to provide a wide variety of graphical program views. Objects are a natural mechanism for this application. They have been widely used for describing the type of structured pictures that are required for visual programming. Moreover, Smalltalk and similar systems have shown the value of objects as a basis for programming.

GARDEN uses objects to represent both programs and data. This provides the flexibility to handle different graphical views. For example, finite state automata can be defined using an object to represent the automata and objects to represent each state and arc. A data flow graph can be defined using objects for each operation and each arc. Control flow can be defined with objects representing the basic control constructs such as a sequence of statements or a loop. GARDEN does not use an underlying programming language. Instead, objects are evaluated directly. Hence the finite state automata objects evaluate by simulating the automata, and data flow objects evaluate by doing data flow. GARDEN includes facilities for rendering and editing natural pictures for the underlying set of objects. This means that finite state automata can be created, editing and displayed using their graphical forms. Moreover, the resultant pictures are directly executable.

This approach to programming requires an object-oriented database system. The objects that compose programs and data and that describe the pictures must be saved between invocations. GARDEN assumes that all objects are persistent and does garbage collection. GARDEN requires that the object basis for a system be shared among the programmers of multiple-person projects. Moreover, GARDEN uses an internal transaction model to protect data between multiple lightweight processes within a run and multiple programmers, to provide an undo facility, and to provide an efficient dependency mechanism.

The object-oriented database system for GARDEN has to be efficient and provide rapid access to large numbers of small objects. This is most important for supporting program execution. Since both programs are represented as objects, it is essential to be able to navigate rapidly around object structures. Since all data is represented as objects, the operation of locking and modifying an object must be fast, especially if it is done repeatedly. The initial object base for GARDEN is currently around 20,000 objects, and we expect this to grow as the system becomes more robust. Moreover, this does not include any of the objects representing the program or data under development.

GARDEN provides these database facilities by implementing an in-core object management facility and using the object server for permanent storage. It distinguishes between objects known only to the in-core manager and those known to the object server. It allows direct addresses to be used for efficient traversal of the object structure. It provides a complex, nested-transaction model suitable for programming and maps this model to the database transaction model provided by the server. It implements garbage collection on in-core objects.

GARDEN supports several types of locks on objects. It supports two types of read locks, one that blocks writes (READ) and one that just accesses the object (NOTIFY). It supports three write locks, a normal WRITE lock that is exclusive based on the relationship of the transaction requesting the lock and that holding the lock, an EXCLUSIVE lock that is always exclusive, and an ALLOCATE lock that is acquired when the object is created. To insure that memory addresses are valid, GARDEN requests NOTIFY locks for all objects accessed. It handles NOTIFY lock messages by invalidating the current copy of an object and forcing the in-core manager to retrieve a new copy from the server on the next access.

The in-core manager is responsible for mapping the locks acquired within GARDEN to locks on the server. NOTIFY and ALLOCATE locks are dealt with internally. READ locks, WRITE locks that are actually exclusive, and EXCLUSIVE locks are all sent to the server the first time they occur in the transaction. The manager uses the requests initiated by the server to minimize the number of objects that are communicated during the session. If the server requires an object from the in-core manager, it sends it a message. The manager will then convert the object to its external form, replacing all addresses with UIDs, and write it out. It also marks the object and all objects it references directly as global. When another process changes an object that is duplicated in core, the server sends a message indicating that the object has been changed. The manager handles this message by flagging the in-core object as invalid. Whenever someone references this object, this flag will be noted and the appropriate new object will be read from the server if necessary and used. This scheme insures that objects are written out only when needed by another user, that objects are read in only the first time they are referenced or changed by another user, and that objects that are created during the run are kept local as long as possible.

At the end of a session with GARDEN or at a user-specified checkpoint, all objects that have been changed since they were read in or that have been created are written out to the server. Before this is done, the garbage collector is run. The garbage collector assumes that all global objects are accessible but will eliminate any local object that is not accessible and is not currently locked. This insures that the large number of temporary objects created during a session with GARDEN, for example while editing or through program execution, are not made a permanent part of the object base.

GARDEN supports a nested transaction mechanism with a marking mechanism similar to that provided by the server. Nested transactions are used for supporting the dynamic creation of threads of control, for handling undo at various levels, and for triggering dependencies at appropriate times. Different classes of transactions are supported. Transactions can be either local or global. Local transactions are known only to the in-core manager; global transactions are known to the database as well. Because the object server supports only one level of transactions, the in-core manager must map the internal transactions to an appropriate database transaction. This transaction begins with the start of a global transaction when there are no open global transactions. It ends at the end of the global transaction that is the last global transaction currently open. This scheme allows nested global transactions and effectively serializes the transactions of the lightweight processes supported by GARDEN.

4   Conclusions and Future Directions

The paper describes a system called ObServer that manages the persistent storage of shared objects, transaction processing, and concurrency control. The system's architecture consists of a single server process and multiple client processes on possibly remote and dissimilar machines. The clients communicate with the server via an interface module called the liaison that resides in each client's process space.

Several decisions made during the design of ObServer were influenced by the transaction model and type systems of the targeted applications. In addition, system performance was a paramount concern. The transaction model that best fit the applications was one of long, interactive sessions controlled by a user at a workstation. In contrast, little similarity was found across the applications' type systems. Consequently, ObServer is typeless; it does not impose a type structure on its users. The transaction model and performance requirements motivated our adoption of an asynchronous communication scheme, a flexible concurrency control mechanism with novel lock types, and a locking protocol in which users are neither suspended nor aborted. Moreover, the system includes an undo facility for interactive users and employs techniques for increasing efficiency in file access and interprocess transfer of objects.

Other issues relevant to object-oriented databases that support design environments were highlighted by the development of ObServer but were not completely resolved in its present implementation. As a result, our continuing research includes work in the areas of concurrency models for parallel design transactions, recovery mechanisms, and segmentation schemes.

The design applications for which ObServer was primarily developed have requirements for transaction processing and concurrency control that are not met by traditional models. Design is an interactive and tentative process. The designer proceeds incrementally and backtracks frequently. The history of the design process is frequently as important as the current state of the design. Design sessions can be long-lived, persisting beyond the point at which the designer logs out. Thus, a unit of recovery smaller than a transaction is desirable in order to save intermediate results, and standard concurrency mechanisms such as aborting or suspending transactions are inappropriate in this interactive and history-dependent setting. Moreover, design environments are not characterized by the insular transaction processes serviced by traditional systems. Instead, designers work in parallel and in collaboration. Several people may be working closely as a team on the same portion of the design, while at the same time other teams may be working on separate, related portions of the design. Components in a design are frequently interdependent so that controlled sharing of transactions' partial results may be required by members of the same or different design teams.

We address several modeling and development issues related to database systems for design environments both in the implementation and the features of ObServer. In particular, the system supports a transaction model for long, interactive processes and offers a new concurrency model as an alternative to serializability that optimizes sharing and performance. In our current research we are further detailing a transaction model that more closely represents the parallel and collaborative nature of the design process. Moreover, we plan to formalize the correctness criteria implemented by a flexible concurrency control scheme [Skar88].

The recovery protocol in ObServer is traditional in that uncommited transactions are undone in the event of a server, client, or network crash. Neither the server nor a client can be reinstated to a mid-transaction point; partial results of transactions are discarded. Clearly, in an environment of long transactions significant amounts of work can be lost. Moreover, the restarting of interactive sessions is not trivial. Consequently, we are designing a recovery scheme in which a client's state with respect to objects written and locks held is saved periodically during a transaction. The frequency of saves would be specified by the client as a ratio of writes to saves and could range from 1:1 (i.e., every write immediately saved) to infinity:1 (i.e., writes are not saved until commit). If a client crashes, read and write locks held by the client are converted to notify locks so that other clients may access the objects. If the objects bearing notify locks are changed while the client is down, messages accumulate for the client. If the client then reopens a session with the server and requests reinstatement, the server sends it copies of objects the client saved as well as any notify messages. If the client's objects have been modified, the client may chose to abort (e.g., a client requiring serializability) or continue. Reinstatement would be available for a period of time specified by the user or the server be default.

Segmentation in an object-oriented database system refers to a grouping of objects for storage and access. A segmentation scheme implements locality of reference, so that objects that are routinely used together can be more efficiently retrieved into an application's work space at the same time. Currently, the granularity in the system is at the level of the object. Objects are referenced explicitly and individually by UID in the communication protocol, in the server file system, and in the locking structure. Objects are never pre-fetched. To alleviate the overhead associated with an object level granularity, we are adding a segmentation scheme to ObServer in which an object's UID encodes its segment. Segment groupings are defined explicitly by clients as part of the type structure, although we are developing heuristics for dynamic regrouping by the system [HoZd87].

5   References

[BeGH], [BeGo], [Chen76], [Codd79], [GLPT76], [GoRo83], [Gray81], [HaMc81], [HoZd87], [KeRi78], [MyBW80], [ReGR86], [Reis86], [RePa86], [Ship81], [Skar88], [SmFL83], [SmSm77b], [Ullm82], [Zdon84], [ZdWe85b], [ZdWe86].

Appendix

The following two tables list the communication primitives used by ObServer and its clients. A mailbox model of communication is used, with bidirectional and asynchronous message transfer occurring between the server and a module called a liaison that is loaded with each client. A client's interaction with ObServer is framed by a session and within a session by transactions; each transaction is made up of a series of messages between the server and client.

CLIENTopen()	*open session*
CLIENTclose()	*close session*
CLIENTtrnsbegin()	*begin transaction*
CLIENTtrnsabort()	*abort transaction*
CLIENTtrnscommit()	*commit transaction*
CLIENTuids(num)	*request num UIDs for newly created objects*
CLIENTmark()	*place a mark for future undo*
CLIENTundo(mark)	*undo current transaction to specified mark*
CLIENTread(uids)	*read objects from database*
CLIENTwrite(objects)	*write objects with write locks to database*
CLIENTreturn(objects)	*return objects with writekeep locks to database*
CLIENTremove(uids)	*delete objects from database*
CLIENTlock(locktype,uids)	*request read or write lock on objects*
CLIENTreceive()	*collect all messages that have arrived from server into queue*
CLIENTmsgread(buffer)	*read first message into buffer and remove from queue*

Table 1: *The functions provided by the liaison with which a client communicates with ObServer. The functions listed each send a specific message to the server except the last two. CLIENTreceive() and CLIENTmsgread() provide for the receipt and reading of messages from the server by the client. A minimal set of parameters for each function is shown to explain the semantics.*

Success
TBOK, tid[#]	*transaction begun, with identifier tid*
TAOK,tid[#]	*transaction aborted, with identifier tid*
TCOK,tid[#]	*transaction committed, with identifier tid*
MOK,mark[#]	*mark placed*
UOK,mark[#]	*undo completed to mark*
WOK,num[#]	*write completed for num objects*
RMOK,num[#]	*deletion completed for num objects*

Delivery
ROK,nbytes,objects[#]	*read completed; deliveryof nbytes block of objects*
WAITREAD,num,UIDs[#]	*requests queued for num UIDs*
UIDOK,num,UIDs[#]	*delivery of num, newly allocated UIDs*

Error
NOOP,error[#]	*undefined client request*
WERR,num,errors[#]	*write error; enumeration of errors by object*
RMERR,num,errors[#]	*delete error; enumeration of errors by object*
RERR,num,errors[#]	*read error; enumeration of errors by object*

Lock
LOK,num,UIDs[#]	*lock granted for num objects*
LERR,num,errors[#]	*lock error; enumeration of errors by object*
WAITLOCK,num,UIDs[#]	*requests queued for num UIDs*
UNWTLOCK,num,UIDs[+]	*queued requests granted locks for num UIDs*
DEADLOCK,num,UIDs[+]	*requests dequeued for num UIDs*

Server
NOTIFY,num,UIDs[*]	*notify message on num UIDs*
REQUEST,num,UIDs[*]	*request return of writekeep locked objects*
ABORT,error[*]	*client has been aborted for an error*

Table 2: *The specific messages sent by ObServer to its clients. Messages are read into a client's buffer by means of the liaison function CLIENTmsgread(). Messages in the table are shown in the following groups: **Success** - successful completion of client request, **Delivery** - delivery of objects from server to client, **Error** - error messages in response to client request, **Lock** - messages related to lock requests, and **Server** - messages initiated by the server. Messages may be sent to a client immediately following a request (#) or after a delay(+). Moreover, messages for a client may be initiated by the server as a result of the actions of another client (*).*

18
Generating Object-Oriented Database Systems with the Data Model Compiler

Fred Maryanski[1,2] , John Bedell[1,2] , Sheilah Hoelscher[1] ,

Shuguang Hong[1] , LouAnne McDonald[1] , Joan Peckham[3] ,

Darrell Stock[1]

Abstract

The Data Model Compiler project represents an effort to automatically produce object-oriented database systems. An analysis of data models of this genre leads to the conclusion that their significant differentiating characteristic is the set of fundamental, or built-in, relationships. This observation has lead to the specification of the basic relationships. Initially, the project focused on the development of a variety of object-oriented models in order to gain an understanding of the problem space. This paper concentrates upon that experience with a brief discussion of future plans. The particular application domains for which models have been constructed include business data processing, mechanical CAD, office information systems, and software performance modelling. The knowledge gained by developing these models served as the basis for the specification of a set of essential relationship characterics. The plan for generating database software corresponding to a user-specified data model revolves around the definition of the fundamental relationships of the model in terms of the aforementioned characteristics.

1 Introduction

As database management systems begin to expand into systems capable of managing objects more complex than the COBOL record, the consistency among modelling approaches breaks down very rapidly. Traditional data

---

[1] The work of this author partially supported by grant ECS-840147 from the National Science Foundation.

[2] The work of this author partially supported by an grant from United Technologies Research Center.

[3] The work of this author partially supported by an IBM Teaching Fellowship.

models have long been divided into three camps - hierarchical, network, and relational, with a number of commercial systems representing each basic model. As database systems begin to describe environments with data not conveniently represented by fixed length strings and with relationships that are not obviously modelled by flat tables, we see a tremendous diversity and very little synergy in the newly proposed data models. This observation holds to some extent because models for complex objects have not yet matured into commercial vehicles and at which point the realities of the marketplace will result in the natural selection of viable approaches. However, it is also true that the diversity in conceptual models for complex objects is a reflection of the diversity of requirements over the numerous application areas. It is upon this latter observation, that the Data Model Compiler (DMC) project is predicated.

The objective of the DMC project is not to define a data model capable of handling all possible problems for any type of object but rather to develop a facility for the automatic generation of database management systems software based upon a range of object-oriented data models. This system could then be utilized by a database professional familiar with the needs of the application environment to produce a data model tailored to a specific problem domain. The function of the DMC is to generate the following components of a database system:

1.   A conceptual data model which is embodied in the software elements listed below.

2.   A database design tool which assists the professional in the production of a schema and a set of operations against that schema.

3.   A translator which maps programs written in the data manipulation language of the conceptual data model onto an underlying physical representation.

4.   A graphical query language which utilizes the diagrams and forms of the design tool in the expression of interactive database operations.

The role of the Data Model Compiler (DMC) is very much akin to that of a compiler-compiler in that it accepts a description of the primitive characteristics of the data model and produces software, a data base manager, corresponding to that description. Th object-oriented data models for which database systems can be generated are variants of the Entity-Relationship model with differing types of inheritance mechanisms.

Fig. 1 positions the Data Model Compiler in the overall database application cycle. The figure references a "data model designer" who is a database professional thoroughly familiar with the requirements of the application environment. The product of the Data Model Compiler is an object-oriented data manager the components of which would be utilized in the traditional manner. In particular, the database design tool is aimed at the individual with a knowledge of a given application, the translator accepts DML programs written by an application programmer, and the query language is oriented toward the needs of the casual end user.

This paper presents a snapshot of the DMC project as it progresses through its middle stages. The major phases of the project are:

1.   Experimentation with an initial model for standard data processing environments.

2.   Development of models for a range of complex objects - the particular problem domains considered are mechanical CAD, office information systems, and software performance evaluation.

3. Abstraction of a set of conceptual modelling primitives to form the basis for the definition of a class of object-based data models.

4. Definition of a methodology for the automatic production of database software conforming to a particular, user-specified, object-oriented model.

5. Implementation of the full DMC software facility.

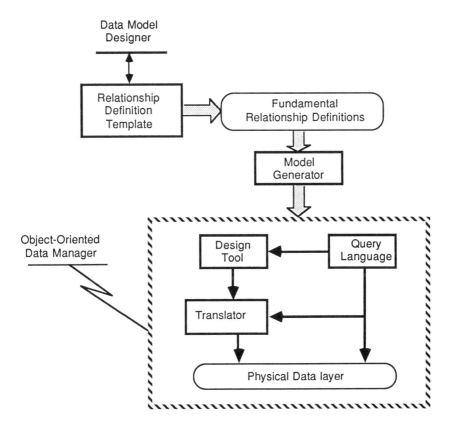

Fig. 1:   *Role of DMC in Application Development*

The emphasis here is upon the first three phases where most of the effort has been concentrated thus far. After a brief discussion of the research projects which have had the greatest influence on the DMC work, each of the three phases are addressed. The final section summarizes the plans for the final stages of the project and analyzes the expected benefits of the DMC.

2   Related Work

As indicated above, the diversity of object-oriented data models is almost frightening. The DMC project has the goal of attempting to unify a substantial subset of this data model space by abstracting the primitive elements of the data models and developing a tool for their generation. The initial data models produced during the first half of the project all were influenced heavily by prior work in their particular subareas.

The initial DMC model has four major relationships IS-A, reference, nest, and association. The particular flavor of IS-A employed in the DMC model relies heavily on the Taxis interpretation by Mylopoulos and his colleagues [MyBW80]. The latter relationship types are variants of the relationships defined by Wiederhold and El-Masri in the Structural Data Model [ElWi80, Wied83]. The SeaWeed design tool was strongly influenced by Studer's [Stud80] work on application specification in which he employed both graphs and forms in the design process. The Database Designer's Workbenches at CCA [Rein84] and Michigan [CoFT84] resemble SeaWeed in functionality and, to some extent, presentation. Surf, the query language for the databases designed using SeaWeed permits expression of queries by form filling using a technique similar, but not identical, to QBE/OBE [Zloo81]. Internally, the ShipWreck translator which maps the object-oriented schema onto a relation physical model bears some resemblance to Nixon's Taxis compiler [Nixo83] although the two systems differ on some fundamental representational issues regarding IS-A hierarchies. For example, ShipWreck trades time for space by storing only keys of parents in child nodes as opposed to storing all inherited attributes.

The three data models defined in the second phase of the project build upon the facilities of the initial model although they all possess unique functionality and distinct principal relationships. Scrimshaw, the object-oriented data manager for 3-D mechanical CAD objects, extends the hierarchical representation scheme proposed by Spooner [Spoo84] into the 3-D domain. The result has some similarity to the system designed by Kim and Batory at MCC [KiBa84] but differs due to the characteristics of its problem domain, mechanical, as opposed to VLSI, CAD.

Compass, the office data model, amalgamates the features of several interactive office information systems in its design and query tools. Gambit [Brae85], ISIS [GGKZ85], the Ingres Forms Package [R85], QBE/OBE [Zloo81], FOBE [LuYa81], and Softform [Huan84] all have impacted the interfaces of Compass.

Finally, the knowledge representation requirements of the PASS system [BoHQ86] have driven the design of TugBoat, the data model for the support of software engineering performance studies. PASS is a performance analysis tool for algorithms expressed in PASCAL. Functionally, TugBoat resembles the SEED package of Glinz and Ludwig [GlLu86] although the fundamental relationships of the two approaches differ considerably. TugBoat uses IS-A and IS-PART-OF while SEED builds upon its own variant of subtype/supertype. The versioning scheme put forth by Zdonik [Zdon85] inspired TugBoat versioning data type.

3   The Initial Model

The first portion of the DMC project focused upon modelling in the traditional data processing domain that has been the target of most database work in the past two decades. The goal of this portion of the project was to develop an object-oriented design and modelling philosophy that would serve as the platform for the later phases of the project. The data model developed is an extended Entity-Relationship model with a subtype/supertype inheritance structure for entities which are defined in terms of their properties, operations, and constraints [Peck85]. The entities and relationships are manipulated by commands in the semantic data manipulation language, Sea [Fran85]. A graphical application design tool, SeaWeed [Hong85, MaHo85], assists the designer in the specification of the entities, relationships, operations, and constraints of a given application domain. Using the information captured by SeaWeed, a semantic-to-relational translator, ShipWreck [Fran85], accepts programs which access the database either through Sea statements or via operations on entities or relationships as specified by the designer. The programs written in Sea are ultimately executed against a relational database. A query language, Surf [Stoc86], processes inquiries expressed using a combination of tables and SeaWeed diagrams and produces transactions against the semantic database.

3.1 Relationships

The initial DMC model [Peck85] directly supports four types of relationships: IS-A, reference, nest, and association. The IS-A relationship is utilized to express generalization/specialization among entity types. The form of IS-A employed here is a template-oriented inheritance mechanism [Brac83] which is very strict in terms of inheritance of properties but does provide for overriding defaults and refining constraints at the subtypes.

The latter three fundamental relationship types are the basis for all user-defined relationships. They have the functionality shown below. The work of El-Masri and Wiederhold [ElWi80, Wied83] strongly influenced the definition of these relationship types.

1.   Reference - a mapping from one entity to another. A reference is realized as an attribute of the referencing entity.

      EXAMPLE - a STUDENT entity references a PROFESSOR entity through the attribute ADVISOR which is of type PROFESSOR.

2.   Nest - a mapping from one entity, the Nest Owner, to a set of entities, the Nest Members. A nest is a set-valued attribute of the owner.

      EXAMPLE - a STUDENT entity contains a nest of the COURSES entities as its COURSE_REQUEST attribute.

3.   Association - a many-to-many mapping between two or more entity types. Associations are represented as independent components of the model with their own properties, operations, and constraints.

      EXAMPLE - TAKE is an association between the STUDENT and COURSE entities that has GRADE as an attribute.

3.2 The SeaWeed Database Design Tool

SeaWeed is designed to aid the application developer in the complete definition of the object types of the application environment. By "complete" is meant that the designer specifies both the static (attributes) and dynamic (operations) properties of each type. The SeaWeed design philosophy is to allow the designer to express the high level features of the application in a diagrammatic fashion and then to provide forms for the specification of detailed information. While SeaWeed permits the designer to proceed in any order through the diagrams and forms which define the application environment, the system has the ability to lead the designer through the process by presenting diagrams and forms in a predefined order. Following this order will also prevent a variety of errors of omission. A SeaWeed design session begins with the creation of an IS-A diagram for each subtype/supertype hierarchy such as that pictured in Fig. 2. SeaWeed traverses the IS-A graph and for each node representing an entity, presents the designer with a form upon which the attributes, relationships, operations, and constraints of the entity are specified. Then the designer is guided through the definition of the entity's relationships, operations, and constraints by means of the presentation of a sequence of graphs and forms. A key difference between SeaWeed and other database design tools is that it provides for the specification of the operations upon the objects as well as the attributes of the objects. The Operation Definition Graph permits the user to graphically express the operation as shown in Fig. 3. SeaWeed automatically generates Sea programs from these graphs. Operations may also be directly coded in Sea.

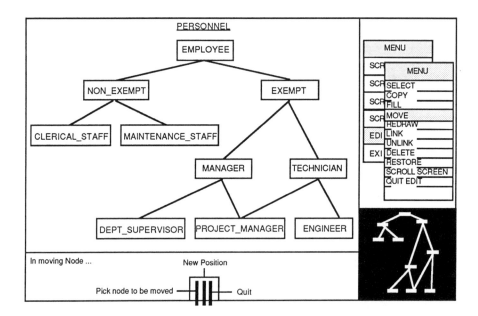

Fig. 2:   *SeaWeed IS-A-Diagram*

3.3 The Surf Query Language

The query language for the initial DMC model, Surf [Stoc86], is closely linked to the SeaWeed design tool. The casual user establishes the context for a Surf query by employing the mouse to navigate through IS-A or entity-Relationship graphs created by the designer to select the entity, or entities, to be involved in the query. Queries upon entities are expressed in a tabular manner as pictured in Fig. 4 which illustrates the expression of the Surf query which retrieves all students whose advisor is older than 35 and whose office is in Room 217. The output of a Surf query is a list of the attributes and values of the selected entities. A distinctive feature of Surf is its use of color to specify the logical OR operation in disjunctive queries. For example, if the previously mentioned queries involved a Boolean OR rather than an AND between the two conditions, the conditions on the AGE attribute and on the ROOM attribute would be entered in different colors. For further discussion of this scheme, see [Stoc86].

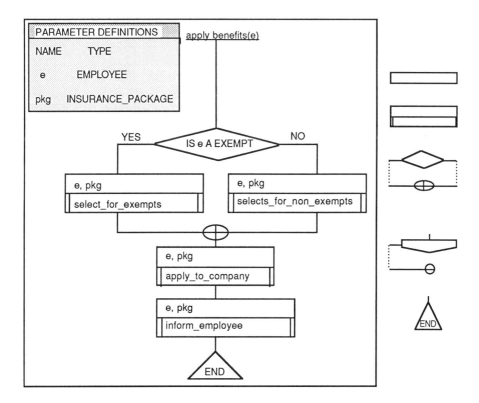

Fig. 3: *SeaWeed Operation Definition Graph*

4   Models of Non-Traditional Data

Once the initial data model had been established, work was initiated on gaining experience with a greater diversity of object-oriented models by attacking a range of application environments. Our goals here are to learn the modelling requirements of these environments with the anticipation that these domains would require differing sets of fundamental relationships. Based upon this experience, we can define a set of primitive relationship characteristics which will serve as the basis for the generation of a class of object-based data models.

RETRIEVE	INSERT	DELETE	MODIFY
student		advisor	
id		id	
name		name	
age		age	> 35
gpa		gpa	
credits		field	
		office	RM217

Fig. 4:   *SURF Query*

In the models described below, the emphasis was upon the definition of a data model that satisfied the requirements of the application space. Each model was the responsibility of an individual who was not a member of the team which developed the initial model. Thus, there was no conscious attempt to force the first model into these other domains although the influence of the earlier work could not be avoided.

4.1   Mechanical CAD Data Model

The first of the non-traditional environments considered was mechanical CAD which provides an example of an image-oriented application. The Scrimshaw system supports the graphical design and manipulation of wireframe and solid images. The conceptual model is an extension of the initial DMC model with particular support for containment and localized changes. Image entities are maintained as a collection of primitive objects which are linked together upon access. The object-based conceptual model is mapped directly onto a relational data manager. Fig. 5 presents the representation of a condominium in Scrimshaw while Fig. 6 illustrates its relational representation.

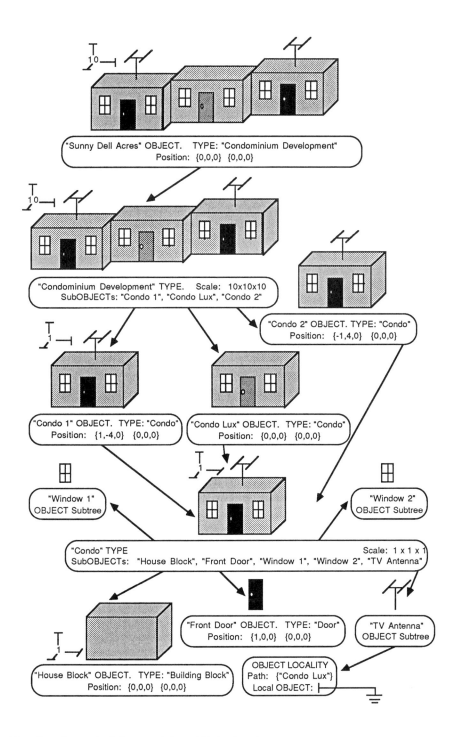

Fig. 5a: Conceptual Representation of Scrimshaw Image

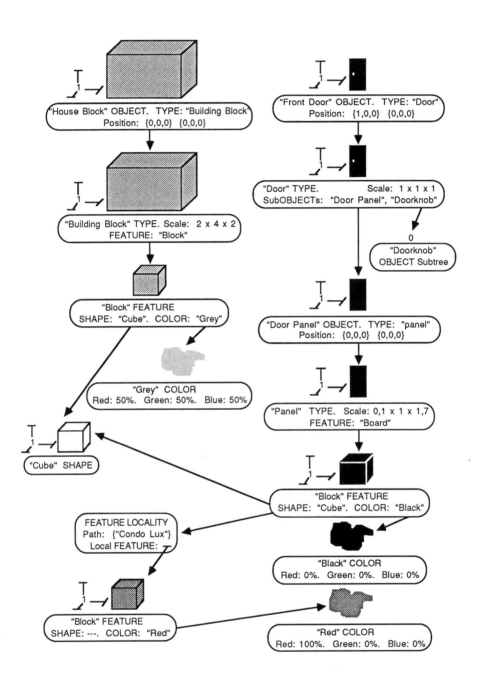

Fig. 5b: Conceptual Representation of Scrimshaw Image

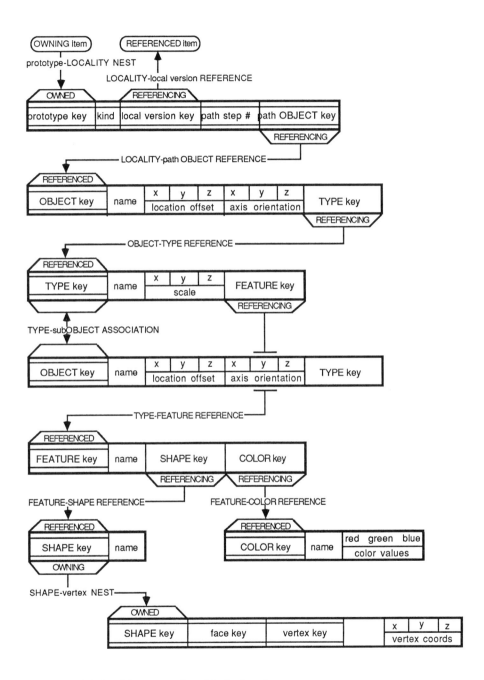

Fig. 6:   *Relational Representation of Scrimshaw Image*

A Scrimshaw image is created by connecting line segments using the mouse. Colors may be chosen from a palette which provides gradients of red, green, and blue. Since a Scrimshaw image is conceptually organized in a hierarchical fashion, components may be easily replicated and altered. Fig. 7 pictures an image of a car during a design session. In order to design a rear-view mirror, the designer descends to the windshield component of the car, creates a new subobject of the windshield (i.e. the attached mirror), shapes it into a rectangle, and positions it properly as in Fig. 8. (N.B. the mirror is also colored appropriately; this is not shown in the black-and-white figure). Whenever a sub-object is altered, the user has the ability to specify if the modifications are to remain local to the particular sub-object or if the object type is to be modified. If the latter course is chosen, the alterations will be reflected throughout the image. In this case, the car has only one mirror of the type designed, so the choice is of little importance.

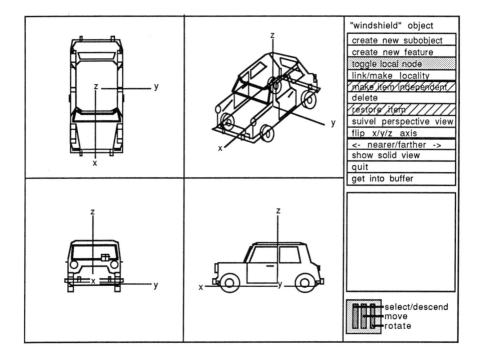

Fig. 7:   *Scrimshaw CAD Image*

Scrimshaw utilizes the capabilities of the IRIS workstation to offer features such as rotation, scaling, and hidden surface removal. The Scrimshaw software also provides shading functionality. All changes to the image during a session are recorded in a log which is processed against the database if the user wishes to save the results of the design session.

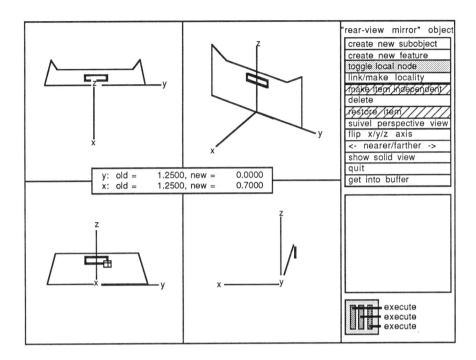

Fig. 8:   *Local Modification in Scrimshaw*

The primary relationships in the Scrimshaw model are:

subtype/supertype with a variant to provide for localized changes and,

IS-PART-OF

4.2   Software Performance Data Model

The data model developed for the software performance analysis environment
is intended to provide the database functionality for the ongoing development
of a suite of software performance tools [BoHQ86]. The basic DMC model
generally fits well in this case. Enhancements are necessary to provide for
inheritance over an IS-PART-OF relationship which varies slightly from that
defined for the graphical database and to support a variety of large
unstructured objects, known as blobs[4].

At the highest conceptual level, a TugBoat schema consists of a collection
of IS-A and IS-PART-OF diagrams. An example of an IS-PART-OF diagram is
pictured in Fig. 9. Inheritance over IS-PART-OF is limited only to the key of the
superpart type. TugBoat's design tool utilizes forms very similar to those

---

[4] Name coined by Barry Rubinson of DEC.

employed by SeaWeed for entity definition, see Fig. 10. The only addition in TugBoat is the subpart/superpart information.

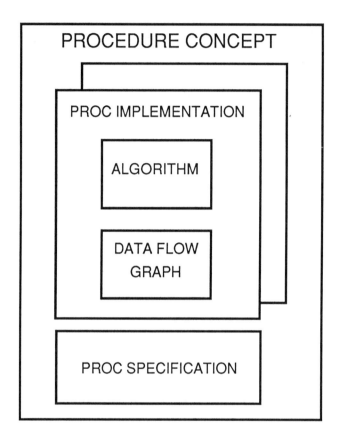

Fig. 9: *Tugboat IS-PART-OF Diagram*

4.2.1 Blobs

Blobs which are incorporated into TugBoat as new primitive types are similar to the "long fields" of Haskin and Lorie [HaLo82]. The following set of values and set of operations define the data type blob:

1. Set of Values -- The set of all possible byte sequences (Anything which could be placed in a file may be represented as a blob).

2. Set of Operations -- create, initialize, update, destroy.

ENTITY DEFINITION FORM

NAME OF ENTITY - procedure implementation

DESCRIPTION - A procedure implementation contains the control flow
and data flow information for a possible
implementation of a procedure.

SUBTYPES	SUPERTYPES
	SYSversioned

SUBPARTS	SUPERPARTS
algorithm data flow graph	procedure concept

ATTRIBUTES

NAME	TYPE
proc_concept_id	string (25)
proc_imp_id	string (25)
version_id	version_num
member_of_version_set	version_set
preceeding_version	version_num
succeeding_version	version_num
version_description	string (250)
performance_results	blob

KEYS

proc_concept_id   proc_imp_id   version_id

RELATIONSHIPS	OPERATIONS	CONSTRAINTS
chosen_together	init_versioning create_new_version delete_version	

Figure 10: Tugboat Entity Definition Form

Fig. 10: Tugboat Entity Definition Form

Blobs may be used to represent source code, object code, specifications, graphs, etc. Sharing of blobs among multiple entities is supported and entities may have multiple distinct blob attributes. TugBoat internally implements blobs as files and as such treats a blob as an unstructured sequence of bytes; it does not recognize any internal fields which can be searched for or joined upon.

4.2.2 IS-PART-OF Relationship

A new basic relationship, IS-PART-OF, will be built into TugBoat to facilitate the description of design pieces which contain subparts. IS-PART-OF is defined as the relationship which exists between an entity and its component entities. For example, a book may be described as an object which is made up of a front cover, a back cover, a binding and a set of pages.

Two types of subparts can be distinguished:

1. unique subparts, such as a book's front cover
2. subparts which form a set in which all members are of the same entity type, such as the pages of a book.

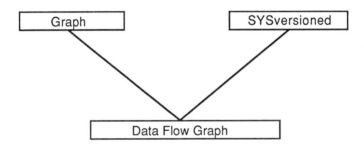

IS-A Graph

Fig. 11: Versioning in Tugboat

A unique subpart shares a common key with its superpart. In the case where a subpart is a set, an additional key attribute must be used to distinguish among members of the set.

The constraints induced by the IS-PART-OF relationship are expressed by the following rules:

1. Insertion of a subpart entity implies insertion of the related superpart entity.
2. Deletion of a superpart entity implies deletion of all its subparts.

4.2.3 Versioning

Versioning is also integrated into the model by providing a VERSIONING type which resembles Zdonik's history bearing entity [Zdon85] and making use of the multiple inheritance property of the IS-A relationship. Fig. 11 depicts the ability of all Data Flow Graph entities to support versioning by defining the Data Flow Graph type as a subtype of the VERSIONING type as well as subtype of the Graph type. The attributes and operations of the SYSversioned type are then inherited by all Data Flow Graph entities. Typical properties of the SYSversioned type include Member_of_Version_Set, Preceding_Version, Succeeding_Version, Version_Description.

4.2.4 User Defined Relationships

Many other relationships can be defined by the modeller to describe the properties of the particular software environment under study. Included among these are:

implements - between an algorithm and a specification

uses - between an algorithm and a data abstraction

chosen-together - between two implementations

Relationships need only to be built into the conceptual model if some value is to be added to the data manager by special support for that type of relationship. For example, if the database design tool contains an inheritance graph for that relationship, then useful information can be incorporated into the model. The above relationships while fundamental to software engineering analysis can be implemented in a straightforward manner using the features already present in the DMC model. Thus, they are not explicitly supported in TugBoat.

4.3 Office Data Model

The office information system portion of the DMC project is predicated on the assumption that forms are an essential ingredient of office life. This supposition has led to the design of a forms-oriented data model and an associated database design and query system (Compass). Compass introduces a new relationship, GIVES-INFORMATION-TO, which is employed to describe the flow of information among forms in an office. Forms and the actions upon them are conceptually described by a Form Information Graph (FIG) as pictured in Fig. 12. Actions are internal or external events which result in the generation of a form instance. In Compass, the form is the primitive system object type and all actions are expressed as operations on form types. The query facility permits the office worker to request information from the database using forms to provide context for the queries.

The GIVES-INFORMATION-TO relationship is analogous to the IS-A relationship employed in the initial DMC model. However, the former supports partial inheritance since not all attributes must flow from one form to another. Actions trigger the information flow between forms and thus are an essential part of the GIVES-INFORMATION-TO inheritance mechanism.

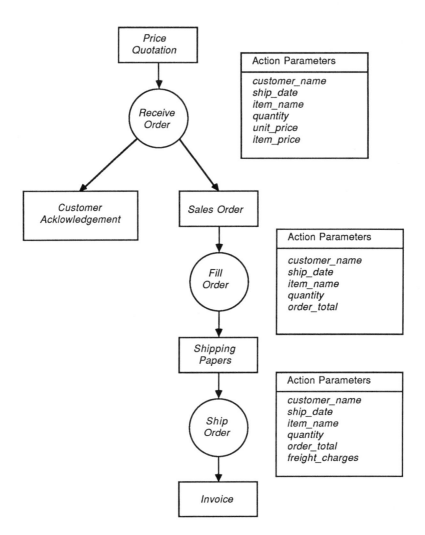

Fig. 12: *Compass Form Information Graph*

4.3.1 Design Tool

The Navigator database design aid is organized along the same basic lines as SeaWeed. In Navigator, the FIG is the focal point for the design. After specifying the high level information flow by drawing a FIG, the designer is provided with a series of Form Definition Templates (see Fig. 13) upon which complete details on each form type are itemized. Operations on the form types are delineated in essentially the same manner as in SeaWeed. Navigator also contains a form imaging component which permits the designer to edit a system provided form layout.

FORM NAME: Sales Order

FORM FIELDS					
name	type	source	change	group	key
order_no	string[6]	*user*	Y		Y
ship_date	string[8]	inherited	N		
item_name	name	inherited	N	items	Y
quantity	integer	inherited	Y	items	
unit_price	real	inherited	Y	items	
item_price	real	inherited	Y	items	
customer_name	name	inherited	N		
cust_street	*name*	*FROM customer list*	N	*address*	
cust_city	*name*	*FROM customer list*	N	*address*	
cust_state	*string[2]*	*FROM customer list*	N	*address*	
cust_zip	*string[10]*	*FROM customer list*	N	*address*	
total_amount	*operation*		N		
discount	*real*		Y		
order_total	*operation*		N		

FORMULAS	
field name	formula
net_total	*total_amount - (discount * total_amount)*
total_amount	*SUM (item_price)*

Fig. 13: Compass Form Definition Template

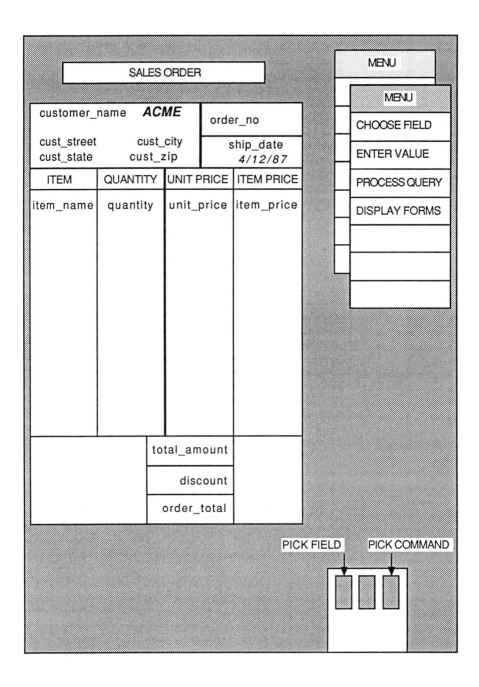

Fig. 14: *Sextant Query*

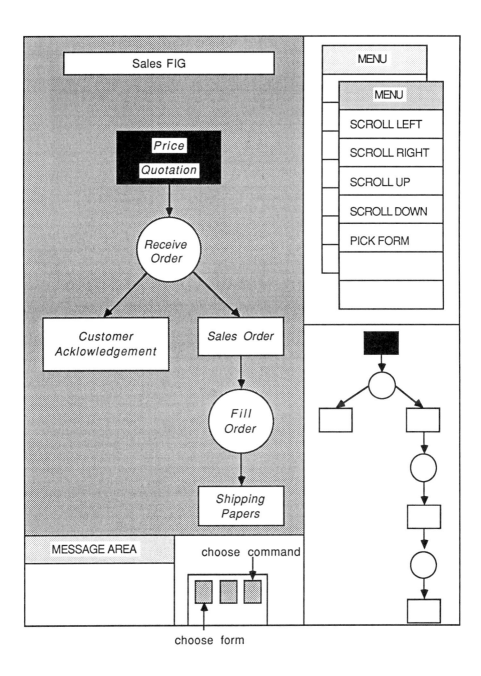

Fig. 15: *Fig Traversal in Sextant*

4.3.2 Query Language

In Compass, forms designed using Navigator serve as the basis for queries that the end user expresses via Sextant. A form filling approach similar to that followed by Surf is employed in Sextant as shown in Fig. 14 which portrays the query which retrieves all Sales Orders for customer Acme with requested ship dates of April 12, 1987. Once a set of forms has been selected by a Sextant query, related forms can be obtained by navigating the FIG. Fig. 15 illustrates the selection of all Sales Quotation forms which are ancestors of the Sales Order forms retrieved by the query of Fig. 14. At any point in the Sextant session, a set of forms may be refined by a further query or a new set obtained by traversing the FIG. Sextant takes advantage of the structure provided by the forms and Form Information Graph designed for the particular environment to offer the end user a comfortable context for query formulation.

5 Modelling Primitives

The experience gained by the development of the above data models has been applied in the specification of a set of parameters for the description of relationships of semantic data models. This parameter set is used to define the primitive relationships of an object-based conceptual model. The values of the parameters for a given relationship are to be specified by the data model designer. Each parameter value will have an associated set of semantic routines which will be linked together to create the software components of an object-oriented database management system.

The parameters are presented below along with the range of meaningful values for each.

1. Cardinality - relationships may be either one-to-one, one-to-many, or many-to-many. The first two values result in the automatic generation of integrity constraints which enforce the appropriate limitation on the number of entities participating in the relationship. Many-to-many relationships are the most flexible and require the most elaborate internal representation.

2. Inheritance - two forms of inheritance are possible:

    a. Type - in which properties, operations, and constraints of one entity type are passed to another.

    b. Value - in which the values of properties are passed from one object to another. Value inheritance implies type inheritance.

    For both forms of inheritance, either all or a part of the properties or values may be inherited via the relationship. In addition, the relationship may support the cancellation property which permits the inheritance mechanism to be overridden at run time. For example, the FACULTY entity type may inherit the MAIL_STOP attribute and value from the DEPARTMENT type. Normally, the value of FACULTY.MAIL_STOP would be identical to that of DEPARTMENT.MAIL_STOP. However, if cancellation were permitted on this attribute, a different MAIL_STOP could be assigned by the user.

3. Insertion constraints - the existence of a relationship between two entity types may imply that if an entity of the target type is inserted into the database, the source entity must already be present. As an example,

consider the ADVISES relationship which could have the associated constraint that each GRAD_STUDENT entity must be related to a FACULTY entity via ADVISES when the GRAD_STUDENT is inserted in that database. For all relationships it is implied that the target entity is either known or null for each source entity.

4. Deletion constraints - for some relationships, the deletion of the source entities implies the deletion of the target entities. An alternative constraint is that all connections of the particular relationship type must be severed before the source entity can be deleted. Thus, a deletion operation on a FACULTY entity could fail if the entity is related to GRAD-STUDENT entities via the ADVISES relationship. An invariant which indicates that the target must be known or null holds over all deletion operations.

5. Arity - indication as to whether the relationship is binary or n-ary. The arity is determined by the number of entity types participating in the relationship.

6. Representation - the relationship may be realized internally as either an attribute of the participating entities, a separate entity, or as an independent element of the model. For independent elements, a graphical representation may also be defined for use in the design tool that will be generated. In the DMC model, the IS-A relationship is an independent model element. It is graphically represented in the design tool by a hierarchy.

7. Properties - relationships may have attributes, constraints, operations, or themselves participate in other relationships. Consider the TAKES relationship between STUDENT and COURSE. This relationship would have the attribute GRADE and operations ASSIGN_GRADE, CHANGE_GRADE.

An example of the description of relationships via these parameters is offered in Table 1 which presents an abbreviated summary of the characteristics of the four fundamental relationships of the initial DMC model.

	IS-A	ASSOC.	NEST	REF.
CARDINALITY	M:N	M:N	1:N	1:N
INHERITANCE	TYPE/FULL	NONE	VALUE/PART	NONE
CANCEL	NO		NO	
INS. CONS.	NONE	OPT.	YES	OPT.
DEL. CONS.	SOUR. -> TARG.	EITHER	SOUR. -> TARG.	EITHER
REQ/OPT	REQ	OPT	REQ	OPT
ARITY	BINARY	N-ARY	BINARY	BINARY
REPRESENTATION	ELEMENT	ENTITY	ATTRIBUTE	ATTRIBUTE
PROPERTIES	NONE	ALL	NONE	NONE

Table1: CHARACTERISTICS OF INITIAL DMC RELATIONSHIPS

The set of all values for the parameters provided above defines the class of data models which can be generated by the Data Model Compiler. Further exploration is required to determine the set of existing models included within the set and, perhaps more interestingly, the set of excluded models. the use of the fundamental relationships of the model as the taxonomical mechanism for data model classification has strong intuitive support [PeMa88].

6   Conclusion

6.1 Current Status

SeaWeed, ShipWreck, Surf, and Scrimshaw are operational while Compass and TugBoat are in the final stages of implementation. The initial design of the data model generation facility has been completed with prototyping to be initiated shortly.

6.2 Future Plans

Thus far, the DMC project has focused upon understanding the fundamental principles of object-oriented data models by designing and implementing a number of distinct models. Based upon the knowledge garnered during the experimental portion of the project, a methodology for generating object-oriented database systems can be formulated. The development of a prototype model generation facility is now underway. One key ingredient in the data model generation process is a special-purpose knowledge base which maintains the component software modules and assembles them based upon the rules for the particular model. The knowledge base concept is receiving further investigation.

The development of a tool for the synthesis of object-oriented database systems based upon user-specified data models is intended to facilitate the expansion of data management technology into non-traditional areas. The Data Model Compiler will permit the application of a model specifically oriented toward the problem domain to the management of data in that domain. Use of an application specific model is expected to produce an isomorphism between the conceptual model of the application designers, implementors, and users and the model of the database system. Moving the data model closer to the human's perception and away from the physical representation within the computer can lead to more productive applications of data management technology. This goal of simplifying the task of designers and end users has been a cornerstone of object-oriented data model research [BoMW84]. The Data Model Compiler is designed to help realize that goal.

7   References

[BoHQ86], [BoMW84], [Brac83], [Brae85], [CoFT84], [ElWi80], [Fran85], [GGKZ85], [GlLu86], [HaLo82], [Hong85], [Huan84], [KiBa84], [LuYa81], [MaHo85], [MyBW80], [Nixo83], [Peck85], [PeMa88], [R85], [Rein84], [Spoo84], [Stoc86], [Stud80], [Wied83], [Zdon85], [Zloo81].

19
Design Issues for Object-Oriented Database Systems

S. L. Osborn

Abstract

A distinction is made between extensible database systems, object-oriented database systems and database system generators. For applications such as computer-aided design and software engineering environments, with complex data, we argue that extensible databases based on the relational model are inadequate for modeling complex aggregation hierarchies, and cannot model generalization hierarchies properly. We also comment on the types of programming activities which are required to support these application areas.

1   Introduction

In recent years, a great deal of research and development in database management has taken place to satisfy the need for database support for complex application areas such as computer-aided design, computer-aided software engineering, office information systems, pictorial and graphics databases, etc. The result of this research is the emergence of a new generation of database management systems. These new systems fall roughly into three categories: extensible database systems, object-oriented database systems and database system generators.

We use the term *extensible database* system to refer to a DBMS which allows an application programmer or database administrator to add new data types and new operations on these new data types to an existing DBMS. In an extensible database system, the underlying DBMS will always be the same in such modules as concurrency control, recovery, basic storage, and query language. Extensible databases may also allow the addition of access methods and hooks to allow the query optimizer to make use of these new access methods. Note that the new operations added usually pertain to operations on what would be the domains in the relational model, and that the major operators of the query language would not be modifiable. Note also that we are assuming that we already have a database system so that persistence of data and data structures from one instantiation of a program to another is already taken care of. Persistence only becomes an issue if such a system is implemented by augmenting a traditional programming language. Some examples of extensible database systems are RAD, ADT-Ingres and POSTGRES [OsHe86, Ston86, StRo86].

An *object-oriented database system* is an extensible database system which incorporates a semantic data model, which in turn is sufficiently powerful to allow reasonably straightforward modelling of complex objects. Complex objects are objects which have a highly nested structure, like a large piece of software or an engineering design. They may also be very large. The semantic data model should be able to model such things as arbitrary levels of aggregation [SmSm77b], components of aggregates which may be sets of other objects or ordered sequences of other objects, and IS-A or generalization hierarchies [SmSm77a] with inheritance of object components and of operations. Some object-oriented database systems also model versions and knowledge. One should be able to define new operations on these objects, which could have the effect of changing the query interface. It is also reasonable to expect that the other pieces of the database management system work at the object level, for example that the objects are passed to the storage manager as a unit, that locking and recovery are done on a per-object basis, etc. Since this definition inherits all the properties of an extensible database system, object-oriented database systems also allow the definition of new data types, operations on them and access methods. They will have the same underlying concurrency control methods, recovery etc. from one instantiation to another, although, being object-oriented, these modules may differ quite a lot from those found in traditional DBMS's. Some examples of object-oriented database systems are GemStone, Probe, and Iris [CoMa84, MaDa86, LyKe86].

The third category of new systems is the *database system generators, customizers* or *compilers*. These systems allow a database system implementor or architect to design and implement a new type of database management system without having to write all the code for this new system from scratch. Using one of these database generators, one could generate different database management systems which differ in virtually all of their modules. The resulting system could be a traditional (non-extensible) DBMS, an extensible one or an object-oriented one. Examples of database generators are EXODUS, the Data Model Compiler and GENESIS [Care, Mary87, Bato86].

The purpose of this paper is to argue that the new database management systems supporting these complex application areas should be based on a semantic data model which is richer or more complex than the relational model. In other words, they should be object-oriented, and not just extensible. Our insight has been gained through our experience with RAD. Thus we will begin with a brief summary of RAD in the next section, followed by an object-oriented description of what the relational model offers. Then we will show how the relational model is inadequate to model both complex aggregations and complex ISA hierarchies. Finally we will make some comments on the programming activities involved in database management and on what kinds of activities should be supported in the new systems.

2   RAD

RAD (which stands for Relations with Abstract Data types) was conceived in the early 1980s as an attempt to address the problems of these challenging application areas, using a simple extension to the relational model, namely allowing the definition of new domains [OsHe86]. The application programmer is allowed to issue a CREATE DOMAIN statement which registers a new domain with the relational database. Along with this goes some code for managing the bytes which these domain values will occupy. These primitive operations include inserting new values, outputing values, updating values, constant validation, and testing for equality and comparisons. The definition of an arbitrary number of predicates involving an arbitrary number of parameters is also allowed. RAD also has a method for defining aggregates on columns of these new data types and for defining arbitrary transformations. Aggregates provide a way of mapping a relation onto a single value of any type. A transformation maps a relation to a relation, thus providing a very general tool for, say, transforming images from one format to another, or coding such things as the group-by construct of SQL or the transitive closure operation of QBE.

3   Object-Oriented Description of Relations

In order to specify exactly what is lacking in the relational model, it is useful to look at an object-oriented description of what is in the relational model. That is, we will describe the object classes the user deals with when interacting with a typical relational database management system. The word object is used here in the sense of Smalltalk-80 [GoRo83]. Objects in an object-oriented system are organized into classes. Objects in the same class exhibit the same behaviour, as defined by the operations they can perform. The members of an object class are called instances. Instances may have some private memory, called instance variables, which they use to carry out these operations. Classes are arranged in an class-subclass hierarchy. Subclasses inherit instance variables and operations from their immediate superclass(es). The encapsulation provided by the class structure is strict in that if an operation is not defined for a class or inherited from one of its superclasses, then it may not be carried out by the instances of that class.

In [Osbo88], both the relational and the Codasyl model were described in an object-oriented manner. For the relational model we used INGRES for two reasons: firstly it is important to model a real DBMS, not just a model, because only then do we see the complete details of the allowed operations as consistently implemented; secondly we did not model an SQL-based system because the way views are handled is inconsistent [Date86]. We briefly summarize this description here.

What the user deals with in INGRES are Databases, Relations, views and domain values. That is, there are data definition statements which allow the creation of databases, and there are various system manager commands for copying them, restoring them, etc. There are a great many operations dealing with relations; some examples are creating them, retrieving from them, appending to them, etc. These commands treat relations as operands, or in the object-oriented paradigm, as instances of a class of Relations. Each **create relname** command defines a new instance (relation) with its own shape - i.e. its own attribute names and attribute types. It is not possible to create a *subclass* of Relations all with the same shape. One can create several relations of the same shape, one relation at a time, but the system does not recognize these as being any different from all the other relations in the database. SQL-based relational databases are the same - each relation is defined as an instance of a general class of Relations.

The other observation arising from this object-oriented point of view is that there is a sharp distinction between the class of Relations and the various domain classes. One set of operators is provided for relations and other operations like arithmetic and pattern matching are provided for numbers and strings respectively. The only operation even remotely in common among all of these classes is some way of displaying objects in response to the print command. Even though the command operates on a relation, some print routine must be used to display all the domain values. Note also that there is no way for the user to manipulate tuples directly, except only fleetingly in the append command.

4   Modelling Aggregation Hierarchies

All of the application areas mentioned in the introduction need to model objects with complex aggregation hierarchies. Indeed, in earlier work these were called complex objects [LoPl83]. For example, in a software engineering system, a software product might be made up of modules, which in turn are made up to data types and procedures, the latter of which have their component parts like the parameter list and code, etc. One might want to be able to represent objects which constitute less than one line of code, such as every occurrence of every variable name. The model of the software product constitutes one complete aggregation hierarchy but there may well be other aggregates referring to the pieces in this hierarchy, such as who wrote each module, and the documentation and design information which is related to each procedure.

One way to store the above information in a relational database is to make the smallest objects one wants to deal with domain values, and use (many) relations to build up the structure. The disadvantage of this approach is that if an application wishes to treat a software product as a single object, the database will have to perform a multitude of joins to gather up all the pieces from the various relations in which it is stored. This would be expensive, and may be required often in all of the application environments mentioned in the introduction.

Rather than completely flattening the objects, which is the first approach, we could (assuming we have one of the extensible systems) construct abstract data types for some of the intermediate objects in the aggregation hierarchy. Thus we could have an abstract data type for procedures, for example, or for various types of documentation. If one chooses too large a portion of the hierarchy to bury in an abstract data type, say a whole software product, then one may be tempted to implement database operations on this data type in order to be able to ask something like "find me all the modules written by Jim Smith". The problem here comes from the fact that the relational model makes such a sharp distinction between relations and domains. On relations, one has operations which query and manipulate sets of objects. On domains, one can perform comparisons and other unary and perhaps binary operations on single objects. With an extensible database, it is very difficult to choose the correct place in such a hierarchy to place the abstract data types. What is needed is some more flexible system which allows both kinds of operations at all levels, and one that treats aggregation hierarchies as single objects.

5   Modelling Generalization Hierarchies

One of the basic components of most object-oriented data models is some way of modeling generalization hierarchies with inheritance of object components and operations. The applications for which these systems are intended are very large and complex. Inheritance of components of an object class by its subclasses is a natural way to model many applications and is becoming well understood. Inheritance of operations on objects can provide an economical implementation of a complex set of activities. It seems that for these new DBMS's to be successful in supporting these application areas, they must include an inheritance mechanism.

There is an inherent difficulty in adding an inheritance mechanism to the relational model. As we have observed above, the relational model in its current implementations treats relations as instances of a single, general class of Relations. One could define inheritance among these instances, but this would be contrary to the way inheritance is usually handled in object-oriented systems, which is as a relationship among *classes*. Adding the capability to model generalization hierarchies to the relational model requires a fundamental change to the structure of the model. If one does model it with an arbitrary number of classes of relations or aggregates, then it should not be called a relational model. People have a fundamental understanding of how inheritance mechanisms work, and of how the relational model is defined, and one would be unwise to introduce a new model combining these concepts in a manner which goes against this intuition.

6   User Interfaces

Traditional DBMS's provided host language interfaces for application programmers and interactive query languages for casual users. They also assumed that a Database Administrator was available to define the database and choose efficient storage structures. For this new generation of database systems, extensible systems will require someone to define the abstract data types and operations for them. Our experience with RAD was that this job could be done by someone with the expertise of an application programmer [Osbo87]. For an object-oriented database system this might or might not be so. The types of objects required by one of these application areas should be known in advance, so the object classes could be specified by someone akin to a Database Administrator. What we feel will be more difficult will be specifying operations on the objects. As end users, who are engineers or scientists, manipulate their objects, they may discover that they wish to perform operations which were not anticipated by the designer of the object classes. The challenge is to provide a way for them to express these operations which plays the role of SQL in traditional DBMS's, without these end users having to be experienced programmers, and especially without them having to be experienced database system implementors.

7   References

[Bato86], [Care], [CoMa84], [Date86], [GoRo83], [LoPl83], [LyKe86], [MaDa86], [Mary87], [Osbo87], [Osbo88], [OsHe86], [SmSm77a], [SmSm77b], [Ston86], [StRo86].

Part VII

Implementation Aspects

20
Associative Access Support in GemStone

Jacob Stein, David Maier

Abstract

The GemStone object server is the first commercially available system to combine the expressive power of an object-oriented language and model with database features for shared, persistent storage. After outlining GemStone's architecture and data model, we explore the issues that arose in incorporating associative access support into the system. The issues include language constructs for specifying associative search, the organization of auxiliary search structures, whether to index on classes or collections and the interaction with other features of GemStone, such as authorization and concurrency. We then describe how these issues were resolved in the design of GemStone, with language and model extensions for paths and typing, multicomponent indexes on long paths, dependency lists connecting objects to indexes, and two varieties of indexes, based on identity and equality. We conclude with a short section on related research.

1   Introduction

The GemStone object server merges object-oriented language concepts with those of database systems. GemStone provides an object-oriented database language called OPAL, which is used for data definition, data manipulation, general computation, and system management.

Conventional record-oriented database systems, such as commercial relational systems, often reduce application development time an improve data sharing among applications. However, these DBMSs suffer from the limitations of a finite set of data types and the need to normalize data [East80, Sidl80]. Object-oriented languages offer flexible abstract data-typing facilities, and the ability to encapsulate data and operations via the message metaphor.

We believe that combining object-oriented language capabilities with the storage management functions of a traditional data management system results in a system that offers further reductions in application development efforts. GemStone's extensible data-typing facilitates storing information not suited to normalized relations. We also believe that our object-oriented language is complete enough to handle database design, database access, and application coding. The GemStone data model and language are similar to Smalltalk [GoRo83] in syntax and semantics. Those readers not familiar with Smalltalk are directed to Goldberg and Robson [GoRo83].

While the choice of Smalltalk as a starting point met some of our design goals, such as providing an extensible data model and a unified language for design, access and application writing, Smalltalk is by no means a database system. Smalltalk is oriented towards a single user on a dedicated processor, with data objects resident in main memory. We report elsewhere [CoMa84, MaOP85, MSOP86] on some of the requirements for making GemStone a multiuser disk-based system, such as concurrency, recovery, authorization and secondary storage management. This paper concentrates on the particular challenges that the Smalltalk model and language present in supporting associative access to objects and supersedes our previous report [MaSt86]. The remainder of this section describes associative access support in relational DBMSs, their analogs in the GemStone model, and the architecture of the GemStone system.

1.1 Associative Access Support in Relational Database Systems and GemStone

Many relational DBMSs provide expressive power through a query language based on relational calculus [Maie83]. The calculus allows a user to define the desired result of a query rather than providing a detailed description of how to produce the result. These relational systems then select an efficient way to compute the desired result from a family of execution plans. The choice of plan is influenced by the presence of auxiliary search structures such as indexes and hash tables. Indexes are especially useful when the user wishes to select a small subset of a relation's tuples based on the value of a specific attribute. In this case, a good execution plan will look up the desired attribute value in the index, then directly retrieve only the page(s) that contain the desired tuples. The presence of these search structures influences the efficiency of producing the result, not the result itself.

In GemStone, the basic need for auxiliary structures is to efficiently select from a collection those members meeting a selection criterion. We want to find all objects in the collection that either contain a given object, or an object equal to a given object, as the value of a particular instance variable. Direct navigation from an object O to objects for which O is the value of an instance variable is not supported by GemStone. References from one object to another are uni-directional. Providing two-way links is problematical, as an object may be the value of an instance variable in several objects. For example, the same *AcademicDepartment* instance can fill the *majoringIn* variable for many *Student* objects. All GemStone objects are independent: no object's existence is constrained to depend on the existence of another object, nor can any object assume that it makes a unique reference to any of its instance variables' values.

One difference between GemStone objects and relational tuples is that objects are not flat. One should be able to index on instance variables that are nested several levels deep in an object, such as the *chairman* variable of the *AcademicDepartment* object that fills a *Student's majoringIn* variable. An important feature of our model is that an object's identity remains the same regardless of changes in its internal state, and objects reference their components by identity, not value. Thus, the *chairman* of a *AcademicDepartment* object can change with no change being apparent in a *Student* object that references that *AcademicDepartment* object. As we shall see in Section 4, this localization of change influences the complexity of index maintenance.

While objects may be viewed as "fancy tuples" that permit attributes to have other tuples as values, it is misleading to equate relations with GemStone classes. A relation serves both to provide the scheme for its component tuples, and to collect all those tuples. In GemStone, a class defines the structure of its instances, but rarely keeps track of all those instances. Instead, collection objects - *Arrays, Bags, Sets* - serve to group those instances. An object may belong to more than one collection, unlike relational, hierarchical or network models, where a record belongs to a single relation, parent or set. Such multiple membership is allowed in the hybrid relational-network model of Haynie [Hayn81].

1.2 GemStone Architecture

A GemStone system consists of a database monitor, GemStone sessions, and application interfaces. The database monitor allocates oops and disk pages, and serves as a critical region monitor for commits and aborts. For each client application, there is one GemStone session. Each GemStone session provides the full functionality of GemStone. Application interfaces exist for C, Parc Place Smalltalk-80 and Smalltalk/V. In addition, there is a command line interface called Topaz that provides direct access to the full functionality of the system.

Fig. 1 shows a possible configuration of a GemStone system. Currently, a VAX, SUN-3 or SUN-4 may serve as the host. Supported workstations include IBM-PCs and compatibles, Apple Macintosh IIs, SUN-3s or SUN-4s, Tektronix 4300 series workstations and Tektronix 4400 series workstations. When using SUN-3s or SUN-4s as workstations, GemStone sessions may be run either on the host computer or the client workstation. Location transparency is provided in that the client need not be aware of whether the GemStone session is resident or running on the host. The ability to run GemStone sessions on client workstations or the host in a mixed SUN environment is our first step toward full heterogeneous network support.

The four principle concepts of GemStone model and language are **object**, **message**, **method and class**. They correspond roughly to record, procedure call, procedure body and record type in conventional systems. An object is a chunk of private memory with a public interface. Objects communicate with other objects by passing messages. The means by which an object responds to a message is a method. So that each object need not carry around its own methods, objects with the same internal structure and methods are grouped together into a class and are called **instances** of the class.

GemStone supports five basic storage formats for objects, **self identifying** (e.g., *SmallInt, Character, Boolean*), **byte** (e.g., *String, DateTime, Float*), **named**, **indexed** and **non-sequenceable** collections. The self identifying format is used for classes whose instances have uniform size and cannot be updated. No storage is allocated for self identifying objects as their state may be deduced from their OOP. The byte format is used for classes whose instances may be considered atomic, but vary in size. The named format supports access to the components of an object by unique identifiers, instance variable names. The indexed format supports access to the components of an object by number, as in instances of class *Array*. This format supports insertions of components into the middle of an object, and can grow to accomodate more components. The non-sequenceable collection (NSC) format is used for collection classes, such as *Bag* and *Set*, in which instance variables are **anonymous**: members of such collections are not identified by name or index, but a collection can be queried for membership, and have members added, removed or enumerated. Both the indexed and NSC format support dynamic growth of objects, and are bounded in size only by the total number of objects in the system and the physical limits of secondary storage. When objects in these formats grow large, their representation switches from a contiguous one to a B-tree that maintains the members by OOP for NSC's, or by offset for indexed object. The byte format also supports dynamic growth in a manner similar to that for the indexed format. Objects into grouped into logical **segments,** which are the unit of ownership for authorization.

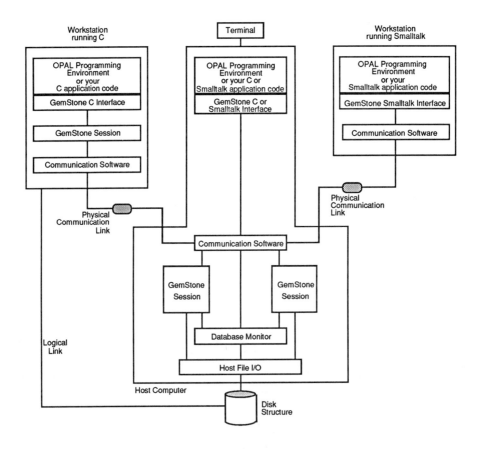

Fig. 1:

GemStone has the capabilities for compiling OPAL **methods** into bytecodes and executing that code, user authentication, authorization and session control. (OPAL bytecodes are similar to the bytecodes used in Smalltalk.) Gem contains the **virtual image**: the collection of OPAL classes, methods and objects that are supplied with every GemStone system. OPAL, being a computationally complete language, can express various associative searches on a collection, such as *aCollection select: aBlock*

which returns a new collection consisting of all elements of *aCollection* for which *aBlock* (a sequence of OPAL statements) returns *true*. In Smalltalk such a search is done by iterating through *aCollection* and evaluating *aBlock* for each member.

2   Associative Access Issues

In this section we elaborate on the problems the GemStone model presents with respect to associative access and indexing. We also present possible solutions to these problems, but leave the details of the solutions actually selected to Sections 3 and 4.

2.1 Language

The two issues here are when to invoke auxiliary access paths for associative searching, and whether indexes should be keyed on an object's structure or its protocol.

How should we indicate or permit the use of indexes in the OPAL language? One solution is to do nothing with the language, and simply provide system classes in the virtual image that the application programmer can use for building and accessing indexes. One drawback with this approach is having to ensure that every application that modifies objects also performs appropriate index maintenance. A second drawback is that having to explicitly deal with an index to support an associative search means application code no longer has physical data independence.

At the other extreme, we could go without modifications to the language, and treat every OPAL expression as a candidate for use of indexing structures in evaluation. OPAL is computationally complete; it is not just a query language. Much of the code operates on single objects, where an index either can't be applied or has no benefit. Indexes are helpful only for operations iterated over members of a large collection. Identifying appropriate iterations for indexing, and determining the intent of the iteration at a high enough level to permit code transformations is a challenging problem in data flow analysis.

Some more moderate positions are to designate certain messages as the only ones for which index use will be attempted, and scan methods for occurrences of those messages, or to add a data sublanguage to OPAL for expressing associative searches, and tailoring the sublanguage to make use of indexes. Adding a sublanguage complicates the language and its compiler. It also introduces the danger of an "impedance mismatch": the sublanguage will be incompatible with the main language as regards data structures or the processing paradigm [CFLR81, Morg83, MaPr84, RoSh79]. If the sublanguage route is chosen, the question is, what kind of sublanguage? It could be a declarative language - an analog to relational calculus. We note that GemStone already has a declarative flavor to it. Messages to objects say what to do; it is left up to the object which method to use - the determination of how the message should be performed. However, the choice is on an individual message basis - there is no ability to take an expression with multiple messages and reorder the message sends or otherwise optimize across methods.

A calculus-like language could support associative searching, extraction of subparts of objects and creation of new objects as the answer to a query. One problem here is, of what class are the resulting objects? Allowing a query to assemble new objects arbitrarily would mean creating classes on the fly. Another problem is whether variables in calculus queries range over classes or collections. Allowing a variable to range over all instances of a class means that a collection of those instances must be maintained. The collection of all instances of a class is not necessarily a semantically useful entity for querying. Usually it is collections of a subset of all instances that are of interest. Also, how do we deal with the situation where a user is only authorized to access some of those instances? Having variables range over collections introduces a problem with binding the query to the specific collections. If the actual collections are not determined until run time, little preprocessing of the query can take place.

One disadvantage of a full calculus sublanguage is that a query must be translated before it can be processed. Being able to interpret a query as regular OPAL code and evaluate it by brute force is useful for avoiding the translation overhead on queries involving small numbers of objects, and to have a "semantic benchmark" for validating associative access routines during system development. A more restricted declarative language might support only selection, avoiding the need to create new classes for the results of queries. The selection conditions could be arbitrary blocks of OPAL code, or have some restrictions. A problem with arbitrary blocks of code is that such code can have side effects on the objects being examined. Side effects make it hard to ensure that evaluating a query with and without an index gives the same answer.

A sublanguage could be more procedural, but still encapsulate iteration - an algebra for collections of objects. Some of the required operations are already present in GemStone, mainly Boolean operations on sets. We have the same problem with join operations as we had with a full calculus language: having a class for the result. While algebras have been proposed for non-1NF relations, we have yet to see a workable algebra for complex objects with identity. In particular, there are semantic difficulties with shared instance variable values, cycles of objects and value-based versus identity-based comparisons.

Another major issue regarding languages is whether indexes are based on the structure - the instance variables - of objects, or the protocol - the responses to messages. For example, if *aStudent* is a *Student* object, we could access that student's last name with some kind of structural notation, such as

>   *aStudent.name.last,*

where *name* and *last* are instance variables, or we can use the message notation

>   *aStudent name last,*

where *name* and *last* are unary messages. If indexes are based on message notation, we must know which updates to an object can influence the result of other messages, so that we know when to update the appropriate indexes. Also, as a method can implicitly change the state of an object, we need assurances that a message will return the same result twice in a row if the structure of the object has not been explicitly changed. The method for a message can be overridden in a subclass, which presents problems in

allowing kinds of[1] a class into a message-based index along with instances of
the class. One problem of other models for message-based indexing not
present in GemStone is attributes inherited through the "component-of"
hierarchy [Brod84]. For example, the absolute position of a machine part could
be computed from its relative position to the assembly that contains it, which
makes an index on absolute position prohibitive to maintain. An OPAL method
may access an object's instance variables, but may not directly access other
objects that contain the object as the value of an instance variable.

Indexing based on structure has the advantage that it can be supported
without involving GemStone's execution model. Indexing on structure violates
the privacy of objects, as it bypasses an object's protocol. One could view an
index on an object as being part of the implementation of the object's class,
and hence being privy to the internal structure of the object. In our experience,
most user-defined classes include methods for setting and fetching each
named instance variable anyway.

2.2 Index Structure

When indexing objects on their internal structure, one question is, how deep
to index? Do we index only the immediate instance variables of an object, or
do we allow indexes on instance variables of instance variables? With a one-
level index, an object is always in hand when a change that can affect its
position in an index occurs. With a multilevel index, as
aStudent.majoringIn.chairman, we have the problem that a change in an
object's position in an index can be caused by a change in a subobject that is
not manifested in the object itself. (An academic department can get a new
chairman without the change being apparent in a student majoring in that
department.)

When indexing on paths with multiple links (multiple instance variables), we
have the choice of a single index for the path, or several indexes, one for each
link in the path. For *aStudent.majoringIn.chairman*, we could have one index
on *majoringIn.chairman* mapping chairmen directly to the students in the
department they chair, or we can have one index on *majoringIn* mapping
departments to students, and another on *chairman*, mapping chairmen to
departments. With a single index on the entire path, there are fewer indexes to
maintain, and fewer consultations needed for an associative lookup. Indexing
on links means more indexes, but not all the indexes will have as many
entries as the index for the entire path. One thousand *Students* may reference
only twenty different *AcademicDepartments* in their *majoringIn* field.

Indexing by links means prefixes of a path are indexed as well: indexing
ability on *aStudent.majoringIn.chairman* implies ability on
aStudent.majoringIn. Supporting a path index as multiple link indexes also
allows sharing between path indexes with a common prefix, such as
aStudent.majoringIn.chairman and *aStudent.majoringIn.division*.

Since GemStone associates types with objects rather than variables, we
can not tell a priori that an object supports a certain path, or the class of the
object at the end of the path. In a collection of Student objects, if we want to
create an index on *aStudent.name.last*, we need to know that the path is
defined for every object in the collection. That is, that the value of the *name*
instance variable is an object that contains a *last* variable. Further, if the index

---

[1] A Object O is a kind of its class and its class's superclasses.

is to be ordered, we need to know that the *last* variables of elements hold comparable values, such as *Strings*. We need typing on collection elements and instance variables to support indexes, unless we want to deal with the complication that not all collection elements will be indexed.

Additionally, we need to consider the following questions concerning typing of instance variables.

1. The link-versus-entire-path question comes up again. We could type *name* in *Student* to always hold a *PersonName* object, and type the *last* variable for the *PersonName* class to always be a *String*. Alternatively, we could declare a single constraint on *Student* that *name.last* be a *String*. Typing on single links is easier to support, while "path typing" might cut down on the number of classes that must be defined.

2. A related question is what to use as types: classes, kinds or some kind of structural or operational template. Classes as types are easiest to check, since an object carries a reference to its class. A kind (a class plus all of its subclasses) requires access to the class hierarchy for checking, but seems more natural for most applications.

3. Is *nil* a member of every type? What about *nil* values along a path? Should they be disallowed? Should selection conditions be given the semantics that the existence of the path is presumed? That is, should both

    > *aStudent.name.last* = 'Smith'

    and

    > *aStudent.name.last* ≠ 'Smith' *(not equal)*

    be false if *aStudent.name* is *nil*? We could interpret the value of any path with *nil* along it as nil for the whole path (in which case the second comparison above will succeed).

4. How much typing? Do we insist that every class have all of its instance variables typed? Complete typing gives us more chances for early binding in queries, but partial typing allows flexibility during applications development and makes OPAL code and classes more reusable.

5. Should an index be based on identity of key objects or their values? An identity index is immune to changes in the key object's state. However, an identity index on *Strings* will not support range queries. On the other hand, if we build an index on *String* objects sorted on their contents, we must detect the case where some method changes the characters of one of those *Strings*. An alternative to detecting changes is to disallow them by constructing immutable subclasses whose instances are not allowed to change after creation.

6. If range indexes are allowed, what comparison operators are allowed for the sort order? If the programmer supplies a method for the comparison, how do we know it is transitive and antisymmetric? Suppose we type by kinds and the comparison method is overridden in a subclass?

2.3 Indexing on Classes versus Collections

Another choice in designing associative access is what to index, classes or collections? Several applications can use instances of the same class, and store them in different collections (like having several relations on the same scheme [Hayn81]). Indexing on the class requires applications that do not use the index to still bear index-related overhead for indexed instances that they use. Further, a classwide index presents authorization problems. No one user may have read access to the set of all instances of the class, so no one is able to request that the index be created. Also, indexing a collection allows the possibility that instances of subclasses be included in a collection that is indexed. Indexing on a class basis makes it easier to trace changes to the state of an object that will cause the object to be positioned differently within an index. We can flag a class-defining object to indicate which instance variables are indexed, and trap to index maintenance routines whenever one of those instance variables is modified.

As an object may participate in many collections, if we index on a class basis, but pose queries against collections, there will be a test for collection membership needed in addition to the index access. On the other hand, if we index by collections, and use references from objects to indexes to support update, each object must be able to reference a number of indexes, not just one. Of course, even if indexing is on classes, it is possible to have a particular class collect all of its instances. If we do index on classes, there is a question of whether a class indexes all the instances of its subclasses as well, or if each subclass must maintain its own index. The latter course probably has unacceptable overhead for a class with more than just a few subclasses.

There is middle ground. We can maintain a single index (per instance variable) per class, but only add members of selected collections to that index [Purd]. With this hybrid scheme, a collection knows if it is indexed, and informs the appropriate class when it adds or deletes elements. However, every instance of the class still pays a penalty on update, as it must be checked for membership in one of the indexed collections, although the penalty is not as large as for indexing by class.

2.4 System Interaction

In determining our indexing strategies, we must take into account how index maintenance affects concurrency, authorization, storage management and performance.

1. Index access requires the same concurrency control as access to any other object. Another factor in the class versus collection decision is that having a class-wide index can cause artificial concurrency conflicts among applications that access disjoint sets of objects.

2. An index should not give away information that is otherwise unavailable to a user. Authorization in GemStone is by single objects; it depends upon which segment they are placed in. A user may have access to a Student object without having access to the value of the *courseHistory* variable of the object (except for its identity). Allowing a user to build an index on *Students* for some path through *courseHistory* could allow him or her to deduce the values of some of the unauthorized information. We could forbid building an index on unauthorized values. However, suppose an index is already built, and permission on some object in it is rescinded what happens to the entry for that object in the index? An alternative is to allow the index to be built, but to check authorization upon access. Another aspect of authorization is that the use of an index might avoid the touching of an object that would be touched if the query were executed without using the index. Generating an access violation in the second case but not the first violates transparency of index use.

3.   Index maintenance clearly will cost in space and time. However, where
      the penalty is paid is important. In some cases we can get an
      improvement in access speed only at the cost of greatly increased cost
      during updates for objects. It is hard to judge if such trade-offs are worth
      while without a good estimate of relative frequency of update versus
      access.

Many of the issues in this section can be addressed by building index
structures in object space. GemStone can then worry about concurrency
control, recovery, mapping large index structures to pages and movement of
index objects between main memory and disk. However, if index and regular
objects were indistinguishable, some opportunities for caching and increased
concurrency may be lost.

3   Typing and Path Expressions in GemStone

In this section and the following one, we outline the actual choices made on
language design and indexing strategy in GemStone. In order to facilitate
associative access, both paths and instance variable typing have been
introduced into OPAL.

3.1 Path Expressions

A **path expression** (or simply a **path**) is a variable name followed by a
sequence of zero or more instance variable names called **links**. The variable
name appearing in a path is called the **path prefix**; the sequence of links, the
path suffix. The value of a path expression $A.L_1.L_2.....L_n$ is defined as
follows:

1.   If n=0, then the value of the path expression is the value of A.

2.   If n>0, then the value of the path expression is the value of instance
      variable L_n within the value of $A.L_1.L_2.....L_{n-1}$ if $A.L_1.L_2.....L_{n-1}$ is defined
      and L_n is an instance variable in the value of $A.L_1.L_2.....L_{n-1}$. Otherwise,
      the value of the path expression is undefined.

A path suffix S is **defined with respect to** a path prefix P if the value of P.S
is defined.

Consider a variable *aStudent* whose value is an instance of *Student*. The
value of the path *aStudent.name* is defined if *name* is an instance variable
defined in *Student.*. Its value would be the value of *aStudent's name* instance
variable. The value of *aStudent.name.first* is defined if the value of
aStudent.name is defined and *first* is an instance variable in the value of
aStudent.name. Its value would be the value of instance variable *first* in the
value of *aStudent.name*.

Path expressions may be used anywhere in OPAL that an expression is
allowed. The evaluation of a path expression is relatively straightforward, and
follows directly from the definition above. It should be noted that determining
whether an instance variable is defined within an object requires accesssing
the object's class, and a list of instance variable names on which string
comparisons must be made. In contrast, unary messages that return the value
of an instance variable are optimized in GemStone. Thus, while path
expressions can be used apart from associative access, such use is less
efficient than the equivalent sequence of unary messages.

In general, given two objects of the same class, A and A', we can not infer that a path suffix is defined with respect to A' from the fact that the suffix is defined with respect to A. The value of *anotherStudent.name.first* might not be defined even though the value of *aStudent.name.first* is defined, and both *anotherStudent* and *aStudent* are of the same class. While *anotherStudent* will contain an instance variable *name* if *aStudent* does, there is no requirement that the value of *name* be of the same class in both objects. However, if we knew that the class of the value of instance variable *name* were the same in all objects of class *Student*, and that the path suffix *name.first* is defined for any object of class *Student*, then we would know that the suffix is defined for all *Student* objects.

3.2 Typing

In OPAL, constraints on the values of named instance variables may be specified when creating classes. For each named instance variable defined in a class C, a class that constrains the allowable values for the instance variable in instances of C may be specified. The constraining class is known as the instance variable's **class-kind**. In an object of class C, a named instance variable constrained to D may only have a value that is either *nil* or a kind of D. One may think of a class-kind constraint being specified for every named instance variable in every class, where the default class-kind constraint is class *Object*.

Consider class *Student* discussed above. If instance variable *name's* class-kind is *PersonName*, and instance variable *first* is defined in *PersonName*, then in any *Student* object *aStudent* where *aStudent.name* is not *nil*, the path suffix *name.first* is defined.

Class-kind constraints are inherited through the class hierarchy. While class-kind constraints may not be removed in a class's subclasses, they can be made more restrictive. For example if in class *Student* instance variable *majoringIn* class-kind were *Academic-Department*, then in *GraduateStudent*, a subclass of *Student*, instance variable *majoringIn's* class-kind could be *GraduateDepartment* if *GraduateDepartment* were a subclass of *AcademicDepartment*.

A path expression is **constrained** when the class-kinds of all the links in the suffix can be inferred. The **class-Kind** of a constrained path is the class kind of the last link in the path's suffix. More formally, a path expression with no suffix is always constrained. The class-kind of a path A is the class of object A. A path $A.L_1.L_2.....L_n$ is constrained if $A.L_1.L_2.....L_{n-1}$ is constrained, and a constrained instance variable L_n is defined within the class-kind of $A.L_1.L_2.....L_{n-1}$. The class-kind of $A.L_1.L_2.....L_n$ is the class-kind of Ln in the class-kind of $A.L_1.L_2.....L_{n-1}$. A path expression $A.L_1.L_2.....L_n$ is **partially constrained** if $A.L_1.L_2.....L_{n-1}$ is constrained. (There is no class-kind for a partially constrained path that is not also constrained.) A path suffix S is **(partially) constrained with respect to** a path prefix P if P.S is a (partially) constrained path.

Note that if S is (partially) constrained with respect to P and P' is an object of the same class as P, then S is (partially) constrained with respect to P'. This observation allows us to say that a path suffix is **(partially) constrained with respect to** a class C if it is (partially) constrained with respect to any, and therefore all, objects of class C. Furthermore, given the inheritance of instance variable constraints, if a path is (partially) constrained with respect to a class, then the path is (partially) constrained with respect to all of the class's subclasses.

In summary, a constrained path always leads to an object that is either *nil* or of a certain kind; a partially constrained path always leads to an object, but we do not know what kind of object it leads to.

Allowing *nil* to be the value of a constrained instance variable slightly complicates the notion of a path suffix. To overcome this complication, we introduce an object *undefined* and redefine the value of a path expression $A.L_1.L_2.....L_n$ whose suffix is partially constrained with respect to its prefix as follows:

1.   If n=0, then the value of the path expression is A.

2.   If n>0, then if the value of $A.L_1.L_2.....L_{n-1}$ is *nil* or *undefined*, the value of the path expression is *undefined.* Otherwise, the path expression's value is that of instance variable L_n in the value of $A.L_1.L_2.....L_{n-1}$.

That the above definition is well formed follows directly from the fact that for any partially constrained path $A.L_1.L_2.....L_n$, if the value of $A.L_1.L_2.....L_{n-1}$ is neither *nil* nor *undefined*, then L_n is an instance variable in the value of $A.L_1.L_2.....L_{n-1}$. What distinguishes a path whose value is *undefined* from one whose value is *nil* is that in the former case the path can not be fully traversed, while in the latter, the path can be traversed, and leads to the value *nil*.

Among *Collection's* subclasses, class Bag and its subclasses are unordered, containing only anonymous instance variables. These are the non-sequenceable collection classes (NSCs) introduced in Section 2, which provide relatively fast identity-based membership, union, intersection and difference operations.

A class-kind constraint may be specified for an NSC class. An NSC may only contain nil and objects of the class-kind specified in the NSC's class. One may view the class-kind constraint specified for an NSC class as a constraint on the anonymous instance variable. If a path suffix is (partially) constrained with respect to the class-kind of an NSC, then the suffix is **(partially) constrained with respect to** both the NSC and its class.

Consider class *Student* discussed above. By creating a subclass of *Bag* or *Set* whose class-kind is *Student*, NSC's can be created that contain only *nil* and objects whose class is a kind of *Student*.

Class-kind constraints for NSCs are inherited throughout the class hierarchy. In the same manner as for named instance variables, class-kind constraints can be made more restrictive in subclasses of an NSC class. For example, given a class *SetOfStudent* whose class-kind is *Student*, a subclass of *SetOfStudent*, say *SetOfGraduateStudent*, can be created whose class-kind is *GraduateStudent*, since *GraduateStudent* is a subclass of *Student*.

4   Indexing in OPAL

4.1 Design Considerations

In OPAL, indexes are attached to NSC's, and are only allowed on constrained and partially constrained paths. By so restricting indexing, the access path that an index represents can be determined at the time of index creation, using only class objects; there is no need to recompute the access path represented by a path expression for each element of an NSC.

OPAL supports two kinds of indexes: identity and equality indexes. Since the identity of an object is independent of its class, identity indexes may be created on partially constrained paths and support the operators == (identical to) and -- (not identical to). Equality indexes support the operators =, ≠, <, <=, > and >=. Equality indexes may be created only on constrained paths. Furthermore, in order to avoid the interpretive execution of the operators supported by equality-indexes, the class-kind of equality indexed paths is restricted to *Boolean, Character, DateTime, Float, Fraction, Integer, Number, String, SmallInteger*, and subclasses thereof. Note that *undefined* is equal and identical to only *undefined*, and is not less than or greater than any object.

The user needs to be aware that if he changes the meaning of one of the supported operators for a subclass of one of the classes above, equality indexes will not support the modified meaning of the operator. However, we consider the likelihood of such modifications low, and in any event, believe that the vast majority of applications will use the default meanings of these operators with respect to the class-kinds upon which equality indexes may be built. Furthermore, the system administrator can, if desired, protect the methods that implement these operators from being overridden.

Consider class *Student* discussed above. In addition to instance variables *name*, let *address* be an instance variable defined in Student that is constrained to *Address*. Further, in *Address* let *state* be an instance variable constrained to String and let *zip* be an instance variable constrained to *SmallInteger*. In *SetOfStudent* objects identity and equality indexes can be created on the suffix *name.first*, *address.state* and *address.zip*. Identity indexes can also be created on *address*, *name*, the empty path and any other path that is partially constrained with respect to *SetOfStudent*.

Even in the absence of indexes, OPAL takes advantage of constrained and partially constrained paths in evaluating queries against NSCs. By being able to apply the same access strategy to each element of an NSC for a given path and being able to evaluate the comparison operator without the use of message sends, terms that use a constrained or partially constrained path and an operator that the path supports can be evaluated efficiently.

For *Boolean, Character* and *SmallInteger* as class-kinds there is no distinction between equality and identity indexes. As the order of OOPs is the same as the order of values for these classes, the operators supported by equality indexes may be applied to objects of these classes by applying the operator to the OOPs of the objects directly. Therefore, when either an equality or an identity index on a path whose class-kind is a kind of one of these classes is created, an identity index is created on the path and is used to support the equality operators. An identity index on a path whose class-kind is *SmallInteger* also supports equality operators, whereas an identity index on a path whose class-kind is *Integer* (whose values and therefore size are unbounded) does not support equality operators. Additionally, an equality index on a path whose class-kind is *SmallInteger* has a more efficient implementation that an equality index on a path whose class-kind is *Integer*.

4.2 Implementation

Indexes on paths are implemented by a sequence of index components, one for each link in the path suffix. For an index into a *SetOfStudent* object on *name.first*, there would be an index component from *name* values of elements of the *SetOfStudent* object to elements of the *SetOfEmployee* objects, and a component from *first* values of *PersonName* objects to *PersonName* objects. The second index component contains only *PersonName* objects that are *name* values of elements of the *SetOfStudent* object. By our method of implementing indexes, creating either an identity or equality index on a path suffix $L_1.L_2.....L_n$ implicity creates n-1 identity indexes on $L_1.L_2.....L_i$, for $1<i<n$.

All data structures used in implementing indexes are stored in object space, and so are managed by GemStone. However, they are objects that are not directly accessible to the user. In this manner, OPAL's concurrency control mechanism handles concurrency conflicts on index structures.

Currently, all index components are implemented using B+-trees. Given the operators supported by identity indexes, it may be preferable to use linear hashing for the components of identity indexes. Unfortunately, this approach would disallow the sharing of components between identity and equality indexes, and prevent identity indexes on *Boolean*, *Character* and *SmallIntegers* from supporting the operators of equality indexes.

If the path suffixes of two or more indexes into an NSC have a common prefix, then the indexes will share the index components on the common prefix. For example, if there were *address.state* and *address.zip* indexes for a *setOfStudent* object, then both indexes would share the component from *Address* objects to elements of the NSC object. Note that this sharing would occur regardless of the varieties of the indexes.

4.3 Index Maintenance

Every object in GemStone that participates in an index is tagged with a **dependency list**. For every index component in which an object is a key value, the object's dependency list will contain a pair of values consisting of the OOP of the index component and the instance variable name for the component (actually the offset of the instance variable within the object). The pair indicates that if the specified instance variable in the object is updated, then an update must be made to the corresponding index component. Additionally, objects that appear as key values of the last component of an equality indexed path whose class-kind has a byte storage format (i.e., *DateTime*, *Float*, *Integer*, *SmallInteger String*, and subclasses thereof) will have a dependency list consisting of the OOPs of index components that must be updated if the value of the object is modified.

4.4 Indexed Lookups

Identity indexes directly support identity (==, --) lookups. Equality indexes and identity indexes on *Boolean*, *Character* and *SmallInteger*, directly support =, ≠, >, >=, <, <= and range lookups. The only differences in evaluating these lookups is the initial access to the last index component of an indexed path. The evaluation of an indexed lookup begins with a B-tree lookup in the last index component of the indexed path's component path. If the indexed path is of length one, then the lookup is complete. Otherwise, the following sequence is repeated n-1 times for an indexed path of length n. Sort the result of the previous B-tree lookup by OOP. Using the sorted list of OOPs, perform a lookup on the B-tree of the previous index component for the preceding link in the path.

Consider the evaluation of the term A.*name.first* = 'Jones', where A is an *SetOfStudent* object with an equality index on *name.first*. Using the B-tree from the second component of the indexed path, all those names with a *first* value of 'Jones' are found. These *personName* values are then sorted by OOP. By performing an incremental search of the B-tree of the first component, using the sorted list of *PersonName* values as lookup keys, the elements of A whose *name* values have a *first* value of 'Jones'are found.

By not having index entries for *nil* elements of an NSC, and not propagating entries for *nil* key values to next-components, indexed lookup never return elements of the NSC for which a path is undefined. Thus, to find those elements of an NSC for which a path is undefined, one forms an NSC containing the values present in the first index component of the path and performs a set difference of it from the indexed NSC. The values present in the first index component are exactly those for which the path is defined.

4.5 The Query Language

We have chosen to provide associative access through a limited calculus sublanguage. However, we have been careful in constructing the language so that associative queries can be viewed procedurally as OPAL code. We support selection on collections with NSC implementations - subclasses of *Set* and *Bag*. Selection conditions are conjunctions of comparisons, where the comparisons are between path expressions and other path expressions or literals. While simple conjunctive selections might seem limited, we not that about the same support for associative access is supplied at the logical level in Cypress [Catt83] and in the internal representation of Adaplex queries [CFLR81], although those systems, as some others [ZdWe85a], select from classes rather than collections. In an object-oriented model, there is no need for many of the joins used in relational systems, as these joins often serve to recompose entities that were decomposed for data normalization. Entities are not decomposed in the first place in an object-oriented model; most joins are replaced by path-tracing, which we support.

An associative query is a variation on a *select* expression:

students select:

> *{aStudent | aStudent.majoringIn.deptName = 'Physics'&*
> *aStudent.gpa > 3.0}*

We have extended all of OPAL to allow path expressions. The meaning of the above query is the same as for the corresponding OPAL expression with a regular *block*.

students select:

> *[aStudent | aStudent.majoringIn.deptName = 'Physics'&*
> *aStudent.gpa > 3.0]*

Thus there is little impedance mismatch between OPAL and its query sublanguage.

Several extensions to the query language are being considered. Although disjunction can currently be specified with the + (union) message, incorporating disjunction directly into the query language would make it easier to phrase such queries and allow for more efficient execution. A projection operator would allow users to more easily ask questions such as, "What are the majors of students whose GPAs are greater than 3.0?" Such a query might appear in OPAL as:

students select:

{aStudent.majoringIn | aStudent.gpa > 3.0 }.

The ability to navigate through collections would allow users to more easily ask questions such as "Which students have failed a course in their major?" Such a query might appear in OPAL as:

students select:

{aStudent | aStudent.courses.grade = $f &
aStudent.courses.department = aStudent.majoringIn },

where *courses* is constrained to *CourseSet*. In the query above, a student's set of courses is existantially quantified. Universal quantification would allow a user to find out which students had failed all of their courses. To fully exploit navigation through collections, a notation for existentially and universally binding variables in queries needs to be developed, and indexing needs to be extended to allow indexing through collections.

5   Related Work

Experimental extensions of System/R to support complex design objects have dealt with the problem of indexing [HaLo82, LoPl83, PKLM84]. There, complex objects are built of a root tuple, plus a tree of components tuples. The resulting object model differs in a fundamental aspect from ours in that the component tuples are dependent on the root tuple. Those component tuples are removed when the root tuple is removed, and they are not shared with other complex objects. (Later versions of the work allow external references to component tuples, but do not enforce referential integrity [Date83] for such references.) The notion of dependent component objects shows up in other models [Gray84, BaBu84, Nier85b, Weis85]. Each complex object is composed from tuples of several relations; these relations can be indexed on values actually stored in the tuple. In the hierarchy of component tuples, each tuple has a reference to its parent tuple, and may have references to other component tuples in the same object, or to roots of other objects. Further, each root tuple maintains an index to its component tuples at all levels, to aid in traversing from parent to child tuple, and for moving or copying the entire object. The techniques for indexing complex objects in System/R were not directly applicable to our problem, since component objects in GemStone can be arbitrarily shared and are not dependent.

Adaplex [Chan82, CFLR81] provides a model similar to GemStone, but again with a significant difference. Entities (objects) may belong to multiple types (classes), unlike GemStone where every object is an instance of a single class. Other models share this multiple multiple-membership property with Adaplex [Zdon84, ZdWe85a, DoKo84]. Since an entity can acquire mappings (attributes) from all the various types it belongs to, the Adaplex designers have chosen to decompose the storage representation of an entity into a logical record for each type to which the entity belongs. (The logical records for an entity can be clustered on physical storage.) Each connected component of the type hierarchy has an entity dictionary - much like our object table - which maps entity identifiers to logical records. The collection of logical records for a given type can be indexed, but on data values only (not entities) and hence not on the substructure of entities. Adaplex allows declarations that two mappings invert each other (such as *manages* and *manager* between *Employee* and *Department*) to support access from an entity to all other entities containing the first entity as the value for a particular mapping. Note that the individual link indexes in GemStone in essence maintain such an inverse mapping for all objects in a collection, although the inverse mapping is not named.

We also note that Adaplex tightly couples its procedural data language with the host language at the expression level, but preprocesses the host language to extract data accesses and encapsulate them in non-procedural "envelopes". In Cypress [Catt83], entities are maintained separately from information about entities (relationships). Entities in a domain (class) are indexed by identity, and relationships can also be indexed. Further, a linked list can be maintained for an entity and all relationship records in which it appears.

An extension to Ingres allows a programmer to add new data types and index support for them [StRG83]. However, Ingres treats instances of those types as uninterpreted sequences of bits, so instances of such types can not reference other database entities directly. A successor to Ingres, Postgres [StRo86], makes some provision for objects, but does so through storing QUEL and C procedures as attribute values. Since complex objects are something the application designer implements on top of Postgres, its hard for the system to give any direct support to indexing complex objects.

6   References

[BaBu84], [Brod84], [Catt83], [CFLR81], [Chan82], [CoKo85], [CoMa84], [Date83], [DoKo84], [East80], [GoRo83], [Gray84], [HaLo82], [Hayn81], [JoSW83], [Kras83], [LoPl83], [Maie83], [MaOP85], [MaPr84], [MaSt86], [Morg83], [MSOP86], [Nier85b], [PKLM84], [Purd], [RoSh79], [Sidl80], [StRG83], [StRo86], [Weis85], [Zdon84], [ZdWe85a].

7   Trademarks

Smalltalk-80 is a trademark of Xerox Corporation

VAX and VMS are trademarks of Digital Equipment Corp.

GemStone is a trademark of Servio Logic Development Corp.

Windows and MS-DOS are trademarks of Microsoft

Smalltalk/V is a trademark of Digitalk Inc.

21
The Efficient Support of Functionally-Defined Data in Cactis

Scott E. Hudson, Roger King

Abstract

Cactis is an object-oriented database management system developed at the University of Colorado. The data model underlying Cactis is based on a principle we call active semantics, and is designed to support complex functionally-defined data. In an active semantics database, each entity is assigned a behavioral specification which allows it to respond to changes elsewhere in the database. Each entity may be a piece of non-derived or (possibly complex) derived data, and may have constraints associated with it. Derived data and constraint specifications are maintained automatically and efficiently by the system. Furthermore, the active semantics data model supports an efficient rollback and recovery mechanism, which enables the user to freely explore the database. Cactis has been implemented and a distributed version is under development.

1 Introduction

The purpose of this paper is to describe an on-going research project at the University of Colorado. We are developing a database management system called Cactis, which supports a data model based on what we call *active semantics*. The goal of Cactis is to allow a user to model and manipulate real world situations in an efficient fashion. In order to provide this capability, the Cactis data model supports complex derived information. In this way, the user can safely deal with one small part of the database and know that the rest remains consistent and correct. A secondary goal of Cactis is to reduce the burden of learning to use the database, by allowing the user to effectively explore and experiment. Thus, Cactis provides a powerful user recovery and reversal (often called Undo) mechanism.

Object-oriented databases has become a very active research area recently; for descriptions of a number of projects dealing with object-oriented databases, see [DiDa86]. Many of these projects are based on data models which stress the importance of supporting derived information in a DBMS. A

This work is being supported in part by NSF under grant DMC-850516, and in part by Hewlett Packard under an American Electronics Association Faculty Development Program fellowship, and in part by ONR under contract N00014-86-K-0054.

large class of such models are commonly called semantic models. A complete discussion of semantic modeling and its relationship to traditional modeling may be found in [KiMc85]. Briefly, traditional database models support record-like structures and/or inter-record links (e.g., the relational, hierarchical, and network models). Semantic models support expressive data relationships; a typical semantic model allows a designer to specify complex objects, and also supports at least one form of derived relationship, generalization (sometimes called subtyping). With generalization, one sort of object can be defined as belonging to a subcategory of a larger category of objects.

Very few semantic models have been actually implemented, although one of the authors of this paper was involved in a semantic database implementation called Sembase (see [FaKM85, King84b]). While this implementation did succeed in providing an effective means of implementing objects and subtyping, it only supports a restricted class of first order predicate-defined subtypes. Sembase does not support the wide class of derived information necessary for many complex applications. Further, the algorithms which support derived subtypes in Sembase, although they are quite efficient, are not as elegant as we would like. In this paper, we present a data model which is much more generalized in its capability to represent derived information than typical semantic database systems. The mechanism used to keep derived data up to date is also simple and easy to program. (For a full discussion of semantic models and the various experimental implementations, see [HuKi87]).

One of the primary goals of Cactis is to support database exploration. Researchers have taken different directions in providing this capability. Hypothetical databases (see [StKe80, Ston81a, WoSt83]) allow the user of a relational database to pose "what if" questions. Different update paths may be pursued, and the various versions of the original database are supported by a differential file mechanism. In this paper, we present an idea which is similar philosophically, but takes a completely different approach in answering "what if" questions. Database exploration is centered around an efficient means of maintaining constraints and derived data, and an efficient rollback and recovery facility. The effectiveness of this last capability is quite important, as databases with complex derived data have the potential of being very difficult to rollback.

Other researchers have stressed the importance of derived data in knowledge based databases [LaSm84, Morg84, ShKe86]. Much of the previous work in this area has come from research in constraint based programming systems [Born81]. While this work shares many common goals with Cactis, it takes a somewhat different conceptual outlook as well as a considerably different algorithmic approach.

Essentially, the Colorado ACTIve Semantics data mode (CACTIS) extends techniques from attribute grammars (see [Knut68, Knut71]) and incremental attribute evaluation (see [DeRT81, ReTD83]) to construct what we call *active semantics* databases. The term active semantics implies that the various pieces of data in the database are *active*, that is each understands its own local semantics and how its local values can be derived, if applicable, from the rest of the database. Such a database supports a powerful data model, capable of representing complex derived data and constraints.

In the next section, the active semantics data model is briefly described. In section three, an example is used to illustrate the utility of the Cactis system. Section four discusses the implementation of Cactis, and section five gives a discussion of ongoing enhancements to Cactis. Section six gives closing remarks.

2   The Cactis Data Model

In a Cactis database, the semantics of the database are described by an unusual data model. In this section, we briefly and informally present this model, which extends techniques derived from Knuth's attribute grammars [Knut68, Knut71] as well as from more recent work on incremental attribute evaluation [DeRT81, ReTD83] used in syntax directed editors. These techniques have been used extensively in compiler construction to represent the semantics of programming language text. In a Cactis database, the data of the database is held in an *attributed graph*. At a high level, an attributed graph is structured like a conventional network model. Each node in the graph is an instance of a particular named type of data. Each such instance represents some semantically meaningful entity and contains a number of named attributes which describe the entity represented by that instance. Each instance in the database can also be connected to other instances in the database by named relationships of various types.

In addition to this conventional entity-relationship style of modeling, the Cactis model allows *attribute evaluation rules* to be attached to certain attributes. These rules allow attributes to be derived from other attributes within a given instance and from the values contained in related instances. Thus, entities may be active in responding to changes in their environment rather than simply passively storing data. Since attribute evaluation rules can be constructed from arbitrary functions of attributes, it is possible to model and manipulate the complicated semantics that real world entities often possess. It should be noted that, in an attributed graph, the attributes of a given instance may be derived only in terms of attribute values passed to it from instances the given instance is directly related to via named relationships. However, attribute values may be passed transitively from instance to instance. Thus, if the data instance A is related to instance B and instance B is related to instance C, A's attributes may be derived in terms of C's attribute values.

There are two kinds of attributes in the attributed graph, derived and intrinsic. Derived attributes have an attribution rule attached to them, while intrinsic attributes do not. This means that only intrinsic attributes may be given new values directly. Derived attributes are only changed indirectly by computations resulting from changes to intrinsic attributes.

An additional property of the Cactis data model is the ability to attach constraints to attributes. In the data model, a constraint is implemented as a derived attribute value which computes a boolean value indicating whether the constraint has been violated. The attribute evaluation rule in this case is simply the predicate defining the constraint. Whenever an attribute which is designated as testing a constraint evaluates to true, rollback of the current transaction is performed. Since constraint predicates are handled in the same manner as normal derived attribute values, the constraint predicate may be formed using any expression which returns a boolean value.

A number of data models have made provisions for functionally derived data. However, the actual implementations of most of these systems use techniques equivalent to triggers [BuCl79] attached to data. While this method is adequate for sparsely interconnected data, it can present problems for more highly interconnected data. Since there is no restriction on the kinds of actions performed by triggers, the order of their firing can change their overall effect. While this allows triggers to be extremely flexible, it can also become very difficult to keep track of the interrelationships between triggers. Hence, it is easy for errors involving unforeseen interrelationships to occur, and much more difficult to predict the behavior of the system under unexpected circumstances.

By contrast, the effects of attribute evaluation computations used in the Cactis system are much easier to isolate and understand. Each data type in the system can be understood in terms of the attribute values it stores, the values it transmits out across relationships, and the values it receives across relationships. This allows the schema to be designed in a structured fashion and brings with it many of the advantages of modern structured programming techniques.

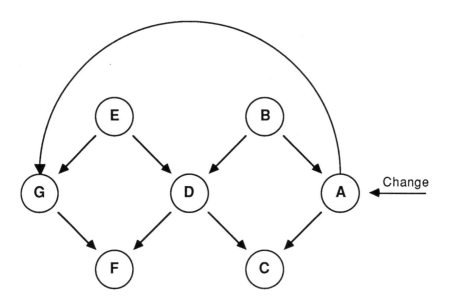

Fig. 1:

Even if we can adequately deal with the unconstrained and unstructured nature of triggers, they can also be highly inefficient. Fig.1 shows the interrelationships between seven pieces of data. The arcs in the graph represent the fact that a change in one piece of data invokes a trigger which modifies another piece of data. For example, modifying the data marked A affects the data items marked B and C. If we choose a naive ordering for recomputing data values after a change, we may waste a great deal of work by computing the same data values several times. For example, a simple trigger mechanism might work recursively, invoking new triggers as soon as data changes. However, in our example, this simple scheme would result in recomputing data value G five times, once for each path from the original change to the data item. In fact, only a few of the many possible orderings of computations does not recompute some data values. Any trigger mechanism which uses a fixed ordering of some sort (e.g. depth first or breadth first) can needlessly recompute some values; in fact, in the worst case can recompute an exponential number of values.

On the other hand, the attribute evaluation technique used in the Cactis system will not evaluate any attribute that is not actually needed, and will not evaluate any given attribute more than once.

While a formal data manipulation language has not yet been defined, Cactis does provide a series of data manipulation primitives which can be used to construct such a language. These primitives include creating and deleting data instances, establishing and breaking relationships between instances, and primitives for retrieving and replacing attribute values. These primitive actions are augmented by the meta-action *Undo*. Undo has the effect of forcing the rollback of one transaction. This meta-action allows the user to freely explore the database, knowing that no actions need have permanent effect.

Whenever changes are made to a database using one of the primitive data manipulation actions, Cactis must ensure that all attribute values in the database retain a value which is consistent with the attribute rules of the system. This requires some sort of attribute evaluation strategy or algorithm. One approach would be to recompute all attribute values every time a change is made to any part of the system. This is clearly too expensive. What is needed is an algorithm for incremental attribute evaluation, which computes only those attributes whose values change as a result of a given database modification. This problem also arises in the area of syntax directed editing systems, so it is not surprising that algorithms exist to solve this problem for the attribute grammars used in that application. The most successful of these algorithms is due to Reps [Reps82]. Reps' algorithm is optimal in the sense that only attributes whose values actually change are recomputed.

Unfortunately, Reps' algorithm, while optimal for attributed trees, does not extend directly to the arbitrary graphs used by Cactis. Instead, a new incremental attribute evaluation algorithm has been designed for Cactis. This new algorithm exhibits performance which is similar to Reps' algorithm, but does have a slightly inferior worst case upper bound on the amount of overhead incurred.

The algorithm works, by using a strategy which first determines what work has to be done, then performs the actual computations. The algorithm uses the *dependencies* between attributes. An attribute is *dependent* on another attribute if that attribute is mentioned in its attribute evaluation rule (i.e. is needed to compute the derived value of that attribute). When the value of an intrinsic attribute is changed, it may cause the attributes which depend on it to become out of date with respect to their defining attribute evaluation rules. Instead of immediately recomputing these values, we simply mark them as *out of date*. We then find all attributes which are dependent on these newly *out of date* attributes, and mark them *out of date* as well.

This process continues until we have marked all affected attributes. During this process of marking, we determine if each marked attribute is *important*. Attributes are said to be *important* if they have a constraint predicate attached to them, or if the user has asked the database to retrieve their values. When we have completed marking attributes during the first phase of the algorithm, we will have obtained a list of attributes which are both *out of date* and *important*. We can then use a demand driven algorithm to evaluate these attributes in a simple recursive manner. The calculation of attribute values which are not *important* may be deferred, as they have no immediate affect on the database. If the user explicitly requests the value of attributes (i.e. makes a query) they become *important*, and new computations of *out of date* attributes may be invoked in order to obtain correct values. A similar implementation approach using lazy evaluation is described in [BuFN82].

Reps' algorithm, which is not demand-driven, has a worst case cost of $O(|\textbf{attributes-changed}|)$, where **attributes-changed** is the set of all attributes whose values actually change, and $|\textbf{X}|$ represents the cardinality of set **X**. Note that this cost analysis is in terms of the number of attributes (not instances) changed. The Cactis algorithm has two phases: marking out of date attributes and reevaluating attribute values. Phase one has worst case cost of $O(|\textbf{could-change}|)$, where **could-change** is the transitive closure of the attribute dependencies starting at the nodes whose primitive values have been updated. Phase 2 also has worst case $O(|\textbf{could-change}|)$.

The above cost analysis gives a worst case for the algorithm. In actual practice the algorithm will often perform much better. In particular, attributes which are not important and have not been accessed (directly or indirectly) can remain in the database with out of date values indefinitely. This means that the first marking phase need not remark these attributes nor any attributes that depend on them when changes are made. This allows computations involving parts of the database which are not currently of interest to be deferred until their values are actually needed. Also, if a given attribute is changed as a result of two different primitive updates to intrinsic attributes, the given attribute will only be reevaluated once (unless of course, the given attribute has been accessed before the second primitive update is performed). As a final note on cost analysis, what we clearly need to develop for the future is a cost measure based on instance fetches, not on attribute reevaluations.

In order to support the primitives which break and establish relationships, a process similar to that used for intrinsic attribute changes is used. When a relationship is broken, the system determines which derived attributes depend on values that are passed across the relationship. These attributes are marked out of date just as if an intrinsic attribute had changed. When a relationship is established, the second half of the attribute evaluation algorithm is invoked to evaluate attributes which are out of date and important. In order to ensure that derived attributes can always be given a valid value, the database ensures that relationships are not left dangling across attribute evaluations. This is either done explicitly by the transaction, or where necessary the system will provide special dummy instances to tie off any dangling relationships. As a final note, the primitive to delete an instance can be treated the same as breaking all relationships to the instance, and the primitive to create an instance does not affect attribute evaluation until relationships are established.

During the evaluation of attributes, certain attributes will have constraint predicates attached to them. After an attribute is evaluated, this constraint predicate is tested. If it evaluates false, a constraint violation exists. By default, this causes the transaction invoking the evaluation to fail and be rolled back or undone. Optionally, a special recovery action associated with the constraint can be invoked to attempt to recover from the violation. In either case, the constraint must be satisfied or the transaction invoking the evaluation will fail and be undone (rollback and recovery will be discussed in section 4).

3   A Sample Session

Fig. 2 is a Parts/Suppliers schema in the Cactis data model. In this application, a middleman buys parts, marks them up, and sells them to his customers. The supplier orders are orders to his suppliers, and customer orders are from his customers. The middleman also has a certain amount of stock on hand, which represents parts that have already been purchased from suppliers, but not delivered to or ordered by any customers yet.

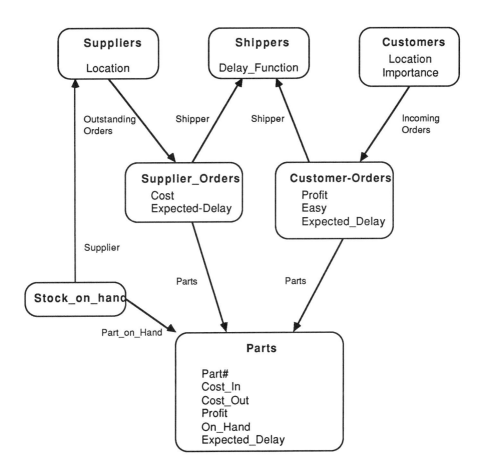

Fig. 2:

3.1 Supporting Derived Data and Constraints

Fig. 3 shows some detail concerning the definition of the derived attributes of Fig. 2. As a simple example, consider the profit attribute of parts. This attribute is defined to be the selling price (Cost Out) less the purchase price (Cost In). Similarly, the profit of a customer order is defined as the sum of the profits for its parts, and the cost of a supplier order is defined as the sum of the cost of its parts. Finally, an attribute is defined for customers which gives their *importance* (computed as the sum of the profits of their orders).

To illustrate the utility of derived information, consider what happens when the middleman changes the selling price of some part. We can expect that this person will be able to find and change the Cost Out attribute of the appropriate part. However, we should not force the user to understand the rest of the database as well. When the user changes the Cost Out attribute of some part, the database will automatically update the profit for that part, as well as the profit for any Customer Order that contains that part, and finally, the database will recompute the Importance attribute of each Customer which is affected. All of this occurs without user intervention, or even user awareness unless a constraint predicate is violated.

Supplier_Orders

    Cost <-- $\Sum$ **over** Parts **of** (Parts . Cost_in)

    Expected_Delay <--

    Apply Shipper.Delay_Function (Outstanding_Orders.Location)

Customer_Orders

    Profit <-- $\Sum$ **over** Parts **of** (Parts . Profit)

    Easy <-- **AND over** Parts **of** (Parts . On_Hand)

    Expected_Delay <--

        Apply Shipper.Delay_Function (Incoming_Orders.Location)

        + Max over Parts **of** (Parts . Expected_Delay)

Customers

    Location   «Intrinsic»

    Importance <-- $\Sum$ **over**

                  Incoming_Orders **of** (Incoming_Orders . Profit)

Parts

    Part#

    On_Hand

    Cost_In

    Cost_Out «Intrinsic»

    Profit <-- (Cost_Out - Cost_In)

        Constraint Profit > 0

    Expected_Delay <--

        Max over Parts **of** (In_Parts . Expected_Delay)

Fig. 3:

If a constraint is violated, the transaction causing the violation fails and is rolled back. In the case of our example, there is a constraint predicate attached to the Profit of Parts. This ensures that a profit is made on each part. As an example, this predicate would fail if the user accidently changed the Cost In attribute when in fact they had intended to change the Cost Out attribute. This sort of a constraint mechanism is particularly important in the case of derived data, since transactions can have wide ranging effects.

3.2 Exploring the Database

As an example of more complex derived information, let's suppose that our middleman is having financial problems. His business is in trouble, and he is looking for a way to cut costs and increase the cash flow into the company. One of the first things he might think of is to adjust his shipper constracts. If he can speed up deliveries, some of his current clients will probably give him more business. So, the middleman tries assigning different shippers to different customer orders. Notice that shippers have an intrinsic attribute: Delay Function. This attribute is in fact a representation of a function which, when given a location, will compute the delay expected for delivery to or from that location. As shown in Fig. 3, this attribute is used to compute an expected delay for each supplier order, then for each part, and finally for each customer order. Each time the middleman assigns a new shipper, Cactis automatically brings the Expected delay attribute up to date for each order, and if the result is not satisfactory, the middleman may quickly reverse the effects of a change by using the Undo command.

Parts

Part#
On_Hand
Cost_In
Min_Cost   «Intrinsic»
Cost_Out <-- **Max** (1.5 * Cost_In, Min_Cost)

Profit <-- (Cost_Out - Cost_In)
      Constraint   Profit > 0
Expected_Delay <--
      Max over Parts **of**   (In_Parts . Expected_Delay)

Fig. 4:

The middleman sees another opportunity for improvement when he notices that often, the Cost In attribute for some part changes. This cuts into his profit. He often does not notice the declining profit for a part until the constraint forcing non-zero profit is violated. Then, the trigger notifies him. Now, with his serious concern over profits, the middleman changes an attribute definition. In

Fig. 4, we see he now has defined Cost Out as 1.5 * Cost In or, an assigned non-derived value, which ever is greater. This ensures him that he will make a significant profit on any part. He no longer needs the constraint on profit.

Both of the above changes will only provide long term help. In order to get his company over the current rough period, the middleman has a smart idea. He will fill the most profitable orders first. However, he realizes that many of his outstanding customer orders require parts that are not on hand. And, of course, buying any new parts would use up what little cash reserve he has.

Customer_Orders

Profit <-- Σ **over** Parts **of** (Parts . Profit)

Easy <-- **AND over** Parts **of** (Parts . On_Hand)

Expected_Delay <--

    Apply Shipper.Delay_Function (Incoming_Orders.Location)

    + Max over Parts **of** (Parts . Expected_Delay)

Emergency_Filling_Order <--

    If Easy **Then** Profit **Else** ∞

Fig. 5:

The attribute Easy already tells the middleman if an order is made up of parts which are all on hand, so, as shown in Fig. 5, he creates a new attribute of Customer Orders called Emergency Filling Order. It is defined as the Profit of the order as long as the Easy attribute is yes; otherwise the Filling Order is infinity. The middleman may now use this new attribute whenever the company has cash problems. It should be noted that as an order is filled and stock on hand is removed, the Easy attribute of other orders will change, but the system will automatically compensate and update the corresponding Filling Order attributes. This implements a greedy algorithm, which while not optimal, is a natural heuristic.

4 The Cactis Implementation

Cactis has been implemented, and consists of approximately 70,000 lines of C code. It runs on a variety of Unix Machines.

4.1 Data Structures

The implementation of the data model at a low level is fairly straightforward. Each instance is given a unique integer identifier. Instances on mass storage are referenced by this identifier using a simple hashed access method. Each instance in the system is structured both in memory and on disk as a header, a block of relationship pointers, and a block of storage for attribute values. The header of each instance contains an index into the schema type table. As would be expected, the schema for the database is kept in memory while the DBMS is running. However, the organization of the schema differs from a conventional database.

A Cactis schema consists of a table of type descriptors. As shown in Fig. 6, these type descriptors encode information about the number of attributes in instances of the type, the number of values transmitted into and out of an instance of this type, and the number and type of relationships that an instance of this type may have with other instances. Type descriptors also contain information about how attributes of an instance of this type are dependent on other attributes within the instance and on values transmitted into the instance across relationships. However, the schema does not directly encode any information about how the storage of attribute values is actually organized (other than the total size of the block of storage that holds the attribute values). Instead, this information is held in compiled code which is responsible for the actual access to information.

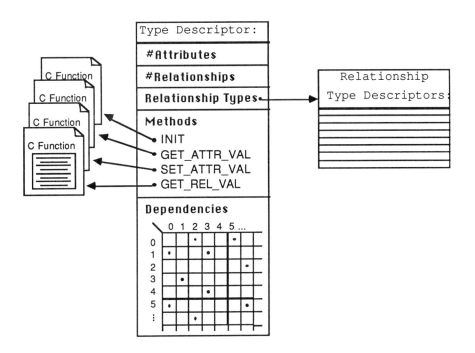

Fig. 6:

In a Cactis database, each instance is implemented as an object which responds to a standard predefined set of messages. These messages include:

Initialize -   assign initial values to attributes of a newly created instance.

Get_Attr_Val - return the value of an attribute within the instance.

Set_Attr_Val - assign an attribute within the instance a new value.

Get_Rel_Val - return a value transmitted out of the instance across a
relationship.

All instances respond to this same set of messages, but instances of
different types will respond to the same message in different ways. One of the
primary tasks of the schema in a Cactis database is to provide the actual
methods which respond to these messages for each type in the system. All
information about how the data is stored is implicitly encoded in the method
routines which are responsible for manipulating the data. In fact, it is not
necessary to actually store all attribute values so long as these values can be
computed when asked for. Consequently, other parts of the schema, such as
the attribute dependency information, need only refer to attributes by an index
and can remain ignorant of the actual storage arrangement used by the
instance.

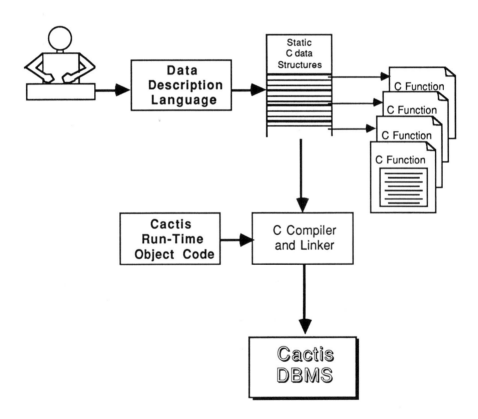

Fig. 7:

Because a Cactis schema contains not only conventional information but
also method routines, it is implemented as statically initialized data stored in

an object file. With this arrangement, the method routines can be implemented as pointers to C functions. The attribute evaluation rules described in some data definition language can then be compiled directly into C functions as shown in Fig. 7. This allows the attribute evaluation rules to use the full power of the C language without reimplementing a special programming language within the database itself.

4.2 Rollback and Recovery

Since Cactis databases are intended to be used in an exploratory manner, they provide a rollback and recovery (or undo) mechanism. The task of rollback and recovery in the presence of complex derived data would seem to be difficult. However, because of the nature of the attribute evaluation algorithms used, Cactis databases can provide this capability with very little additional effort.

The key to rollback and recovery in a Cactis database is that all changes to derived data occur as a result of the automatic attribute evaluation process that is invoked whenever intrinsic attributes are changed. Because of this fact, we can completely reverse the effects of a change to an intrinsic attribute simply by restoring the old value. The same attribute evaluation process that was used to derive information in the first place can be used to *un-derive* the information when rollback and recovery is performed. Because of this, the system need only retain the old value of any changed intrinsic attributes to be able to completely undo the changes. Just as the user can ignore the automatic information derivation process, the system need only concern itself with restoring intrinsic attributes, and need not try to retain information about how these attributes affect other parts of the database.

Because rollback and recovery uses precisely the same mechanisms as the original update process, it is equally efficient. In addition, very little complexity is added to the database. The database need only remember a series of old values and the location of changes along with a (nested) set of markers which delineate the boundaries of (nested) transactions. When a transaction fails, or the user explicitly requests an undo, the system simply restores the saved values back to the appropriate transaction boundary marker. The normal attribute evaluation mechanism then automatically restores the effected derived information.

5   Improving Efficiency

If we ignore the process of attribute evaluation required for updates, a Cactis database can be seen as a simple object-oriented database. Consequently, many of the standard optimization techniques for databases, such as algebraic query manipulation, indexing and clustering [Ullm82], can be used for a Cactis database. Below, we discuss how the known techniques of deferred updates, batching, and clustering have been used to address the specific performance problems associated with the Cactis attribute update algorithm.

Although the attribute evaluation algorithm discussed in section 2 is efficient in terms of the number of attribute evaluations, it was originally designed for use with a relatively small amount of data residing in high speed memory. The rest of this section discusses optimization techniques that have been used in Cactis databases with large amounts of data residing in slower (disk based) storage.

5.1 Deferred Computations

Recall that the attribute evaluation algorithm has two phases: first, a series of attributes are marked *out of date*; then, an evaluation is made of attributes which are *out of date* and *important*. Note that attributes which are not of immediate interest to the user nor have constraint predicates attached (i.e. not *important*) need not be evaluated. Once they have been marked as *out of date* they may remain in the database with their old invalid values until they are actually needed. Only then will they be actually evaluated. In this way, we can defer a significant amount of computation. In addition, this avoids the inefficiency of updating a value several times even though intermediate values are never actually used.

In addition to deferring computations in a long term sense, a Cactis database also defers computations in the short term by using the common technique of batching. Batching is done on a sub-transaction level. The actual transactions given by the user are broken into *transaction fragments*. These transaction fragments are such that the intermediate results of the fragment are not needed until after the fragment has been executed. An example of this would be a series of updates, without intervening queries. No actual attribute evaluations occur until the end of a transaction fragment is reached. Only at the end of a fragment do we begin to mark attributes as *out of date* or perform any actual evaluations. By using batching, we are able to make a more intelligent selection of update ordering, as we will see below.

5.2 Using Concurrency to Improve Evaluation Efficiency

Evaluation of functionally defined data in a Cactis DBMS is performed in a purely applicative manner. By using this applicative model we are not constrained to perform evaluations in a fixed order but need only observe the partial order required by attribute dependencies. Conceptually, many computations may be done concurrently. Even when only one processor is available we may perform the evaluations in the order which is most efficient.

At any one time the system will have a set of values that are *pending*. These are values which are needed to complete some computation(s). Since the order in which these computations are performed cannot effect the result the system may choose to perform them in the order which is most efficient. For example, to evaluate an attribute A we may need the values of attributes B, C, and D while to evaluate an attribute E we may need the values of attributes F, G, and H. If the system can determine that evaluating attributes B, C, and D would likely be inexpensive (e.g. the values happened to already be cached in memory) it can choose to evaluate A first.

In general the system will choose to perform computations involving values that are currently cached in memory first. When all such computations have been performed the system will choose computations which appear to be least expensive based on some hueristic. We are currently experimenting with several such hueristics with the goal of minimizing the number of disk reads needed to complete the computation. For example, we are keeping dynamic statistics about the past I/O cost for computing a particular attribute value and then use this to estimate how much new I/O is likely to take place if we choose to evaluate this attribute next. Using this scheme the system can be self-adaptive using past performance information to choose the most efficient evaluation order.

In addition to information I/O performance for computing particular attribute values, the system also keeps statistics about the frequency of traversal of relationships in the database. This information is then used to periodically reorganize the database to improve its clustering using a simple greedy algorithm. With a well clustered database, when we are forced to read a new block into memory, there is some likelyhood that a number of computations may be performed involving that block before it must be replaced by another.

While this sort of clustering will improve the performance of attribute evaluations, it should be noted that it may conflict with the clustering that might be used in a normal network database to optimize frequently executed queries. A tradeoff may be necessary to balance fast updates with fast query response. This tradeoff will be governed by the relative frequency of updates, and the importance of answering "what if" types questions.

6 Final Remarks

Cactis is a DBMS that has been developed at the University of Colorado. The goal of Cactis is to support very complex derived information in as efficient a fashion as possible. In this paper, we have tried to establish the generality of the Cactis model, the power it provides, and its efficiency.

We are currently experimenting with Cactis for use as the database support for a software environment. Due to Cactis' ability to represent complex derived data and a time and space efficient rollback mechanism, we see it as an ideal database for supporting such derived computations as compilations and configurations, and for supporting versioning. Also, a distributed version of Cactis is in progress, and we plan to experiment with Cactis as the basis of a distributed workstation-based software environment.

7 Acknowledgements

We would like to thank the Cactis implementation team: Pam Drew, Shehab Gamalel-din, Carla Mowers, Loraine Neuberger, Evan Patten, Tom Rebman, Jerry Thomas, and Gary Vanderlinden.

8 References

[Born81], [BuCl79], [BuFN82], [DeRT81], [DiDa86], [FaKM85], [HuKi87], [KiMc85], [King84b], [Knut68], [Knut71], [LaSm84], [Morg84], [Reps82], [ReTD83], [ShKe86], [StKe80], [Ston81a], [Ullm82], [WoSt83].

22
Managing Complex Objects in the Darmstadt Database Kernel System

U. Deppisch, H.-B. Paul, H.-J. Schek, G. Weikum

Abstract

Complex objects are required in many new applications of databases. A common feature is that objects use other (sub-)objects for their description. So, retrieval or update of complex objects may include some or all of their subobjects. The kernel of DASDBS, the DArmStadt DataBase System, is described which was designed and implemented with the objective to provide a storage system for a variety of complex object notions. This paper concentrates on the mapping of hierarchically structured complex records to sets of pages and shows how set-orientation in the operations at the kernel interfaces can be preserved and transformed to operations on sets of pages.

1 Introduction

Recently, research and development in the DBMS area has been oriented more and more towards advanced or non-standard applications. Such applications comprise office information systems, geographical database systems, and especially engineering information systems to support CAD/CAM applications. The following characteristics are required in order to provide better functionality than conventional database systems, and - related to this - to improve performance of a database system, when applied as a basis for advanced applications.

Object-orientation: Molecules [BaBu84, BaKi85a] or complex objects [BaKh86, Daya87, Lori85, Lum85] must be supported in such a way that objects as a whole as well as subobjects can be manipulated by the DBMS. All meta information should be stored as database objects, and the DBMS must provide extensibility of data types and access methods [AMKP85, Care, DaSm86, Ditt86, ScWa86, Schw86, StRG83, Ston].

Set-orientation: Whatever notion of complex objects is convenient for an application, sets of objects should be transferred from the database to the application program. Especially in engineering applications, algorithms often operate on large sets of data as opposed to traditional applications, e.g.

This research was partly supported by the Scientific Center Heidelberg of IBM Germany within the project "Databases in Server-Workstation Environment".

banking transactions. The internal DBMS interfaces should support operations on sets of their objects as well. Even the page management layer and the operating system layer which does the disk I/O should store and retrieve set of pages (blocks). It has been stated that I/Os are the main performance bottleneck in DBMS. On the other hand, it is also known that accessing a set of contiguously stored disk blocks better utilizes the disk's maximum bandwidth than performing single block transfers repeatedly. Basically, this benefit of set-oriented I/O is due to minimizing rotational delays, avoiding diskhead movements whenever possible, and reducing CPU overhead of I/O handling.

In the sequel we will describe how the kernel of DASDBS (see Fig. 1) meets these two requirements. The main focus of this paper is the description of the storage structures which have been designed and implemented under the main objective of set-orientation for the execution of the basic operations. We call this component of the DASDBS kernel Complex Record Manager (CRM). In our architecture it is the next higher layer above the page-oriented Stable Memory Manager which will not be discussed further.

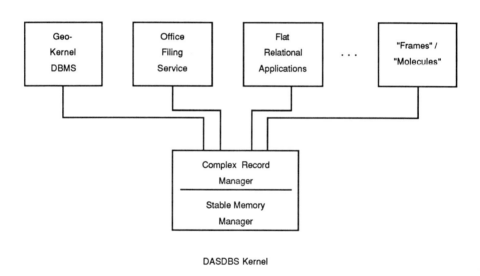

Fig. 1:   DASBDS Architecture: The Kernel and its Extensions

We also do not address other important topics like version support and transaction management (see [Paul87]). Index structures are mapped to kernel objects and therefore discussed only shortly. Applications of the kernel system are described in [ScWa86, ScPS87].

Chapter 2 describes the kernel objects and the operations at the interface of the CRM. Chapter 3 presents the implementation through the appropriate storage structure and the addressing concept. We show in chapter 4 how an operation on a complex record is processed within the DASDBS kernel and how the required set-orientation can be kept. Chapter 5 describes brief examples how indexes and shared subobjects are supported by the kernel. Finally we compare our solution to related work.

2   Complex Records and Operations

2.1 Kernel Objects

The objects of the kernel interface are sets of hierarchically structured and therefore "complex" records. They may be regarded as tuples of the nested relational model, sometimes referred to as NF^2 tuples [ScSc86]. Two kinds of attributes can occur as components of each tuple of a relation: atomic attributes and relation-valued attributes. A relation-valued attribute (subrelation) contains a set of subtuples (subrecords) which again consist of a sequence of atomic and/or a sequence of relation-valued attributes. Note, however, that similar to the RSS component of System R [Astr76] the kernel system has no knowledge about data types like integer, real or more specific data types, except for one data type, namely bytestrings. Atomic attributes have variable length and may even be very long, i.e. span more than one page.

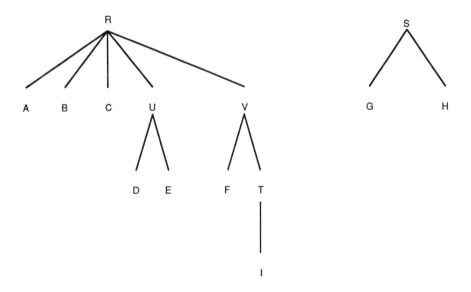

Fig. 2.1: *Schema of internal NF^2 Relations R and S*

In the example in Fig. 2.1, relation S contains the two atomic attributes G and H, and no relation-valued attributes. In contrast to this "flat" relation, the nested relation R consists of the atomic attributes A, B, C and of the relation-valued attributes U and V. The subrelation U consists of two atomic attributes

D and E, whereas the subrelation V contains the atomic attribute F and the relation-valued attribute T with the atomic attribute I.

2.2 Operations on Complex Records

Generally, all CRM operations allow retrieval or update on both entire complex record sets and single attribute values. However, they do not allow to generate a new complex record by a join operation or other composition operators. Because the storage system serves as a kernel system for higher, more application-specific layers, only basic operations are implemented: All CRM operations are performed on one single relation in one single pass through the corresponding pages. they transfer and process a set of complex records. So, the CRM offers single table, single scan, set-oriented operations. In the following we distinguish between retrieval and update operations.

2.2.1 Retrieval by Nested Selection and Projection

The retrieval operations provide not only fast access for complete complex records but also direct access to subrelations and atomic attributes of complex records. Additionally, simple filters can be applied in selections at each level of a hierarchically structured complex record. The retrieval operations are formally characterized by a subset of the NF^2 relational algebra [Sche85, ScSc86]. In short, the RETRIEVE operation provides the following functions:

a) Scan: Get the whole relation, e.g. all complete complex records of relation R.

b) Projection: Get particular parts of the whole relation, e.g. attributes B, C, and U, i.e. all subrecords of subrelation U out of all complex records of R.

c) Nested Projection: Get particular parts of subrelations, e.g. attributes A, U', and V' of all complex records of R where U' contains attribute E of all subrecords of U and V' contains the subrelation T of all subrecords of V.

d) Atomic Selection: Select complex records by (a conjunction of) filters on their atomic attributes, e.g. complete complex records which have a value greater than 25 in attribute A and a value of abc in attribute B.

e) Projection-Selection: Select subrecords by (a conjunction of) filters on their atomic attributes, e.g. all complex records with complete attributes, A, B, C and U, in subrelation V only those complete subrecords which have a value of 100 or less in attribute F.

f) Set-Selection: Select complex records or subrecords by a selection condition on a relation-valued attribute. To retain the single scan property, only comparisons with the empty set are allowed, e.g. select complex records which have at least one subrecord in subrelation V.

g) Nested-Selection: Select complex records or subrecords by an existential quantifier ranging over a relation-valued attribute, which again has a selection condition on some of its attributes, e.g. select complex records which have at least one subrecord in subrelation V which has a value of 100 or less in attribute F.

h) Combinations of the above operations at different nodes of the schema tree, e.g. if there exists any subrecord in subrelation V with an F value greater than or equal to 200, then the query result contains the attribute A and the attribute T of all subrecords matching the search condition.

A RETRIEVE operation is specified by marking a schema tree as shown in Fig. 2.2. Note that the example h is obtained by a combination of the basic retrieval types (b, c, d, e, f, g).

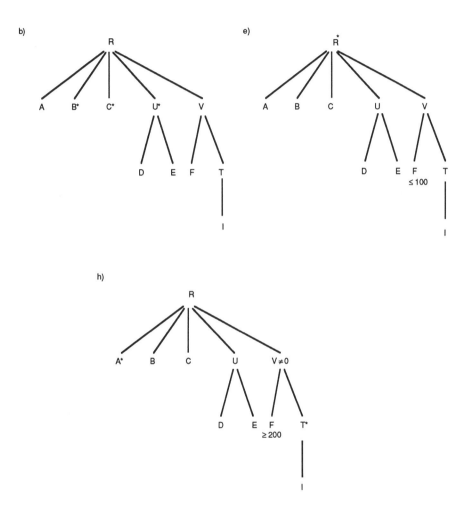

Fig. 2.2: *Examples for Marking the Schema Tree for the RETRIEVE Operation*

Queries are constructed by entering a project-select query on any non-leaf node of the schema tree. Each such node represents a relation; a project-select expression attached to it replaces the original relation by the related result.

2.2.2 Retrieval by Address Selection

In addition to the algebraic operations, we may select complex records and subrecords also by their addresses, which is called address selection. The desired query result is restricted by a specified address relation AR which is again an NF^2 relation according to the hierarchical structure of the complex records. Addresses are used as references in indexes and as system controlled surrogates for the representation of n:m-relationships. They are managed by higher level components using the kernel system (see examples in chapter 5).

2.2.3 Update Operations

Update operations provide for changes of specific small parts of a complex record directly and for insertion, deletion, update and replacement of sets of complex records or subrecords by one CRM call. Again only single table, single pass operations are allowed. In particular, there are four basic operations INSERT, DELETE, REPLACE and UPDATE with the following features:

INSERT a set of new complete complex records into an existing relation. Optionally, a tentative address can be provided for each complex record. Also a set of complete subrecords can be inserted into a subrelation of an existing complex record.

DELETE a set of complex records or a set of subrecords of one subrelation belonging to a complex record.

REPLACE a set of entire complex records or a set of complete subrecords by new values for these complex records or subrecords including all subrecords of subrelations of these (sub-) records. This is a form of bulk update in place, i.e. the changed records have the same addresses as before and are - apart from growing and shrinking - on the same pages as before.

UPDATE a set of atomic attributes in one (sub-) record.

Except the insert operation, all update operations specify the set of complex records or subrecords to be changed by a set of addresses. Though the described update operations are powerful, some operations which might have been considered too, must be realized by several CRM calls. For example, we can not add a constant to an attribute value because the CRM has no knowledge of arithmetic computations on bytestrings. Several kernel calls are also needed to move a subrelation from one complex record to another.

3 Storage Architecture

In this chapter we develop the storage architecture for complex records according to the different types of accesses.

3.1 Access to Entire Complex Records

Generally we have to deal with complex records that consist of several atomic and several relation-valued attributes. Since subrelations are not fixed in cardinality, a complex record in general has variable length, and will usually not fit into one single page. Moreover, there might even be a particular atomic attribute value within the complex record, that spans several pages, i.e. a long field. Therefore a complex record normally covers a set of pages.

The key mechanism to support access to entire complex records is appropriate clustering of the data on disk. Clustering means that related data are stored near to each other, i.e. within the same page or on closely allocated pages within a page set, in order to utilize set-oriented I/O [WeNP87]. We introduce the concepts of address space and its exclusiveness to achieve the desired clustering.

Address Space: A complex record is stored clustered in as few pages as possible. This set of pages is the dynamic address space of the complex record and all information to interpret this space is located inside the complex record. An address space descriptor contains the list of pages which forms the address space. It is stored on the so-called root page which is the first page of a complex record.

Exclusiveness: If a complex record is smaller than a page it must not be divided into fragments scattered across several pages. If it is larger than a page, its address space does not contain other complex records. The principle of exclusive address spaces guarantees that a whole complex record can be accessed in a minimum number of page accesses. Normally, extracting an entire complex record is performed in two page accesses: First we fetch the root page and read the address space descriptor. Then all the other pages of the address space are requested in a set-oriented I/O.

The performance gain through set-oriented I/O depends on the clustering of pages on disk. Due to growth and shrinkage of a complex record the contiguity of its page set on disk may deteriorate. Therefore, there is an obvious need for periodic reorganization of storage clusters, though our implementation of set-oriented I/O does not require strict contiguity and still yields very good performance if, e.g., all pages of an address space are allocated in the same disk cylinder.

In the case of reorganization, the concept of object-oriented address spaces is useful once more. As we will show in following chapters, all internal pointers of a complex record refer only to relative page ids of an address space and are translated through the address space descriptor. Therefore, it is pretty inexpensive to move disk pages in order to reestablish a higher degree of contiguity. Maintenance costs are restricted to modifications of the address space descriptor, so that even dynamic reorganization as a background task may be viable.

3.2 Access to Subrecords

A subrelation might have relation-valued attributes again, and this can repeat up to an arbitrary but fixed depth. As our list of operations in chapter 2 has shown, CRM operations may require data of a complex record at several different levels. Therefore, besides access to complex record as a whole, fast random access to any subrecord or subrelation on an arbitrary level in the hierarchy is required. Our efficient solution to this requirement is based on the following storage structure.

A complex record or any subrecord may or may not have subrelations. In the first case a link segment is always introduced to a record. Such a link segment consists of as many pointer arrays as subrelations exist in the record. Further it contains exactly one pointer to the concatenation of atomic attribute values, called data segment in the following. Each pointer array contains the pointers to all subrecords of the related subrelation. If these subrecords again consist of at least one subrelation, the pointers address the link segments of these subrecords. Otherwise, i.e. if they contain only atomic attributes, the pointer array consists of pointers to the corresponding data segments directly.

So every complex record is built of three basic types of segments: the address space descriptor, the link segments and the data segments. All data segments are stored clustered in depth-first strategy. Link segments, which represent subrecords with subrelations, are stored clustered in a breadth-first strategy. All link segments and the address space descriptor form the record directory of a complex record. This record directory begins on the root page and is separated from the data segments.

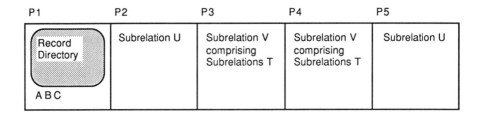

Fig. 3.1: *Allocation of a Complex Record*

Fig. 3.1 illustrates the allocation of a complex record of relation R (see Fig. 2.1). The first page (P1) contains the data segment of the first hierarchy level (attributes A, B and C) and the record directory. The record directory includes the address space descriptor (the page ids P1, P2, P3, P4, P5) and the link segments for the subrelations. The pages P3 and P4 contain data segments representing subrecords of V. For each subrecord of V one data segment containing the value of F and a set of data segments representing the subrecords of T are stored, preferably in the same page. The pages P2 and P5 contain data segments representing the subrecords of U. Here, the subrelation U has grown after the initial insertion of the complex record. Therefore, after filling up the page P2, the new page P5 was acquired.

Fig. 3.2 describes the storage structure in more details. The record directory starts with the address space descriptor, which is tied to the first level link segment. This link segment contains a single pointer to the data segment with the values of the attributes A, B and C. Further it consists of a pointer array for the subrelation U, where each pointer leads to the corresponding data segment, and a pointer array for the subrelation V, where each pointer indicates a link segment, representing a subrecord of V. Each link segment of V contains a pointer for data segments with an F value and a pointer array for the data segments of I. (A description following the storage architecture model [Bato85] is contained in [DePS86]).

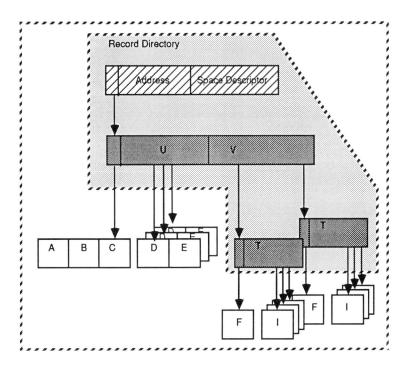

Fig. 3.2: *Storage Structure of a Complex Record*

By segmentation of internal links and data we restrict the number of requested pages in case of projections. Together with the address space descriptor this facilitates the utilization of the set-oriented I/O. The record directory centralizes all necessary internal pointer and page information. Access to a subrecord will be performed in three basic steps: First, the root page with the address space descriptor is accessed. Second, the pages containing the record directory are requested if the record directory occupies more than one page. We evaluate the record directory and determine the set of additional pages necessary to execute the operation. This page set is requested in a further page manager call. Thus we do not request the complete page set of a complex record from the page manager if this can be avoided. If the record directory fits in the root page we need only two page accesses. In the example given in Fig. 3.1, a projection of subrelation U results in a request for page P1 and a second call requesting the pages P2 and P5.

3.3 Access by Addresses

Addresses available at the interface of the kernel are used as surrogates for the representation of n:m-relationships and to reference complex records, subrelations and subrecords in access paths. An address selection is a fast operation, independent from the hierarchy level of the complex record on which it is applied. The addresses are kept stable w.r.t. relocations within a page as well as w.r.t. migration across pages.

To distinguish the addresses used above the kernel from the addresses used inside a complex record, we call the former external addresses and the latter internal addresses or pointer. External addresses are hierarchically organized. They consist of a tuple identifier (TID) for the beginning of the complex record in the root page and of a sequence of subrelation numbers and subrecord sequence numbers. An entire complex record is addressed by the TID. An address of a subrecord or subrelation is composed of the TID of the complex record and the relative subrelation numbers and subrecord sequence numbers of all its predecessors in the hierarchy of a complex record.

The TID gives the page id of the root page within the underlying file. It locates the address space descriptor, which is the beginning of the record directory. Since the TID is a direct address technique, fast access is provided. If a relocation of the entire complex record to another page or page set occurs, a substitute consisting of the new valid TID replaces the address space descriptor in the old page to guarantee address stability. A relocation of an entire complex record can only occur to complex records which were smaller than the page size and then have grown. Otherwise the complex record is in a stable phase concerning its address, i.e. for each big complex record the root page containing its address space descriptor is pinned. If a big complex record shrinks and becomes smaller than the page size, it leaves the stable phase and looses the exclusiveness of its address space. That is, other small complex records can share its page.

External hierarchical addresses are translated to internal addresses via the record directory. The link segments realize translation tables for every subrelation at every level in the hierarchy. For access to inner subrecords we use the subrelation number and the subrecord sequence number as an index into the link segments. In the dereferencing process the address yields a path through the record directory. By a relative subrelation number we find the pointer array of the addressed subrelation. The subrecord sequence number gives the pointer to the link segment which represents the referenced subtuple or the data segment for a flat subrecord. Note that the positions of pointers within a pointer array are bound to external addressing. Since external addresses are to be kept stable, we cannot close a gap in the pointer array which results from a deletion of a subrecord. Instead we mark it and reuse it for a new insertion.

In the example given in Fig. 3.3 the address of the whole complex record is the TID <P1.2>. The second subrecord of the first subrelation (U) has the address <P1.2;1.2>. The second existing subrecord of subrelation V, which is the second subrelation, is represented by the address <P1.2;2.3> indicating the collection of segments contained in page P4 and their parent link segment. Note that the second entry in the pointer array for subrelation V is empty due to deletion of a subrecord. The second and third subrecord in first subrelation of subrecord <P1.2;2.3> are addressed by <P1.2;2.3;1.{2,3}>. This way, we can even address sets of subrecords.

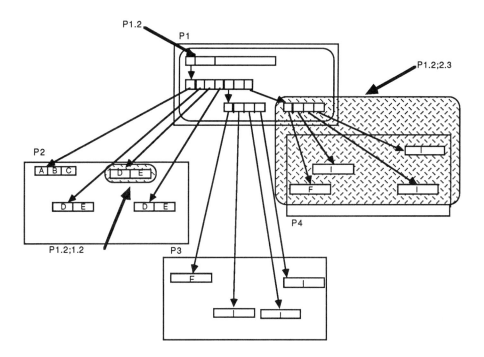

Fig. 3.3: External Addressing of a Complex Record

3.4 Implementation of Pointers

Internal addresses, the pointers in link segments, are only known within the scope of a complex record. They are realized as so-called mini-tids as also used in [Dada86]. Similar to the TID concept a mini-tid consists of a page identifier and a page-local entry number. But the page identifier only refers to the address space of the complex record, and is therefore called relative page identifier. We apply no substitution technique if a segment is moved to another page, because its mini-tid is known only locally.

The relative page identifier is an index in the address space descriptor. The corresponding entry consists of the real page identifier within the underlying file. If the complex record shrinks and a real page id is removed from the address space descriptor, this causes a gap. Such gaps are reserved for a later insertion. If a page id is to be inserted and no gap is available, a new entry extends the corresponding page set in the address space descriptor. So, also the relative page identifiers are kept stable.

If a segment grows but still fits in its page, then we relocate this segment and possibly others in this page, and change only the corresponding page-local byte addresses in the entries of the page trailer. The internal addresses in the record directory still remain the same. A relocation of a segment to another page might occur due to expansions of the segment or expansions of the complex record's address space. In this case its internal address should be updated immediately, because it is stored only once, viz in the parent link segment within the record directory of the same complex record. In accessing a segment we always visit the parent link segment. So we need no substitution technique here to provide stability.

3.5 Long Fields

A long atomic field (e.g. code, image, text, etc.) is divided into variable length fragments which are mapped to data segments. A special pointer array with length information (similar to [HaLo82]) substitutes the field in the normal data segment. On a long field we support a "from-to" byte extraction. If a part in the long field is deleted, the variable length fragments shrink within the affected pages, and possibly entire pages are released. Fragments on neighbouring pages are merged to a single page whenever possible. Correspondingly, fragments are split in the expansion case when additional pages are needed. We apply the same approach also to large pointer arrays in link segments and in a slightly altered way to fixed length data segments of a subrelation (see [DePS86]).

3.6 Discussion

Concerning the access costs we suppose that complex records usually are larger than a page. Then no overflow substitute occurs. We further suppose that the address space descriptor usually fits into the root page. Thus, a whole complex record can be fetched in two page fetches. The first call of the page manager delivers the address space descriptor from which we get the ids of the page set containing the rest of the complex record. These pages are fetched in the second call. Access to a small complex record normally requires one page access. If an overflow occured due to growth of a small complex record, an additional page access is necessary. Random access to a subrecord involves no more than two page accesses independent of the depth of that subrecord, provided the record directory fits in the root page. After the first call, the CRM evaluates the record directory and requests only those pages which are really needed. In the case of a large record directory, an additional call can be made to reduce the number of requested pages by evaluating the directory information.

The hierarchical structure of external addresses is useful for query processing of complex objects. Particularly they support nested selections. Suppose we have an index on attribute I of subrelation T. The reference lists in the index contain the external addresses of the T-subrecords. For the retrieval of complex records of relation R specified by an existence condition on I, we get the addresses of complex records of R directly by the index. Generally, this holds for every nested selection condition independent of the depth of the subrelation it is applied to. Due to the hierarchical addressing scheme we need no parent pointer in links, because the parent link segment is visited during processing anyway. So, hierarchical access is well supported. Although we apply an indirect addressing concept, we do not need to introduce further complexity through additional translation tables. Instead we use the pointer arrays in link segments for the representation of subrelations and for addressing their subrecords.

Due to the page-structured design of the storage clusters the page manager is not required to store pages of complex records in contiguous frames of the database buffer. Consequently no fragmentation problem occurs. To reorganize the storage cluster on disk, the contents of pages belonging to a complex record can be copied into other page blocks without costly maintenance. We just change corresponding page ids in the address space descriptor on the root page. All internal addresses are relative within the address space, so that the rest of the storage structure remains the same. This feature also guarantees that whole complex records can be easily transferred in distributed systems, e.g. in an engineering environment of a server and workstations (see [BuCe85, DeOb87, HaLo82]).

4   Internal Processing

In this chapter we describe how the CRM executes the operations described in chapter 2 based on the storage structures introduced in the last chapter.

4.1 Buffers

The CRM maps the operations on sets of NF^2 tuples to operations on sets of pages, i.e. it transfers the complex records to pages and vice versa. For that purpose two types of data containers called buffers are introduced:

-    Page Buffer: this is the usual database buffer containing pages which are transferred to and from external devices by operating system primitives. In a multi-user environment it is shared among all users as usual.
-    Object Buffers: each of these contains a set of complex records of a single relation type. The object buffers are the means of transporting data from the CRM interface to higher levels. They are not shared.

Each object buffer has one predefined cursor and optionally additional cursors. Using the main cursor, navigational as well as read, write and update operations are possible, whereas only navigational and read operations are allowed for additional cursors. The calling modules are responsible for coping with cursors becoming undefined due to deletion of a (sub-) record. All operations only allow to navigate within the object buffer or to manipulate atomic attributes, i.e. only one atomic attribute at a time can be put into a bytestring variable of the programming language and passed to the calling module.

Note that this kind of object buffers is a straightforward solution for embedding complex records into a programming language at the user's (= programmer's) level. In contrast to classical database systems this is not a simple problem, because each complex record has a set of subrecords in each subrelation and its cardinality is not known before the query is executed. In our case the problem is even harder because we want to transfer sets of complex records.

For object buffers the following navigational operations are available:
-    navigate to the next/prior (sub-) record
-    navigate down/up within the hierarchy of a complex record
-    reset a cursor to the beginning of the object buffer
-    read/write a specified atomic data attribute of the current (sub-) record
-    insert a new (sub-) record before or after the current one

- delete a specified number of (sub-) records beginning with the current one
- generate a new or destroy an existing object buffer or an additional cursor

The CRM RETRIEVE operation fills one object buffer which contains the set of requested complex records. If there is enough space for the result it will be totally transferred with one RETRIEVE operation. Otherwise an implicit scan is opened, to which a following sequence of NEXT operations may refer. The CLOSE operation terminates an opened scan. On the other side, the INSERT operation passes an object buffer to the CRM containing the set of complex records which are to be stored. As a result another object buffer is filled containing the addresses of the stored complex records.

4.2 Execution of Kernel Operations

4.2.1 Retrieval Operations

The parameters of the RETRIEVE operation are given by a marked schema tree as introduced in chapter 2.2 and an object buffer containing addresses of the records to be retrieved. The operation generates an object buffer containing the requested complex records. The main steps of the RETRIEVE algorithm are:

1. for each complex record address in the address buffer do
    a) fix the root page
    b) if the record directory spans more than one page: fix all these pages by one set-oriented page buffer call
    c) determine those data pages of the record address space which contain the required data segments by evaluating the link segments in the record directory according to the marked nodes of the schema tree
    d) fix all the determined pages containing the desired data segments by one set-oriented page buffer call
    e) perform recursively at each level of the schema tree on the current (sub-) record:
        e1) test whether it matches the query according to the selection filters of that level
        e2) and if it does, move the requested part into the object buffer according to the projection list of that level
    f) unfix all fixed pages of the current complex record by one page buffer call
2. if the output object buffer is completely filled up before all complex records are processed: prepare the NEXT operation.

To process CRM operations some catalog information is needed, e.g. to get all pages with the address space descriptors of a given relation. After the pages of the record directory are fixed (step 1b) it is possible to determine all pages with data segments using the marked schema tree and the link segments of the corresponding complex record only because all internal addresses are local. Obviously, this is the step where our object-oriented storage scheme is most profitable. So, all data page fetches are preplanned (step 1c) and may be executed by one call of the page manager (step 1d). Thus, our set-oriented page buffer interface is fully utilized and performance is gained by using set-oriented I/O (see [WeNP87] for implementation details and measurements). After all pages are fixed - and we assume that the page buffer can satisfy the page set request - the execution of the query starts. Step 1e is the crucial step to realize the single scan philosophy. The CRM interface has been carefully designed such that each segment has to be touched only once. Besides we recognize early as possible whether the complex record or subrecord does not match the current selection condition. Thus we avoid to move (sub-) record parts which are not needed in an early phase of the execution. Note that the single scan property forbids collecting intermediate results, which would be processed repeatedly.

4.2.2 Update Operations

The INSERT operation gets an object buffer containing the complex records which are to be stored. It generates an object buffer containing the addresses of these stored records.

The main steps of the INSERT operation are: first we compute for each complex record in the object buffer how many pages are necessary to store it. If the complex record is larger than one page, the corresponding page ids are requested from the internal catalog, which contains all ids of free pages. These pages are fixed by one page buffer call. Otherwise a page with enough space is searched and fixed. The the corresponding segments are created and filled by recursive insert procedures. Finally, all pages are unfixed and the corresponding catalog information is updated. Other update operations are processed similarly. Note that set-orientation of CRM calls and the resulting page accesses is applied to update operations as well, and accounts for considerable performance enhancements, particularly in the case of bulk updates, i.e. very large records.

5   Support for References

There are two main cases where external addresses (references) of complex records are stored: access paths and shared subobjects. A discussion whether the record addresses should be interpreted and evaluated within or on top of the kernel system is given in [Paul87]. In DASDBS these mechanisms will be implemented utilizing the Complex Record Manager. This chapter gives one example for each case.

5.1 Access Paths

The well-known access path method B+-tree, which is needed for most of the applications, may be modelled as shown in Fig. 5.1. The relation Data-Node is the inverted list for an atomic attribute, e.g. attribute A of relation R (see Fig. 2.1). The relation Index-Node is the actual B+-tree built on the inverted list. In this relation a complex record is at most as long as one page, i.e. the node of the B+-tree.

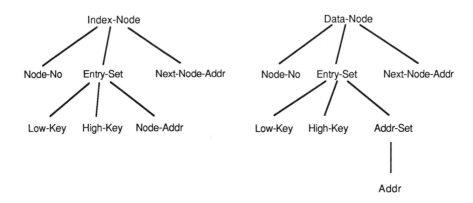

Fig. 5.1: *Access Path Relations*

A selection on relation R with condition A=100 could be processed by calling the CRM with a marked schema tree (see section 2.2). As explained in section 4.2 the CRM must perform a sequential scan on all complex records of R and match the condition on A. Therefore the higher level query processor is in charge to make use of the access path on A and start a sequence of CRM calls on relation Index-Node as shown in Fig. 5.2, where ARI and ARD are the address relations to the relation Index-Node or Data-Node, respectively.

The first RETRIEVE (Fig. 5.2a) selects the root node of the B+-tree by its address from the catalog. The result contains attribute Node-Addr of the requested subrecord of subrelation Entry-Set with an interval <Low - Key> .. <High - Key> containing the value 100. The value of Node-Addr is the input for the next RETRIEVE call, again with an address selection as shown in Fig. 5.2a. A sequence of this call follows until we get an address of the Data-Node relation. The RETRIEVE operation on that relation (see Fig. 5.2b) returns the required set of addresses of those complex records of relation R which match the selection condition. Finally, a last RETRIEVE operation with a set of addresses of records of relation R gives the same result as the original RETRIEVE on R. The sequence of CRM calls on the Index-Node relation is necessary because this transitive closure operation is not single scan processible.

5.2 Shared Subobjects

Shared subobjects are subobjects which are in relationships to several complex objects. For example, see the objects of the n:m-relationship between VE and SE in the Entity-Relationship-Model (ERM) diagram shown in Fig. 5.3. There are different possibilities of modeling the shared subobjects utilizing the DASDBS kernel (see [ScPS87]). The complex records R and S in Fig. 2.1 are one of many possibilities. Here the subrelation T of subrelation V in complex record type R contains references to the complex record type S. This realizes the n:m-relationship. To process a join operation between V and S we call the CRM in the following way: First a RETRIEVE operation on R fetches all subrecords of T besides other attributes. In the next call these subrecords of T are used as the address parameter for a query on S. Therefore, in that realization we get the join result by two CRM calls.

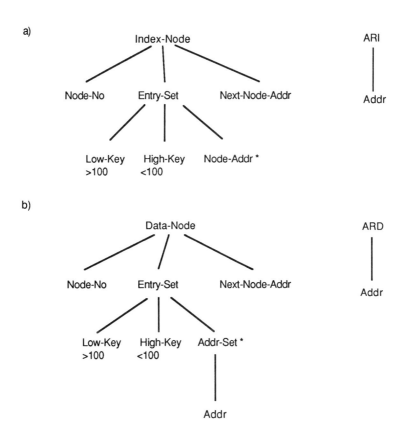

Fig. 5.2: *Marked Schema Tree for Access Path Queries*

6   Comparison with Related Work

Compared to the storage architecture of other extensible database systems, our approach has some similarities with the one in EXODUS [CDRS86]. The main difference is that our structure is based on the notion of hierarchically structured bytestring records. So, it should be easier to map different notions of complex objects onto the kernel. The EXODUS storage structure implements arbitrary long bytestrings by a B+-tree on bytestring fragments where each fragment is mapped to a particular page. Extremely long flat bytestrings are supported very well, whereas the size of a complex record in DASDBS is bound by the maximum size of an address space descriptor.

Consequently, it seems to be promising to adopt the EXODUS technique to implement long segments generally.

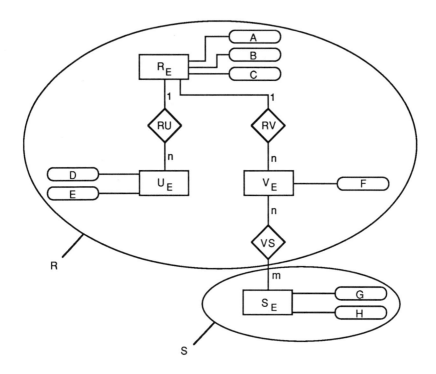

Fig. 5.3:   *ERM-Diagram Example*

In contrast to GENESIS [Bato86] we provide only one storage schema in the kernel and realize different storage techniques by the design of the internal schema (cf. [ScPS87]). Compared to AIM-P [Dada86, Lum85] there is no intermediate stage of flat records ("subtuple manager") which can be seen outside the DASDBS kernel. Set-orientation may be lost at such an interface. We enforce clustering of the complex records by their schema and avoid repeated calls to a "subtuple manager" in order to collect all necessary segments together. The storage structure of AIM-P can support sorted subrelations immediately by its mini-directory structure. On the other side, our implementation technique of addresses makes reorganization less frequent compared to the AIM-P addressing technique where an external address is composed of the TID and subsequent mini-tids.

The storage structures used in PRIMA [HMMS87] are simpler than ours, as hierarchies have maximum depth 1 there. To cope with redundancy that might be useful in case of frequent read access to shared subobjects, a sophisticated address translation structure has been proposed. Other implementation techniques for complex objects are described in [Chan82, HoZd87, Lori85, MaSt, VaKC86].

7 Summary

This paper describes the main concepts of the Complex Record Manager (CRM), the main component of the DASDBS kernel, which provides operations on hierarchically structured bytestring records. Our concern was the internal (object) model and its mapping to pages of physical storage devices. The problem to be solved was the transformation of the set-orientation of the Complex Record Manager interface to the page layer. Two key concepts proved to be useful here: Clustering and encapsulation of each complex record are the basis of the object-orientation of our kernel, and processing of complex records is substantially speeded up by accessing the whole sets of pages in a single set-oriented call of the I/O system. Altogether these concepts account for efficient execution of the kernel operations. A first implementation of the DASDBS kernel is running, and a comprehensive performance evaluation is underway. Further ongoing work is devoted to application-specific layers, especially the DBMS for geometrical objects and the flat relational frontend.

8 Acknowledgement

Many discussions with P. Dadam, J. Guenauer, K. Kuespert and G. Walch at the IBM Scientific Center Heidelberg are gratefully acknowledged.

9 References

[AMKP85], [Astr76], [BaBu84], [BaKh86], [BaKi85a], [Bato85], [Bato86], [BuCe85], [Care], [CDRS86], [Chan82], [Dada86], [DaSm86], [Daya87], [DeOb87], [DePS86], [Ditt86], [HaLo82], [HMMS87], [HoZd87], [Lori85], [Lum85], [MaSt], [Paul87], [Sche85], [Schw86], [ScPS87], [ScSc86], [ScWa86], [Ston], [StRG83], [VaKC86], [WeNP87].

Part VIII

Conclusions

Summary

Umeshwar Dayal

Object-oriented database management is a new technology that aims to provide data management support to applications (such as computer-aided design, computer-aided software engineering, geographic information processing, and office automation) that currently are not well served by conventional, record-oriented database management systems (DBMSs).

Conventional DBMSs provide only a small, fixed set of data types (e.g., integers, reals, strings) and conceptual data structures (e.g., records, relations) that were designed for business data processing applications. These data types and structures have been found to be inadequate for representing the richly structured, complex objects (e.g., maps, documents, programs, part assemblies) encountered in the new applications. Furthermore, conventional DBMSs provide only a fixed repertoire of operations for manipulating records or relations, and a fixed set of access methods and processing strategies for efficiently implementing these operations. This requires the application programmer to coerce the objects and operations of his application domain into those supported by the DBMS; such mappings are clumsy and inefficient at best, and often impossible because conventional database query languages are computationally incomplete.

Conventional "modern" programming languages are computationally complete and have rich type systems. However, they are inconvenient, inefficient, and inadequate for applications that require access to shared, persistent data, i.e., data whose lifetime is longer than a single program execution. They provide only files for the storage and retrieval of persistent objects; before a persistent object can be manipulated, it must be retrieved from the file and translated into an "internal" format; afterwards, it must be translated back into the "external" format suitable for secondary storage, and then stored in the file. Sharing is at the level of mutual exclusion over files provided by the operating system.

The conventional approach to supporting application development has been to embed a database query language in a programming language (e.g., SQL embedded in PL/1 or C). The complex structures and complex operations of the application are implemented over transient data in the host programming language; calls are made from the program to the DBMS to store persistent data into records in the database, or to retrieve persistent data into the program's data structures. This approach does not eliminate the translation problem: since arbitrary objects cannot be made to persist, there still are two different type systems to deal with, each with its own set of operations. The application programmer has to learn two different languages. Also, the translations are likely to be inefficient, since each complex operation may require several database operations, which cannot be optimized *in toto* by the DBMS.

Object-oriented database systems lie at the confluence of research in DBMSs and programming languages. Their goal is to simplify application development by alleviating, and ultimately eliminating, the translation problem. The papers in this book reflect two approaches to developing object-oriented database systems that are being actively pursued by the research community. The two approaches differ in their starting points: one approach seeks to extend existing DBMS *concepts* (not necessarily the *software*) with data and procedural abstractions; the other approach embellishes existing programming languages with persistence and sharing.

1   The Extended DBMS Approach

This approach is rooted in the well-understood concepts of relational DBMSs: *relations, tuples, attributes, and scalar domains* comprise the data model (type system) of a relational DBMS; *transactions* are the basic unit of computation for sharing and recovery; and persistent data in the database is accessed through set-at-a-time, associative *queries* expressed in a query language.

The first stage beyond relational DBMSs was the development of DBMSs based on *semantic* data models. These DBMSs retained the powerful concepts of transactions and set-at-a-time queries, but introduced enhanced data modelling features in support of "structural object orientation." *Entities* were introduced to model real-world objects; each entity was uniquely identified by a system-generated identifier, rather than by a user-supplied key; entities existed even if their attributes had not been assigned any values. Attributes were allowed to be non-scalar; this permitted the direct modelling of entity-to-entity relationships, and as a special case, the structure of complex objects. In these semantic models, entities were *typed* and the entity types participated in *type hierarchies*, down which attributes were *inherited*.

Progress towards object-oriented DBMSs has required extending semantic DBMSs with concepts to support "behavioural object orientation." These include user-defined type-specific *operations* or *methods* (which are implemented by procedures or rules), computed and derived attributes, single and multiple inheritance of attributes and operations down type hierarchies, and *encapsulation* of structure and behaviour with the object types. Encapsulation means that, while the implementor of a type can see its internal representation and the procedures that implement its operations, the user of the type sees only its interface, i.e., the name of the type and the signatures of its operations. Several papers in this volume (in particular, the papers on Iris, PDM, Exodus, and Postgres) illustrate this approach to object-oriented data management.

The research issues that have to be addressed in this approach include the following:

- Type systems: Rich data models that match the type systems of modern programming languages and support strong type-checking have to be constructed. These type systems will need to incorporate powerful inheritance mechanisms, especially to support multiple inheritance.

- Query languages: Powerful query languages that support both set-at-a-time operations over objects and object-at-a-time operations, and both associative queries (retrieval based on properties or attributes of objects) and navigational queries (retrieval based on inter-object references), are required. Also, these query languages have to be extended computationally to allow the formulation of queries over complex objects, and especially of recursive queries. Finally, because arbitrary procedures can be invoked from the query language, computational completeness is achieved (at the expense of guaranteed termination and optimizability).

- Access methods, clustering, and buffering techniques for large and small objects: Relational DBMSs typically cluster tuples of a relation on physical storage. Different clustering tactics appear to be needed for complex objects, e.g., should all the components of a complex object be clustered? Does it pay to precompute the results of complex operations or to prefetch components of a complex object? Should complex views be materialized? New access methods (e.g., indexing schemes) are needed to support the mixed associative and navigational queries.

- Query optimization: Relational query optimizers work with a fixed set of operations, access methods, and processing strategies. Optimizers for object-oriented DBMSs will need to be extensible (description-driven) in order to accomodate arbitrary user-defined operations and their implementations. Also, these optimizers will need to know how to optimize recursive and other kinds of queries over complex objects, and both set-at-a-time queries and object-at-a-time queries.

- Protection: Because object-oriented DBMSs allow arbitrary user-supplied procedures to be linked into the system, techniques are needed for validating and registering these procedures, to ensure that the system is not inadvertently or maliciously corrupted by them.

- Application-specific features: The applications that are driving the design of object-oriented DBMSs typically require special features that are not provided by conventional DBMSs. Examples of these features are versioned objects, flexible concurrency control (e.g., the support of long transactions or new lock modes), constraint checking and exception handling, active objects or triggers, and specialized user interfaces (e.g., graphics or hypertext, instead of a linear query language).

- Design and programming tools: In addition to tools for the database administrator and the application programmer, tools are also needed for the *database implementor*, who customizes the generic object-oriented DBMS for an application domain by defining and implementing the appropriate object types. This role requires more sophistication than that of a database administrator for conventional DBMSs.

2 The Persistent Programming Language Approach

Conventional programming languages (e.g., Algol, Pascal, C, Lisp) provided procedural abstraction, together with facilities for constructing complex types from primitive types. Modern languages such as Modula, CLU, and Ada added data abstraction (abstract data types with type-specific operations, encapsulation of representation and behaviour, and strong type checking). Object-oriented languages (e.g., Smalltalk, Loops, Flavors, Object Pascal, Galileo, Owl/Trellis, C++, Objective C) add inheritance to the data and procedural abstraction facilities. (These languages differ widely in their syntax, and in the semantics of their type systems. Also, some of them use a message passing metaphor for invoking operations on objects; we do not see this as an essential feature of an object-oriented programming language.)

There is considerable ongoing research aimed at providing access to persistent, shared data from these languages. The goal is to provide *orthogonal persistence* (i.e., any object of any type can be made to persist, not just objects of specific types). Also, the DBMS notion of *transaction* as the unit of concurrency control and recovery is being incorporated into these persistent, object-oriented programming languages. The papers on

Owl/Trellis, GemStone, and Galileo in this volume are illustrative of this approach.

The important research issues in this approach complement those of the first approach:

- Choice of a persistent object server: Should the persistent language be implemented over a full-functionality DBMS or over a persistent object store? A DBMS will provide not just storage and retrieval of objects and sharing, but also a data model, query language, access methods, and query optimization. A persistent object store is usually just a file system, perhaps with some special support for large, structured objects. Whether the object store should understand the semantics of the programming language's type system is a related issue.

- Mapping between transient and persistent stores: The representation of an object in transient storage may be quite different from that in persistent storage. For example, data structures in transient storage may embed a large number of physical pointers; for persistent storage, these may have to be translated into symbolic references. This mapping will have to be performed automatically by the system every time an object is moved from one store to the other. The efficiency of the translation has a major impact on performance.

- Storage and buffering of objects: Conventional storage and buffering techniques are based on uniform page sizes. Because a persistent programming system may have to deal with objects of vastly different sizes, and vastly different access patterns, a variety of storage and buffering techniques, based on objects rather than pages, may be necessary. Storage reclamation for persistent languages is also an issue.

- Integration with a data model: If the persistent programming language is implemented over a DBMS, the translation between transient and persistent data, the type checking of persistent data, and type evolution will all be simplified if the data model of the DBMS and the type system of the programming language are closely matched. A counterpoint, however, is the emerging requirement for multilingual programming environments: the same persistent object server will need to work with a variety of languages so as to enable the sharing of objects among programs written in different programming languages.

- Queries: A language that provides persistence but no aggregate types (e.g., sets, sequences, bags) would be of limited utility, because persistence is so often associated with collections of objects. Integrating set-at-a-time and associative queries with navigational, object-at-a-time manipulation is an important issue. In addition to language design, the optimization of programs written in such a language is a challenging problem, since it combines elements of code optimization and query optimization.

- Sharing: It is generally conjectured that persistent programming systems require more flexible concurreny control and recovery models than those provided by DBMSs. It is important to identify these requirements.

- Single address space abstraction: Some efforts (notably the LISP Persistent Memory described in this book) are aimed at presenting a single persistent virtual memory to every program. This eliminates the need for mapping between the representations of transient and persistent data. However, there are performance tradeoffs because of increased system bookkeeping; also, the issues of distributed virtual memory have not yet been addressed.

3   Predictions

In the near future, we will see a family of post-relational DBMSs exhibiting subsets of the features of an object-oriented DBMS (more powerful data models and query languages; support for procedures, triggers, and rules; and access methods for large objects). Similarly, we will see a family of persistent programming languages interfaced to object servers that provide storage and retrieval of objects, and some sharing and recovery. In the long term, the two paths will converge, and we will see seamlessly integrated, persistent, object-oriented programming environments that incorporate an object-oriented DBMS. These environments will include computationally complete programming languages with rich type systems and inheritance; high-level aggregate types and queries; orthogonal persistence; optimization; efficient translation, storage, buffering, and reclamation schemes; flexible concurrency control and recovery; and design and programming tools.

References

[ABLN85]   Almes, G.T., Black, A.P., Lazowska, E.D., Noe, J.D.: "The Eden system: a technical review", IEEE Trans. on Software Eng., SE-11 (1), pp. 43-59, January 1985.

[Abri74]   Abrial, J.R.: "Data Semantics", In: Data Base Management, Klimbie, J.W., Koffman, K.L., (Eds.), North-Holland, Amsterdam, pp. 1-59, 1974.

[AbSu85]   Abelson, H., Sussman, G.J.: "Structure and Interpretation of Computer Programs", MIT Press, Cambridge, MA, 1985.

[AbWi86]   Abarbanel, R.M., Williams, M.D.: "A Relational Representation for Knowledge Bases", Unpublished manuscript, April 1986.

[AdLi80]   Adiba, M.E., Lindsay, B.G.: "Database Snapshots", IBM San Jose, Res. Tech. Rep. RJ-2772, March 1980.

[AiNa86]   Ait-Kaci, H., Nasr, R.: "Logic and Inheritance", Proc. of the 1986 POPL Conference, St. Petersburg, FL, January 1986.

[AitK84]   Ait-Kaci, H.: "A lattice theoretic approach to computation based on a calculus of partially ordered type structures", Ph.D. thesis, University of Pennsylvania, 1984.

[Alba83]   Albano, A.: "Type Hierarchies and Semantic Data Models", ACM SIGPLAN 1983: Symposium on Programming Languages Issues in Software Systems, San Francisco, CA, pp. 178-186, 1983.

[AlCO85]   Albano, A., Cardelli, L., Orsini, R.: "Galileo: A Strongly Typed, Interactive Conceptual Language", ACM TODS, Vol. 10, No. 2, pp. 230-260, June 1985.

[AlGO88]   Albano, A., Ghelli, G., Orsini, R.: "The Implementation of Galileo's Values Persistence", In: Data Types and Persistence, Topics in Information Systems, Atkinson, M.P., Buneman, P., Morrison, R., (Eds.), Springer-Verlag, 1988.

[AlHS76]   Allman, E., Held, G., Stonebraker, M.: "Embedding a Data Manipulation Language in a General Purpose Programming Language", Proc. 1976 SIGPLAN-SIGMOD Conference on Data Abstraction, Salt Lake City, UT, March 1976.

[AlOO88]   Albano, A., Occhiuto, M.E., Orsini, R.: "Galileo Reference Manual, Version 2.0", Servizio Editoriale Universitario di Pisa, Italy, February 1988.

[AMKP85]   Afsarmanesh, H., McLeod, D., Knapp, D., Parker, A.: "An Extensible Object-Oriented Approach to Databases for VLSI/CAD", Proc. 11th International Conference on VLDB, Stockholm, Sweden, 1985.

[AnCl85]   Anderson, T.L., Claghorn, B.B.: "ADE: Mapping between the External and Conceptual Levels", In: Information Systems: Theoretical and Formal Aspects, Sernadas, A., Bubenko, J., Olive, A., (Eds.), North Holland, 1985.

[AnEM86a]   Anderson, T.L., Ecklund, E.F., Maier, D.: "Proteus Bibliography: Representation and Interactive Display in Databases", In: ACM-SIGMOD Record, Vol. 15, No. 3, September 1986.

[AnEM86b]   Anderson, T.L., Ecklund, E.F., Maier, D.: "PROTEUS: Objectifying the DBMS User Interface", Proc. Int. Workshop on Object-Oriented Database Systems, In: [DiDa1986].

[Astr76]   Astrahan, M., et al.: "System R: Relational Approach to Database Management", ACM TODS, Vol. 1, No. 2, June 1976.

[Atki83]   Atkinson, M.P., Bailey, P.J., Chisholm, K.J., Cockshott, P.W., Morrison, R.: "An Approach to Persistent Programming", The Computer Journal, Vol. 26, No. 4, pp. 360-365, December 1983.

[Atki84]   Atkinson, M.P., Bailey, P.J., Cockshott, W.P., Chisholm, K.J., Morrison, R.: "Progress with Persistent Programming", Technical Report ROR-8-84, Department of Computer Science, University of Edinburgh, Edinburgh, Scotland, February 1984.

[Atwo85a]   Atwood, T.: "An Object Oriented DBMS for Design Support Applications", Proc. IEEE COMPINT 85, Montreal, Canada, September 1985.

[Atwo85b]   Atwood, T.: "An Object-Based Platform for Design Support Applications", Technical Report, Mosaic Technologies Inc., Billerica, MA, July 1985.

[BaBu84]   Batory, D.S., Buchmann, A.P.: "Molecular Objects, Abstract Data Types, and Data Models: A Framework", Proc. 1984 VLDB, Singapore, 1984.

[BaDa77]   Bachman, C., Daya, M.: "The Role Concept in Database Models", Proc. 1977 VLDB Conference, Tokyo, Japan, October 1977.

[BaKh86]   Bancilhon, F., Khoshafian, S.: "A Calculus for Complex Objects", Proc. PODS 1986, Cambridge, MA, 1986.

[BaKi85a]   Batory, D., Kim, W.: "Modeling Concepts for VLSI CAD Objects", ACM TODS, Vol. 10, No. 3, September 1985.

[BaKi85b]   Batory, D., Kim, W.: "Supporting Versions of VLSI CAD Objects", M.C.C. Technical Report, Austin, TX, 1985.

[BaRa85]   Barbic, F., Rabitti, F.: "The Type Concept in Office Document Retrieval", In: Proc. 11th International Conference on VLDB, Pirotte, A., Vassiliou, Y., (Eds.), Stockholm, Sweden, August 1985.

[BaSc77]   Bayer, R., Schkolnick, M.: "Concurrency of Operations on B-trees", Acta Informatica 9, 1977.

[Bato85]   Batory, D.S.: "Modeling the Storage Architectures of Commercial Database Systems", ACM TODS, Vol. 10, No. 4, 1985.

[Bato86]   Batory, D., Barnett, J., Garza, J., Smith, K., Tsukuda, K., Twichell, C., Wise, T.: "GENESIS: A Reconfigurable Database Management System", Technical Report, TR-86-07, Department of Computer Sciences, University of Texas at Austin, TX, March 1986.

[BCPB84]   Barbic, F., Carli, M., Pernici, B., Bracchi, G.: "A Tool for Form Definition in Office Information Systems Specification", In: New Applications of Data Bases, Gardarin, G., Gelenbe, E., (Eds.), Academic Press, 1984.

[BeBC80]   Bernstein, P., Blaustein, B., Clarke, E.: "Fast Maintenance of Semantic Integrity Assertions Using Redundant Aggregate Data", In: Proc. 6th International Conference on VLDB, October 1980.

[BeCD69]   Bensoussan, A., Clingen, C.T., Daley, R.C.: "The MULTICS Virtual Memory", In: Proc. 2nd Symp. Operating Systems Principles, Princeton University, pp. 30-42, October 1969.

[BeFe83]   Beech, D., Feldman, J.S.: "The Integrated Data Model: A Database Perspective", In: Proc. 9th International Conference on VLDB, Florence, Italy, October 1983.

[BeGH]   Bernstein, P.A., Goodman, N., Hdzilacos, V.: "Recovery Algorithms for Database Systems", Aiken Computation Laboratory, Technical Report.

[BeGo]   Bernstein, P.A., Goodman, N.: "A Sophisticate's Guide to Distributed Database Concurrency Control", Aiken Computation Laboratory, Technical Report.

[Beki74]   Bekic, H., Bjorner, D., Henhapl, W., Jones, C.B., Lucas, P.: "A Formal Definition of a PL/1 Subset", Technical Report, IBM Vienna Laboratory, December 1974.

[BiNe78]   Biller, H., Neuhold, E.J.: "Semantics of Databases: The Semantics of Data Models", Information Systems, Vol. 3, pp. 1-30, 1978.

[Bish77]   Bishop, P.B.: "Computer Systems with a Very Large Address Space and Garbage Collection", Technical Report TR-178, Laboratory for Computer Science, Cambridge, MA, May 1977.

[BjJo78]   Bjorner, D., Jones, C.B., (Eds.): "The Vienna Development Method: The Meta-Language", Lecture Notes in Computer Science, Vol. 61, Springer-Verlag, May 1978.

[BjLo82]   Bjorner, D., Lovengren, H.H.: "Formalization of Database Systems - And a Formal Definition of IMS", In: Proc. 8th International Conference on VLDB, Mexico City, Mexico, September 1982.

[BjOe80]   Bjorner, D., Oest, O.N., (Eds.): "Towards a Formal Description of Ada", Lecture Notes in Computer Science, Vol. 98, Springer-Verlag, 1980.

[BoHQ86]   Booth, T.L., Hart, R., Qin, B.: "High Performance Software Design", Proc. Hawaii Int. Conf. on Sys. Sci., Vol. II, pp. 41-52, January 1986.

[BoKi87]   Bobrow, D., Kiczales, G.: "Common Lisp Object System Specification", Draft X3 Document 87-001, Am. Nat. Stand. Inst., February 1987.

[BoMW84]   Borgida, A., Mylopoulos, J., Wong, H.K.T.: "Generalization/ Specialization as a Basis for Software Specification", In: On

Conceptual Modeling, Brodie, M.L., Mylopoulos, J., Schmidt, J.W., (Eds.), Springer-Verlag, New York, 1984.

[Borg85]   Borgida, A.: "Language Features for Flexible Handling of Exceptions in Information Systems", ACM TODS, Vol. 10, pp. 565-603, 1985.

[Born81]   Borning, A.: "The Programming Language Aspects of ThingLab, A Constraint-Oriented Simulation Laboratory", In: ACM Transactions on Programming Languages, Vol. 3, No. 4, pp. 353-387, October 1981.

[Born85]   Borning, A.: Defining Constraints Graphically, University of Washington TR 85-09-06, Seattle, WA, September 1985.

[Born86]   Borning, A.: "Classes vs. Prototypes in Object-Oriented Languages", Proc. FJCC, Dallas, TX, November 1986.

[BoSt83]   Bobrow, D.G., Stefik, M.: "The LOOPS Manual", In: LOOPS Release Notes, Xerox Corporation, Palo Alto, CA, 1983.

[Brac83]   Brachman, R.J.: "What IS-A Is and Isn't: An Analysis of Taxonomic Links in Semantic Neworks", IEEE Computer Magazine, pp. 37-41, October 1983.

[Brae85]   Brägger, R.P., et al.: "Gambit: An Interactive Database Design Tool for Data Structures, Integrity Constraints, and Transactions", IEEE Trans. on Soft. Eng., Vol. (SE-11,7), pp. 574-582, July 1985.

[BrCr85]   Broverman, C.A., Croft, W.B.: "A Knowledge-Based Approach to Data Management for Intelligent User Interfaces", In: Proc. 11th International Conference on VLDB, Pirotte, A., Vassiliou, Y., (Eds.), Stockholm, Sweden, August 1985.

[Brem86]   Bremser, J.: "COOLE: C Object-Oriented Language Extension, Reference Manual", Technical Report, Center for Interactive Computer Graphics, Rensselaer Polytechnic Institute, Troy, NY, 1986.

[BrHu86]   Bryce, D., Hull, R.: "SNAP: A Graphics-Based Schema Manager", In: Proc. of the IEEE International Conference on Data Engineering, Los Angeles, CA, February 1986.

[Brod80]   Brodie, M.L.: "The Application of Data Types to Database Semantic Integrity", Information System, Vol. 5, No. 4, pp. 287-296, 1980.

[Brod84]   Brodie, M., Blaustein, B., Dayal, U., Manola, F., Rosenthal, A.: "CAD-CAM Database Management", Database Engineering 7:2, June 1984.

[BrRi84]   Brodie, M., Ridjanovic, D.: "On the Design and Specification of Database Transactions", In: On Conceptual Modeling, Brodie, M.L., Mylopoulos, J., Schmidt, J.W., (Eds.), Springer-Verlag, New York, 1984.

[BuCe85]   Buchmann, A.P., Celis, C.P.: "An Architecture and Data Model for CAD Data Bases", Proc. 11th International Conference on VLDB, Stockholm, Sweden, August 1985.

[BuCl79]   Buneman, O.P., Clemons, E.K.: "Efficiently Monitoring Relational Databases", ACM TODS, Vol. 4, pp. 368-382, September 1979.

[BuCV86]   Buchmann, A., Carrera, R., Vazquez-Galindo, M.: "A Generalized Constraint and Exception Handler for an Object-Oriented CAD-DBMS", In: [DiDa1986].

[BuFN82]   Buneman, P., Frankel, R.E., Nikhil, R.: "An Implementation Technique for Database Query Languages", ACM TODS, Vol. 7, No. 2, pp. 164-186, June 1982.

[BuGe85]   Buchmann, A.P., Gerzso, J.M.: "Handling Hetergeneously Formatted Data in an Object-Oriented Database Environment", National Computer Graphics Association, Dallas, TX, April,1985.

[Butl86]   Butler, M.H.: "An Approach to Persistent LISP Objects", In: Proc. COMPCON, IEEE, San Francisco, CA, pp. 324-329, March 1986.

[CaDe85]   Carey, M., DeWitt, D.: "Extensible Database Systems", Proc. of the Islamorada Workshop on Large Scale Knowledge Base and Reasoning Systems, February 1985.

[CaDS85]   Carey, M., DeWitt, D., Stonebraker, M.: Personal Communication, July 1985.

[CaDV88]   Carey, M.J. DeWitt, D.J., Vandenberg, S.L.: A Data Model and Query Language for EXODUS, Proc. ACM SIGMOD, 1988.

[Camm86]   Cammarata, S.: "An Object-Oriented Data Model for Managing Computer-Aided Design and Computer-Aided Manufacturing Data Bases", Ph.D. Thesis, Computer Science Department, University of California at Los Angeles, CA, 1986.

[Card84]   Cardelli, L.: "A Semantics of Multiple Inheritance", In: Semantic of Data Types, Lecture Notes in Computer Science, Vol. 173, Springer Verlag, pp. 51-67, 1984.

[Care]   Carey, M.J., DeWitt, D.J., Frank, D., Graefe, G., Muralikrishna, M., Richardson, J.E., Shekita, E.J.: "The Architecture of the EXODUS Extensible DBMS", in this volume.

[Cart86]   Carter, H.M.: "Computer-Aided Design of Integrated Circuits", Computer, Vol. 19, No. 4, pp. 19-36, April 1986.

[Catt80]   Cattell, R.G.G.: "An Entity-Based Database User Interface", In: Proc. ACM-SIGMOD International Conference on the Manipulation of Data, Santa Monica, CA, May 1980.

[Catt83]   Cattell, R.G.G.: "Design and Implementation of a Relationship-Entity-Datum Data Model", Xerox PARC Technical Report CSL 83-4, May 1983.

[CCA83]   CCA: "ADAPLEX: Rationale and Reference Manual", Technical Report CCA-83-03, Computer Corporation of America, 1983.

[CDRS86]   Carey, M.J., DeWitt, D.J., Richardson, J.E., Shekita, E.J.: "Object and File Management in the EXODUS Extensible Database System", Proc. International Conference on VLDB, Kyoto, Japan, August 1986.

[CeGT90]   Ceri, S., Gottlob, G., Tanca, L.: Logic Programming and Databases. Springer, 1990.

[CFLR81]   Chan, A., Fox, A.A., Lin, W.-T.K., Ries, D.: "Design of an ADA
            Compatible Local Database Manager (LDM)", TR CCA 81-09,
            Computer Corporation of America, November 1981.

[Cham76]   Chamberlin, D.D., et al.: "SEQUEL 2: A Unified Approach to Data
            Definition, Manipulation, and Control", IBM Journal of Research
            and Development, Vol. 20, No. 6, 1976.

[Chan82]   Chan, A., Danberg, A., Fox, S., Lin, W.-T.K., Nori, A., Ries, D.:
            "Storage and Access Structures to Support a Semantic Data
            Model", Proc. 8th International Conference on VLDB, Mexico
            City, Mexico, September 1982.

[ChDe85]   Chou, H.-T., DeWitt, D.: "An Evaluation of Buffer Management
            Strategies for Relational Database Systems", Proc. International
            Conference on VLDB, Stockholm, Sweden, August 1985.

[Chen76]   Chen, P.: "The Entity-Relationship Model - Towards a Unified
            View of Data", ACM TODS, Vol. 1, No. 1, pp. 9-36, March 1976.

[ClMe81]   Clocksin, W., Mellish, C.: "Programming in Prolog", Springer-
            Verlag, New York, 1981.

[ClTa85]   Clifford, J., Tansel, A.: "On an Algebra for Historical Relational
            Databases: Two Views", Proc. 1985 SIGMOD Conference,
            Austin, TX, May 1985.

[Cock84]   Cockshott, W., Atkinson, M., Chisholm, K., Bailey, P., Morrison, R.:
            "Persistent Object Management System", Software Practice and
            Experience, 14, pp. 49-71, 1984.

[Codd70]   Codd, E.F.: "A Relational Model of Data for Large Shared Data
            Bases", CACM, June 1970.

[Codd79]   Codd, E.F.: "Extending the Database Relational Model to Capture
            More Meaning", ACM TODS, Vol. 4, No. 4, December 1979.

[Codd86]   Codd, E.F.: "Missing Information (Applicable and Inapplicable) in
            Relational Databases", SIGMOD Record, Vol. 15, No. 4,
            December 1986.

[CoFT84]   Cobb, R.E., Fry, J.P., Teorey, T.J.: "The Database Designer's
            Workbench", CRL-TR-18-84, University of Michigan, March 1984.

[CoKo85]   Copeland, G., Koshafian, S.N.: "A Decomposition Storage
            Model", Proc. ACM-SIGMOD International Conference on the
            Management of Data, 1985.

[CoLy88]   Connors, T., Lyngbaek, P.: "Providing Uniform Access to
            Heterogeneous Information Bases", In: Advances in Object-
            Oriented Database Systems, Dittrich, K.R., (Ed.), Lecture Notes in
            Computer Science 334, Springer Verlag, 1988.

[CoMa84]   Copeland, G., Maier, D.: "Making Smalltalk a Database System",
            Proc. 1984 ACM-SIGMOD Conference on Management of Data,
            Boston, MA, pp. 316-325, June 1984.

[CoMu88]   Cohen, B., Murphy, G.L.: "Views and Objects in OBI: A PROLOG-
            based View-Object-Oriented Database, Tech. Rep. PRRL-88-TR-
            005, SRI Sarnoff Laboratory, Princeton, NJ, March 1988.

[Cout84]   Coutaz, J.: "The Box, A Layout Abstraction for User Interface Toolkits", CMU Technical Report #CMU-CS-84-167, Carnegie Mellon University, December 1984.

[Dada86]   Dadam, P., Kuespert, K., Andersen, F., Blanken, H., Erbe, R., Günauer, J., Lum, V., Pistor, P., Walch, G.: "A DBMS Prototype to Support Extended NF^2 Relations: An Integrated View on Flat Tables and Hierarchies", Proc. ACM-SIGMOD International Conference, Washington, D.C., June 1986.

[DaLW84]   Dadam, P., Lum, V., Werner, H.-D.: "Integration of Time Versions into a Relational Database System", Proc. International Conference on VLDB, Singapore, August 1984.

[Dani82]   Daniels, D., et al.: "An Introduction to Distributed Query Compilation in R*", Proc. 2nd Intl. Symp. on Distributed Databases, Berlin, West-Germany, September 1982.

[DaNy66]   Dahl, O., Nygaard, K.: "Simula, an Algol-based Simulation Language", CACM, Vol. 9, pp. 671-678, 1966.

[DaSm86]   Dayal, U., Smith, J.M.: "PROBE: A Knowledge-Oriented Database Management System", In: Brodie, M.L., Mylopoulos, J., (Eds.): On Knowledge Base Management Systems: Integrating Artificial Intelligence and Database Technologies, Springer Verlag, Berlin 1986.

[Date81]   Date, C.J.: "Referential Integrity", Proc. 7th International VLDB Conference, Cannes, France, September 1981.

[Date83]   Date, C.J.: "An Introduction to Database Systems", Vol. 2, Addison-Wesley, 1983.

[Date86]   Date, C.J.: "A Critique of the SQL Database Language", In: Relational Database: Selected Writings, Addison-Wesley, pp. 269-311, 1986.

[Daya85]   Dayal, U., et al.: "PROBE - A Research Project in Knowledge-Oriented Database Systems: Preliminary Analysis", Technical Report CCA-85-03, Computer Corporation of American, 1985.

[Daya87]   Dayal, U., et al.: "Simplifying Complex Objects: The PROBE Approach to Modeling and Querying Them" , Proc. GI-Conference on Data Base Systems in Office, Engineering and Scientific Applications, Darmstadt, West-Germany, April 1987.

[DDGO87]   Dayal, U., Dewitt, M., Goldhirsch, D., Orenstein, J.: "PROBE Final Report", Technical Report CCA-87-02, Computer Corporation of America, 1987.

[DeKL85]   Derrett, N., Kent, W., Lyngbaek, P.: "Some Aspect of Operations in an Object-Oriented Database", IEEE Database Engineering Bulletin, December 1985.

[DeOb87]   Deppisch, U., Obermeit, V.: "Tight Database Cooperation in a Server-Workstation Environment", Proc. International Conference on Distributed Computing Systems, Berlin, West-Germany, 1987.

[DePS86]   Deppisch, U., Paul, H.-B., Schek, H.-J.: "A Storage System for Complex Objects", In: [DiDa86].

[Derr86]   Derrett, N.P., Fishman, D., Kent, W., Lyngbaek, P., Ryan, T.: "An Object-Oriented Approach to Data Management", Proc. 1986 COMPCON Conference, San Francisco, CA, February 1986.

[DeRT81]   Demers, A., Reps, T., Teitelbaum, T.: "Incremental Evaluation for Attribute Grammars with Application to Syntax Directed Editors", Conference Record of the 8th Annual Symposium on Principles of Programming Languages, pp. 105-116, January 1981.

[DiDa86]   Dittrich, K., Dayal, U., (Eds.): Proc. International Workshop on Object-Oriented Database Systems, IEEE Computer Society Press, Washington, September 1986.

[DiDB]   Dittrich, K.R., Dayal, U., Buchman, A., (Eds.): Object-Oriented Database Systems, in this volume.

[Ditt86]   Dittrich, K.R.: "Object-Oriented Database Systems: The Notion and the Issues", In: [DiDa86].

[Ditt88]   Dittrich, K.R.: Preface, In: Dittrich, K.R. (ed.): Advances in Object-Oriented Database Systems, Lecture Notes in Computer Science, Vol. 334, Springer, 1988.

[DoKo84]   Dolk, D.R., Konsynski, B.R.: "Knowledge Representation for Model Management Systems", IEEE Transactions on Software Engineering, 10:6, November 1984.

[Donz80]   Donzeau-Gouge, V., et al.: "Formal Definition of the Ada Programming Language", (preliminary version for public review), I.N.R.I.A., Le Chesnay, France, November 1980.

[East80]   Eastman, C.M.: "System Facilities for CAD Databases", Proc. IEEE 17th Design Automation Conference, June 1980.

[EgEl87]   Ege, A., Ellis, C.: "Design and Implementation of GORDION, an Object Base Management System", Proc. 3rd Data Engineering Conference, IEEE, Los Angeles, CA, February 1987.

[EGLT76]   Eswaran, K.P., Gray, J.N., Lorie, R.A., Traiger, I.L.: "The Notions of Consistency and Predicate Locks in a Database System", CACM, 19 (11), pp. 624-633, November 1976.

[ElWi80]   El-Masri, R., Wiederhold, G.: "Properties of Relationships and their Representation", Proc. NCC, Vol. 49, pp. 319-326, May 1980.

[FaKM85]   Farmer, D., King, R., Myers, D.: "The Semantic Database Constructor", IEEE Transactions on Software Engineering SE-11, pp. 583-590, July 1985.

[Feld79]   Feldman, S.: "Make - A Program for Maintaining Computer Programs", Software - Practice and Experience, Vol. 9, 1979.

[Fish87]   Fishman, D., et al.: "Iris: An Object-Oriented DBMS", ACM Transactions on Office Information Systems, Vol. 5, No. 2, April 1987.

[Forg81]   Forgy, C.L.: "OPS5 Reference Manual", Computer Science Technical Report 135, Carnegie-Mellon University, 1981.

[Fox79]   Fox, M.S.: "On Inheritance in Knowledge Representation", Proc. 1979 International Joint Conference on AI, 1979.

[Fran85]   Francis, S.M.: "Implementing a Semantic Data Model on Top of a Relational Database System, M.S. Thesis, EECS Dept., University of Connecticut, 1985.

[FrBK82]   Friedell, M., Barnett, J., Kramlich, D.: "Context-Sensitive, Graphic Presentation of Information", Computer Graphics, Vol. 16, No. 3, pp. 181-188, July 1982.

[Frey85]   Freytag, C.F.: "Translating Relational Queries into Iterative Programs", Ph.D. Thesis, Harvard University, September 1985.

[FrGo86]   Freytag, C.F., Goodman, N.: "Translating Relational Queries into Iterative Programs Using a Program Transformation Approach", Proc. 1986 ACM-SIGMOD Conference, May 1986.

[GeBu85]   Gerzso, J.M., Buchmann, A.P.: "TM: An Object-Oriented Language for CAD and Required Database Capabilities", In: Chang, S.K., (Ed.), Languages for Automation, Plenum Press, 1985.

[GGKZ85]   Goldman, K.J., Goldman, S.A., Kanellakis, P.C., Zdonik, S.B.: "ISIS: Interface for a Semantic Information System", In: Navathe, S., (Ed.), Proc. ACM-SIGMOD 1985 International Conference of Management of Data, Austin, TX, pp. 328-342, May 1985.

[GlLu86]   Glinz, M., Ludewig, J.: "SEED - A DBMS for Software Engineering Applications Based on the Entity-Relationship Approach", Proc. International Conference on Data Eng., pp. 654-660, February 1986.

[GLPT76]   Gray, J.N., Lorie, R.A., Putzolu, G.R., Traiger, I.L.: "Granularity of Locks and Degrees of Consistency in a Shared Data Base", Proc. of the IFIP TC-2 Working Conference on Modeling in Data Base Management Systems, January 1976.

[Gold81]   Goldberg, A.: Introducing the Smalltalk-80 System, BYTE Magazine, August 1981.

[Gord79]   Gordon, M.J.C.: "The Denotational Description of Programming Languages", Springer-Verlag, 1979.

[GoRo83]   Goldberg, A., Robson, D.: "Smalltalk-80: The Language and its Implementation", Addison-Wesley, Reading, MA, 1983.

[Gray79]   Gray, J.: "Notes on Database Operating Systems", In: Operating Systems: An Advanced Course, Bayer, R., Graham, R., Seegmuller, G., (Eds.), Springer-Verlag, 1979.

[Gray81]   Gray, J.N.: "The Transaction Concept: Virtues and Limitations", Proc. International Conference on VLDB, September 1981.

[Gray84]   Gray, M.: "Databases for Computer-Aided Design", In: New Applications of Databases, Garadarin, G., Gelenbe, E., (Eds.), Academic Press, 1984.

[GrDe86]   Graefe, G., DeWitt, D.: "The EXODUS Optimizer Generator", submitted for publication, December 1986.

[Gutt84]   Guttman, T.: "R-Trees: A Dynamic Index Structure for Spatial Searching", Proc. 1984 ACM-SIGMOD Conference, Boston, MA, May 1984.

[HaFe86]   Hagman, R., Ferrari, D.: "Performance Analysis of Several Back-End Database Architectures", ACM TODS, Vol. 11, No. 1, pp. 1-26, March 1986.

[HaHT75]   Hall, P.A.V., Hitchcock, P.J., Todd, S.J.P.: "An Algebra of Relations for Machine Computation", Proc. 2nd ACM Symp. on Principles of Programming Languages, Palo Alto, CA, January 1975.

[Hall84]   Hall, P.A.V.: "Relational Algebras, Logic, and Functional Programming", Proc. 1984 ACM-SIGMOD Conference, Boston, MA, May 1984.

[HaLo82]   Haskin, R., Lorie, R.: "On Extending the Functions of a Relational Database System", Proc. International ACM-SIGMOD Conference on the Management of Data, pp. 207-212, Orlando, FL, 1982.

[HaMa85]   Hartzband, D.J., Maryanski, F.J.: "Enhancing Knowledge Representation in Engineering Databases", Computer, Vol. 18, No. 9, pp. 39-48, September 1985.

[HaMc75]   Hammer, M.M., McLeod, D.J.: "Semantic Integrity in a Relational Data Base System", Proc. International Conference on VLDB, September 1975.

[HaMc81]   Hammer, M.M., McLeod, D.J.: "Database Description with SDM: A Semantic Database Model", ACM TODS, Vol. 6, No. 3, pp. 351-386, September 1981.

[HaOB87]   Halbert, D., O'Brien, P.: "Using Types and Inheritance in Object-Oriented Programming", IEEE Software, Vol. 4, No. 5, September 1987.

[Hard87]   Hardwick, M.: "Why ROSE is Fast: Five Optimizations in the Design of an Experimental Database System for CAD/CAM Applications", Proc. ACM-SIGMOD Conference, San Francisco, CA, May 1987.

[Harr86]   Harrison, D., et al.: "Data Management and Graphics Editing in the Berkeley Design Environment", Proc. ICCAD, Santa Clara, CA, November 1986.

[HaSi86]   Hardwick, M., Sinha, G.: "A Data Management System for Graphics Objects", Proc. 2nd Data Engineering Conference, IEEE, Los Angeles, CA, February 1986.

[HaSp87]   Hardwick, M., Spooner, D.: "Comparison of Some Data Models for Engineering Objects", Computer Graphics and Applications Magazine, IEEE, March 1987.

[HaSS87]   Hardwick, M., Samaras, G., Spooner, D.: "Evaluating Recursive Queries in CAD Using an Extended Projection Function", Proc. 3rd International Data Engineering Conference, IEEE, Los Angeles, CA, February 1987.

[Hayn81]   Haynie, M.N.: "The Relational/Network Hybrid Data Model for Design Automation Databases", Proc. IEEE 18th Design Automation Conference, 1981.

[HeLi83]   Hewitt, C., Liebermann, H.: "A Real-Time Garbage Collector
            Based on the Lifetime of Objects", CACM, Vol. 26, No. 6, pp. 419-
            429, 1983.

[Hero80]   Herot, C.F.: "SDMS: Towards Spatial Data Management
            System", ACM TODS, Vol. 5, No. 4, pp. 493-514, April 1980.

[HeRo85]   Heiler, S., Rosenthal, A.: "G-Whiz, A Visual Interface for the
            Functional Model with Recursion", In: Proc. 11th International
            Conference on VLDB, Pirotte, A., Vassiliou, Y., (Eds.), Stockholm,
            Sweden, August 1985.

[HMMS87]   Härder, T., Meyer-Wegener, K., Mitschang, B., Sikeler, A.: "PRIMA
            - A DBMS Prototype Supporting Engineering Applications", Proc.
            13th International Conference on VLDB, Brighton, England,
            1987.

[Holl85]   Holland, L.: "Engineering Support System Sortware", Micro, Vol.
            5, No. 5, pp. 17-21, October 1985.

[Hong85]   Hong, S.: "DBDT - A Database Design Tool for the Design of
            Semantic Data Models", M.S. Thesis, EECS Dept., University of
            Connecticut, 1985.

[HoZd87]   Hornick, M.F., Zdonik, S.B.: "A Shared, Segmented Memory
            System for an Object-Oriented Database", ACM TOOIS 5.1,
            January 1987.

[Huan84]   Huan, K.T., et al.: "SOFTFORM - A Two Dimensional Interactive
            Form Design Language", IEEE Workshop on Language for
            Automation, November 1984.

[HuKi87]   Hull, R., King, R.: "Semantic Database Modeling: Survey,
            Applications, and Research Issues", ACM Computing Surveys,
            September 1987.

[IBM80]   IBM General Systems Division: IBM System/38 Technical
            Developments, Technical Report G580-0237-1, IBM, July 1980.

[IGES84]   IGES: Experimental Solids Proposal, National Bureau of
            Standards, Washington, September 1984.

[JeWi75]   Jensen, K., Wirth, N.: Pascal: User Manual and Report, Springer-
            Verlag, New York, 1975.

[JoSW83]   Johnson, H.R., Schweitzer, J.E., Warkentine, E.R.: "A DBMS
            Facility for Handling Structural Engineering Entities",
            Engineering Design Application, Proc. SIGMOD Database Week,
            May 1983.

[KaCB86]   Katz, R., Chang, E., Bhateja, R.: "Version Modeling Concepts for
            Computer-Aided Design Databases", Proc. ACM-SIGMOD
            Conference, Washington, D.C., May 1986.

[KaCh87]   Katz, R. H., Chang, E.: "Managing Change in a Computer-Aided
            Design Database", Proc. 13th International Conference on VLDB,
            Brighton, England, September 1987.

[Kaeh81]   Kaehler, T.: "Virtual Memory for an Object-Oriented Language",
            Byte 6, 8, August 1981.

[KaKr83]   Kaehler, T., Krasner, G.: "LOOM - Large Object-Oriented Memory
             for Smalltalk-80 Systems", In: Smalltalk-80: Bits of History, Words
             of Advice, Krasner, G., (Ed.), Addison Wesley, Reading, MA, May
             1983.

[KaLe84]   Katz, R.H., Lehman, T.J.: "Database Support for Versions and
             Alternatives of Large Design Files", IEEE Transactions of
             Software Engineering SE-10, No. 2, pp. 191-200, March 1984.

[Katz83]   Katz, R.H.: "Managing the Chip Design Database", Computer
             Magazine, Vol. 16, No. 12, December 1983.

[Katz85]   Katz, R.H.: "Information Management for Engineering Design",
             Springer-Verlag, 1985.

[Katz86]   Katz, R.H., et al.: "Version Modeling Concepts for Computer-
             Aided Design Databases", Proc. ACM-SIGMOD International
             Conference on Management of Data, Washington, D.C., May
             1986.

[Katz87]   Katz, R.H., et al.: "Design Version Management", IEEE Design &
             Test Magazine, Vol. 4, No. 1, February 1987.

[Kell86]   Keller, A.M.: "Choosing a View Update Translator by Dialog at
             View Definition Time", Computer, January 1986.

[Kent78]   Kent, W.: "Data and Reality", North-Holland, 1978.

[Kent83a]   Kent, W.: Private Communication.

[Kent83b]   Kent, W.: "Fact-Based Data Analysis and Design", In: Entity-
             Relationship Approach to Software Engineering, Davis, C.G.,
             Jajodia, S., Ng, P.A., Yeh, R.T., (Eds.), Elsevier Science
             Publishers B.V. (North-Holland), 1983.

[KeRi78]   Kernighan, B.W., Ritchie, D.N.: The C Programming Language,
             Prentice-Hall, Englewood Cliffs, NJ, 1978.

[Kers86]   Kerschberg, L., (Ed.): "Expert Database Systems", Proc. 1st
             International Workshop, The Benjamin-Cummings Publishing
             Company, Inc., Menlo Park, CA, 1986.

[KeSc86a]   Kersten, M.L., Schippers, F.H.: "Godal: A General Object-
             Centered Database Language", CS-R8615, Centre for
             Mathematics and Computer Science, April 1986.

[KeSc86b]   Kersten, M.L., Schippers, F.H.: "Using the Guardian
             Programming Paradigm to Support Database Evolution", Proc.
             Working Conference on Knowledge and Data, November 1986.

[KeSn86]   Kempf, J., Snyder, A.: "Persistent Objects on a Database", Report
             STL-86-12, Sftw. Tech. Lab., HP Labs, September 1986.

[KeWa81]   Kersten, M.L., Wasserman, A.I.: "The Architecture of the PLAIN
             Data Base Handler", Software - Practice and Experience, Vol. 11,
             pp. 175-186, 1981.

[KhVa87]   Khoshafian, S., Valduriez, P.: "Sharing, Persistence, and Object
             Orientation: A Database Perspective", DB-106-87, MCC, April
             1987.

[KiBa84]   Kim, W., Batory, D.S.: "A Model and Storage Technique for
             Versions of VLSI CAD Objects", MCC Database Program

Document 18, Microelectronics and Computer Technology Corp., December 1984.

[Kilb62]   Kilburn, T.: "One-level storage system", IRE Trans. Electronic Comput., EC-11 (2), April 1962.

[KiLo89]   Kim, W., Lochovsky, F.H.: Object-Oriented Concepts, Databases, and Applications, ACM Press, 1989.

[Kim90]   Kim, W.: Research Directions in Object-Oriented Databases, MCC Technical Report, ACT-OODS-013-90, 1990.

[KiMc85]   King, R., McLeod, D.: "Semantic Database Models", In: Database Design, Yao, S.B., (Ed.), Prentice Hall, 1985.

[KiMe84]   King, R., Melville, S.: "SKI: A Semantics Knowledgeable Interface", In: Proc. 10th International Conference on VLDB, Dayal, U., Schlageter, G., Lim Huat Seng, (Eds.), Singapore, August 1984.

[King84a]   King, R.: "A Database Management System based on the Object-Oriented Model", Proc. International Workshop on Expert Database Systems, pp. 443-468, October 1984.

[King84b]   King, R.: "Sembase: A Semantic DBMS", Proc. 1st International Workshop on Expert Database Systems, Kiawah Island, SC, pp. 151-171, October 1984.

[KiNN89]   Kim, W., Nicolas, J.-M., Nishio, S. (Eds.): Proceedings of the First International Conference on Deductive and Object-Oriented Databases, Kyoto, Japan, 1989.

[Knut68]   Knuth, D.E.: "Semantics of Context-Free Languages", Math. Systems Theory J. 2, pp. 127-145, June 1968.

[Knut71]   Knuth, D.E.: "Semantics of Context-Free Languages: Correction", Math. Systems Theory J. 5, pp. 95-96, March 1971.

[Kort84]   Korth, H., et al.: "System/U: A Database System Based on the Universal Relation Assumption, ACM TODS, September 1984.

[Kosh86]   Koshafian, S.: Discussion at Object-Oriented Workshop, Monterey, CA, 1986.

[Krab85]   Krablin, G.L.: "Building Flexible Multilevel Transactions in a Distributed Persistent Environment, Persistence and Data Types", Papers for the Appin Workshop, Univ. of Glasgow, August 1985.

[Kras83]   Krasner, G.: "Smalltalk-80: Bits of History", Words of Advice, Addison-Wesley, Reading, MA, 1983.

[KSUW85]   Klahold, P., Schlageter, G., Unland, R., Wilkes, W.: "A Transaction Model Supporting Complex Applications in Integrated Information Systems", Proc. 1985 ACM-SIGMOD Conference, Austin, TX, May 1985.

[Kulk83]   Kulkarni, K.G.: "Evaluation of Functional Data Models for Database Design and Use", Ph.D. Thesis, University of Edinburgh, 1983.

[Lamp81]   Lampson, B.W.: "Atomic Transactions", In: Lampson, B.W., Paul, M., Siegert, H.J., (Eds.), Distributed Systems, chapter 11, Springer Verlag, New York, NY, 1981.

[LaSJ86]   Law, K., Spooner, D., Jouanah, M.: "The Abstraction Model for Modeling Engineering Data", to appear in Engineering with Computers, Vol. 2, Springer-Verlag, March 1987.

[LaSm84]   Lafue, G.M.E., Smith, R.G.: "Implementation of a Semantic Integrity Manager with a Knowledge Representation System", Proc. 1st International Workshop on Expert Database Systems, Kiawah Island, SC, 172-185, October 24-27 1984.

[Lieb85]   Lieberman, H.: "There's more to Menu Systems than Meets the Screen", Computer Graphics, Vol. 19, No. 3, pp. 181-189, July 1985.

[Lieb86]   Lieberman, H.: "Using Prototypical Objects to Implement Shared Behavior in Object Oriented Systems", Proc. OOPSLA'86 Conference, Portland, OR, September 1986.

[Lisk81]   Liskov, B., Atkinson, R., Bloom, T., Moss, E., Schaffert, C., Scheifler, R., Snyder, A.: "CLU Reference Manual", Springer-Verlag, 1981.

[Litw80]   Litwin, W.: "Linear Hashing: A New Tool for File and Table Addressing", Proc. International Conference on VLDB, Montreal, Canada, October 1980.

[Loch86]   Lochovsky, F., (Ed.): Database Engineering, Vol. 8, No. 4, Special Issue on Object-Oriented Systems, 1986.

[Lohm83]   Lohman, G., et al.: "Remotely Senses Geophysical Databases: Experience and Implications for Generalized DBMS", Proc. 1983 ACM-SIGMOD International Conference on Management of Data, San Jose, CA, May 1983.

[LoPl83]   Lorie, R., Plouffe, W.: "Complex Objects and Their Use in Design Transactions", Proc. Eng. Design Applications of ACM-IEEE Data Base Week, San Jose, CA, May 1983.

[Lori77]   Lorie, R.A.: "Physical Integrity in a Large Segmented Database", ACM TODS, Vol. 2, No. 1, pp. 91-104, March 1977.

[Lori85]   Lorie, R., Kim, W., McNabb, D., Plouffe, W., Meier, A.: "Supporting Complex Objects in a Relational System for Engineering Databases", In: Kim, Reiner, Batory, (Eds.), Query Processing in Database Systems, Springer Verlag, Berlin, 1985.

[LSAS77]   Liskov, B., Snyder, A., Atkinson, R., Schaffert, C.: "Abstraction Mechanisms in CLU", Comm. ACM, 20 (8), August 1977.

[Lum85]   Lum, V., Dadam, P., Erbe, R., Guenauer, J., Pistor, P., Walch, G., Werner, H., Woodfill, J.: "Design of an Integrated DBMS to Support Advanced Applications", Proc. International Conference on Foundations of Data Organization, Kyoto Univ., Japan, May 1985.

[LuYa81]   Luo, D., Yao, S.B.: "Form Operation By Example - A Language for Office Information Processing", Proc. ACM-SIGMOD Conference, pp. 212-233, May 1981.

[LyKe86]   Lyngbaek, P., Kent, W.: "A Data Modeling Methodology for the Design and Implementation of Information Systems", In: [DiDa86].

[LyMc84a]   Lyngbaek, P., McLeod, D.: "Object Management in Distributed Information Systems", ACM Transactions on Office Information Systems, Vol. 2, No. 2, pp. 96-122, April 1984.

[LyMc84b]   Lyngbaek, P., McLeod, D.: "A Personal Data Manager", In: Proc. 10th International Conference on VLDB, Singapore, August 1984.

[LyVi87]   Lyngbaek, P., Vianu, V.: "Mapping a Semantic Database Model to the Relational Model", In: Proc. ACM-SIGMOD International Conference on the Manipulation of Data, San Francisco, CA, May 1987.

[MaDa86]   Manola, F., Dayal, U.: "PDM: An Object-Oriented Data Model", In: [DiDa86].

[MaHo85]   Maryanski, F., Hong, S.: "A Tool for Generating Semantic Database Applications", IEEE COMPSAC, pp. 368-375, October 1985.

[Maie83]   Maier, D.: "The Theory of Relational Databases", Computer-Science Press, Rockville, MD, 1983.

[Maie86]   Maier, D.: "Why Object-Oriented Databases can Succeed where Others have Failed", In: [DiDa86].

[MaNG86]   Maier, D., Nordquist, P., Grossman, M.: "Displaying Database Objects", In: "Proc. 1st International Conference on Expert Database Systems, Kiawah Island, SC, pp. 15-30, April 1986.

[Mani89]   Atkinson, M., Bancilhon, F., DeWitt, D., Dittrich, K., Maier, D., Zdonik, S.: The Object-Oriented Database System Manifesto (A Political Pamphlet). Proc. DOOD 89, Kyoto, Japan, December 1989.

[Mano87]   Manola, F.: PDM: "An Object-Oriented Data Model for PROBE", Technical Report CCA-87-03, Computer Corporation of America, 1987.

[MaOD87]   Manola, F., Orenstein, J., Dayal, U.: "Geographic Information Processing in the PROBE Database System", Proc. 8th International Symposium on Automation in Cartography, American Congress on Surveying and Mapping, March 1987.

[MaOP85]   Maier, D., Otis, A., Purdy, A.: "Object-Oriented Database Development at Servio Logic", Database Engineering 8:4, December 1985.

[MaOr86]   Manola, F.A., Orenstein, J.A.: "Toward a General Spatial Data Model for an Object-Oriented DBMS", Proc. 12th International Conference on VLDB, Kyoto, Japan, August 1986.

[MaPr84]   Maier, D., Price, D.: "Data Model Requirements for Engineering Applications", In: [Kers86].

[Mark85]   Mark, L.: "Self-Describing Database Systems - Formalization and Realization", Ph.D. Thesis, University of Maryland, April 1985.

[Mary87]   Maryanski, F., et al.: "The Data Model Compiler: A Tool for Generating Object-Oriented Database Systems", Unpublished manuscript, Elect. Eng. Comp. Sci. Dept., Univ. of Connecticut, 1987.

[MaSt]   Maier, D., Stein, J.: "Indexing in an Object-Oriented DBMS", in this volume.

[MaSt86]   Maier, D., Stein, J.: "Indexing in an Object-Oriented DBMS", Proc. Int. Workshop on Object-Oriented Database Systems, In: [DiDa1986].

[McDa89]   McCarthy, D.R., Dayal, U.: The Architecture of an Active Database Management System, Proc. ACM-SIGMOD, 1989.

[McDe82]   McDermott, J.: "R1: A Rule-Based Configurer of Computer Systems", Artificial Intelligence, Vol. 19, pp. 39-88, 1982.

[McEn86]   McEntee, T.J.: "An Overview of Garbage Collection in Symbolic Computing", Texas Instruments Engineering Journal, 3 (1), pp. 130-139, January 1986.

[McKe84]   McKewon, D.M.: "Digital Cartography and Photo Interpretation from a Database Viewpoint", In: Gardarin, G., Gelenbe, E., (Eds.), New Applications for Data Bases, Academic Press, pp. 19-42, 1984.

[McKi81]   McLeod, D., King, R.: "Database Description with SDM: A Semantic Database Model", ACM TODS, Vol. 6, No. 3, September 1981.

[McMc81]   McDonald, N., McNally, P.J.: "VGQF: Video Graphics Query Facility Database Design", In: Proc. ACM-SIGMOD/SIGSMALL Workshop, pp. 96-101, 1981.

[McNR83]   McLeod, D., Narayanaswamy, K., Rao, K.: "An Approach to Information Management for CAD/VLSI Applications", Proc. Database Week: Engineering Design Applications, IEEE, San Jose, CA, May 1983.

[Merr84]   Merrett, T.H.: Relational Information Systems, Reston, 1984.

[Meyr86]   Meyrowitz, N.: "Intermedia: The Architecture and Construction of an Object-Oriented Hypermedia System and Applications Framework", Proc. 1986 ACM-OOPSLA Conf., Portland, OR, September, pp. 186-201, 1986.

[MiBK86]   Mittal, S.J., Bobrow, D.G., Kahn, K.M.: "Virtual Copies: At the Boundary of Between Classes and Instances", Proc. OOPSLA'86 Conference, Portland, OR, September 1986.

[Mish84]   Mishkin, N.: "Managing Permanent Objects", Technical Report YALEU/DCS/RR-338, Department of Computer Science, Yale University, New Haven, CT, November 1984.

[Moon84]   Moon, D.A.: "Garbage Collection in a Large Lisp System", In: Proc. 1984 ACM Symp. Lisp and Functional Programming, pp. 235-246, August 1984.

[Morg83]   Morgenstern, M.: "Active Databases as a Paradigm for Enhanced Computing Environments", In: Proc. 9th International Conference on VLDB, Schkolnick, M., Thanos, C., (Eds.), Florence, Italy, October 1983.

[Morg84]   Morgenstern, M.: "The Role of Constraints in Databases, Expert Systems, and Knowledge Representation", Proc. 1st International Workshop on Expert Database Systems, Kiawah Island, SC, pp. 207-223, October 24-27 1984.

[Moss89]   Moss, J.E.B.: Object-Orientation as Catalyst for Language-Database Integration. In: [KiLo89].

[MPBR82]   Manola, F., Pirotte, A., Blaustein, B.T., Ries, D.R.: "A Family of Data Model Specifications for DBMS Standards", Technical Report CCA-82-03, Computer Corporation of America, (May 25, 1982), Available as NBS-GCR-82-419, National Bureau of Standards, Washington, D.C., May 1982.

[MSOP86]   Maier, D., Stein, J., Otis, A., Purdy, A.: "Development of an Object-Oriented DBMS", Proc. Conference on Object-Oriented Programming Systems, Languages and Applications, ACM SIGPLAN Notices, Vol. 21, No. 11, pp. 472-482, Portland, OR, September 1986.

[MyBW80]   Mylopoulos, J., Bernstein, P.A., Wong, H.K.T.: "A Language Facility for Designing Database-Intensive Applications", ACM TODS, Vol. 5, No. 2, pp. 185-207, June,1980.

[Myer82]   Myers, G.J.: "Advances in Computer Architecture", Wiley-Interscience, New York, NY, 2nd edition, 1982.

[Mylo85]   Mylopoulos, J., et al.: "A Language Facility for Designing Interactive Database-Intensive Systems", ACM TODS, Vol. 10, No. 4, December 1985.

[NgFG82]   Nguyen, G.T., Ferrat, L., Galy, H.: "A High-Level User Interface for a Local Network Database System", Proc. of the IEEE Infocom, pp. 96-105, 1982.

[Nier85a]   Nierstrasz, O.M., "Hybrid: A Unified Object-Oriented System", IEEE Database Engineering, Vol. 8, No. 4, pp. 49-57, December 1985.

[Nier85b]   Nierstrasz, O.M.: "An Object-Oriented System", In: Office Automation: Concepts and Tools, Tsichritzis, D.C., (Ed.), Springer-Verlag, 1985.

[NiHS84]   Nievergelt, J., Hinterberger, H., Sevcik, K.C.: "The Grid File: An Adaptable, Symmetric Multikey File Structure", ACM TODS, Vol. 9, No. 1, March 1984.

[Nixo83]   Nixon, B.: "A TAXIS Compiler", Computer Systems Research Group TR-33, University of Toronto, Canada, May 1983.

[Nixo84]   Nixon, B.: "TAXIS 84': Selected Papers", CSRG-160, June 1984.

[NoMi86]   Norris-Sherborn, A., Milne, W.J.: "A Practical Approach to Data Modeling in Spatial Applications", Software-Practice and Experience, 16 (10), pp. 893-913, October 1986.

[OBri85]   O'Brien, P.: "Trellis Object-Based Environment: Language Tutorial", Digital Equipment Corporation, Technical Report DEC-TR-373, November 1985.

[OBBS86]   O'Brien, P., Bullis, B., Schaffert, C.: "Persistent and Shared Objects in Trellis/Owl", In: [DiDa1986].

[OpDa81]   Oppen, D.C., Dalal, Y.K.: "The Clearinghouse: A Decentralized Agent for Locating Named Objects in a Distributed Environment", Technical Report OPD-T8103, Systems Development Department, Xerox Corporation, Palo Alto, CA, October 1981.

[Oren86]   Orenstein, J.: "Spatial Query Processing in an Object-Oriented Database System", Proc. 1986 ACM-SIGMOD International Conference on Management of Data, 1986.

[OrMa88]   Orenstein, J., Manola, F.: "PROBE Spatial Data Modeling and Query Processing in an Image Database Application", IEEE Transactions on Software Engineering, Vol. 14, No. 5, May 1988.

[Osbo87]   Osborn, S.L.: "Extensible Databases and RAD", Database Engineering, 10 (2), pp. 10-15, June 1987.

[Osbo88]   Osborn, S.L.: "An Object-Oriented Critique of Traditional Data Models", July 1988, submitted for publication.

[OsHe86]   Osborn, S.L., Heaven, T.E.: "The Design of a Relational Database System with Abstract Data Types for Domains", ACM TODS, Vol. 11, No. 3, pp. 357-373, 1986.

[Ozso85]   Ozsoyoglu, G., et al.: "A Language and a Physical Organization Technique for Summary Tables", Proc. 1985 ACM-SIGMOD International Conference on Management of Data, Austin, TX, June 1985.

[Paul87]   Paul, H.-B., Schek, H.-J., Scholl, M.H., Weikum, G., Deppisch, U.: "Architecture and Implementation of the Darmstadt Database Kernel System", Proc. ACM-SIGMOD 1987, San Francisco, CA, 1987.

[Peck85]   Peckham, J.: "A Formal Model for the Design of Semantic Databases", M.S. Thesis, EECS Dept., University of Connecticut, 1985.

[PeMa88]   Peckham, J., Maryanski, F.: "Semantic Data Models", ACM Computing Surveys, September 1988.

[Pilo83a]   Pilote, M.: "A Programing Language Framework for Designing User Interfaces", In: Proc. 1983 ACM-SIGPLAN Symposium on Programming Language Issues in Software Systems, San Francisco, CA, June 1983.

[Pilo83b]   Pilote, M.: "A Data Modeling Approach to Simplify the Design of User Interfaces", In: Proc. 9th International Conference on VLDB, Schkolnick, M., Thanos, C., (Eds.), Florence, Italy, October 1983.

[Piro76]   Pirotte, A.: "Explicit Description of Entities and their Manipulation in Languages for the Relational Data Base Model", Report R336, MBLE Research Laboratory, Brussels, Belgium, September 1976.

[PKLM84]   Plouffe, W., Kim, W., Lorie, R., McNabb, D.: "A Database System for Engineering Design", Database Engineering, Vol. 7, No. 2, June 1984.

[PoKW81]   Pollack, F.J., Kahn, K.C., Wilkinson, R.M.: "The iMAX-432 Object Filing System", In: Proc. 8th ACM Symp. Operating Systems Principles - ACM SIGOPS Operating Systems Review, ACM SIGOPS, Pacific Grove, CA, pp. 137-147, December 1981.

[Powe83]   Powell, M.: "Database Support for Programming Environments", Proc. Eng. Design Applications of ACM-IEEE Data Base Week, San Jose, CA, May 1983.

[Purd]   Purdy, A.: Personal Communication.

[R85]   An Introduction to INGRES, Relational Technology Inc., 1985.

[ReGR86]   Reiss, S.P., Golin, E.J., Rubin, R.V.: "Prototyping Visual Languages with the GARDEN System", Proc. IEEE Symposium on Visual Languages, June 1986.

[Rein84]   Reiner, D., et al.: "The Database Design and Evaluation Workbench (DDEW) Project at CCA", IEEE Database Engineering, Vol. 7,No. 4, pp. 10-15, December 1984.

[Reis86]   Reiss, S.P.: "GARDEN Tools: Support for Graphical Programming", Proc. Workshop on Advanced Software Development Environments, June 1986.

[Rent81]   Rentsch, T.: "Object-Oriented Programming", ACM-SIGPLAN Notice 17 (9), pp. 74-86, 1981.

[RePa86]   Reiss, S.P., Pato, J.N.: "Displaying Program and Data Structures", Brown University, Technical Report, April 1986.

[Reps82]   Reps, T.: "Optimal-Time Incremental Semantic Analysis for Syntax-Directed Editors", Conference Record of the 9th Annual ACM Symposium on Principles of Programming Languages, pp. 169-176, January 1982.

[ReTD83]   Reps, T., Teitelbaum, T., Demers, A.: "Incremental Context-Dependent Analysis for Language-Based Editors", Trans. Progr. Lang. and Systems 5, pp. 449-477, July 1983.

[ReTe84]   Reps, T., Teitelbaum, T.: "The Synthesizer Generator", Proc. ACM-SIGSOFT/SIGPLAN Software Engineering Symposium on Practical Software Development Environments, Pittsburgh, PA, Apr. 23-25, 1984, Appeared as joint issue: SIGPLAN Notices (ACM) 19, 5, May, 1984, and Soft. Eng. Notes (ACM) 9, 3, pp. 42-48, May 1984.

[Reut80]   Reuter, A.: "A fast Transaction-Oriented Logging Scheme for UNDO Recovery", IEEE Trans. Software Eng., SE-6 (4), pp. 348-356, July 1980.

[ReVo83]   Requicha, A., Voelcker, H.: "Solid Modeling: Current Status and Research Directions", Computer Graphics and Applications, IEEE, October 1983.

[RiCa86]   Richardson, J., Carey, M.: "Programming Constructs for Database System Implementation in EXODUS", 1986.

[Ries83]   Ries, D.R., et al.: "Decompilation and Optimization for ADAPLEX: A Procedural Database Language", Technical Report CCA-82-04, Computer Corporation of America, September 1983.

[Robi81]   Robinson, J.T.: "The k-d-B-tree: A Search Structure for Large Multidimensional Dynamic Indexes", Proc. of the 1981 SIGMOD Conference, June 1981.

[RoKB85]   Roth, M., Korth, H., Batory, D.: "SQL/NF: A Query Language for 1NF Relational Databases", Tech Report, TR-85-19, Computer Science Department, University of Texas, September 1985.

[Rose86]   Rosenthal, A., et al.: "Traversal Recursion: A Practical Approach to Supporting Recursive Applications", Proc. ACM-SIGMOD International Conference on Management of Data, ACM, Washington D.C., May 1986.

[RoSh79]   Rowe, L.A., Shoens, K.A.: "Data Abstraction, Views and Updates in RIGEL", Proc. ACM-SIGMOD International Conference on the Management of Data, Boston, MA, May 1979.

[RoSt87]   Rowe, L.A., Stonebraker, M.R.: "The POSTGRES Data Model", In: Proc. 13th International Conference on VLDB, Brighton, England, September 1987.

[Rowe]   Rowe, L.: "A Shared Object Hierarchy", in this volume.

[Rowe83]   Rowe, N.: "Top-Down Statistical Estimation on a Database", Proc. 1983 ACM-SIGMOD International Conference on Management of Data, San Jose, CA, May 1983.

[Rowe85]   Rowe, L.: " 'Fill-In-The-Form' Programming", In: Proc. 11th Int. Conference on VLDB, Pirotte, A., Vassiliou, Y., (Eds.), Stockholm, Sweden, August 1985.

[RoWi87]   Rowe, L.A., Williams, C.B.: "An Object-Oriented Database Design for Integrated Circuit Fabrication", submitted for publication, April 1987.

[RuCa87]   Rubenstein, W.B., Cattell, R.G.G.: "Benchmarks for Database Response Time", Proc. ACM-SIGMOD, 1987.

[RTI85]   Relational Technology Inc.: "INGRES Reference Manual, Version 4.0", Alameda, CA, November 1985.

[Salt78]   Saltzer, J.H.: "Naming and Binding of Objects", In: Bayer, R., Graham, R.M, Seegmuller, G., (Eds.), Operating Systems: An Advanced Course, pp. 99, Springer-Verlag, New York, 1978.

[ScCW85]   Schaffert, C., Cooper, T., Wilpolt, C.: "Trellis Object-Based Environment: Language Manual", Digital Equipment Corporation, Technical Report DEC-TR-372, November 1985.

[Scha86]   Schaffert, C., et al.: "An Introduction to Trellis/Owl", Proc. Object-Oriented Programming Systems, Languages, and Applications Conference, ACM, Portland, OR, September 1986.

[Sche85]   Schek, H.-J.: "Towards a Basic Relational NF^2 Algebra Processor", Proc. International Conference on Foundations of Data Organization, Kyoto, Japan, 1985.

[Schm77]   Schmidt, J.: "Some High Level Constructs for Data of Type Relations", ACM TODS, Vol. 2, No. 3, September 1977.

[Schm78]   Schmidt, J.W.: "Type Concepts for Database Definition", In: Database: Improving Usability and Responsiveness, Schneidermann, B., (Ed.), Academic Press, pp. 215-244, 1978.

[Schm86]   Schmucker, K.: "Object-Oriented Languages for the Macintosh", Byte, Vol. 11, No. 8, August 1986.

[Schw86]   Schwarz, P., et al.: "Extensibility in the Starburst Database System", In: [DiDa86].

[ScPS87]   Scholl, M.H., Paul, H.-B., Schek, H.-J.: "Supporting Flat Relations by a Nested Relational Kernel", Proc. International Conference on VLDB, Brighton, England, 1987.

[ScSc86]   Schek, H.-J., Scholl, M.H.: "The Relational Model with Relation-Valued Attributes", In: Information Systems 11.2, 1986.

[ScSp84]   Schwarz, P.M., Spector, A.Z.: "Synchronizing Shared Abstract Data Types", ACM Transactions on Computer Systems, Vol. 2, No. 3, August 1984.

[ScWa86]   Schek, H.-J., Waterfeld, W.: "A Database Kernel System for Geoscientific Applications", Proc. International Symposium on Spatial Data Handling, Seattle, WA, 1986.

[Ship81]   Shipman, D.: "The Functional Data Model and the Data Language DAPLEX", ACM TODS, Vol. 6, No. 1, March 1981.

[ShKe86]   Shepherd, A., Kerschberg, L.: "Constraint Management in Expert Database Systems", In: [Kers86].

[Shop79]   Shopiro, J.: "Theseus - A Programming Language for Relational Databases", ACM TODS, Vol. 4, No. 4, December 1979.

[Sidl80]   Sidle, T.W.: "Weaknesses of Commercial Data Base Management Systems in Engineering Applications", Proc. IEEE 17th Design Automation Conference, June 1980.

[Sigp86]   SIGPLAN Object-Oriented Programming Workshop, June 9-13, 1986, ACM-SIGPLAN Notice 21 (10), October 1986.

[Skar]   Skarra, A.H., et al.: "An Object Server for an Object-Oriented Database System", in this volume.

[Skar88]   Skarra, A.H.: "A Model of Concurrency Control for Cooperating Transactions", Ph.D. Thesis Proposal, Dept. of Computer Science, Brown University, September 1988.

[SmFL83]   Smith, J.M., Fox, S., Landers, T.: "ADAPLEX: Rationale and Reference Manual", 2nd edition, Computer Corporation of America, Cambridge, MA, 1983.

[SmSm77a]   Smith, J., Smith, D.: "Database Abstractions: Aggregation and Generalization", ACM TODS, Vol. 3, No. 3, July 1977.

[SmSm77b]   Smith, J., Smith, D.: "Data Abstractions: Aggregation", Communications of the ACM, Vol. 20, No. 6, June 1977.

[SnAh85]   Snodgrass, R., Ahn, I.: "A Taxonomy of Time in Databases", Proc. 1985 ACM-SIGMOD International Conference on Management of Data, Austin, TX, June 1985.

[SpHS87]   Spooner, D., Hardwick, M., Samaras, G.: "Some Conceptual Ideas for Extending SQL for Object-Oriented Engineering Database Systems", Proc. International Conference on Data and Knowledge Systems for Engineering and Manufacturing, IEEE, Hartford, CT, October 1987.

[SpMF86]   Spooner, D., Milicia, M., Faatz, D.: "Modeling Mechanical CAD Data with Abstract Data Types and Object-Oriented Techniques", Proc. 2nd International Conference on Data Engineering, IEEE, Los Angeles, CA, February 1986.

[SpMi84]   Spooner, D., Milicia. M.: "ADG Data Structures for the GDP Solid Modeler", In: Industrial Associates Technical Review, Center for Interactive Computer Graphics, Rensselaer Polytechnic Institute, Spring 1984.

[Spoo84]   Spooner, D.: "Database Support for Interactive Computer Graphics, Proc. 1984 ACM-SIGMOD International Conference on Management of Data, Boston, MA, pp. 90-99, June 1984.

[StBo86]   Stefik, M., Bobrow, D.G.: "Object-Oriented Programming: Themes and Variations", The AI Magazine 6, 4, pp. 40-62, 1986.

[Stee84]   Steele, G.L.: "Common Lisp - The Language", Digital Press, 1984.

[StGu84]   Stonebraker, M., Guttman, A.: "Using a Relational Database Management System for Computer Aided Design Data - an Update", IEEE Database Engineering, Vol. 7, No. 2, pp. 56-60, June 1984.

[StHH87]   Stonebraker, M.R., Hanson, E., Hong, C.H.: "The Design of the POSTGRES Rules System", IEEE Conference on Data Engineering, Los Angeles, CA, February 1987.

[StKa82]   Stonebraker, M., Kalash, J.: "TIMBER: A Sophisticated Relation Browser", In: Proc. 8th International Conference on VLDB, Mexico City, Mexico, September 1982.

[StKe80]   Stonebraker, M., Keller, K.: "Embedding Expert Knowledge and Hypothetical Databased into a Database System", Proc. ACM-SIGMOD Conference, 1980.

[Stoc86]   Stock, D.: "SURF: A Graphical Language for Semantic Database Interaction", M.S. Thesis, Computer Science and Engineering Dept., University of Connecticut, December 1986.

[Ston75]   Stonebraker, M.: "Implementation of Integrity Constraints and Views by Query Modification", ACM-SIGMOD International Conference on Management of Data, June 1975.

[Ston81a]   Stonebraker, M.: "Hypothetical Data Bases as Views", Proc. 1981 ACM-SIGMOD Conference, Boston, MA, May 1981.

[Ston81b]   Stonebraker, M.: "Operating System Support for Database Management", Communications of the ACM, Vol. 24, No. 7, pp. 412-418, July 1981.

[Ston83a] Stonebraker, M., Stettner, H., Lynn, N., Kalash, J., Guttman, A.: "Document Processing in a Relational Database System", ACM Transactions on Office Information Systems, Vol. 1, No. 2, April 1983.

[Ston83b] Stonebraker, M., et al.: "Application of Abstract Data Types and Abstract Indexes to CAD Data", Proc. Engineering Applications Stream of 1983 Data Base Week, San Jose, CA, May 1983.

[Ston84] Stonebraker, M., et al.: "QUEL as a Data Type", Proc. 1984 ACM-SIGMOD Conference on Management of Data, Boston, MA, June 1984.

[Ston85a] Stonebraker, M.: "Triggers and Inference in Data Base Systems", Proc. Islamoora Conference on Expert Data Bases, Islamoora, FL, February 1985.

[Ston85b] Stonebraker, M.: Personal Communication, July 1985.

[Ston86a] Stonebraker, M.: "Inclusion of New Types in Relational Data Base Systems", Proc. 2nd Data Engineering Conference, Los Angeles, CA, pp. 262-269, February 1986.

[Ston87] Stonebraker, M.: "Extending a Relational Database System with Procedures", to appear ACM TODS, 1987.

[Ston] Stonebraker, M.: "Object Management in POSTGRES Using Procedures", in this volume.

[StRG83] Stonebraker, M., Rubenstein, B., Guttman, A.: "Application of Abstract Data Types and Abstract Indices to CAD Databases", Proc. Database Week - Engineering Design Applications, San Jose, CA, May 1983.

[StRo84] Stonebraker, M., Rowe, L.: "Database Portals - A new Application Program Interface", Proc. International Conference on VLDB, Singapore, August 1984.

[StRo86] Stonebraker, M., Rowe, L.: "The Design of POSTGRES", Proc. 1986 ACM-SIGMOD Conference on Management of Data, Washington, D.C., pp. 340-355, May 1986.

[Stro86] Stroustrup, B.: The C++ Programming Language, Addison-Wesley Publishing Company, Reading, MA, 1986.

[Stud80] Studer, R.: "Dialogue Interface for Data Base Applications", VLDB Conf., pp. 167-182, October 1980.

[Sun86] Sun Microsystems, Inc.: "SunSimplify 1.0 Manuals", Order Number SunSimplify-09, Sun Microsystems, Mountain View, CA, 1986.

[Symb85] Programming the User Interface, Symbolics Corp., Cambridge, MA, 1985.

[Texa85a] Texas Instruments Incorporated, Data Systems Group: EXPLORER Programming Concepts and Tools, Part No. 2243130-0001, May 1985.

[Texa85b] Texas Instruments Incorporated, Data Systems Group: EXPLORER Technical Summary, Part No. 2243189-0001, May 1985.

[That85]   Thatte, S.M.: "Persistent Memory for Symbolic Computers", Technical Report TR-08-85-21, Central Research Laboratories, Texas Instruments Incorporated, Dallas, TX, July 1985.

[That86]   Thatte, S.M.: "Persistent Memory: Merging AI-knowledge and Databases", Texas Instruments Engineering Journal, 3 (1), pp. 151-159, January 1986.

[That]   Thatte, S.M.: "Persistent Memory: A Storage Architecture for Object-Oriented Database Systems", in this volume.

[Trai82]   Traiger, I.L.: "Virtual Memory Management for Database Systems", ACM Operating System Review, 16, pp. 26-48, October 1982.

[Tsic82]   Tsichritzis, D.: "Form Management", Communications ACM, Vol. 25, No. 7, pp. 453-478, July 1982.

[Ullm82]   Ullman, J.D.: Principles of Database Systems, Computer Science Press, Rockville, MD, 1982.

[Ullm85]   Ullman, J.: "Implementation of Logical Query Languages for Databases", ACM TODS, September 1985.

[Unix83]   Unix System Manual, Programming Tools, Sun Microsystems Inc., 1983.

[VaKC86]   Valduriez, P., Khoshafian, S., Copeland, G.: "Implementation Techniques of Complex Objects", Proc. International Conference on VLDB, Kyoto, Japan, 1986.

[Verh78]   Verhofstad, J.: "Recovery Techniques for Database Systems", ACM Computing Surveys, Vol. 10, No. 2, June 1978.

[VMS82]   VAX/VMS Code Management System, Digital Equipment Corporation, 1982.

[WaPP77]   Warren, D.H., Pereira, L.M., Pereira, F.: "PROLOG - The Language and its Implementation Compared With Lisp", Proc. ACM SIGART-SIGPLAN Symp. on AI and Programming Languages, 1977.

[Webe78]   Weber, H.: "A Software Engineering View of Database Systems", Proc. International Conference on VLDB, pp. 36-51, 1978.

[Weis85]   Weisner, S.P.: "An Object-Oriented Protocol for Managing Data", Database Engineering, 8:4, December 1985.

[WeNP87]   Weikum, G., Neumann, B., Paul, H.-B.: "The Concept and Realization of a Set-Oriented Page-Interface Supporting the Efficient Access To Complex Objects", (in German), Proc. GI-Conference on Data Base Systems in Office, Engineering and Scientific Applications, Darmstadt, West-Germany, 1987.

[WeSc84]   Weikum, G., Schek, H.-J.: "Architectural Issues of Transaction Management in Multi-Layered Systems", Proc. International Conference on VLDB, Singapore, August 1984.

[Weth82]   Wetherell, C.S.: "Error Data Values in the Data-Flow Language VAL", ACM Trans. Prog. Languages and Systems, Vol. 4, No. 2, April 1982.

[Wied83]   Wiederhold, G.: Database Design, 2nd Edition, McGraw-Hill, 1983.

[Wied]   Wiederhold, G.: "Views, Objects, and Databases", in this volume.

[WiLi85]   Wiehl, W., Liskov, B.: "Implementation of Resiliant Atomic Data Types", ACM Transactions on Programming Languages and Systems, Vol 7, No. 2, April 1985.

[Wilk85]   Wilkins, M.W., et al.: "Relational and Entity-Relationship Model Databases and Specialized Design Files in VLSI Design", Proc. ACM-DA 22, pp. 410-516, 1985.

[WoKa80]   Wong, E., Katz, R.: "Logical Design and Schema Conversion for Relational and DBTG Databases", Proc. 1980 E-R-Conference, 1980.

[WoKL85]   Woelk, D., Kim, W., Luther, W.: "An Object-Oriented Approach to Multimedia Databases", MCC Technical Report, Number DB-172-85.

[WoKu82]   Wong, H.K.T., Kuo, I.: "GUIDE: Graphical User Interface for Database Exploration", Proc. 8th International Conference on VLDB, Mexico City, Mexico, September 1982.

[WoSt83]   Woodfill, J., Stonebraker, M.: "An Implementation of Hypothetical Relations", Proc. 9th International Conference on VLDB, Florence, Italy, December 1983.

[Xero83]   Xerox Corporation: Xerox Interslip Reference Manual, October 1983.

[Zani83]   Zaniolo, C.: "The Database Language GEM", Proc. 1983 ACM-SIGMOD Conference on Management of Data, San Jose, CA, May 1983.

[Zani86]   Zaniolo, C., Ait-Kaci, H., Beech, D., Cammarata, S., Kerschberg, L., Maier, D.: "Object Oriented Database Systems and Knowledge Systems", In: [Kers86].

[ZdMa90]   Zdonik, S.B., Maier, D., (Eds.): Readings in Object-Oriented Database Systems. Morgan Kaufmann Publishers, 1990.

[Zdon84]   Zdonik, S.B.: "Object Management System Concepts", Proc. 2nd SIGOA Conference on Office Information Systems, Toronto, Canada, June 1984.

[Zdon85]   Zdonik, S.: "Object Management Systems for Design Environments", IEEE Database Engineering, December, pp. 23-30, 1985.

[ZdWe85a]   Zdonik, S.B., Wegner, P.: "Towards Object-Oriented Database Environments", Brown University TR, 1985.

[ZdWe85b]   Zdonik, S.B., Wegner, P.: "A Database Approach to Languages Libraries and Environments", Proc. of the Workshop on Software Engineering Environments for Programming-in-the-Large, June 1985.

[ZdWe86]   Zdonik, S.B., Wegner, P.: "Language and Methodology for Object-Oriented Database Environments", Proc. International Conference on System Sciences, January 1986.

[Zhu86]   Zhu, J.: "Prototype Implementation and Storage Design for an Engineering Data Model", Research Paper, Oregon Graduate Center, 1986.

[Zloo77]   Zloof, M.M.: "Query-by-Example: A Data Base Language", IBM Systems Journal, Vol. 16, No. 4, pp. 324-343, 1977.

[Zloo81]   Zloof, M.M.: "QBE/OBE: A Language for Office and Business Automation", Computer, Vol. 14, No. 5, pp. 13-22, May 1981.

Contributors

A. Albano, G. Ghelli, M.E. Occhiuto, R. Orsini
Università di Pisa, Italy
(Albano is now with Università de Udine, Italy)

T.L. Anderson, E.F. Ecklund, Jr.
Tektronix Inc., USA
(Anderson is now with Servio Logic Corporation, USA; Ecklund is now with Mentor Graphics, USA)

A.P. Buchmann, R.S. Carrera, M.A. Vazques-Galindo
National University, Mexico
(Buchmann is now with GTE Laboratories, USA)

M.J. Carey, D.J. DeWitt, D. Frank, G. Graefe, J.E. Richardson, E.J. Shekita, M. Muralikrishna
University of Wisconsin, Madison, USA
(Graefe is now with University of Colorado, Boulder, USA)

U. Dayal, F. Manola
Computer Corporation of America, USA
(Dayal is now with Digital Equipment Cambridge Research Laboratory, USA; Manola is now with GTE Laboratories, USA)

U. Deppisch, H.-B. Paul, H.-J. Schek, G. Weikum
TH Darmstadt, Germany
(now with ETH Zürich, Switzerland)

K.R. Dittrich
Forschungszentrum Informatik (FZI), Germany
(now with Universität Zürich, Switzerland)

S.E. Hudson
University of Arizona at Tucson, USA

R.H. Katz, E.E. Chang
University of California at Berkeley, USA

M.L. Kersten, F.H. Schippers
Centre for Mathematics and Computer Science, Netherlands

R. King
University of Colorado at Boulder, USA

T. Learmont, R. Cattell
Sun Microsystems, USA

P. Lyngbaek, W. Kent
Hewlett-Packard Laboratories, USA

D. Maier
Oregon Graduate Institute of Science and Technology, USA

F. Maryanski, J. Bedell, S. Hoelscher, S. Hong, L. McDonald, J. Peckham, D. Stock
University of Connecticut at Storrs, USA

P. O'Brien, B. Bullis, C. Schaffert
Digital Equipment Corporation, USA

S.L. Osborn
University of Western Ontario at London, Canada

L.A. Rowe
University of California at Berkeley, USA

A.H. Skarra, S.B. Zdonik, S.P. Reiss
Brown University, USA

D.L. Spooner
Rensselaer Polytechnic Institute, USA

J. Stein
Servio Logic Corporation, USA

M. Stonebraker
University of California at Berkeley, USA

S.M. Thatte
Texas Instruments, USA

G. Wiederhold
Stanford University, USA

Glossary

A

F

G

H

P

Q

R

S